ANALYSES IN MACROECONOMIC MODELLING

Advances in Computational Economics

VOLUME 12

The titles published in this series are listed at the end of this volume.

Analyses in Macroeconomic Modelling

edited by

Andrew Hughes Hallett
University of Strathclyde

and

Peter McAdam
University of Kent at Canterbury

Kluwer Academic Publishers
Boston/Dordrecht/London

Distributors for North, Central and South America:
Kluwer Academic Publishers
101 Philip Drive
Assinippi Park
Norwell, Massachusetts 02061 USA
Telephone (781) 871-6600
Fax (781) 871-6528
E-Mail <kluwer@wkap.com>

Distributors for all other countries:
Kluwer Academic Publishers Group
Distribution Centre
Post Office Box 322
3300 AH Dordrecht, THE NETHERLANDS
Telephone 31 78 6392 392
Fax 31 78 6546 474
E-Mail <orderdept@wkap.nl>

Electronic Services <http://www.wkap.nl>

Library of Congress Cataloging-in-Publication Data
Analyses in macroeconomic modelling / edited by Andrew Hughes Hallett and Peter McAdam.
p. cm. -- (Advances in computational economics; v. 12)
Includes bibliographical references and index.
ISBN 0-7923-8598-5
1. Macroeconomics--Mathematical models. 2. Rational expectations (Economic theory) -- Mathematical models. I. Hughes Hallett, Andrew. II. McAdam, Peter. III. Series.
HB 172.5.A5 1999
339'.01'5195 -- dc21 99-44507
CIP

Printed on acid-free paper.

Printed in the United States of America

TABLE OF CONTENTS

PART FOUR: LONG RUN AND CLOSURES IN MACRO MODELS

LIST OF CONTRIBUTORS

Gary S. Anderson
Federal Reserve Board of Governors

Stephen Hall
Imperial College of Science Technology and Medicine

Andrew J. Hughes Hallett
University of Strathclyde

Sean Holly
University of Cambridge

Michel Juillard
University Paris 8 and CEPREMAP

David A Kendrick
University of Texas

Douglas Laxton
International Monetary Fund

Coung Le Van
CEPREMAP

Peter McAdam
University of Kent at Canterbury

Warwick McKibbin
Australian National University and the Brookings Institution

Pierre Malgrange
CEPREMAP

P. Ruben Mercado
University of Texas

Scott Moss
Manchester Metropolitan University

Hope Pioro
Bank of Canada

Werner Roeger
European Commission

Esther-Mirjam Sent
University of Notre Dame

Steven Symansky
International Monetary Fund

Paul Turner
University of Sheffield

Jan in't Veld
European Commission

PART ONE

SOLUTION METHODS

CHAPTER 1

SOLUTION METHODS AND NON-LINEAR FORWARD-LOOKING MODELS[1]

Michel Juillard, Douglas Laxton, Peter McAdam and Hope Pioro

1. INTRODUCTION

In this paper, we compare the performance of two leading algorithms now regularly used to solve large forward-looking models. In particular we relate traditional Fair-Taylor 'extended path' algorithms to the newer breed of stacked Newton Raphson ones.[2] As a testing ground for these solution methods we use the IMF's world econometric model,MULTIMOD (Mason et al,1990) which may be considered typical of many current forward-looking large macro-models.[3]

The organisation of the paper is as follows: in section II we review the structure of both types of algorithms and review their general convergence properties. Section III extends the discussion to forward-looking looking models. In section IV we compare the performance of the Fair-Taylor algorithm and a new state-of-the-art Newton Raphson algorithm called NEWSTACK that is available in portable TROLL. Section VI provides some illustrative simulation times from NEWSTACK that were obtained from several different macroeconomic models and computer platforms. Finally, in section VII we offer conclusions.

2. TRADITIONAL SOLUTION METHODS

In this section, we illustrate the mechanics and convergence properties of our chosen solution methods. These results are already well known and so merely motivate and support the remainder of the paper. We first deal with first order then discuss

---

[1] We thank Ralph Bryant, Don Coletti, Peter Hollinger, Andrew Hughes Hallett, Ben Hunt, Tiff Macklem, Guy Meredith, Susanna Mursula, Steve Symansky, Bob Tetlow, Jakob Toftgard and Jan in't Veld for helpful comments and for providing simulation analyses on several models. The usual disclaimer applies.

[2] This is not to suggest that they are the *only* methods of solving forward-looking models only that they would appear to be the most popular - viable alternatives include Penalty function methods (Holly and Zarrop,1983) and shooting methods (Lipton et al,1982).

[3] MULTIMOD is an annual estimated econometric model containing the G7 countries as well as distinct other country blocks. Each country incorporates 53 equations (of which 34 are identities) and for which there are roughly 19 exogenous variables including, principally, monetary target, government expenditure, debt target, oil price and population etc. A full description of MULTIMOD's properties and simulation characteristics is given in Masson et al (1990) and model vintages in Helliwell et al (1990) and Mason et al (1988).Exercises in cross model comparisons may be found in Bryant et al (1988,1993) and Mitchell et al (1995) ,amongst others. Finally note that for these exercises we use the basic production vintage of the MULTIMOD model - MULTAR. With some exceptions - such as the ERM members' (cubic) monetary reaction function and the obvious case of price deflators and log-linear functional forms - the model is highly linear and so should, in principle, be relatively straight forward to solve.

Newton-type methods. We also deal with the necessary extensions to these algorithms to solve models with lead variables separately in section three.

In linear systems, solutions methods merely require the substitution of exogenous (and pre-determined) variables into the reduced form. To illustrate given a structural estimated model,

$$AY + BX = U$$

we can solve for the reduced form - assuming that the A matrix is square and of full rank:

$$Y = \Pi X + V$$

where, $\Pi = -(A)^{-1} B$; $V = (A^{-1}) U$.

In non-linear systems, however, the impact and dynamic multipliers embodied Π are base and perturbation dependent and so yield <u>no</u> unique reduced form. Such systems therefore are solved iteratively with the initial search based on a series of "first-guesses" or "starts" for each endogenous variable, usually their lagged values.

2.1 First Order Algorithms

In a first-order solution (Gauss-Seidel, Jacobi or variants) the iterative solution is of the form:

$$y^s = Gy^{s-1} + b_s$$

In Gauss-Seidel (GS) we progress by solving equations sequentially (based on first-guesses for the endogenous variables Y^{s-1} or Y^0 in the case of the first iteration) with an exogenous variable set. In other words:

$$Y^{s1t} = \Sigma^n_{j=2}\, b_{ij}\, Y^{s-1}{}_{jt} + b_{1t}$$

$$Y^{s2t} = b_{21} Y^s{}_{1t} + \Sigma^n_{j=3}\, b_{ij}\, Y^{s-1}{}_{jt} + b_{2t}$$

$$Y^{s3t} = b_{31} Y^s{}_{1t} + b_{32} Y^s{}_{1t} + \Sigma^n_{j=4}\, b_{ij}\, Y^{s-1}{}_{jt} + b_{3t}$$

.

.

.

.

$$Y^s{}_t = LY^s{}_t + UY^{s-1}{}_t + b_t$$

collecting terms,

$$Y^s_t = (I-L)^{-1}UY^{s-1}_t + (I-L)^{-1}b_t$$

The iteration pattern therefore depends on values already solved for (indicated L for lower) and values for which there is not yet a new solution because they are solved further down in the model (indicated U for upper).This last equation can be re-written as:

$$Y^s_t = GY^{s-1}_t + k_t \qquad (1)$$

where $G = (I-L)^{-1}U$ and $k = (I-L)^{-1}b_t$.

This iterative process terminates only when the values of the endogenous variables in successive iterations converge to a pre-set tolerance(δ):

$$\max_j \left| (y^s - y^{s-1})/y^{s-1} \right| < \delta$$

for all j,j=1,2,3,..,n,subject to a maximum iterations setting.

Popular extensions to this basic GS scheme include Successive Over-relaxation (SOR) and Fast-Gauss-Seidel (FGS) in which the Gauss-Seidel result are further damped or extrapolated according to the iteration matrices:

$$G^{SOR} = (I-\alpha L)^{-1}(\alpha U + (1-\alpha)I)$$

$$G^{FGS} = \gamma(I-\alpha L)^{-1}(\alpha U + (1-\alpha)I) + (1-\gamma)I \qquad (2)$$

Note that variations are nested within (2) - with (α=1,γ=1) retrieving (pure) Gauss-Seidel,($\alpha \neq 1$,γ=1) retrieving Gauss-Seidel plus SOR and (α=1,$\gamma \neq 1$) yielding Fast Gauss-Seidel with no SOR.[4]

The convergence properties for these schemes are reasonably well know. Equation (1) converges if the spectral radius (i.e., the absolute value of the largest eigenvalue) of the iteration matrix, G, is less than unity - see Young (1971). The FGS case converges for some non-zero γ if the real parts of the eigenvalues of G are all less than unity - see Hughes-Hallett (1981). In the SOR case there are limited convergence results; it is convergent if the for some $\alpha \neq 0$ (where we require $0<\alpha<2$ for convergence) if all the roots of (I-B) are less than unity in real parts.[5] However the *general* properties of SOR are well known to programmers and modellers alike (see Dorn and McCracken

[4] There are also the much less popular Jacobi and Jacobi Over-Relaxation Methods; in the case of the Jacobi iteration pattern we use only past iteration values in the current iteration update whilst GS uses (where possible) the value of current iterations in solving forward. Gauss-Seidel tends to be considered the faster of the two (Fair,1984). In the context of our previous discussion this yields :
$Y^s_t = GY^{s-1}_t + k_t$; where $G = U$ and $k = b_t$.

[5] Note an $\alpha \approx 0$ setting converges super quick but is a meaningless one since the simulation tends to the (uncooked) baseline as the new iterated values are 'damped away'.

(1972) for a simple example and Hughes-Hallett (1981) for SOR searches on a range of vintage US models) with the iteration number-SOR space a unique minimum.

Equivalent results hold for non-linear models: the iteration matrix, G^{s-1}, and the forcing function, k , will be base and iteration dependent:

$$Y^s_t = G^{s-1} Y^{s-1}_t + k_s$$

Convergence requires that the spectral radius of the iteration matrix evaluated at the true Solution , G^{YSol}, is less than unity.

2.2 Newton Raphson Algorithms

Given a non-linear model where y and x represent endogenous and exogenous variable sets respectively and f, the model's functional form,

$$f_i(y,x) = 0 \quad i=1,2,...,n$$

then the Newton Raphson (NR) solution is based on an expansion around a starting solution y^{s-1}:

$$y^s = y^{s-1} - (F^{s-1})^{-1} f(y^{s-1},x)$$

Where F, the Jacobian, is the matrix of partial derivatives evaluated at the present iteration :

$$F^{s-1} = [\partial f/\partial y]_{y(s-1)}$$

The convergence results for NR methods are relatively straight forward; if the form of the functional form f(.) is continuously differentiable over a convex set D containing the unique true solution, Y^{Sol}, where $f(Y^{Sol})$ in non-singular and $f(Y^{Sol,x})=0$ then there exists around Y^{Sol} an open set C such that

$$F^{s-1} = [\partial f/\partial y]_{y(s-1)}$$

converges from any starting values in the set of C. Furthermore if

$$\| F(Y)-F(Y^{Sol}) \| \leq d \| (Y-Y^{Sol}) \|$$

holds with d>0 the rate of convergence becomes:

$$\| Y^s - Y^{Sol} \| \leq \delta \| Y^{s-1} - Y^{Sol}) \|^{1+q}$$

Where s is the current iteration number. Thus convergence is quadratic (as opposed to linear as under First-Order systems) with q=1 and δ>0. Indeed quadratic convergence rates is the norm if C is sufficiently small when

$$f_i(y,x) = 0$$

is twice differentiable around Y^{Sol}.

Thus convergence to Y^{Sol} is *guaranteed* once the iterates (or indeed any arbitrary starts) are within some open set C - without the need for damping or acceleration parameters.[6]

However despite these seemingly trivial convergence requirements traditional NR solutions are computational problematic because of the need to evaluate, invert and update F, the Jacobian (which is of the order of the model) at each iteration and that problem worsens if we have inappropriate first-guesses[7] or if the Jacobian is near singular around the solution. Therefore, unless the system can be decomposed or the algorithm takes advantage of the sparseness of the Jacobian the solution remains unambiguously inefficient for large systems. We now present a simple example of how such sparseness in the Jacobian manifests itself.

2.3 A Simple Example Of Sparse Jacobians.

Consider the following traditional closed-economy Income-Expenditure model:

Consumption Function.
$C_t = a*Y^d + b*C_{t-1}$
Disposable Income Identity.
$Y^d_t = Y_t - T_t$
National Income Identity
$Y_t = C_t + G_t + I_t$
Non-Linear Tax Yield
$T_t = (RY)_t$
Tax Rate
$R_t = c + d*Y_t$

We can build up the (first-iteration) Jacobian matrix, F_o :

$$\begin{matrix} 1 & -a & 0 & 0 & 0 \\ 0 & 1 & -1 & 1 & 0 \\ -1 & 0 & 1 & 0 & 0 \\ 0 & 0 & -R_o & 1 & -Y_o \\ 0 & 0 & -d & 0 & 1 \end{matrix}$$

where the subscript $_o$ indicates starting (or lagged) values.

Thus it can be seen that over 50% (13 out of 25) of the elements in the Jacobian are sparse (i.e., zero). Indeed sparseness is very much a feature of identified

---

[6] In practise damping is useful in the armoury of NR users and of the form:
$y^s = y^{s-1} - \alpha(F^{s-1})^{-1} f(y^{s-1},x)$, where $0<\alpha\leq 1$.

[7] i.e., $Y^{s-1} \notin c$.

macro-models (and certainly not just a construct of this particular example) since typically not all of the endogenous variables appear in every single equation in a system.

Here of course continual evaluation, inversion and updating of the Jacobian is negligible given its trivial dimensions (5*5) however this would not carry over to ,say, a 100+ equation model.

For Newton techniques to be tractable therefore invariably implies that programmers minimise their computational burden.

NR techniques can be simplified by for example rank updating schemes (which avoid the need for continual Jacobian inversion) or only re-evaluating the Jacobian at discreet pre-set points. In the last case the more the steps to re-evaluation the more we tend to traditional NR methods, the fewer ($\text{Limit}_{\to\infty}$) the more the initial Jacobian matrix is used throughout all subsequent calculations.[8]

Furthermore NR methods are often based on models re-ordered into recursive and simultaneous blocks because if the simultaneous block is small then computational savings are made (relative to the formerly ordered model) from solving the equation system on a recursive basis - assuming those blocks are themselves easy to solve.

However, NR algorithms which exploit the sparseness and block structure of the Jacobian matrix hold out perhaps the most promising means of accelerating NR methods. Although there is nothing new about such methods - see for example Duff(1977),Duff et al(1986),Press et al(1992) - they have become relatively more well known and more successful recently with the common implementation of a new breed of Stacked-Newton algorithms - see for example Laffargue (1990),Boucekkine(1995) and Juillard (1996).However we reserve a discussion of those techniques until section III which deals specifically with algorithms for solving models with lead variables.

2.4 A General Comparison Of FO and NR Methods.

FO methods require an explicit normalisation and in turn are sensitive to equation ordering; simulations may converge slowly or not at all (even when a well-defined stable solution exists), depending on whatever equation ordering call exists. Moreover, in case of convergence difficulties there are practical difficulties in arranging an alternative successful ordering.[9] Normalisation itself is also important : models can be written in any number of (algebraically equivalent) ways but may fail to solve depending on whatever normalisation is employed.

NR methods (which require no explicit normalisation) are sensitive to the choice of starting values and so, where $Y^{s-1} \notin C$, convergence (in non-linear models) is certain to fail. In most contemporary macro-models this does not - it should be admitted - present too much of a practical problem since invariably 'starts' are derived from

---

[8] This however will reduce the rate of convergence from Superlinear to linear ; a clear trade off therefore.

[9] Individual modellers will of course follow their own practises such as calling the least embedded equations first,solving for flows before stocks, solving the (uncovered interest parity) exchange rate equation first etc. However there exists a considerable literature on reordering techniques – for example Stewart(1962),Don and Gallo(1987),Hughes Hallett and Piscitelli (1998) and Hughes Hallett and Fisher (1990) investigate others.

lagged or steady state values.[10] However the overwhelming problem with Newton methods remains that - as they stand - they are rarely computationally feasible since the solution method requires evaluation, inversion and updating of the Jacobian, F, *at each iteration* : for models of ≥ 100 equations the computational burden involved is non-trivial. In addition, that problem worsens if we have inappropriate first-guesses or if the Jacobian is near singular around the solution. Therefore *workable* Newton methods require some decomposition of the Jacobian.

3. EXTENSIONS TO MODELS WITH 'RATIONAL' EXPECTATIONS (RE).

Normal First Order or Newton methods have to be changed to accommodate RE models otherwise they would treat the lead as exogenous in the same way as FT Type 1 solution.

3.1 First Order Techniques For RE Models.

For First-Order Techniques invariably the Fair-Taylor algorithm is used - we fix the expectational terms at their baseline values and solve the system as in the conventional case period by period with normal Gauss-Seidel iterative techniques (or indeed any solution method),[11] having done this 'Type 1' or 'inner loop' we then update the lead terms, for each variable in turn. We then return to the inner or Type 1 loop with the expectational terms updated and perform another iteration - until the tolerance between successive iteration on both loops respects the pre-set convergence criteria - which may be set differently across loops. We therefor have a two-part scheme - an inner or Type1 loop, which solves for the current, and lagged parts of the model with fixed expectations and an outer or Type 2 loop, which solves the model consistently. When the outer or Type 2 loop has converged the model has consistently solved subject to iteration tolerance.

To illustrate ,consider the model :

$$Y_t = BY_{t-1} + CY^e_{t+1|t} + U_t$$

which stacked over time yields:

---

[10] Although of course that in itself is no guarantee that these values are within C either.

[11] In these exercises we have chosen to solve the type 1 loop of the FT runs with Newton matrix inversion methods since in the authors' experience this has proved more robust at solving and developing this particular model. Solving the model with Gauss methods was examined in Poiro et al (1996) using different software (Fisher's (1990) SLIM) and a vintage of the model (MULTAQ) but with far less successful results in terms of generating convergent scenarios for the FO methods.

$$\begin{bmatrix} I & -C & 0 & 0 \\ -B & I & -C & 0 \\ 0 & -B & I & -C \\ 0 & 0 & -B & I \end{bmatrix} * \begin{bmatrix} Y_t \\ . \\ . \\ Y_T \end{bmatrix} = \begin{bmatrix} U_t \\ . \\ . \\ U_T \end{bmatrix} + \begin{bmatrix} B \\ 0 \\ 0 \\ 0 \end{bmatrix} * Y_0 + \begin{bmatrix} 0 \\ 0 \\ 0 \\ C \end{bmatrix} * Y_{T+1}$$

which can be written more compactly as:

$$HY_t = b_t$$

with b_t containing predetermined variables such as lags, residuals, exogenous terms and perhaps forward terms if expectations are fixed. A solution only exists if H^{-1} is defined with the matrix H itself being unit block diagonal with upper and lower triangular sub-matrices of U^{s-1} and L^{s-1}. The lower triangle can by solved by any solution method keeping expectations fixed with the upper block triangle solved by setting expectational terms equal to (or as a weighted average of solved and baseline estimates of) their forward solution from the lower triangle.

Often modellers have sought to take advantage of this splitting of the solution procedure with the most popular method the so-called incomplete inner iterations method.[12] This may be explained as follows : since the solutions of the inner or Type 1 loop will be updated with every outer or Type 2 loop the practise choose is to avoid these extra and unnecessary calculations - we can therefore set the convergence criteria for the inner or Type 1 loop looser relative to the outer (Rational Expectations) loop. Alternatively we may require the Type 1 loop to have tighter or the same convergence criteria as the Type 2.[13] Alternatively rather than loosen convergence criteria (cc) we could vary the maximum number of iterations allowed over each loop.

3.2 Newton Techniques For RE Models

Fundamentally we have two approaches for solving RE models with Newton Techniques. First we simply use Newton for calculating the inner or type 1 loop (rather than First Order methods) and so yielding essentially the same type of analysis of section II.I,[14] the other is to use a single loop NR method in which we endogenous leads. In this paper we compare FT methods (with Newton on the inner) and a single-loop Newton method. We have found elsewhere (Poiro et al (1996) , Juillard et al (1998)) that first order methods have performed particularly poorly in the case of Multimod.[15]

As suggested operational NR techniques often require some decomposition of the Jacobian matrix to reduce the computational burden to manageable levels; for

---

12 Fisher (1992) and Fisher et al (1986) discuss many more types of splitting - according to their own classification the method presented here is their (preferred) c method.

13 The (TROLL) FT macro that we use was developed by Faust, Tyron and Gagnon at the Federal Reserve Board Of Governors and interestingly would seem to have CC_Type1 < CC_Type2 as its default.

14 Although the convergence requirements follow that given in section II.II rather than II.1 .

15 We have also found that another Newton based one loop procedure - discussed in Armstrong et al(1995) - performed badly and therefore excluded it from our analysis.

example in the MULTAR vintage of MULTIMOD with 466 equations and ,say, 120 simulation periods we would have a Jacobian of dimension 56,852 by 56,852 (i.e.,[n*(T+2)]*[n*(T+2)].[16] However as is shown in Laffargue(1990) the structure of this matrix is such that its triangularization can be handled recursively and so there is no need to store the entire Jacobian at any one time; the matrix stored need only in fact be of order 55,920 by 112 (ie,n*T by TNLV - where TNLV = Total Number Of Lead Variables).

In this paper we concentrate on an extension of such techniques based on Laffargue (1990), Boucekkine (1995) and Juillard (1996). In accordance with modern programming parlance we shall call this algorithm *NEWSTACK* although it has also been variously called 'LBJ' - after the aforementioned authors - in Juillard et al(1998) and the 'Stacked-Time Simulator' in Hollinger (1996).

3.3 A New NR Method For RE Models: NewStack

We can write the equations of a model as

$$f(z_t) = \begin{bmatrix} g_1(y_{t-1}, y_t, y_{t+1}, x_t, \theta) \\ . \\ . \\ . \\ . \\ . \\ g_n(y_{t-1}, y_{t+1}, x_t, \theta \end{bmatrix}$$

for t-1,2,..,T and z_t=[y'_{t-1},y'_t,y'_{t+1}]'. That is to say as a stacked non-normalised equation set over time.

Solving all periods simultaneously we can build up the vector of endogenous variables:

$$Y' = [y'_0, y'_1, \ldots, y'_T, y'_{T+1}]'.$$

We know the initial and terminal points:

$$f_o = (y_o - y_o^*) = f_{T+1} = (y_{T+1} - y_{T+1}^*) = 0$$

and so the entire system forms a (T+2)*n equation system:

16 The problem here is essentially a two-point boundary problem accommodating initial and terminal conditions hence the 2 in 'T+2'.

$$F(Y) = \begin{bmatrix} f_0(y_0) \\ f_1(z_1) \\ . \\ . \\ . \\ f_T(Z_T) \\ f_{T_{+1}}(Y_{T_{+1}})) \end{bmatrix} = 0$$

Now recall the general NR structure:

$$y^t = y^{t-1} - (F^{t-1})^{-1} f(y^{t-1},x)$$

or

$$\Delta y^t = -(F^{t-1})^{-1} f(y^{t-1},x)$$

$$(F^{t-1}) \Delta y^t = -f(y^{t-1},x)$$

which here in full matrix form becomes:

$$\begin{bmatrix} I & 0 & 0 & 0 & 0 & 0 & 0 \\ L_1 & C_1 & F_1 & 0 & 0 & 0 & 0 \\ 0 & . & . & . & 0 & 0 & 0 \\ 0 & 0 & L_t & C_t & F_t & 0 & 0 \\ 0 & 0 & 0 & . & . & . & 0 \\ 0 & 0 & 0 & 0 & L_T & C_T & F_T \\ 0 & 0 & 0 & 0 & 0 & 0 & I \end{bmatrix} * \Delta Y = -\begin{bmatrix} 0 \\ f_1(z_1) \\ . \\ f_t(z_t) \\ . \\ f_T(z_T) \\ 0 \end{bmatrix}$$

where L,C and F are the partial Jacobian for lagged, contemporaneous and forward variables ,i.e.,

$F_t = \partial f_t(z_t)/\partial y_{t+1}$
etc.

The approach of Newstack is to remove elements below or above the main diagonal (here we remove below but the solution is invariant to whether you end up with an upper or lower block Jacobian) and so the solution can proceed recursively either backwards or forwards.

Consider the first period solution :

$$L_1\, \Delta Y_o + C_1\, \Delta Y_1 + F_1\, \Delta Y_2 = -f_1(z_1) \tag{3}$$

Given Δy_o=0 this reduces to :

$$\Delta Y_1 + M_1\, \Delta Y_2 = d_1$$

where,$M_1=(C_1)^{-1}*F_1$ and $d_1=-(C_1)^{-1}*f_1(z_1)$

For the second period:

$$L_t\, \Delta Y_1 + C_t\, \Delta Y_t + F_t\, \Delta Y_{t+1} = -f_t(z_t)$$

ΔY_1 can be retrieved from (3) and substitution Y_{t-1} for Y_1 yields:

$$\Delta Y_t + M_t\, \Delta Y_{t+1} = D_t$$

where $M_t=(C_t-L_tM_{t-1})^{-1}*F_t$ and $d_t=-(C_t - L_t\, M_{t-1})^{-1}*[f_1(z_1) + L_td_{t-1}\,]$

We can do this for all subsequent periods but clearly this M and d pattern is emerging. Thus the system can be recomposed as

$$\begin{bmatrix} I & 0 & 0 & 0 & 0 \\ 0 & I & M_1 & 0 & 0 \\ 0 & 0 & . & . & 0 \\ 0 & 0 & 0 & I & M_T \\ 0 & 0 & 0 & 0 & I \end{bmatrix} * \Delta Y = \begin{bmatrix} 0 \\ d_1 \\ . \\ d_T \\ 0 \end{bmatrix}$$

And the value of ΔY can be retrieved through backward substitution:

$$\Delta Y_t = d_t - M_t\, \Delta Y_{t+1}$$

And so in this approach it is only the M_t and d_t block, for t=1,2,..,T which require storage. And further storage reduction can be achieved by taking into account the sparse columns of the Jacobians using conventional sparse matrix techniques - see for example Duff et al(1986),Press et al(1992).

4. THE SIMULATION FRAMEWORK : THE SIMULATIONS UNDERTAKEN

In these exercises we run the following deterministic simulations on the US country :

(A) A permanent increased in Government Expenditure of 5% of real baseline GDP.

(B) A permanent 5% decreases in the Debt target.

(C) A permanent 5% increases in the monetary target.

(D) A permanent 50% increases in World Oil Production.[17]

Whilst these scenarios are by no means exhaustive they are certainly representative; for a wider selection see Poiro et al (1996). Furthermore to test for robustness and any non-linearities involved (in the timing and accuracy dimension) we also doubled both the size of these shocks (from 5% to 10% etc) and the simulation horizon (from T to 2T).Specifically, we perform these shocks for the US economy.[18]

Finally in these exercise - as in Armstrong et al (1995) - we set a common convergence setting of:[19]

$$\max_{j} \left| (y^{s} - y^{s-1})/(y^{s-1}+5) \right| < \delta.$$

Where δ, the convergence tolerance, is changed at various junctures to accommodate incomplete inner iterations. Such a rule may be justified as a mixture of relative and absolute convergence criteria since the '5' in the denominator prevents division by zero for variables which may take values around zero (e.g., the trade balance) - it makes the convergence criteria approximate an absolute one for small iterated values of y and a relative one for larger values.

Specifically (and to accommodate incomplete-inner-iterations) we follow the following codes for the FT simulations : we start off with three types (A,B,C) where we set a common Type 2 convergence criteria of 0.001 which matches that of Newstack. As we move from A to B however we progressively tighten the type 1 convergence criteria from ten times looser (0.01) to ten times tighter (0.0001) the type 2 one. Thereafter (D to F) we perform the same pattern although with tighter type 2 convergence criteria at 0.0001. The reason for the latter scenario is our prior knowledge that Newstack is

---

[17] Note that this is a shock to oil production rather than oil prices - the former is exogenous whilst the latter is endogenous. For Oil Price Shocks see Juillard et al(1998).

[18] All in all this involves running 32 simulations. These jobs were performed on batch mode overnight on a Pentium PC with 32mb of Ram and a 200Mhz clock at Strathclyde University. Any further information on these simulation can be directed to *p.mcadam@ukc.ac.uk*. For all the simulations we used the TROLL simulation software,Hollinger and Spivakovsky(1996).

[19] In TROLL parlance:CONOPT STOP 200 CONCR 0.001 GAMMA 5;.

exceptionally accurate - in the sense that (whatever the differences in timing) it takes a very tight convergence criteria on FT to replicate its results.

Key

FT_III : FAIR_TAYLOR (incomplete inner iterations)
CC_TYPE1=0.01:CC_TYPE2=0.001

FT_EI : FAIR_TAYLOR (equal iterations)
CC_TYPE1=0.001:CC_TYPE2=0.001 (ie,CC_TYPE1=CC_TYPE2)

FT_TO : FAIR_TAYLOR (tight outer iterations)
CC_TYPE1=0.0001:CC_TYPE2=0.001

NEWSTACK:CC=0.001

5. COMPARISONS

Table 1 shows that in the overwhelming majority of cases Newstack outperforms the FT variants both in terms of solution times and numerical accuracy , table 2.Typically FT meets the cc at its margins whereas Newstack yields a solution well below it . For example in the US_G 5% (t=60) the percentage error of the last convergent variable before global convergence was declared was 1.03e-007 whereas for FT it was 7.00e-004 for a common cc of 0.001.

Indeed tightening the cc will not overly disrupt the solution times for NewStack – which is exactly what we would expect with its quadratic convergence pattern. It is clear however that (although it still performs relatively poorly compared to NewStack) simple acceleration strategies are feasible for the Newton FT variant – loosening the Type 1 cc brings a significant time saving with no real cost in terms of accuracy (relative to FT_EI). Clearly tightening the type 2 cc (in FT_TO) is approximating the more accurate Newstack results (and so is also making smaller errors compared to FT-III and FT_EI) but is doing so at a high (and probably unacceptable) cost in relative solution terms .

6. SOME RECENT EXPERIENCES WITH NEWTON-RAPHSON ALGORITHMS IN PORTABLE TROLL

The availability of two state-of-the-art Newton-Raphson algorithms in portable TROLL has made it considerably easier to solve non-linear forward-looking econometric models. These two Newton-Raphson algorithms are referred to as NEWSTACK (NS) and OLDSTACK (OS) in portable TROLL. The algorithms differ in their approach for exploiting the sparse structure of the Jacobians that arise in forward-looking macroeconomic models. For some initial documentation on the performance of these two algorithms see Armstrong and others (1998) and Juillard and others (1999). Because the performance of NS tends to dominate the performance of OS, the main results that we focus on in this chapter is for the former, but in some cases we will also report results for OS when this algorithm solves faster than the NS algorithm. Both algorithms have an extremely desirable property in that extremely accurate solutions can be obtained in a few Newton-Raphson iterations if the model is approximately linear.

This section reports on some simulation experiences of several TROLL users in the model building community. The users were asked to provide simulation times under NS for representative simulation experiments that they conduct on a regular basis. In addition, they were asked to provide information such as: (1) the number of Newton-Raphson iterations to achieve convergence; (2) the number of equations in their model; (3) the number of periods that the simulation was carried out over; and (4) their experiences with first-order methods versus the second-order Newton-Raphson methods that are available in portable TROLL.

Overall Experiences First-Order and Second-Order Methods

All of the model builders that were surveyed reported that they had encountered significant convergence problems with first-order methods in the past and most model builders reported that they have abandoned first-order methods for this reason. One model builder reported that on highly non-linear models it is sometimes necessary to move to hybrid methods that combine first-order iterations and with second-order methods. One multicountry model builder reported that it was more efficient to use NS to solve for each country block conditional on guesses for the solutions for the other countries and then to use first-order Jacobi iterations to reach full convergence for the entire system.

Solution Times on Various Computer Platforms and Individual Experiences

Table 3 reports solution times and the other information that was requested for a number of macroeconomic models of nontrivial dimension (greater than 50 equations). We do not report estimates for models that have less than 50 equations because these two Newton-based algorithms are so fast that the results are uninteresting for most applications.[20] Table 3 reports estimates of simulation times for models that vary in size between 56 and 1031 equations. These simulations were conducted by model users and developers on several different types of computer platforms. Each model simulator was asked to perform a typical simulation that might be conducted on these models.

1. Small Model of World Government Debt

This is a small annual model of the world economy that was used by Faruqee et al. (1997) to study the crowding out effects of world government debt. The model consists of 56 equations and can be solved in 4 NS iterations in under one second on an RS/6000 machine, model 595, Power2 SC (135 MHz CPU with 640 megabytes of RAM). The model users report that they obtain similar times for open-economy versions of this model as well as other models that have a similar number of equations. They also obtain similar performance with the OLDSTACK algorithm

---

[20] Because of their speed and robustness these algorithms have also been used for conducting stochastic simulations on small forward-looking models to examine the implications of uncertainty for the design of monetary policy rules—for example, see Laxton, Rose and Tambakis (1998).

in portable TROLL. The solution times under NS are roughly proportional to the number of periods solved so doubling the number of periods approximately doubles the solution times.

2. IMF Multicountry Model (MULTIMOD Mark III): Canada Submodel

This is one of the individual country models in the Mark III version of MULTIMOD—for documentation, see Laxton and others (1998). The model can be used to study the effects of various shocks as well as the effects of different monetary and fiscal policy rules. A novel feature of the model is that it contains a significant non-linearity in the unemployment-inflation process so the effects of fiscal and monetary policy shocks will depend on the initial state of the business cycle. For example, the real short-run effects of positive monetary and fiscal shocks will be greater when there is significant slack in the economy than when the economy is characterised by excess demand. The model consists of 92 equations and can be solved in about 3 seconds on an RS/6000 machine, model 595, Power2 SC (135 MHz CPU with 640 megabytes of RAM).

3. The Federal Reserve Board of Governors' US Model (FRB/US): Canada Submodel

FRB/Global is a large-scale quarterly multicountry macro model developed by the staff of the Federal Reserve Board. Simulation experiments conducted with FRB/Global assist the Board in analysing exogenous shocks and alternative policy responses in the United States and foreign economies. Expectations are modelled explicitly, and the model can be solved under the assumption of adaptive or rational expectations. The Canadian block of the model consists of 161 equations and can be solved in about 7 seconds on a Sparc Ultra 2, (300 MHz CPU with 512 megabytes of RAM). For documentation on the model and its properties see Levin, Rogers and Tryon (1997). The users solve the multicountry model by using a mixture of first-order and second order methods. NS is used to solve for each country block conditional on guesses for the solutions for the other countries and then they use Jacobi iterations to reach full convergence for the entire system.

4. Canadian Policy Analysis Model (CPAM)

CPAM is a quarterly model of the Canadian economy that has been designed to study monetary and fiscal policy issues. The model consists of 177 equations and can be solved in about156 seconds on a Sparc Ultra 2, (296 MHz CPU with 524 megabytes of RAM). In this case the modellers report significant timesavings from using OS instead of NS. For documentation on the model and its properties see Black and Rose (1997).

5. RBNZ's Forecasting and Policy System Model (FPS)

FPS is a quarterly model of the New Zealand economy that was constructed by Richard Black, David Rose and staff the Reserve Bank of New Zealand. It has been designed to support quarterly economic projections and conduct policy analysis. Since June 1997, FPS has been used to prepare the RBNZ's published quarterly economic projections and has enabled the publication of several alternative scenarios that highlight keys risks to those projections. A body of research work examining efficient policy rules for inflation targeting regimes has also been produced using FPS. The model consists of 185 equations and can be solved in about 244 seconds on a Compac Dual Processor, Model 6000 (300 MHz CPU with 256 megabytes of RAM). For documentation on the model and its properties see Black and others (1997).

6. Small Two Country Model (Bryant, 1999)

The model has been designed to study the own-country and spillover effects of alternative fiscal policies. For documentation of the model and its properties see Bryant (1999). The model consists of 236 equations and can be solved in about 118 seconds on a Dell Pentium Pro (266 MHz CPU with 64 megabytes of RAM).

7. The Federal Reserve Board of Governors' US Model (FRB/US)

FRB/US is a medium-sized non-linear macroeconometric model of the United States. First brought into production in 1996, FRB/US can be simulated using either expectations generated from a small-scale VAR, or 'rational' expectations. When simulated under rational expectations, the model has 38 non-predetermined variables. The various versions of the model are used for both forecasting and policy analysis exercises at the U.S. Federal Reserve Board of Governors. For documentation of the model and its properties see Brayton and Tinsley (1996), Brayton and others (1997) and Bomfim and others (1997). The model consists of 280 equations and can be solved in about 245 seconds on a Sun Ultra 4 (296 MHz with 2 gigabytes of RAM).

8. Bank of Canada's Quarterly Projection Model (QPM)

QPM is a quarterly model of the Canadian economy designed to serve a dual purpose. First, as its name implies, the model is intended for use by Bank of Canada staff in preparing economic projections. Second, the model is designed as a research tool, to be used when analysing important changes to the economy or to macroeconomic policies which require a deeper understanding of the longer-term equilibrium forces that influence economic behaviour over time. The model consists of 402 equations and can be solved in about 779 seconds on a Sparc Ultra 2, (296 MHz CPU with 524 megabytes of RAM). For documentation on the model and its properties see Black and others (1994) and Coletti and others (1996).

9. IMF Multicountry Model (MULTIMOD Mark III)

MULTIMOD is a modern dynamic multicountry macro model of the world economy that has been designed to study the transmission of shocks across countries as well as the short-run and medium-run consequences of alternative monetary and fiscal policies. It has several variants, the current versions of which are referred to as the Mark III generation. The core Mark III model includes explicit country sub-models for each of the seven largest industrial countries and an aggregate grouping of 14 smaller industrial countries. The remaining economies of the world are then aggregated into two separate blocks of developing and transition economies.

Extended versions of MULTIMOD include separate sub-models for many of the smaller industrial countries, and work has been initiated on expanding the analysis of the developing and transition economies. The model consists of 601 equations and can be solved in about 261 seconds on an RS/6000 machine, model 595, Power2 SC, (135 MHz CPU with 640 megabytes of RAM). For documentation of the model and its properties see Laxton and others (1998).

10. IMF Multicountry Model with Endogenous TFP (MULTIMOD Mark III)

This is an extended version of the Mark III version of MULTIMOD that allows for endogenous trend total factor productivity. This type of model is significantly more difficult to solve because of the simultaneity between demand and supply. The model consists of 625 equations and can be solved in about 2000 seconds on an RS/6000 machine, model 595, Power2 SC, (135 MHz CPU with 640 megabytes of RAM). For documentation of the model and its properties see Bayoumi, Coe and Laxton (1998).

12. Representative Industrial Country Block of MULTIMOD Mark II (ICB)

The model is a variant of a representative industrial country block contained in the Mark II version of MULTIMOD. The model can be used to construct long-run baseline scenarios for an individual country using the IMF staff's medium-term WEO forecast as a starting point. Simulations involving policy shocks and other changes to the exogenous variables can then be run around this baseline solution. The model has been used extensively to analyze the long-run equilibrium path for the Japanese exchange rate, including the effects of alternative policy actions on the exchange rate path in the presence of a liquidity trap that prevents nominal interest rates from becoming negative. In its fully forward-looking mode, a typical simulation can be performed in about 10 seconds on a Toshiba Tecra 550CDT (266 MHz CPU with 64 megabytes of RAM).

13. European Commission's Quarterly Multicountry Model (QUEST)

This is the largest model of the group and consists of 1031 equations. QUEST was designed to analyse the economies of the member states of the European Union. It includes structural submodels for each of the EU member states, the US and Japan, and 11 smaller trade feedback models for the remaining regions of the world. The model is based on principles of dynamic optimisation of households and firms, but incorporates standard Keynesian features in the short run since it allows for imperfectly flexible wages and prices, adjustment costs for investment and labour hoarding. The QUEST model has been intensively used to analyse the macroeconomic effects of fiscal and monetary policy, tax and various other structural reforms in Europe. This model can be solved on a Digital Alpha 8200 (440 MHz with 400 megabytes of RAM) in 1373 seconds or about 23 minutes. Slightly longer simulation times were reported on a Dell XPS R400 (Pentium II 400MHz) with 384 MB RAM. For documentation on the model and its properties see Werner and in 't Veld(1997).

7. CONCLUSION

In this paper we have compared a traditional forward-looking algorithm (Fair-Taylor) with a Newton inner loop with Newstack ,a stacked Newton algorithm which exploits the sparseness and block structure of the Jacobian matrix and treats leads endogenously

It is clear from these exercises that Newstack massively dominates the (Newton) Fair Taylor runs: Newstack is - in most of the scenarios - faster than FT and that advantage is increasingly sharply with tightened Type 2 convergence criteria. We also know that Newstack is accurate since it has low 'errors' relative to the pre-set convergence criteria and indeed we require *tighter* Type 2 convergence criteria to approximate that accuracy.

This algorithm would also indicate great robustness : it would seem to be linear in the time dimension and (in iteration number) invariant to the dimension of the shock or the length of the simulation horizon.

REFERENCES

Armstrong, J., D. Black, D. Laxton, and D. Rose, (1998), "A Robust Method for Simulating Forward-Looking Models," *Journal of Economic Dynamics and Control*, Vol. 22, pp. 489-501.

Bayoumi, Tamim, David Coe, and Douglas Laxton, (1998), "Liberating Supply: Technological Innovation in a Multicountry Econometric Model" IMF Working Paper 98/95, June.

Black, R., and D. Rose, (1997), "The Canadian Policy Analysis Model: CPAM," Bank of Canada Working Paper 97-16.

Black, R., D. Laxton, D. Rose, and R. Tetlow, (1994), "The Steady-State Model: SSQPM," The Bank of Canada's New Quarterly Projection Model, Part 1, Technical Report No. 72, (Ottawa: Bank of Canada).

Black, R., V. Cassino, A. Drew, E. Hansen, D. Rose, and A. Scott, (1997), "The Forecasting and Policy System: The Core Model", Research Paper No. 43 (Wellington, New Zealand: Reserve Bank of New Zealand).

Blanchard, O, Kahn, C (1980), "The Solution Of Linear Difference Equations Under Rational Expectations", *Econometrica*, Vol. 48, pp. 1305-11.

Bomfim, Antulio, Robert Tetlow, Peter von zur Muehlen, and John Williams, (1997), "Expectations, Learning and the Costs of Disinflation: Experiments Using the FRB/US Model", Finance and Economics Discussion paper series 1997-42, Board of Governors of the Federal Reserve System (August).

Boucekkine, R (1995), "An Alternative Methodology For Solving Non Linear Forward Looking Models", *Journal Of Economic Dynamics and Control*, Vol. 19, pp. 711-34.

Brayton, Flint, and Peter Tinsley, (1996), "A Guide to FRB/US: A Macroeconoetric Model of the United States," Finance and Economics Discussion paper series 1996-42, Board of Governors of the Federal Reserve System (October).

Brayton, Flint, Eileen Maukopf, David Reifschneider, Peter Tinsley, and John C. Williams, (1997), "The Role of Expectations in the FRB/US Macroeconometric Model", Federal Reserve Bulletin (April), pp. 227-245.

Bryant, R, Hooper and C Mann (1993), "Evaluating Policy Regimes: New Research in Empirical Macroeconomics", Brookings Institution, Washington DC.

Bryant, R, (1999), "The Government's Budget and Economic Prosperity", forthcoming, Brookings Institution, Washington DC.

Bryant, R, Henderson, D W, Holtham, G and Symansky, S (1988), "Empirical Macroeconomics For Interdependent Economies", Brookings Institution, Washington DC.

Coletti, D, Hunt, B, Rose, D, and Tetlow, R, (1996), The Bank of Canada's New Quarterly Projection Model, Part 3, The Dynamic Model: QPM Technical Report No. 75 (Ottawa: Bank of Canada)

Dorn, W and McCracken, D (1972), "Numerical Methods With Fortran IV Case Studies", Wiley, New York.

Duff, I (1977), "A Set Of Fortran Routines For Sparse Unsymmetric Equations", Technical Report R-8730, AERE Harwell Laboratory.

Duff, I, Erisman, A, Reid, J (1986), "Direct Methods For Sparse Matrices", Oxford University Press.

Fair, R C (1979), "Analysis of a macro-econometric model with rational expectations in the bond and stock market.", *American Economic Review*, Vol. 69, pp. 539-552.

Fair, R C, and Taylor, JB (1983), "Solution and Maximum Likelihood Estimation of Dynamic Non-Linear rational Expectation Models", *Econometrica*, Vol. 51, pp. 1169-1186

Faruqee, Hamid, Douglas Laxton, and Steve Symansky, (1996), "Government Debt, Life- Cycle Income and Liquidity Constraints: Beyond Approximate Ricardian Equivalence," IMF Working Paper 96/140 and IMF Staff Papers, Vol. 44 (September 1997), pp. 374-82 (Washington: International Monetary Fund).

Fisher, P G and Hughes Hallett, A J (1987), "The Convergence Characteristics Of Iterative Techniques For Solving Econometric Models", *Oxford Bulletin Of Economics and Statistics*, May 1987, Vol. 49, No. 2, p. 231-44.

Fisher, P G (1992), "Rational Expectations In Macro-economic Models", Kluwer, Dordrecht and Boston.

Fisher, P G, Holly, S, Hughes Hallett, A J (1986),"Efficient Solution Techniques For Dynamic Non-Linear Rational Expectations Models", *Journal Of Economic Dynamics and Control*, Vol. 10, pp. 139-45.

Helliwell, J, Meredith, G and Bagnloi, P (1990), "Intermod 1.1: A G7 version of the IMF's Multimod", *Economic Modelling*, (January).

Hollinger, P (1996), "The Stacked-Time Simulator in TROLL: A Robust Algorithm For Solving Forward Looking Models", Paper presented at the Second International Conference On Computing in Economics and Finance, Geneva, Switzerland, June 26 - 28,1996.

Hollinger, P, Spivakovsky, L (1996), "Portable Troll", Intex Solutions.

Holly, S, Zarrop, M (1983), "On Optimality and Time Consistency when Expectations are Rational", *European Economic Review*, 20, pp. 23-40.

Hughes Hallett, A J (1981), "Some extensions and comparisons in the theory of Gauss-Seidel Iterative Techniques For solving large equation systems" in Charatsis D (ed) Computer Simulation Experiments with models of Economic systems, North Holland, Amsterdam.

Hughes Hallett, A J, and Fisher, P G (1990), "On Economic Structures and Solution Methods: Or should econometricians use Newton methods for Model Solution?", *Oxford Bulletin Of Economics and Statistics*, Vol. 52, No. 3, p. 317-30.

Hughes Hallett, A J, Ma Y, and Pin, Y P (1996), "Hybrid Algorithms With Automatic Switching For Solving Non-Linear Equation Systems", *Journal Of Economic Dynamics and Control*, Vol. 20, pp. 1051-71.

Hughes Hallett, A J, Piscitelli, L (1998), "Simple Reorderiong Techniques For Expanding the Convergence radius of First Order Iterative Techniques", *Journal Of Economic Dynamics and Control*, Vol. 22, pp. 1319-33.

Juillard, Michel, Douglas Laxton, Peter McAdam, and Hope Pioro, (1998), "An Algorithm Competition: First-Order Iterations Versus Newton-Based Techniques", *Journal of Economic Dynamics and Control*, Vol. 22, pp. 1333.

Juillard, M (1996), "DYNARE:A Programme for the Resolution and Simulation Of Dynamic Models With Forward Variables Through The Use Of A Relaxation Algorithm.",CEPREMAP Working Paper No. 9602.

Laffargue, J P (1990) "Resolution d'un Modele Macro-Economique Avec Anticipations Rationelles", *Annales D'Economie et Statistique*, Vol. 17.

Laxton, Douglas, David Rose, and Demosthenes Tambakis, (1998), "The U.S. Phillips Curve: The Case for Asymmetry", IMF Working Paper (forthcoming; Washington: International Monetary Fund).

Laxton, Douglas, Peter Isard, Hamid Faruqee, Eswar Prasad, and BartTurtleboom (1998), "MULTIMOD Mark III: The Core Dynamic and Steady-State Models," IMF Occasional Paper 164, IMF, Washington DC.

Levin, Rogers, and Ralph Tryon, (1997), "A Guide to FRB/Global," Federal Reserve Bulletin, October.

Lipton, D, Poterba J, Sachs J, Summes, L (1982), "Multiple Shooting In Rational Expectations models", *Econonometrica*, 50, pp. 1329-33.

Masson, P, S Symansky and G Meredith (1990), "MULTIMOD: Mark II: A Revised and Extended Model", IMF Occasional Paper 71, IMF, Washington DC.

Meredith, G. (1998), "The Yen: Past Movements and Future Prospects," in *Structural Change in Japan*, B. Aghevli, T. Bayoumi, and G. Meredith eds., IMF, Washington DC.

Meredith, G. (1998), "A Dynamic Extension of the Macroeconomic Balance Approach," in *Exchange Rate Assessment*, IMF Occasional Paper 167, IMF, Washington DC.

Mitchell, P R, Sault, J, Smith, P N, Wallis, K (1995), "Comparing Global Econometric Models", Discussion Paper No. 40, University Of Warwick.

Nepomiastchi, P, and Ravelli, A (1978), "Adapted methods for solving and optimising Quasi Triangular Econometric Models", *Journal Of Economic Dynamics and Control*, Vol. 6, pp. 555-562.

Norman, A L, Lasdon, L S, and Hsin, J (1983), "A comparison of methods for solving and optimising Large Non-Linear economic Models", *Journal Of Economic Dynamics and Control*, Vol. 6, pp. 3-24.

Poiro, H (1995), "Faster Simulation Times For QPM: Saving the LU Decomposition Indices In TROLL", Bank Of Canada, mimeo, April 4th, 1995.

Poiro, H, McAdam, P, Laxton, D (1996), "Solving MULTIMOD with First-Order and Newton Based Techniques", *International Centre For Macroeconomic Modelling* Discussion Paper No.37, University Of Strathclyde, Glasgow.

Press, W, Teukolsky, S, Vetterling, W and Flannery, B (1992), "Numerical Recipes in C : The Art of Scientific Computing", Cambridge University Press, Cambridge.

Roeger, Werner, and Jan In't Veld, (1997), "QUEST II: A Multi Country Business Cycle and Growth Model," Economic Papers no. 123, Directorate General for Economic and Financial Affairs, European Commission (October), Brussels

Young, D (1971), "Iterative Solutions to Large Linear Systems", Academic Press, New York.

Table 1.
Solution Comparisons

US_G 5% T = 60

Iteration No	Time-to-Solve [Seconds]
Newstack	4
252	
FT_III	87
1,147	
FT_EI	87
1,512	
FT_TO	134
2,448	

US_G 5% T = 120	Iteration No
Time-to-Solve	
Newstack	4
484	
FT_III	95
6,882	
FT_TO	173
16,707	

US_G 10% T = 60	Iteration No
Time-to-Solve	
Newstack	4
323	
FT_III	110
1,412	
FT_EI	110
1,771	
FT_TO	160
2,720	

US_G 10% T = 120	Iteration No
Time-to-Solve	
Newstack	4
797	
FT_III	149
7,963	
FT_EI	149
10,240	
FT_TO	200
14,074	

US_MT 5% T = 60	Iteration No
Time-to-Solve	
Newstack	3
312	

FT_III 42
693
FT_EI 42
834
FT_TO 90
1,853

US_MT 10% T = 120 Iteration No
Time-to-Solve
Newstack 4
655
FT_III 39
1,227
FT_EI 39
1,423
FT_TO 122
4,534

US_MT 10% T = 60 Iteration No
Time-to-Solve
Newstack 4
352
FT_III 65
1,201
FT_EI 65
1,475
FT_TO 95
1,956
US_MT 10% T = 120 Iteration No
Time-to-Solve
Newstack 4
774
FT_III 57
1,259
FT_EI 57
1,551
FT_TO 132
4,914

US_BT 5% T = 60 Iteration No
Time-to-Solve
Newstack 3
164
FT_III 4
69
FT_EI 4
83

US_BT 5% T = 120	Iteration No
Time-to-Solve	
Newstack	3
331	
FT_III	4
137	
FT_EI	4
154	
FT_TO	33
1,241	

US_BT 10% T = 60	Iteration No
Time-to-Solve	
Newstack	3
268	
FT_III	7
138	
FT_EI	7
142	
FT_TO	35
694	

US_BT 10% T = 120	Iteration No
Time-to-Solve	
Newstack	3
538	
FT_III	7
198	
FT_EI	7
253	
FT_TO	49
1,782	

Oil production (50%) T = 60	Iteration No
Time-to-Solve	
Newstack	4
197	
FT_III	27
403	
FT_EI	27
485	
FT_TO	87
2,600	

Oil production (50%) T = 120	Iteration No
Time-to-Solve	
Newstack	4
384	
FT_III	32
934	

FT_EI 32
1,108
FT_TO 118
2,899

Oil production (100%) T = 60 Iteration No
Time-to-Solve
Newstack 4
353
FT_III 39
700
FT_EI 39
703
FT_TO 90
4,194

Oil production (100%) T = 60 Iteration No
Time-to-Solve
Newstack 4
770
FT_III 39
1,300
FT_EI 39
1,351
FT_TO 140
8,020

Table 2.
Solution Times (Seconds) of NEWSTACK in TROLL

No.	Model	Equations	Periods	Iterations	Solution Time	User Experience
1.	Faruqee et al. (1997)	56	180	4	1	A,C
2.	CAMOD: Mark III	92	50	5	3	B,C
3.	FR/Global: Canada	161	100	7	7	D
4.	CPAM	177	100	3	156	A,C
5.	FPS	185	100	6	244	A,C
6.	Bryant (1999)	236	214	26	118	A
7.	FRB/US (1998)	280	200	5	245	A,C
8.	QPM	402	100	4	779	A,C
9.	MULTIMOD: Mark III	601	50	6	261	B,C
10.	Bayoumi et al. (1998)	625	300	7	2000	A,C
11.	DEMOD: Mark III	673	50	3	376	A
12.	ICB: Mark III	50	80	19	10	A,C
13.	Quest (1998)	1031	280	4	1373	A,C

Notes on Modelers' Experiences: (A) Do not currently use first-order methods because the newer breed of Newton-based algorithms are extremely efficient and reliable; (B) Ocassionally use first-order and hybrid methods for highly nonlinear models but mainly use the newer breed of Newton-based algorithms because they work very reliably; (C) Have experienced lots of difficulties with first-order methods in cases where Newton-based algorithms work quite reliably; (D) Generally use a combination of first-order and second-order methods.

CHAPTER 2

FROM HERE TO ETERNITY: THE ROBUSTNESS OF MODEL SOLUTIONS TO IMPERFECT STARTING VALUES[1]

Peter McAdam and Andrew Hughes Hallett

1. THE GENERAL PROBLEM OF SELECTING STARTS

It is rare that a model builder has *no* idea about possible starts. For example with empirical macro models, the parameters of the equations will be estimated from realised data. That makes it easier to guess good start values: (usually lagged historical values of the endogenous variables). This does not *in itself* preclude non-convergence. But if it does occur, it will usually be for other reasons – e.g. failing Blanchard-Kahn stability conditions, inappropriate normalisations and equation orderings, simultaneous equation bias, unstable feed backs, explosive calibrated policy rules, inappropriate dampening factors etc.

Similarly, users will tend to know something of the *logical* structure of their model. For example, various parameter restrictions – e.g. that constant-returns production function parameters sum to one – and variable constraints – e.g. non negativity in unemployment and nominal interest rates etc - can guide their choice of starts.

However the general problem of starts searches tend to be most acute in nonlinear models constructed from optimising behaviour; or in models with forward looking expectations terms. If such models are solved numerically there may be insufficient information to tie down first guesses: other than an uninformative zero solution.[2] Nevertheless, even in estimated macro models (with historical lags) starts may be a problem; particularly with diagnostic simulations (such as stochastic simulations) or, for example, where users wish to test alternative dynamic paths to the steady state. This for example is quite a common problem in simulating large multi-country models (with Solow-type closures) where users may have to guesstimate or impose an artificial dynamic path to long run balanced growth. In such a case, even the historical starts may be so far from the implied dynamic path that the solution breaks down. Of course, one might want to also include certain mainly negative deterministic shocks or counter-factual historical tracking exercises that cause general solution problems.

It is in this context that it is important to know something of the robustness of the standard model solution algorithms to imperfect or poorly chosen start values.

[1] We are grateful to Peter Hollinger for TROLL support. The usual disclaimer applies.

[2] Although in some cases a base zero solution would be applicable – as with an impulse-response model.

That is a subject which has not been studied before. This paper provides a first analysis of the problem.

2. GENERAL SOLUTION ALGORITHMS

2.1 Standard Newton Techniques

Consider the problem of solving a non-linear econometric model:

$$f_i(y,z)=0 \qquad i=1,\ldots,n \tag{1}$$

where $y \in R^n$ and $z \in R^m$ are real vectors containing the endogenous and exogenous (predetermined) parts of each equation respectively and where $f_i(\cdot)$ are arbitrary real-valued functions. Assume for simplicity that the vector valued function representing the entire model, $f(y,z)=0$, has at least one real solution (y^*) for the known or projected values of z. The Newton method for solving (1), given z, is based on a first order expansion about some trial solution value $y^{(s)}$:

$$y^{(s)}=y^{(s-1)}-F^{-1}f\left(y^{(s-1)},z\right) \tag{2}$$

where $F=\left[\partial f/\partial y\right]_{y^{(s-1)}}$ is a matrix of partial derivatives evaluated at the current iteration.

The convergence conditions for (2) can be summarised as follows (Ortega and Rheinboldt, 1970, p.312). If $f(\cdot)$ is continuously differentiable over a convex set D containing y^*, where $f(y^*,z)=0$ and $F(y^*)$ is non-singular, then there exists an open set C about y^* such that (2) converges at least linearly from any $y^{(0)} \in C$. If, in addition, the Lipschitz condition $\|F(y)-F(y^*)\| \le c\|y-y^*\|$ holds for $y \in C$ and some $c>0$, the rate of convergence becomes quadratic.

Each step of (2) is computationally expensive because the inversion of F is both laborious for large econometric systems and prevents us from exploiting the sparseness of F when solving for each new iterate. The method becomes particularly expensive if the convergent neighbourhood is very small (requiring good start values), or if F approaches singularity at or near y^*.

2.2 Modified Newton Methods

There are three ways of reducing the computation per step of (2). They involve cheap ways of evaluating F and F^{-1}, or obtaining F^{-1} without inversion.

(a) Numerical Derivative Evaluations

The matrix F can be constructed using information from past iterates rather than by differentiation. Ortega and Rheinboldt (1970) suggest various schemes, but to identify all the elements of F requires n initial iterations (where n is typically very large). Zero restrictions on F reduce the convergence rate and ultimately produce first order methods (Hughes Hallett, 1982).

(b) Avoiding Repeated Matrix Inversions

The solution to (2) could be obtained by solving a simultaneous equation by first order methods rather than by inverting F. Another method of avoiding repeated inversions is to re-evaluate F and hence F^{-1}, every m^{th} step. However, the rate of convergence then falls to (m+1)/m (Ortega and Rheinboldt, 1970, p.316).

(c) Obtaining the Inverse Directly

The matrix F^{-1} can be built up from information in the iterates themselves avoiding any inversions or derivative calculations, using updating schemes based on an arbitrary start. Examples are Broyden's rank one updating scheme and the Fletcher-Powell rank two method. Convergence is at least linear, and might be superlinear (Dennis and More, 1977).

2.3 First Order Iterative Techniques

First order iterative methods for solving (1) take the non-stationary form:

$$y^{(s)} = G^{(s-1)}y^{(s-1)} + k_s \tag{3}$$

where the iteration matrix and forcing function $G^{(s-1)}$ and k_s, depend on the solution path $y^{(s-1)},\ldots,y^{(1)}$ and starting values $y^{(0)}$. Convergence is achieved when

$$\max_i \left|\left(y_i^{(s)} - y_i^{(s-1)}\right) / \left(y_i^{(s-1)} + \epsilon\right)\right| < \tau$$

for small values of τ and ϵ (we set ϵ=.01 in what follows). These methods have linear convergence rates.

Three simple versions of (3) are routinely used in econometrics: the Jacobi overrelaxation (JOR) method, the Gauss-Seidel (SOR) method, and the Fast-Gauss-Seidel (FGS) method. Imposing some normalisation, on (1) $y_i=g_i(y,z)$ for i=1,...,n the JOR, SOR and FGS iterations are special cases of (3) where:

$$\begin{aligned}
&\text{JOR: } G^{(s-1)} = \gamma B^{(s-1)} + (1-\gamma)I \\
&\text{SOR: } G^{(s-1)} = \left(I - \alpha L^{(s)}\right)^{-1}\left(\alpha U^{(s-1)} + (1-\alpha)I\right) \\
&\text{FGS: } G^{(s-1)} = \delta\left(I - \alpha L^{(s-1/2)}\right)^{-1}\left(\alpha U^{(s-1)} + (1-\alpha)I\right) + (1-\delta)I
\end{aligned} \tag{4}$$

and $B^{(s-1)} = [\partial g / \partial y]_{y^{(s-1)}}$ has upper and lower triangular submatrices $U^{(s-1)}$

and $L^{(s-1)}$. The convergence of (3) to a solution y*, given an arbitrary start within a neighbourhood of y*, then follows if $\rho(G^*)<1$ where G* is $G^{(s-1)}$ evaluated at y* and $\rho(\cdot)$ denotes spectral radius (Ostrowski, 1966) i.e., if and only if the characteristic roots of B and $(I-\alpha L)^{-1}(\alpha U+(1-\alpha)I)$, respectively, are all less than unity in real part. The value of γ which maximises the rate of convergence, together with the maximum value of γ which permits convergence, have also been determined (Hughes Hallett, 1984).

2.4 Forward Looking (Rational Expectations) Models

Many economic models now put a great deal of emphasis on modelling the behaviour of market agents who react anticipated future events, as well as current and past developments. This poses problems for solving the model. A conventional difference equation system can be written as

$$Ay_t = Dy_{t-1}+u_t \tag{5}$$

where u_t represents all strictly exogenous and random variables. Such a model can be solved recursively forward in time, $t=1,\ldots,T$, since (at each t) y_{t-1} is predetermined. Hence y_t may be found conditional on y_0 and given values of $u_1,\ldots,u_t$. In fact (5) takes the form of (1) for each value of t. However, rational expectations models include lead terms to represent expected future developments:

$$Ay_t = D_1y_{t-1}+C_0y_{t|t}+C_2y_{t+1|t}+u_t \tag{6}$$

where $y_{t+j|t} = E(y_{t+j}|\Omega_t)$, for $j\geq 0$, is an expectation conditional on the information available at the start of period t. Each expectation in (6) is the same as the next period's forecast value obtained by solving the model conditional on the information set Ω_t. Hence the expectations are linked forward in time and to solve (6) for each y_t in period 1 requires each $y_{t+j|t}$ $j=1,\ldots,T-t$ and a terminal condition $y_{T+1|t}$. If $A_1=A-C_0$, (5) implies

$$\begin{bmatrix} A_1 & -C_1 & & 0 \\ -D_1 & \ddots & \ddots & \\ & \ddots & \ddots & -C_1 \\ 0 & & -D_1 & A_1 \end{bmatrix} \begin{bmatrix} y_{1|1} \\ \vdots \\ y_{T|1} \end{bmatrix} = \begin{bmatrix} u_{1|1} \\ \vdots \\ u_{T|1} \end{bmatrix} + \begin{bmatrix} D_1 \\ 0 \\ \vdots \\ 0 \end{bmatrix} y_0 + \begin{bmatrix} 0 \\ \vdots \\ 0 \\ C_1 \end{bmatrix} y_{T+1|1}. \tag{7}$$

Evidently (7) can be written as $\tilde{A}y = \tilde{b}$ where $\tilde{A}$ is the block tridiagonal matrix; y is the stacked vector of endogenous variables conditioned on Ω_1; and $\tilde{b}$ is the stacked vector of terms on the right of (7).

The solution of dynamic rational expectations models therefore takes exactly the same form as that for a conventional model. The differences are only that:

(i) the unknowns of different time periods will be determined simultaneously rather than recursively;

(ii) the Jacobian matrix A has been replaced by the expanded matrix $\tilde{A}$; and

(iii) the exogenous elements in b have been augmented by the terminal condition $y_{T+1|1}$. Fisher, Holly and Hughes Hallett (1986) therefore use the same first order iterative techniques as a cheap way of constructing numerical solutions to rational expectations models.

The problem here is that (7) represents an extremely large equation system (given that we are stacking n equations across T time periods, 1,000 equations and upwards - e.g. 500 equations over 20 periods - is not unusual) and several modifications are necessary in order to keep the computational burden within reasonable bounds. And the crucial difference between (1) and (7) is that, whereas the ordering of the elements in y of (1) has no special significance, the equations in (7) are ordered by time periods. Thus, in a conventional model when $C_1=0$, solutions may be generated recursively forwards through the block recursive structure of $\tilde{A}$ and the only relevant splittings are those in A_1 itself. But when $C_1 \neq 0$ that block recursive structure is lost and we need to consider splitting of $\tilde{A}$ over time periods as well as over equations within a given period. The three main possibilities are:

(a) Splittings of $\tilde{A}$, element-by-element, without regard to its block structure. This defines a family of simple first-order iterations on (7) treated as one large equation system.

(b) Splittings of $\tilde{A}$, element-by-element *within* each diagonal block, to define equation-by-equation iterations for each time period (solved sequentially forwards) with expectations temporarily fixed: and a separate block-by-block splitting for the above diagonal sub-matrices to define the iterative steps which update those expectations terms. These splittings define a two-part iteration: an *inner* iteration which solves for the current and lagged variables of each period, and an *outer* iteration which updates the forward expectations terms.

(c) Type (b) splittings in which the inner iterations are not taken to convergence at each outer loop step. This can be done by setting a substantially weaker convergence criterion on the inner loop, or by testing for convergence only on those variables for which forward looking expectations are formed. Computational savings are made because computation is not wasted in getting a full inner loop solution which is then going to be changed again by the values generated in the next outer loop step.

Different specifications of the various iterative schemes which follow from the three types of splittings of $\tilde{A}$ are considered by Fisher and Hughes Hallett (1988), and the associated convergence results are derived there. However three special cases appeared earlier in the literature. Fair and Taylor (1983) proposed a type (b) scheme, and Fisher et al (1986) showed how that proposal could be improved by introducing both incomplete inner iterations and extrapolated inner and outer iterations. Hall's (1985) suggestion can be classified as either a type (a) scheme, or a type (c) scheme with a single inner step per outer loop step. Finally the multiple shooting method (Lipton et al (1982)) can be written as an expanded version of a type (a) scheme. Any of these iterations may be extrapolated in the same way as (4); and type (b) and (c) methods allow different extrapolations for the inner and outer loops.

Other methods without an iterative base (e.g. the eigenvalue method of Blanchard and Khan (1980)) have also been proposed, but only iterative techniques have proved to be sufficiently robust and of sufficient generality for everyday use. The alternative is to work directly on (6), or to recast it as (5) with multiple lags. But nonlinear models cannot always be reformulated into the conventional recursive structure of (5), and it may not be cheap or easy to do that for linear systems either. Similarly it is not easy to check on the sensitivity of the solution to the terminal condition, or to introduce multiple leads or lags while retaining the splittings/accelerations which maintain computational costs at reasonable levels, unless the solution fits into the framework of (7). But we can always work directly with (6), or its nonlinear equivalent.

We do not consider variations in the terminal conditions in this paper; type 3 iterations in Fair-Taylor terminology. Inner and outer loop iterations may be called type 1 and type 2 iterations respectively.

2.5 The Algorithms used in this Study

Newstack [NS] and OldStack [OS]

These stacked algorithms are essentially a single loop Newton algorithm suitable for simulating models with consistent leads. The n time periods are "stacked" together and the model is solved consistently for its leads by solving multiple time periods simultaneously.

Given a general non-linear model:

$$f_t\left(y_{t-1}, y_t, E_t y_{t+1}, x_t\right) = 0$$

Where f_t is a vector of n non-linear dynamic equations and $\mathbf{y}_t$ and $\mathbf{x}_t$ are vectors of endogenous and exogenous variables. If we stack the model for all time periods – namely from its historical to its lead positions:

$$F(z, x; t) = \begin{bmatrix} f_t(z_t, x_t) \\ \vdots \\ f_{t+j}\left(z_{t+j}, x_{t+j}\right) \\ \vdots \\ f_{t+T}\left(z_{t+T}, x_{t+T}\right) \end{bmatrix} = 0$$

where $z_{t+j}=(y_{t+j-1}, y_{t+j}, E_t y_{t+j+1})$. We solve this equation system by Newton-Raphson given a predetermined variable $\mathbf{y}_{t-1}$ and the terminal side condition y_{t+T+1}.

For a large system of equations, the inversion of the Jacobian - F, being the matrix of first order derivatives of the same as the model – is not a trivial operation computationally, especially if the equations have to be started over many time periods as in (7). The Stacked algorithms makes use of the repetitive structure of this stacked system, which is block triangular with the blocks corresponding to the different time periods. By taking advantage of the sparsity within the single period blocks, the numerical and computational burden is significantly reduced by inverting the matrix by blocks (for Oldstack see Armstrong et al, 1995; for NewStack see Juillard et al, 1998a, b). Comparing the two algorithms we have;

Similarities

1. They are both single loop Stacked Newton solution methods suitable for simulating models with consistent leads. The n time periods are "stacked" together and the model is solved consistently for its leads by solving multiple time periods simultaneously.

2. They both take advantage of sparsity (i.e. zero elements) within the Jacobian and its associated factored blocks.

Differences

1. OLDSTACK does not use any a priori knowledge about the repetitive structure of the Jacobian and so solves the model as if it were backward looking but with separately coded equations for the leads. In fact it is often faster than NEWSTACK for repetitive solutions; but it can be much slower the first time, given that the information on the repetitive structure of the Jacobian is not saved from one simulation task to another.[3]

FT_GAUSS [FT_GS]

The Fair Taylor algorithm with Gauss Seidel (GS) solving the inner or type 1 loop where expectations are fixed.

FT_NEWTON [FT_N]

The Fair Taylor algorithm with Newton solving the inner or type 1 loop where expectations are fixed.

---

[3] Although the algorithm *can* be made to retain information on its repetitive structure in repeated simulations - see Poiro, 1995.

3. THE SIMULATIONS AND MODELS UNDER CONSIDERATION

We use four models to test algorithm robustness to starting values. All of our test models are small relative to the most popular national or multi-national macro models. Small models were chosen in order to make our experiments more transparent. But having said that there seems to be a trend amongst policy institutions to use such small analytical models , like the Dornbush Exchange rate model, for specialised policy analysis - see Fisher and Whitely (1997), Whitely(1997). And so whilst our choice of models is never going to be entirely representative they are certainly in the range of those popularly used, and possess variously forward leads[4] and significant non-linearity.

Our four test models are specified equation by equation in the appendix to this paper. They represent four different aspects of the typical econometric model:

1. A forward Looking **Inflation-Output Gap** model.[5]

2. A linear forward looking Exchange Rate Overshooting model - a **Dornbush model**.

3. A non-linear Growth model (**Growth**).

4. A non-linear forward looking simulation model (**FLSIM**).

In each case, our first step is to solve each model to produce a baseline or reference solution as a point of comparison for all later solutions and algorithm comparisons. We already know from Juillard et al (1988a) that Newstack, when it solves, is likely to be the most numerically accurate of all the algorithms we test. So we use that algorithm to establish the baseline solution for each model. In each case, too, we check the percentage errors from this baseline in the main lead variable (i.e. the one to which the other variables are most sensitive, and hence last lead variable to converge) when each of the other solution techniques was used. We do this because, given the initial jump onto the saddle path, this is the variable where errors are most likely to originate (Poiro et al, 1996). If those percentage errors remain quite small the baseline solution is accepted as the correct solution - and the one as the central projection in the subsequent algorithm comparisons, given the possibility of multiple equilibria. However since the actual (analytic) solution was not known in any of these models, one arbitrary set of start values was maintained for each model solution in the subsequent exercises. The only exception was the model FLSIM, where there is a historical database from which lagged values of the historical values were used as starting values of the endogenous variables. That corresponds to common practice.[6]

---

[4] It is important to point out that it is mainly the degrees of simultaneity, non-linearity and the functional forms (exponents, logarithms etc), and *not* specifically forward-looking components, that are important in the solution algorithm. For example under the Fair-Taylor (1983) algorithm the first solution stage exogenises leads and is therefore equivalent to repeatedly solving a backward looking model.

[5] This model was taken from Laxton et al, 1995. We thank Douglas Laxton for permission to use it but do not wish to implicate him in our conclusions.

[6] Were we solving a forward looking model into the future, the usual practice would be to use values projected from their historical trend.

Having done this preparatory work, our second step is to shock each model in turn with a standardised shock, typically a 1% increase in a policy or exogenous variable. Each model is then resolved, using each algorithm in turn, using our chosen start values; and then again using a series of modifications to those start value for the endogenous variables; in this case by taking starts which are reduced (or increased) by 10%, in steps of 10%, to 90% below (or above) their original values in the same scenario. The performance of each algorithm on the given model can then be compared across the different shocks to the starts. In certain cases, we extend the variations in the starts to below 90% of their original values to trace out any further differences (sensitivities) in the algorithms.

For all simulations, and across all models, we use a proportional convergence criterion of $\tau=10^{-6}$ for the inner loop and $\tau=10^{-12}$ for the outer one (type 1 and type 2 loops respectively). These convergence tests are probably much tighter than is necessary, and they could certainly be loosened further for the inner loop of the Fair-Taylor type algorithms. Indeed Fisher et al (1986) and Fisher and Hughes Hallett (1988) have shown that incomplete inner iterations, obtained by putting a weaker convergence criterion on the inner loop iterations, are a necessary part of constructing a computationally efficient version of those algorithms. We have not pursued this theme further so the FT algorithms may be at a disadvantage to the Newton ones. Similarly we have not examined the possibility of accelerating these algorithms with SOR(α) or FGS(δ) type relaxations in the inner loop.

4. NUMERICAL SOLUTIONS AND COMPARISONS

We define algorithm performance across this 'shocking' process as :

Differences in simulation times
Differences in iterations
Differences in numerical accuracy
Differences in numerical stability
Differences in solution paths
Available remedies for delinquent solution paths

4.1 Algorithm Comparisons on the Output Gap Model

This model has proved attractive since it implies that the Phillips-Curve relationship depends on excess demand (equation 1 in the appendix) and is thus non-linear in the output gap and forward-looking in its term structure. That generates significant amount of non-linearity in the monetary transmission mechanism. The model has 4 equations and one lead variable (in inflation) and one purely simultaneous block.

Despite its complexity, it can be seen that as far as a starts problem is concerned this model provides no great problems: all algorithms perform alike and are not greatly affected by the start values chosen. In addition numerical accuracy is not a problem. The worst percentage error relative to Newstack is of the order of 10^{-10}. Finally the solution times and the number of iterations to reach a solution are effectively independent of the start values chosen in each algorithm. Furthermore we could not find any non-zero shock that caused any generalised break down .This suggests that under general conditions there may be no practical reason to expect one algorithm to perform any worse than another in the face of imperfect starts. And in terms of time taken, given that we have not exploited the remaining possibilities for accelerating the Fair-Taylor algorithms, the ranking of speed of convergence is NS or OS, FT-N, FT-GS.

4.2 Algorithm Comparisons on the Dornbush Model

This is a popular policy simulation model and has undergone many refinements. Being linear, we can directly check for signs of Blanchard-Kahn stability .Also being linear it will require no Newton damping.

This model has eleven equations , three forward looking variables (in exchange rates and prices) and seven blocks : six recursive and one simultaneous. The convergence results show the Newton based models converge in one step, which is as expected since the model is linear. For the same reason, those algorithms are convergent irrespective of the start values chosen. FT-GS however had a convergence rate which decreased the further the starts were away from their original (reference) values: that is the smaller the start values in this case. However that problem was never so serious that FT-GS failed to converge. It just gets slower compared to Newton on linear models.

4.3 Algorithm Comparisons on the Growth Model

Here we found that all algorithms survive the shock process from 10% down to 90% below base. However, for even smaller ranges we found the Stacked Newton algorithms broke down. For example when multiplying the starts by $5x10^{-5}$, OS failed although NS, FT_GS, and FT_N generated identical solutions to the baseline. More generally, the Newton methods are much more sensitive to badly chosen start values than FT-GS. Indeed the latter proved insensitive to that problem altogether.

This raises the problem of how one handles starts failure in Newton systems. The *generalised* remedies to algorithm failure include the following:

1. ***Re-normalisation of the equations.***
2. ***Re-ordering of the equations.***

---

3. ***Transforming the model (de-Log the equations etc).***
4. ***Changing Step size (i.e. more damping) to avoid illegal solution paths.***[7]

[7] An illegal solution path is one requiring the algorithm to perform "illegal arithmetic" to evaluate a variable at some step along the way to the final solution (which won't, in itself, require illegal arithmetic).

5. ***Constraining the solution path to non-negative ranges.***
6. ***Applying looser convergence criteria.***

---

7. ***Controlling the number of times the Jacobian is recalculated in simulations.***

Notice that there is a natural division between these options: whilst options 3-6 can apply to any algorithm or algorithm type, options 1-2 are purely of use in first order algorithms.[8] And option 7 is one of many possible modifications of the Newton algorithm which can be used to reduce the computational burden of each step, described in Section 3. The advantage here is that such modifications also slow the Newton algorithms of rate convergence (Hughes Hallett, 1990) and hence make it less likely to step into an area of illegal arithmetic.

The easiest remedy for nonconvergence is to change the internal loop relaxation (or damping) parameter, γ, in an attempt to avoid stepping into an area of illegal arithmetic.[9] Reducing the relaxation factor will of course reduce the step length. In the previous exercise we had used starts reduced by factors of between 0.9 to 0.1 below the reference solution and γ=0.5. Reducing the relaxation factor to γ=0.1 allowed all algorithms - including the Newton based Oldstack and Newstack methods - to retrieve the reference solution, although of course more iterations were necessary. Similarly for starts reduced by a factor of 10^{-5} below the reference solution and a relaxation parameter of γ=0.1 all algorithms converged (where this was the point at which Newstack had previously failed to converge). Our next exercise was to reduce the starting values to close to zero - zero starts are frequently recommended when the final solution is unknown (see Young 1971). In this case neither the Oldstack, nor the Newstack-Newton algorithms would solve for any relaxation parameter, however small. On the other hand, none of the Fair-Taylor algorithms had any problems in this case. For example FT GS (and FT N) continued to find the solution without difficulty and for a very wide range of relaxation parameters.

The question arises, why do the stacked Newton algorithms fail in this case? Each breakdown could be traced to K, the capital stock in equations 1 and 4, turning negative at some point along the iteration path. Although in principle it might have turned positive again at a later iteration, a negative capital stock has no meaning in economics and causes the algorithm to break down at that point since equation 1 then requires a negative number to be raised to a negative or fractional power; A was set equal to 0.33. Consequently, so long as the algorithm is restricted to real arithmetic, it necessarily breaks down at this step and cannot go on to a point at which K turned positive again. Notice that this breakdown is caused by the more rapid convergence speed, and hence longer step length, of the stacked Newton algorithms. Their

---

Illegal arithmetic might involve taking the log or the root of a negative number, or inverting a function outside its domain, or raising a negative number to a fractional power. We have not considered the possibility of extending these algorithms into the complex domain.

[8] Transforming the model will change the numerical composition of the Jacobian but Newton solution methods are invariant to equation ordering and normalisation.

[9] i.e. in the case of a Newton algorithm we replace (2) by $y^{(s)} = \gamma(y^{(s-1)} - F^{-1}f(y^{(s-1)},z)) + (1-\gamma)y^{(s-1)}$; and for the others we use (3) with $G^{(s-1)} = \gamma B^{(s-1)} + (1-\gamma)I$.

solution paths therefore overshoot to the extent that they stray into the area of illegal arithmetic. As a result, the breakdowns are not due to a singularity in the final solution path or at the solution (i.e. the system's Jacobian matrix becoming singular, temporarily or within a neighbourhood of the final solution). Nor is it a problem of divergence in the algorithm (because the starts are sufficiently far away from the solution as to lie <u>outside</u> the set C for which convergence is guaranteed). Either of the latter problems could also have prevented convergence, but equally they could have been fixed by experimenting with larger step sizes (larger values of the relaxation parameters) unless the solution was undefined because of singularity at the point of breakdown. That is not the case since the Fair-Taylor algorithms continued to find the solution without difficulty, and since larger step sizes (larger relaxation parameters) led to break downs just the same.

This example therefore just shows how sensitive the Newton based algorithms may be to poorly chosen starts, leading to break down rather than divergence as such, even when a well defined solution exists. Other algorithms - in this example at least - do not have the same sensitivity and frequency of breakdowns.

Can the Newton methods be rescued in this case? Since varying the step size is no longer an option, we are left with options 5 and 7 of our list above. First, option 5. To implement this, we constrained <u>all</u> endogenous variables (rather than just K) to be nonnegative in <u>all</u> the stacked Newton runs. This represents an "if, then else ..." loop: *if* any endogenous variable becomes negative, *then* we reset at a value in a positive neighbourhood of zero (arbitrarily chosen to be 10^{-9} here) subject to a maximum number of times that it can be reset: *else* do nothing. This in effect adds another nonlinear constraint to the solution path, if it is ever activated. We should therefore expect the modified algorithm to take rather more steps to convergence than in other cases (it does), but nonetheless to converge.

This intervention successfully recovered the reference solution when either stacked Newton algorithm was used with the usual range of starts and the usual relaxation parameter value of γ=0.5 (also if γ<0.5). Nevertheless for larger values of γ, or smaller values of the start values down to zero, the stacked Newton algorithms still ran into problems that the Fair-Taylor algorithms had never even hinted at. Once again the result of inappropriately chosen starts is not divergence as such, but a break down through getting into an area of illegal arithmetic. And it may be that such breakdowns cannot be avoided by imposing nonnegativity constraints because the latter may simply mean that the algorithm simply stops and "marks time" at those constrained zero values - being unable ever to get away from them again. Thus the problem for the user is that we may not know enough, a priori, about the final solution to be able to specify start values that are sufficiently close to that solution to avoid this problem of breakdown through illegal arithmetic, "marking time" or divergence - especially where we have to guess start values for endogenous variables which lie far into the future in a rational expectations model. The other problem is that economic models so frequently have this kind of nonlinear structure - i.e. variables to fractional powers in production functions, or potential output and wealth functions; or variables in log-linear functions - that we should expect to see this kind of sensitivity to ill chosen starts frequently with the Newton based algorithms.

However this still leaves us with the puzzle of why Stacked Newton methods fell into this hole when the first order methods (which are potentially un-robust in other dimensions – Juillard et al, 1998b) did not. Once again the reason must be closely linked with step size. Whilst the Fair-Taylor methods process a great many small and computationally cheap steps, stacked Newton will take huge and computationally expensive ones and that means that – here at least - they can break down quite easily and irretrievably unless they can be stopped going down certain paths. Irretrievably in the sense that no parameter search will remedy the break down .

As an further interesting experiment, we allowed the Jacobian fewer inversions (option 7). This may mean – at the possible loss of some accuracy or speed – that they were less likely to stray into illegal paths. However if we set it at just two inversions – and for unshocked starts – we still found that the model could not solved under Stacked Newton. This option was of no help, therefore.

4.4 Algorithm Comparisons on the FLSIM Model

Now let us consider the policy simulation model.

This model :

*1: LOG(P) = LOG(P(-1))+A*LOG(GNP(-1))+ADD.P,*
*2: LOG(M/P) = N*LOG(GNP)-G*RS+ADD.M,*
*3: LOG(GNP) = D*LOG(ER/P)+ADD.GNP,*
4: RS = RW.RS+100(ER(1)-ER)/ER,;*

is clearly non-linear (given the price deflator in equations 2 and 3 and the exchange rate growth in the uncovered interest parity condition (UIP) in equation 4.) Although it is log-linear otherwise.

Here we find that NS , OS and FT_N solve satisfactorily onto the control from the .9 to .1 shocks (see table). FT_GS however fails at and below 0.5 of the usual lagged endogenous starts. The problem cannot be solved by damping parameter searches; nor incidentally can it be solved by non-negativity constraints. This is because – as we can infer from a successful iteration path (the first 24 outer-loop iterations) - the solution path goes negative. But if we impose a non-negativity constraint, the model diverges.

What other options could be used to make this algorithm work for small start values? Out of our list in Section 4.3, we have only the following possibilities.

1. Re-normalisation of the equations.
2. Re-ordering of the equations.
3. Transforming the model (de-Log the equations etc).

Let us first try re-normalising. Presently the model has the following ordering

1 • P
2 • GNP
3 • ER
4 • RS

and an incidence matrix (see Appendix) which shows that P can be solved recursively with respect to a simultaneous block consisting of the other three endogenous variables. The only alternative normalisation is therefore:

Normalisation A
1 • P
2 • RS
3 • GNP
4 • ER

We found that normalisation A would not solve the model under the original start values. The original normalisation however worked under the original starts, but failed when we reduced the starts to 0.5 of their original size or lower.

There remains the possibility of reordering the equations as they stand, rather than renormalising them. This is an option which has worked well in the past (Hughes Hallett and Fisher, 1990), and with a four equation model we have 24 different reorderings to try. Solving all 24 orderings with the FT_GS algorithm produced an interesting result – of the 24 possible reorderings only 6 worked at starts down to 0.1 of their original size.[10] All of these 6 reorderings had something in common: they each solved the UIP equation (i.e. equation 4) first. Any ordering that placed the UIP below the first equation failed at very low starts.

The exchange rate equation of course represents the only forward looking component in this model. It might be therefore that the structure of GS solutions in forward-looking models requires lead equations to be solved first or among the first. Clearly this result is open to further verification, but it is a notable one. And it does support our earlier finding that the best way to accelerate Fair-Taylor type algorithms is to conduct incomplete inner iterations, in which a loose convergence criterion is placed only on these variables which have forward expectations of variables appearing elsewhere in the model (Fisher et al 1986, Fisher and Hughes Hallett 1998). We have not experimented with these or other (SOR type) accelerations of the inner or outer loop iterations, so the scope for making the Fair-Taylor algorithms more robust, or faster, has not been fully exploited. Nevertheless equation ordering would seem to be far more important for precluding illegal starts problems and accelerating convergence, than renormalisation.

As a final option, we can transform the model. Retaining the original ordering, we can de-log the model as follows:

---

[10] But all of these successful six had their limit at 0.01 shocks .The other algorithms – NS, OS and FT_N – however could survive at 0.01 and beyond.

P = exp (LOG (P(-1))+A*LOG(GNP(-1))+ADD.P),
GNP = exp((LOG(M/P)+G*RS-ADD.M)/n),
er=p*exp((LOG(GNP)-ADD.GNP)/d),
RS = RW.RS+100*(ER(1)-ER)/ER,

Again we performed the same 0.9 to 0.1 shocks (see Table 5). When the model is de-logged, it becomes much more robust; FT_GS can satisfactorily solve on to control (with relative errors in common with FT_N at around e-04). This result accords with the common practice of first order modellers to normalise their models since in doing so they often preclude "illegal arithmetic" and this is what we found here. Although of course in so doing they can often "inappropriately" normalise their model and inject other errors into their solution procedure. For example this is what Poiro et al (1996) found when normalising the IMF's MULTIMOD model.

As a final exercise let us examine the case where we shock the starts up , considering both logged and de-logged model versions with the original ordering. Here we shock the starts equivalently by factors of 1.1 to 1.9 *above* base. We can see that shocking upwards is not so dramatic – the algorithms all track the control comfortably and FT_GS does not break down. If we put the model into de-logged form (Table 6), a shock of up to 1.9 shock is accommodated although again – as with the down-starts – at a reasonable cost in terms of accuracy.

The starts problem therefore – at least for FT_GS - is asymmetric: whilst numerical accuracy and solution stability is not a problem for “up-starts” it very much is more acute for “down-starts”.

5. CONCLUSIONS

This paper was a first look at a relatively neglected area of algorithm comparison. Our tests cannot be representative of all of the problems (or all of the solutions!) to imperfect starts across algorithms. But we can make a few broad points:

(i) Given the small models that we have considered here, there is no reason to expect first order methods to be any less robust to imperfect starts than stacked Newton.

(ii) Downsized starts seem more problematic than upsized starts.

(iii) Knowledge of a model’s internal structure can often used to preclude bad starts searches.

(iv) The most common form of algorithm breakdown, and the most difficult to remedy, was illegal arithmetic. It was not divergence or singularity at some point in the solution path.

(v) Inequality constraints would appear more useful for fixing breakdowns in Newton algorithms, but renormalisation or reordering work well for Fair-Taylor schemes. Experience suggests that these options may become more important on larger models, such as MULTIMOD, Quest or NIGEM.

(vi) The superior speed of the Newton algorithms in a neighbourhood close to the final solution give them an advantage when the problem consists of a series of smallish variations around an existing solution - such as in "fine tuning" a certain policy strategy for example. But further away from that known solution, and when the simulation horizon is quite long with forward looking expectations in particular, both types of algorithm can break down (or fail to converge).

Table 1. Results from the Output Gap Model.
No. of Outer Loop Iterations; and time taken in seconds to full convergence (in brackets).

	Algorithm:	NS	OS	FT-GS	FT-N
Start Values	1.0	19 (0.66)	19 (0.64)	61 (10.0)	61 (5.0)
[factor reduction	0.9	19 (0.66)	19 (0.45)	61 (9.8)	61 (5.1)
relative to base	0.5	19 (0.38)	19 (0.49)	61 (10.1)	61 (4.8)
line starts].	0.1	19 (0.33)	19 (0.46)	61 (10.3)	61 (4.5)

Table 2. Results From The Dornbusch Model
No. of outer loops iterations; and time taken in seconds to full convergence (in brackets).

	Algorithm:	NS	OS	FT-GS	FT-N
Start Values	1.0	1 (0.9)	1 (0.92)	716 (136.8)	41 (2.4)
[factor reduction	0.9	1 (1.15)	1 (0.95)	739 (139.7)	41 (2.5)
relative to base	0.8	1 (1.30)	1 (0.91)	750 (142.7)	41 (2.0)
line starts].	0.5	1 (0.9)	1 (0.96)	768 (132.5)	41 (1.9)
	0.1	1 (0.99)	1 (1.10)	786 (141.7)	41 (2.2)
	0.01	1 (0.91)	1 (0.96)	790 (144.7)	41 (2.0)

Table 3. Results from the Growth Model
No. of outerloop iterations; and time taken in seconds to full convergence (in brackets).

	Algorithm:	NS	OS	FT-GS	FT-N
Start Values	1.0	44 (4.0)	44 (3.8)	112 (23.0)	37 (2.1)
[factor reduction	0.9	44 (1.2)	44 (1.2)	112 (23.0)	37 (3.5)
relative to base	0.8	44 (1.2)	44 (0.71)	112 (20.0)	37 (4.0)
line starts].	0.7	44 (1.4)	44 (0.74)	112 (18.0)	37 (4.1)
	0.6	44 (1.2)	44 (0.80)	112 (22.0)	37 (4.1)
	0.5	45 (1.3)	44 (0.84)	112 (31.0)	37 (3.8)
	0.4	45 (1.2)	44 (0.90)	112 (28.0)	37 (3.9)
	0.3	46 (1.3)	45 (0.90)	113 (17.0)	37 (4.1)
	0.2	46 (1.2)	45 (1.06)	113 (18.0)	37 (4.1)
	0.1	49 (4.3)	48 (1.41)	113 (21.0)	37 (4.2)
	$5x10^{-5}$	65 (3.6)	∞	113 (20.0)	37 (4.1)
	$1x10^{-5}$	∞	∞	113 (20.0)	37 (4.5)
	$1x10^{-5}$	82 (6.9)	82 (7.6)	113 (20.0)	37 (4.3)

Table 4. The FLSIM Model
No. of outerloop iterations; and time taken in seconds to full convergence (in brackets).

	NS	OS	FT-GS	FT-N
1.0	18 (0.5)	18 (0.60)	85 (26.17)	86 (4.9)
0.9	21 (0.55)	21 (0.68)	85 (11.6)	86 (4.9)
0.8	23 (0.55)	23 (0.68)	85 (11.9)	86 (4.9)
0.7	24 (0.55)	24 (0.68)	85 (11.8)	86 (4.99)
0.6	25 (0.54)	25 (0.66)	85 (11.6)	86 (5.4)
0.5	25 (0.50)	25 (0.62)	∞	86 (5.5)
0.4	26 (0.50)	26 (0.60)	∞	86 (5.5)

Table 5. The FLSIM Model, in de-logged form
No. of outerloop iterations; and time taken in seconds to full convergence (in brackets).

	NS	OS	FT-GS	FT-N
1.0	18 (.44)	18 (.55)	86 (6.08)	86 (4.7)
0.9	22 (.90)	21 (.70)	86 (6.29)	86 (4.7)
0.8	23 (.56)	23 (.69)	86 (6.4)	86 (4.9)
0.7	25 (.56)	24 (.66)	86 (6.7)	86 (4.5)
0.6	27 (.60)	25 (.70)	86 (6.9)	86 (5.13)
0.5	30 (.65)	26 (.69)	86 (6.9)	86 (5.9)
0.4	34 (.94)	28 (.92)	86 (7.05)	86 (4.9)
0.3	37 (.95)	28 (.89)	86 (7.01)	86 (4.7)
0.2	40 (1.01)	29 (.91)	86 (7.38)	86 (4.6)
0.1	43 (1.06)	30 (.90)	86 (10.98)	86 (6.2)

Table 6. The FLSIM Model; increasing the start values
No. of outerloop iterations; and time taken in seconds to full convergence in brackets.

	NS	OS	FT-GS	FT-N
1.0	18 (.42)	18 (.57)	86 (14.3)	86 (4.9)
1.1	21 (.45)	21 (.55)	86 (11.4)	86 (5.9)
1.2	22 (.40)	22 (.53)	86 (11.2)	86 (6.7)
1.3	22 (.40)	22 (.44)	86 (10.9)	86 (5.4)
1.4	23 (.60)	23 (.59)	86 (10.6)	86 (5.2)
1.5	23 (.58)	23 (.70)	86 (17.3)	86 (4.9)
1.6	24 (.58)	24 (.70)	86 (11.8)	86 (4.7)
1.7	24 (.54)	24 (.67)	86 (11.9)	86 (5.8)
1.8	24 (.51)	24 (.63)	86 (11.9)	86 (5.6)
1.9	24 (.49)	24 (.62)	86 (21.0)	86 (5.9)

REFERENCES

Armstrong, J, Black, R, Laxton, D and Rose, D (1995), "A Robust Method For Simulating Forward Looking Models", Technical Report No. 73 , Bank Of Canada .

Blanchard, O and Kahn, C (1980), "The Solution Of Linear Difference Equations Under Rational Expectations", *Econometrica*, Vol. 48, pp. 1305-11.

Dennis, J and More, J J (1977), "Quasi-Newton Methods, Motivation and Theory", *SIAM Review*, Vol. 19, pp. 46-89.

Fair, R C and Taylor, J B (1983), "Solution and Maximum Likelihood Estimation of Dynamic Non-Linear Rational Expectation Models", *Econometrica*, Vol. 51, pp. 1169-1186.

Fisher, P G, Holly, S and Hughes Hallett A J (1986), "Efficient Solution Techniques for Dynamic Nonlinear Rational Expectations Models", *J. Econom. Dynamics and Control*, Vol. 10, pp. 139-145.

Fisher, P G and Hughes Hallett, A J (1998), "An Efficient Strategy for Solving Nonlinear Rational Expectations Models, *J. Econom. Dynamics Control*, Vol. 12, pp. 635-657.

Fisher, P and Whitely, J (1997), "Macro Economic Models at the Bank Of England", mimeo, Bank of England.

Hall, S G (1985), "On the Solution of Large Econometric Models with Consistent Expectation, *Bull Econom. Res.*, Vol. 37, pp. 157-161.

Hughes Hallett, A J (1982), "Iterative Techniques for Solving Systems of Nonlinear Equations", *Journal of Computational and Applied Mathematics*, Vol. 8, pp. 35-48.

Hughes Hallett, A J (1984), "Simple and Optimal Extrapolations for First Order Iterations", *International Journal of Computer Mathematics*, Vol. 16, pp. 309-18.

Hughes Hallett, A J and Fisher, P G (1990), "On Economic Structures and Model Solution Methods", *Oxford Bulletin of Economics and Statistics*, Vol. 52, pp. 317-330.

Hughes Hallett, A J (1990), "A Note on the Difficulty of Comparing Iterative Processes with Differing Rates of Convergence", *Computer Science in Economics and Management*, Vol. 3, pp. 273-279.

Juillard, M, Laxton, D, McAdam, P, Poiro, H (1998a), "An Algorithm Competition: First Order Iterations versus Newton Based Techniques", *Journal of Economic Dynamics and Control* , Vol. 22, pp. 1275-1289.

Juillard, M, Laxton, D, McAdam, P, Poiro, H (1998b), "Solution Methods and Nonlinear Forward Looking Models", this volume .

Laxton, D, Meridith, G, Rose, D (1995), "Asymmetric effects of economic activity on Inflation", IMF Staff Papers , Vol. 42, pp. 8.

Lipton, D, Poterba, J, Sachs, J and Summers, L (1982), "Multiple Shooting in Rational Expectations Models", *Econometrica*, Vol. 50, pp. 1329-1330.

Ortega, J M and Rheinboldt, W D (1970), *Iterative Solution of Nonlinear Equations in Several Variables*, Academic Press, New York.

Ostrowski, A M (1966), *Solutions to Equations and Systems of Equations* (2nd edition), Academic Press, New York.

Poiro, H (1995), "Faster Simulation Times for QPM: Saving the LU Decomposition Indices in TROLL", Bank of Canada, mimeo, April 4th, 1995.

Poiro, H, McAdam, P, Laxton, D (1996), "Solving MULTIMOD with First Order and Newton Raphson techniques", University of Strathclyde, ICMM Discussion Paper no 37.

Whitely, J (1997), "Economic models and Policy Making", *Bank Of England Quarterly Bulletin*, May.

Young, D M (1971), *Iterative Solution of Large Linear Systems* (Academic Press, New York).

APPENDIX MODEL DESCRIPTION

Model One: An Inflation-OutPut Gap Model

ENDOGENOUS : PDOT RR RS Y
EXOGENOUS : EY G

Equations:

1: PDOT = 0.414*PDOT(1)+(1-0.414)*PDOT(-1)+0.916*(G**2/(G-Y)-G)+
0.276*(G**2/(G-Y(-1))-G)
2: RR = RS-0.414*PDOT(1)-(1-0.414)*PDOT(-1)
3: RS = 3*PDOT+Y
4: Y = 0.304*Y(-1)-0.098*RR+EY

Horizon:

Min	Max	Symboltype	Symbolname
-1	1	ENDOGENOUS	PDOT
0	0	ENDOGENOUS	RR
0	0	ENDOGENOUS	RS
-1	0	ENDOGENOUS	Y

The model has 1 block, including 1 simultaneous block.
The largest block has 4 equations and the next largest has 0.

Block	Size	Eqn	Var
1	4	1	PDOT
		2	RR
		3	RS
		4	Y

Variable Used Unlagged in Equations

PDOT	1	3		
RR		2	4	
RS		2	3	
Y		1	3	4

Model Two - The Dornbush Model

ENDOGENOUS: EX P PC PCF PCGP PCGPF PF R RF Y YF
EXOGENOUS : G M MF UE UP UPF UR URF UY UYF
PARAMETER : A1O A1U A2O A2U A3O A3U A4O A4U A5O A5U A6O A6U A7O A7U
Equations:

```
 1:  Y = -A4U*(P-EX-PF)-A5U*(R-P(1)+P)+G+UY
 2:  EX = EX(1)-(R-RF+UE)
 3:  P = P(-1)+PC(-1)-PC(-2)+A1U*Y(-1)+A2U*(Y(-1)-Y(-2))+UP
 4:  PF = PF(-1)+PCF(-1)-PCF(-2)+A1O*YF(-1)+A2O*(YF(-1)-YF(-2))+UPF
 5:  PC = A3U*P+(1-A3U)*(PF+EX)
 6:  PCF = A3O*PF+(1-A3O)*(P-EX)
 7:  YF = -A4O*(PF+EX-P)-A5O*(RF-PF(1)+PF)+G+UYF
 8:  R = A6U*Y-A7U*(M-P)+UR
 9:  RF = A6O*YF-A7O*(MF-PF)+URF
10:  PCGP = PC-PC(-1)
11:  PCGPF = PCF-PCF(-1)
```

Horizon:

Min	Max	Symboltype	Symbolname
0	1	ENDOGENOUS	EX
-1	1	ENDOGENOUS	P
-2	0	ENDOGENOUS	PC
-2	0	ENDOGENOUS	PCF
0	0	ENDOGENOUS	PCGP
0	0	ENDOGENOUS	PCGPF
-1	1	ENDOGENOUS	PF
0	0	ENDOGENOUS	R
0	0	ENDOGENOUS	RF
-2	0	ENDOGENOUS	Y
-2	0	ENDOGENOUS	YF

The model has 7 blocks, including 1 simultaneous block.
The largest block has 5 equations and the next largest has 1.

Block	Size	Eqn	Var
1	1	3	P
2	1	4	PF
3	5	1	Y
		2	EX
		7	YF
		8	R
		9	RF
4	1	5	PC
5	1	6	PCF
6	1	10	PCGP
7	1	11	PCGPF

Variable	Used	Unlagged in Equations				
EX	1	2	5	6	7	
P	1	3	5	6	7	8
PC	5	10				
PCF	6	11				
PCGP		10				
PCGPF		11				
PF	1	4	5	6	7	9
R	1	2	8			
RF	2	7	9			
Y	1	8				
YF	7	9				

Model Three - A Small Growth Model (SGM)

MODCOM Small Growth Model
ENDOGENOUS : C K X Y Z
EXOGENOUS : SHK
PARAMETER : A BETA DELTA ROH SIGMA TAO
FUNCTION : LOG
Equations:

```
1:    C**(-TAO) = BETA*A*K**(A-1)*X(1)+BETA*DELTA*Y(1)
2:    X = C**(-TAO)*Z
3:    Y = C**(-TAO)
4:    K = Z*K(-1)**A-C+DELTA*K(-1)
5:    LOG(Z) = ROH*LOG(Z(-1))+SIGMA*SHK
```

Horizon:

Min	Max	Symboltype	Symbolname
0	0	ENDOGENOUS	C
-1	0	ENDOGENOUS	K
0	1	ENDOGENOUS	X
0	1	ENDOGENOUS	Y
-1	0	ENDOGENOUS	Z

The model has 4 blocks, including 1 simulatenous block.
The largest block has 2 equations and the next largest has 1.

Block	Size	Eqn	Var
1	1	5	Z
2	2	1	C
		4	K
3	1	2	X
4	1	3	Y

Model Four - A Forward Looking Simulation Model (FLSIM)

ENDOGENOUS : ER GNP P RS
EXOGENOUS : ADD.GNP ADD.M ADD.P M RW.RS
COEFFICIENT : A D G N
FUNCTION : EXP LOG

Equations:

1: LOG(P) = LOG(P(-1))+A*LOG(GNP(-1))+ADD.P,
2: LOG(M/P) = N*LOG(GNP)-G*RS+ADD.M,
3: LOG(GNP) = D*LOG(ER/P)+ADD.GNP,
4: RS = RW.RS+100*(ER(1)-ER)/ER,;

Horizon:

Min	Max	Symboltype	Symbolname
0	1	ENDOGENOUS	ER
-1	0	ENDOGENOUS	GNP
-1	0	ENDOGENOUS	P
0	0	ENDOGENOUS	RS

The model has 2 blocks, including 1 simultaneous block.
The largest block has 3 equations and the next largest has 1.

Block	Size	Eqn	Var
1	1	1	P
2	3	2	GNP
		3	ER
		4	RS

Variable	Used Unlagged in Equations		
ER	3	4	
GNP	2	3	
P	1	2	3
RS	2	4	

ACCELERATING NON LINEAR PERFECT FORESIGHT MODEL SOLUTION BY EXPLOITING THE STEADY STATE LINEARIZATION

Gary S. Anderson

1. A NON-LINEAR EXTENSION OF THE ANDERSON-MOORE TECHNIQUE

1.1 General Model Specification

Consider the model

$$h(x_{t-\tau}, x_{t-\tau+1}, \ldots, x_{t+\theta-1}, x_{t+\theta}) = 0 \qquad (1)$$
$$t = 0, \ldots, \infty$$

Where $\chi \in \Re^{L}$ and $h: \Re^{L(\tau+1+\theta)} \rightarrow \Re^{L}$. We want to determine the solutions to Equation 1 with initial conditions

$$x_i = \bar{x}_i \; for \; i = -\tau, \ldots, -1 \qquad (2)$$

$$\lim_{t \to \infty} x_t = x^*. \qquad (3)$$

satisfying

This paper shows how to adapt the methods of (Anderson & Moore,1985) to determine the existence, and local uniqueness of the solution to Equation 1.

1.2 Asymptotic Linearization

If *h* were linear, we could immediately apply the methods of (Anderson & Moore, 1985) to determine the existence and uniqueness of a perfect foresight solution and to compute the solution. Since *h* is non-linear, we will compute approximate solutions to system 1 by using the nonlinear *h* constraints in Equation 1 for the initial part of the trajectory, and using a system of linear constraints which reflect the asymptotic properties of the system for the remainder of the trajectory.

This technique can be thought of as a generalization of the approach used by Fair-Taylor (Fair & Taylor, 1983). This paper describes a procedure which, unlike the Fair-Taylor approach, allows the solution to lie in the *stable subspace* of a linear system characterizing the asymptotic properties of the nonlinear system.

The steady state value x^* satisfies

$$h(x^*, \ldots, x^*) = 0 \tag{4}$$

$$h(x_{t-\tau}, \ldots, x_{t+\theta}) \approx \sum_{i=-\tau}^{\theta} H_i|_{x^*} (x_{t+i} - x^*) \tag{5}$$

Near the steady state, the linear first-order Taylor expansion of h about x^* provides a good approximation to the function h.

The technique presented in (Anderson & Moore, 1985) can determine the existence and uniqueness of perfect foresight solutions near the steady state of linear models. The asymptotic analysis of the linear model determines convergence properties before burdensome calculations of the nonlinear solutions. That stability analysis produces a matrix, Q, which restricts values of the endogenous variables to the stable subspace of the linearized system.

For trajectories which approach a steady state, one can ultimately replace the non-linear system with the constraints codified in the matrix Q.

$$Q \begin{bmatrix} x_{T-\tau} - x^* \\ \vdots \\ x_T - x^* \\ \vdots \\ x_{T+\theta} - x^* \end{bmatrix} = 0 \tag{6}$$

Consequently, for solutions which converge to the steady state, we can, in principal, compute solutions to whatever accuracy required by increasing the magnitude of T.

1.3 Relationship to Traditional Approach Using Fixed Points

The more traditional Fair-Taylor approach also increases T to increase accuracy, but it imposes Equation 7

$$I \begin{bmatrix} x_{T+1} - x^* \\ \vdots \\ x_{T+\theta} - x^* \end{bmatrix} = 0 \tag{7}$$

instead of equation 6.

Since Equation 6 more accurately characterizes the dynamics of the nonlinear system near the steady state the approach described in this paper converges more quickly. It will be convenient to normalize the Q matrix so that there is the negative of the identity matrix in the rightmost block. (Anderson & Moore, 1985) shows that such a normalization exists for models which have uniquely convergent

$$Q^N = \begin{bmatrix} -B_1 & I & & & \\ -B_2 & & I & & \\ \vdots & & & \ddots & \\ -B_{\theta-1} & & & & I \\ -B_\theta & & & & & I \end{bmatrix} \tag{8}$$

saddle points paths from arbitrary initial conditions.

Thus, the traditional approach of setting the end of the trajectory to the steady state would be equivalent to zeroing out the left half of the normalized Q matrix. Using AIM to Restrict the end of the trajectory to the asymptotic stable linear subspace provides a better approximation of the asymptotic behavior of the non linear function. This improvement in the approximation is reflected in the length of the trajectory needed to achieve a given level of accuracy for the values at the beginning of the trajectory. In order to achieve a specific number of significant digits in the computation of the points near the beginning of the trajectory, setting the end of the trajectory equal to a specific constant would force us to compute a longer solution path than adopting our approach of restricting the solution to the asymptotic linear space.

2. TWO NON-LINEAR EXAMPLES

2.1 A Money Demand Model

Consider the three equation non-linear system

$$\ln \frac{m_t}{p_t} = \alpha + \beta \ln(\rho + (\frac{p_{t+1} - p_t}{p_t})) \tag{9}$$

$$m_t - m_{t-1} = \gamma(m_{t-1} - \mu) + \delta s_t \tag{10}$$

$$s_t = \lambda s_{t-1}(1 - s_{t-1}) \tag{11}$$

Where $L = 3, \tau = 1, \theta = 1,$ and $0 \leq \lambda, \alpha < 0, \beta < 0, \rho > 0, \gamma < 0$ and $\mu > 0$ exogenously given. This example augments a simple forward looking money demand function (Equation 9) and a money supply rule (Equation 10) with an easy to manipulate and much studied nonlinear function, the quadratic map (Equation 11). Including the quadratic map provides a convenient way to study the impact of model parameters on asymptotic behavior. The parameter λ in the quadratic map provides a simple nonlinear function that can generate fixed points, limit cycles, and chaotic invariant sets, but this paper will study values of λ associated with fixed points.

The points $m^* = \mu - \frac{-\delta s^*}{\gamma} p^* = m^* \exp^{-(\alpha + \beta \ln(\rho))}$, where $s^* = 0$ or $s^* = \frac{\lambda - 1}{\lambda}$, are fixed points for the system. We can linearize the system and investigate the dynamics of the system near either steady state.

We want to investigate the model with initial conditions

$m_0 = \overline{m}_0$

$p_0 = \overline{p}_0$

$s_0 = \overline{s}_0$

and terminal conditions

$$\lim_{t \to \infty} \begin{bmatrix} m_t \\ p_t \\ s_t \end{bmatrix} = \begin{bmatrix} m^* \\ p^* \\ s^* \end{bmatrix}$$

Applying the methods of (Anderson & Moore, 1985) near the fixed point, the state space transition matrix is

$$A = \begin{bmatrix} (1+\gamma) & 0 & -\delta\lambda(2s^* - 1) \\ \frac{\rho/\beta}{m^*/p^*} & \frac{\beta-\rho}{\beta} & 0 \\ 0 & 0 & -\lambda(2s^* - 1) \end{bmatrix}$$

Which has three non zero eigenvalues, $(1+\gamma), \lambda(1-2s^*)$, and $\frac{\beta-\rho}{\beta}$.

The first two eigenvalues are smaller than one in magnitude provided:

$$-2 < \gamma < 0$$

and

$$s^* = \begin{cases} 0 & \text{and} \quad |\lambda| < 1 \\ \frac{\lambda-1}{\lambda} & \text{and} \quad 1 < \lambda < 3 \end{cases}$$

The last eigenvalue has magnitude bigger than one since $\frac{\rho}{\beta} < 0$.

The Q matrix of constraints imposing the saddle point property consists of two auxiliary initial conditions and one unstable left eigenvector if $0 < \lambda < 1$ or $1 < \lambda < 3$

$$Q = \begin{bmatrix} -(1+\gamma) & 0 & 0 & 1 & 0 & -\delta \\ 0 & 0 & \lambda(2s^* - 1) & 0 & 0 & 1 \\ 0 & 0 & 0 & -\frac{(-\beta+\beta\lambda+\rho-2\beta\lambda s^*)}{(\beta\delta\lambda(1-s^*))} & -\frac{m^*(\beta\gamma+\rho)(-\beta+\beta\lambda+\rho-2\beta\lambda s^*)}{\rho p^*(\beta\delta\lambda(1-s^*))} & 1 \end{bmatrix}$$

$$Q^N = \begin{bmatrix} 1+\gamma & 0 & \delta\lambda - 2\delta\lambda s^* & -1 & 0 & 0 \\ \frac{(1+\gamma)\rho p^*}{(\beta\gamma+\rho)m^*} & 0 & \frac{\delta\lambda\rho(-\beta+\rho)p^*(-1+2s^*)}{(\beta\gamma+\rho)m^*(\beta-\beta\lambda-\rho+3\beta\lambda s^*)} & 0 & -1 & 0 \\ 0 & 0 & \lambda - 2\lambda s^* & 0 & 0 & -1 \end{bmatrix} \quad (12)$$

$$= \begin{bmatrix} B_1 & -I \end{bmatrix} \quad (13)$$

2.2 Boucekkine's Non Linear Example

Boucekkine (Boucekkine, 1995) presents the following example nonlinear model. For $t > 0$

$$z_t - 5 y_{1,t}^{0.15} x_{1,t}^{0.75} = 0 \tag{14}$$

$$0.15 \frac{y_{1,t+1}}{y_{1,t}} + 5 x_{1,t}^{a} - 0.25 = 0 \tag{15}$$

$$y_{2,t+1} - 3 \frac{y_{2,t}^{1.65}}{x_{1,t-1}} w_{t-3} = 0 \tag{16}$$

$$x_{2,t} - 0.75 \frac{y_{1,t-1}}{y_{2,t}} + 1.25 = 0 \tag{17}$$

$$y_{1,t+1}^{b} - c \frac{x_{2,t-1}}{y_{2,t+1}} y_{1,t} = 0 \tag{18}$$

$$w_t = 1 \tag{19}$$

Solving for fixed point solutions x_1^*, x_2^*, y_2^*, z^* in terms of y_1^* produces

$$w_1^* = 1.$$

$$x_1^* = 50.^{\frac{-1.}{a}}$$

$$x_2^* = -1.25 + 4.06531\, 50.^{\frac{1.53846}{a}}\, y1$$

$$y_2^* = \frac{0.184488}{50.^{\frac{1.53846}{a}}}$$

$$z^* = \frac{5.\, y1^{\frac{3}{20}}}{50.^{\frac{0.75}{a}}}$$

provided y_1^* satisfies

$$y1^{b} - \frac{5.42042\, c\, y1 \left(-5. + 16.2613\, 50.^{\frac{1.53846}{a}}\, y1\right)^{d}}{4.^{1.d}\, 50.^{\frac{-1.}{a}\frac{20}{13}}} = 0. \tag{20}$$

Fixing a, b, and c produces a version of the mode whose asymptotic behavior depends only on d. In the text that follows,

$$\left\{a \rightarrow -3, b \rightarrow \frac{3}{2}, c \rightarrow \frac{5}{2}\right\}.$$

Figure 1 graphs solutions for 20 as a function of d. Note that for values of d between 0.0700073 and 0:38472 y_1 is complex valued. This paper will analyze model solutions over the range of d for which the solutions for y_1 are real valued.

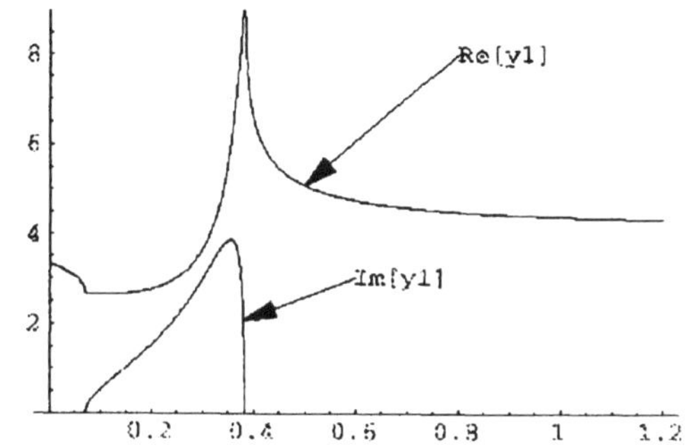

Figure 1: y_1 Solutions versus d with $\left\{a \to -3, b \to \frac{3}{2}, c \to \frac{5}{2}\right\}$

In constructing the transition matrix, the AIM algorithm discovers 4 auxiliary initial conditions. Figure 2 graphs the magnitude of the second and third largest eigenvalues as a function of d. The model will have locally unique convergent solutions when there are exactly two eigenvalues with magnitudes bigger than one. When the second largest eigenvalue has a magnitude less than one, there are multiple solutions converging to the steady state. When the third largest eigenvalue has a magnitude greater than one, there are no solutions converging to the steady state.

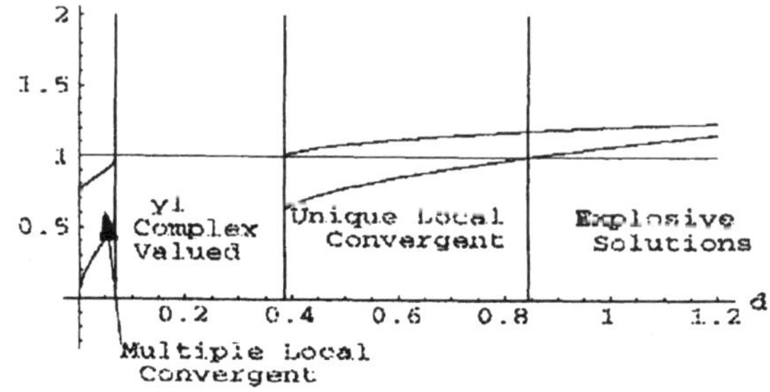

Figure 2: Magnitude of Second and Third Largest Eigenvalues versus d

Table 1 displays the eigenvalues for the asymptotic linearization when $d = 1.0$. Since there are 4 roots with magnitudes larger than one and 4 auxiliary initial conditions, there are no solutions converging to the fixed point from arbitrary initial starting points.

Fixed Point	{1., 3.68403, 1.14926, 4.38784, 1.37162, 16.5978}
Eigenvalues	{2.12643, -0.345383 −1.01957 *i*, 1.21433, −0.345383 + 1.01957 *i*}
Magnitudes	{2.12643 1.07649, 1.21433, 1.07649}

Table 1: Solution characteristics for d=1.0

Table 2 displays the eigenvalues for the asymptotic linearization when $d = 0.05$. Since there are 4 auxiliary initial conditions and only one eigenvalue with magnitude greater than one, there are multiple solutions converging to the fixed point.

Fixed Point	{1., 3.68403, 0.412629, 3.04066, 1.37162}
Eigenvalues	{1.91557, -0.0795795 −0.402948 *i*, 0.893593, -0.0795795 +0.402948 *i*}
Magnitudes	{1.91557, 0.410731, 0.893593, 0.410731}

Table 2: Solution characteristics for d=0.05

Table 3 displays the eigenvalues for the asymptotic linearization when $d = 0.5$. Since there are 4 auxiliary initial conditions and two eigenvalues with magnitude greater than one, so long as the auxiliary initial conditions and the eigenvectors associated with the two roots with magnitudes greater than one are linearly independent, there are unique solutions converging to the steady state from arbitrary initial conditions.

Fixed Point	{1., 3.68403, 1.53089, 5.08577, 1.37162, 16.9694}
Eigenvalues	{1.99626, -0.216796 − 0.743478 i, 1.08733, -0.216796 + 0.743478 i}
Magnitudes	{1.99626, 0.774441, 1.08733, 0.774441}

Table 3: Solution characteristics for d=0.5

Table 4 presents the Q and normalized Q matrices.

Appendix B provides additional detail describing the transition matrix and the auxiliary initial conditions.

$$Q = \begin{bmatrix} 0 & 0 & 0 & 0 & 0 \\ 0 & 0 & 0 & 0 & 0 \\ 0 & 0 & 0 & 0 & 0 \\ 0 & 0 & 0 & 0 & 0 \\ 0 & -0.345841 & 0 & 0 & 0 \\ 0 & -0.890678 & 0 & 0 & 0 \end{bmatrix} \cdots$$

$$\begin{matrix} \\ \end{matrix} \begin{bmatrix} 0 & 0 & 0 & 0 & 0 \\ 0 & 0 & 0 & 0 & 0 \\ 0 & 0 & 0 & 0 & 0 \\ 0 & 0 & 0 & 0 & 0 \\ 0 & -0.345841 & 0 & 0 & 0 \\ 0 & -0.890676 & 0 & 0 & 0 \end{bmatrix}$$

$$Q^N = \begin{bmatrix} 0 & 0 & 0 & 0 & 0 & 0 & 0 & 0 & 0 & 0 & 0 & 0 & 0 & 0 & 0 & 0 & 0 & 0 & -1 & 0 & 0 & 0 & 0 & 0 \\ 0.0569869 & 0 & 0 & 0 & 0 & 0 & 0.883257 & 0 & 0 & 0 & 0 & 0 & 0.96277 & -0.0154686 & 0.422868 & 0.0144885 & 0 & 0 & 0 & -1 & 0 & 0 & 0 & 0 \\ 1.59759 & 0 & 0 & 0 & 0 & 0 & 0.743063 & 0 & 0 & 0 & 0 & 0 & 0.319599 & -0.438653 & -0.0330743 & 0.316313 & 0 & 0 & 0 & 0 & -1 & 0 & 0 & 0 \\ -1.0019 & 0 & 0 & 0 & 0 & 0 & -2.83148 & 0 & 0 & 0 & 0 & 0 & -3.56987 & 0.271957 & -0.742194 & -0.32505 & 0 & 0 & 0 & 0 & 0 & -1 & 0 & 0 \\ -0.78798 & 0 & 0 & 0 & 0 & 0 & -0.366502 & 0 & 0 & 0 & 0 & 0 & -0.157636 & 0.213981 & 0.0459071 & 0.0140297 & 0 & 0 & 0 & 0 & 0 & 0 & -1 & 0 \\ -0.304576 & 0 & 0 & 0 & 0 & 0 & 1.6342 & 0 & 0 & 0 & 0 & 0 & 0.507439 & 0.0826745 & 1.08039 & -0.0098128 & 0 & 0 & 0 & 0 & 0 & 0 & 0 & -1 \end{bmatrix}$$

Table 4: Asymptotic Linear Constraints for Boucekkine Example: $(\{a \to -3, b \to \frac{3}{2}, c \to \frac{5}{2}, d \to 0.5\})$

Components of the Algorithm for Computing the Convergent Path

One can apply Newton's Algorithm to compute the solution to the non linear system Equations 1-3. With

$$y_t = \begin{bmatrix} x_{t-\tau} \\ x_{t-\tau+1} \\ \vdots \\ x_{t+\theta-1} \\ x_{t+\theta} \end{bmatrix} \tag{21}$$

$$z(T) = \begin{bmatrix} x_{-\tau} \\ x_{-\tau+1} \\ \vdots \\ x_{T+\theta-1} \\ x_{T+\theta} \end{bmatrix} \tag{22}$$

Equations 1-3 become

$$\aleph(z(T), \mho) = \begin{bmatrix} \begin{bmatrix} x_{-\tau} - \bar{x}_{-\tau} \\ \vdots \\ x_{-1} - \bar{x}_{-1} \end{bmatrix} \\ h(y_1) \\ h(y_2) \\ \vdots \\ h(y_{T-1}) \\ h(y_T) \\ \mho \begin{bmatrix} x_{T+1-\tau} - x^* \\ \vdots \\ x_{T+\theta} - x^* \end{bmatrix} \end{bmatrix} \quad \text{where } \mho = \begin{cases} Q & \text{for AIM} \\ \begin{bmatrix} 0 & I \end{bmatrix} & \text{for FP} \end{cases} \tag{23}$$

Figures 3 and 4 present pseudo code describing the algorithms for analyzing the steady state and computing the convergent path.

3.1 Improved Model Diagnostics

It is possible to choose the parameters of the model and initial conditions so that the number of time periods to convergence is arbitrarily large.

```
begin
if ¬ succeedsQ  (xStar := computeFixedPoint  (h, xGuessFP ))
then failcomment: unable to compute fixed point
else H := linearize(h, xStar )
if ¬hasSaddlePointPropertyQ (Q := andersonMoore(H))
then failcomment: no saddle point property at this fixed point
else
if ¬hasConvergedQ(xPath :=
   convergentPath  (xHistory ; h; Q ; T_MIN ; T_MAX ))
then failcomment: path has yet to converge
else success  (xPath )
fi
fi
fi
end
```

Figure 3: Nonlinear Extension of Anderson-Moore Algorithm: Initial Setup

```
begin
T := T_MIN
xPathOld := solveNonLinearSystem(xHistory ; h; Q ; T_MIN ; xGuessPath )
T := T + ΔT
xPathNew := solveNonLinearSystem(xHistory, h, Q, T)
while (xPathOld ≠ xPathNew) ^ (T ≤ T_MAX) do
xPathOld := xPathNew
T := T + ΔT
xPathNew := solveNonLinearSystem (xHistory, h, Q, T) od
end
```

Figure 4: Nonlinear Extension of Anderson-Moore Algorithm: convergentPath

Thus, for some parameter settings, procedures which depends on failure to converge will have trouble determining the appropriateness of the asymptotic stability conditions. The asymptotic linearization approach provides this information near the beginning of computation before undertaking many costly computations leading to uncertain results.

3.1.1 Computational Results

The approach of this paper focuses computational resources on computing saddle point paths for models which have saddle point paths. The analysis of the previous section indicates that the money demand model will have convergent perfect foresight paths to the $s = 0$ fixed point for $0 < \lambda < 1$ and to the $s = \frac{\lambda-1}{\lambda}$ for $1 < \lambda < 3$. There is no need to attempt solutions for models with values of λ outside this range.

The analysis of the previous section indicates that the Boucekkine model will have convergent perfect foresight paths for $0.38472 < d < 0.843407$. There is no need to attempt solutions for models with values of d outside this range.

3.2 Improved Initial Path Guess

The Newton iteration requires an initial guess, $z^0(T)$. Define

$$z^*(T^0, \mho) \ni \aleph(z^*(T^0, \mho), \mho) = 0 \tag{24}$$

The $z^*(T^0, \mho)$ represent solutions to Equation 21 using T^0 non linear time periods before applying asymptotic constraint $\mho$. Using iterative techniques to get a solution for $z^*(T, \mho)$, $T > T^0$ will require an initial guess $z^0(T)$

3.2.1 Steady State Bootstrap

The traditional approach augments the shorter solution trajectory $z^0\ (T^0)$

$$z^0(T) = \begin{bmatrix} z^*(T^0, \begin{bmatrix} 0 & I \end{bmatrix}) \\ x^*_{T^0+1} \\ x^*_{T^0+2} \\ \vdots \\ x^*_{T+\theta-1} \\ x^*_{T+\theta} \end{bmatrix} \tag{25}$$

with the fixed point values.

3.2.2 Aim Bootstrap

Alternatively, one could augment the shorter solution trajectory $z^0\ (T^0)$ with values consistent with the asymptotic behavior of the non linear system near the fixed point.

$$z^0(T) = \begin{bmatrix} z^*(T^0, Q) \\ \hat{x}_{T^0+1} \\ \hat{x}_{T^0+2} \\ \vdots \\ \hat{x}_{T+\theta-1} \\ \hat{x}_{T+\theta} \end{bmatrix} \tag{26}$$

with

$$\hat{x}_t = x^* + B_1 \begin{bmatrix} (\hat{x}_{t-\tau} - x^*) \\ \vdots \\ (\hat{x}_{t-1} - x^*) \end{bmatrix} \forall t > T_0 \tag{27}$$

Where B_1 comes from the first few rows of Q^N of equation 12.

Appendix A presents equations describing the AIM bootstrap applied to the Money Demand Model.

3.2.3 Computational Results

Using B_1 reduces the number of Newton steps required to compute a path of given horizon length whether or not using Q for the asymptotic constraint. Figure 5 and 6 show the number of newton steps needed to move from the initial guess to the solution for each horizon length. The line labeled "FP Initialization" shows the number of steps required when setting the entire initial path guess to the fixed point values. The line labeled "Q Initialization" shows the number of steps required when setting the initial path guess to the result of applying the B_1 matrix to the initial conditions given in equation 2. The line labeled "FP Extension" shows the number of steps required when applying the Steady State Bootstrap to the solution from a horizon on period shorter. The line labeled "Q Extension" shows the number of steps required when applying the AIM Bootstrap to the solution from a horizon one period shorter. The "Q Extension" and "Q Initialization" lines show the number of Newton steps required to solve equation 24 with $\mho = Q$. The "FP Extension" and "FP Initialization" lines show the number of Newton steps required to solve equation 24 with $\mho = [\,0 \quad I\,]$. These results are typical for applying the two initial path guess strategies to the two models.

The AIM Bootstrap minimizes the number of Newton steps for finding the $z^*(T^0, \mho)$ for both models. Figure 5 presents computational results for the Money Demand Model. For example, Figure 5 indicates that at a horizon of 5 periods, initializing the path to the steady state lead to 13 newton steps. Initializing the path to the solution obtained by applying the asymptotic linearization to the initial conditions alone lead to 7 Newton steps. Extending the 4 period solution by adding one period of fixed point values leads to 5 Newton steps. Using AIM to augment the 4 period solution leads to 3 Newton Steps.

Figure 6 presents computational results for the Boucekkine Model. Figure 6 indicates that at a horizon of 7 periods, initializing the path to the steady state lead to 5 newton steps. Initializing the path to the solution obtained by applying the asymptotic linearization to the initial conditions alone lead to 4 Newton steps. Extending the 6 period solution by adding one period of fixed point values leads to 3 Newton steps. Using AIM to augment the 6 period solution leads to 3 Newton Steps. Extending the path using the Fixed Point Bootstrap or the AIM Bootstrap lead to the same number of Newton steps. The next section will show that the AIM Bootstrap dominates since the "FP" algorithms require more iterations to converge to the same accuracy than the "Q" algorithms.

Shorter Computation Horizon for Given Computation Error

When solving models with the saddle point property near the steady state, the two approaches compute equivalent paths. However, using Q improves the tradeoff between computation horizon and solution accuracy. For a given level of precision, the asymptotic linearization approach obtains the solution with a shorter computation horizon. At any given computation horizon, the asymptotic linearization approach computes a more accurate solution.

This paper defines numerical convergence for the algorithms using a measure of relative error. The algorithms terminate when

$$\|D^T(x - \hat{x})\| \leq m\|D^T\hat{x}\|$$

$$D^T = \begin{cases} \{1., 1., 1.\} & \text{Money Demand Model} \\ \{1., 0.27144, 0.65321, 0.19663, 0.72906, 0.05893\} & \text{Boucekkine Model} \end{cases}$$

$$\|\epsilon\| = \sqrt{(\epsilon^T\epsilon)}$$

$$x - \hat{x} = S_{1k}z^k(T) - S_{2k}z^{k-1}(T)$$

$$\text{with } S_{1k} = \begin{bmatrix} I_{nL} & 0 \end{bmatrix} \text{ and } S_{2k} = \begin{bmatrix} I_{nL} & 0 \end{bmatrix}$$

Where S_{1k} and S_{2k} are chosen to select comparable parts of the state vector.

If $m = 10^{-k}$ then larger components of *Dx* have k significant digits(Numerical Algorithms Group, 1995). The numerical calculation for this paper set $k \approx 8$.

3.3.1 Computational Results

Table 5 presents some computational results for the Money Demand Model. The last column demonstrates the equivalence between the convergent solution paths obtained by

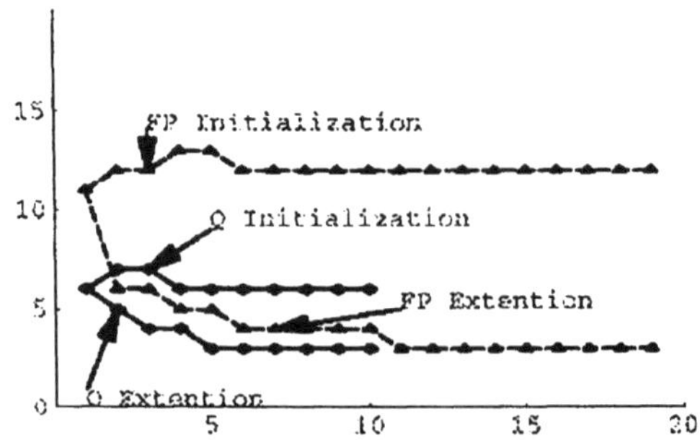

Figure 5: Newton Steps as Function of Horizon Length for Various Initial Guesses for Money Demand Model

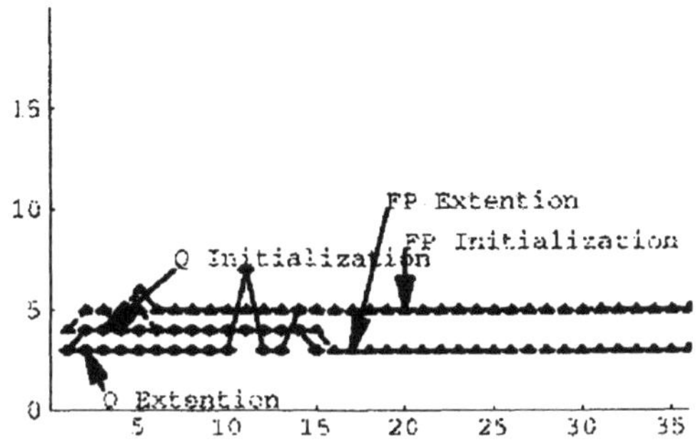

Figure 6: Newton Steps as Function of Horizon Length for Various Initial Guesses for Boucekkine Model

using the asymptotic linearization and those obtained using the traditional fixed point constraint. The computations using Q and using FP each used a convergence tolerance of 10^{-8}. The $\| \cdot \|_2$ difference between the initial portions of the trajectories are also within the supplied convergence tolerance of 10^{-8}.

λ	Fixed Point	Largest EVal	Convergence		$\|\chi_Q - \chi_{FP}\|$
			Q	FP	
1.5	0.467, 0.693, 0.333	0.5	11	22	2.17835 10^{-9}
1.9	0.242, 0.359, 0.474	0.1	10	19	4.45944 10^{-9}
2.3	0.0957, 0.142, 0.565	− 0.3	9	18	2.43792 10^{-9}

Table 5: Asymptotic Linearization and Fixed Point Solution Characteristics

The following figures employ two measures of error to characterize the rate of convergence of the two algorithms: approximation error and change in path error. The approximation error is $\|D(S_{1k}(T\,)_{X\text{-}now} - S_{2k}(T\,^*)_{X\ converged})\|_2$. The change in path error is $\|D(S_{1k}(T+1)_{X\ next} - S_{2k}(T)_{X\ now})\|_2$.

The top half of Figure 7 reports the variation in approximation error as a function of the computation horizon when $\lambda = 1.5$. For any given horizon, the approximation error is always about 6 times larger when using the fixed point instead of the asymptotic linearization. The bottom half of Figure 7 emphasizes this point by reporting the variation in approximation rescaled so that the initial approximation errors are the same.

Without prior knowledge of the convergent solution, algorithms rely on the change in the solution path to determine convergence. Figure 8 reports the variation in the change in path error as a function of the computation horizon when $\lambda = 1.5$. The asymptotic linearization algorithm would signal convergence before the fixed point algorithm. The accuracy of the solution does not suffer since the aggregate errors are so much less for any given computation horizon.

Figure 9 reports the variation in approximation error as a function of the computation horizon when $\lambda = 1.9$. Again, for any given horizon, the approximation error is always significantly less when using the asymptotic linearization.

Figure 10 reports the variation in the change in approximation error as a function of the computation horizon when $\lambda = 1.9$. The asymptotic linearization algorithm would signal convergence before the fixed point algorithm.

Figure 11 reports the variation in approximation error as a function of the computation horizon when $\lambda = 2.3$. For any given horizon, the approximation error is always significantly less when using the asymptotic linearization.

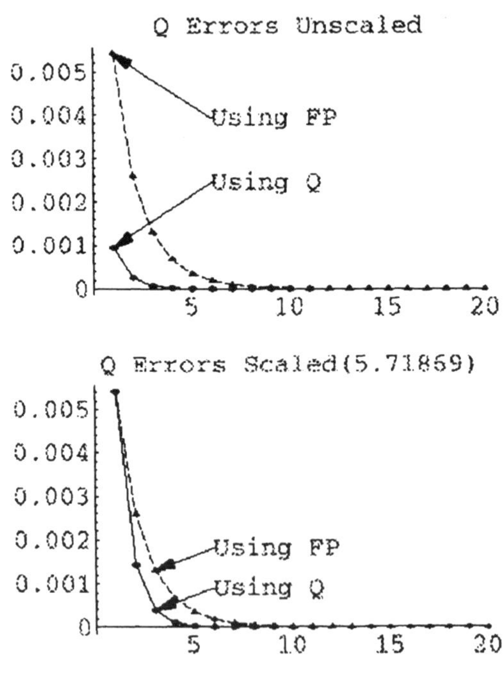

Figure 7: Approximation Error as Function of T for $\lambda = 1.5$.

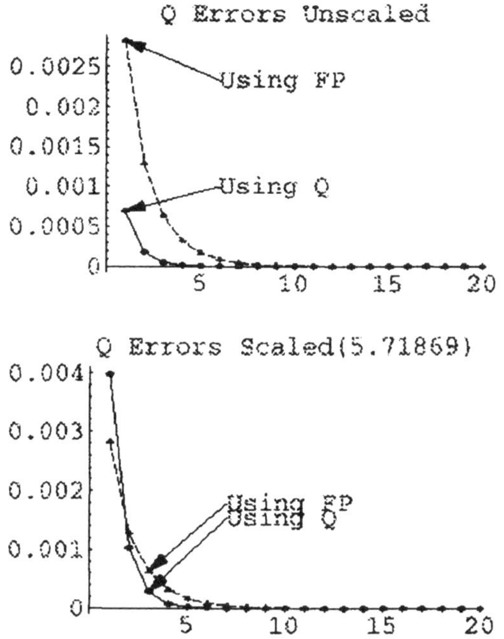

Figure 8: Change in Path Error as Function of T for λ = 1.5.

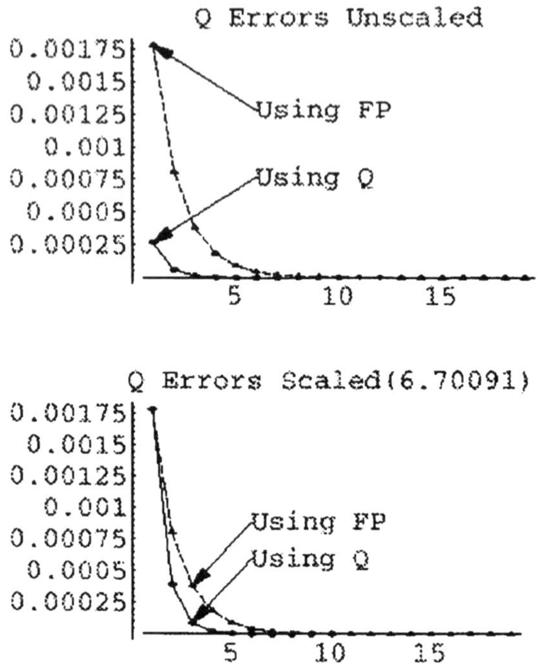

Figure 9: Approximation Error as Function of T for λ = 1.9.

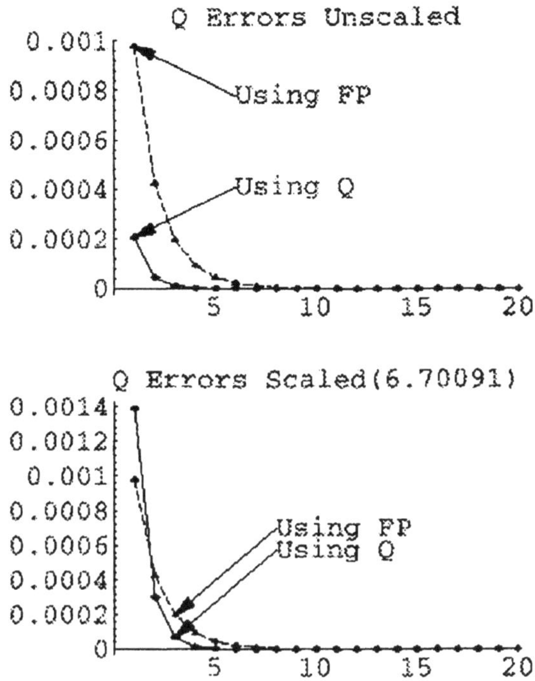

Figure 10: Change in Path Error as Function of T for λ = 1.9.

Figure 11 reports the variation in approximation error as a function of the computation horizon when λ = 2.3. For any given horizon, the approximation error is always significantly less when using the asymptotic linearization.

Figure 12 reports the variation in the change in approximation error as a function of the computation horizon when λ = 2.3. The asymptotic linearization algorithm would signal convergence before the fixed point algorithm.

Figure 13 presents a density plot comparing the number of horizons required for convergence for the two algorithms as a function of the initial conditions. Since m_0 and s_0 depend only on initial conditions they will not vary as the horizon length, T_0, changes, but p_0 will depend on the future values and the terminal conditions and will vary with the horizon length. The asymptotic linearization converges faster than the fixed point for all initial conditions.

Figures 14 - 16 present some computational results for the Boucekkine Model. Figure 14 reports the approximation error while Figure 15 reports the variation in the change in approximation error as a function of the computation horizon when d = 0.5 For any given horizon, the approximation error is always significantly less when using the asymptotic linearization. The asymptotic linearization algorithm would signal convergence before the fixed point algorithm.

The accuracy of the solution does not suffer since the aggregate errors are so much less for any given computation horizon.

Figure 16 presents a graph comparing the number of horizons required for convergence for the two algorithms as a function of the initial conditions for w. The asymptotic linearization converges faster than the fixed point for all initial conditions.

4. CONCLUSIONS

Linearizing non linear models about their steady state makes it possible to use the Anderson-Moore Algorithm(AIM) to investigate their saddle point properties and to efficiently compute their solutions. Using AIM to check the long run dynamics of non linear models avoids many of the burdensome computations associated with alternative methods for verifying the saddle point property. In addition, for models that have the saddle point property, AIM provides a set of terminal conditions for solving the non linear model that work better than the traditional approach of setting the end of the trajectory to the steady state values. Furthermore, the asymptotic linear constraints can also generate initial conditions for the solution path that are better than initializing the solution path to the steady state values. Using the improved asymptotic constraints typically halves the computational burden associated with solving the nonlinear problem.

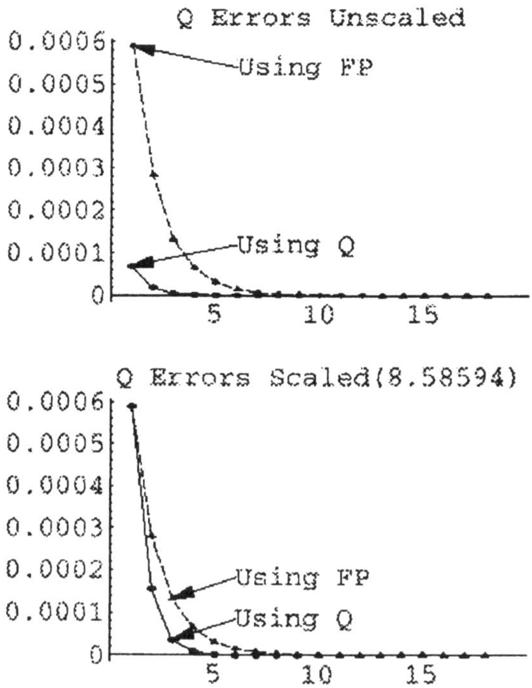

Figure 11: Approximation Error as Function of T for λ = 2.3

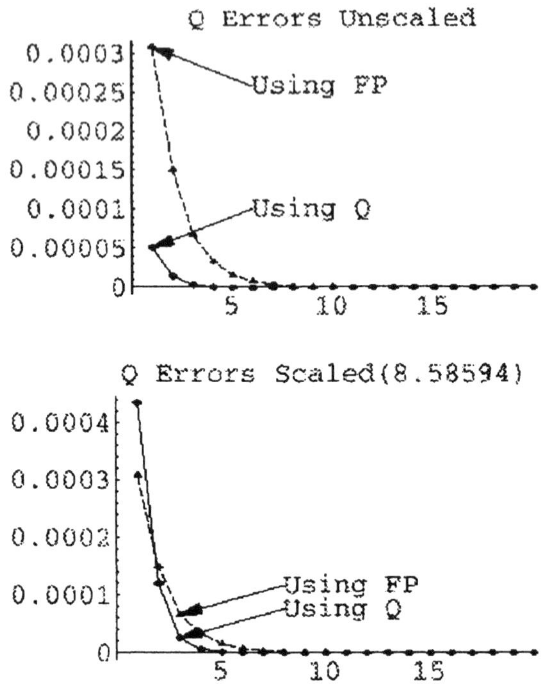

Figure 12: Change in Path Error as Function of T for λ = 2.3

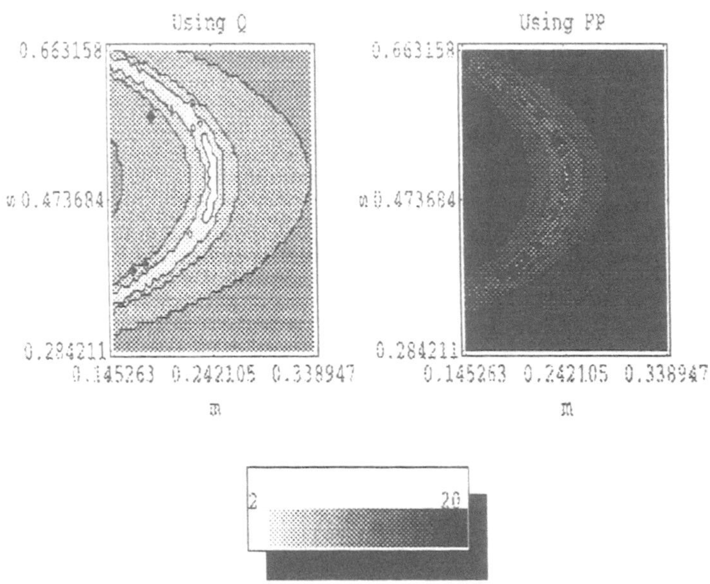

Figure 13: Horizon Length as a Function of Initial Conditions

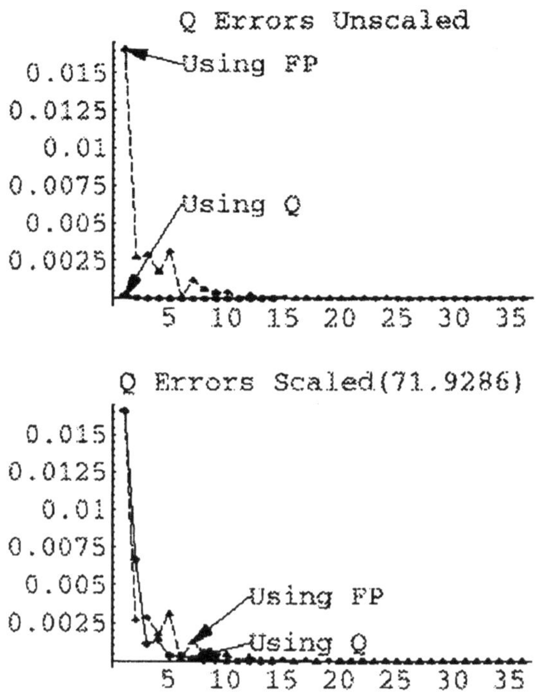

Figure 14: Variation in Approximation Error as Function of *T* for $\mathbf{a} = -3, \mathbf{b} = \frac{3}{2}, \mathbf{c} = \frac{5}{2}, \mathbf{d} = \frac{1}{2}$

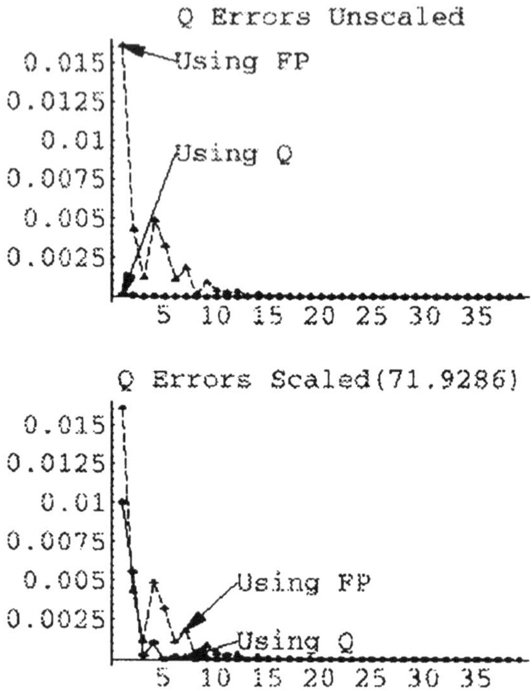

Figure 15: Change in Path Error as Function of *T* for
$a = -3, b = \frac{3}{2}, c = \frac{5}{2}, d = \frac{1}{2}$

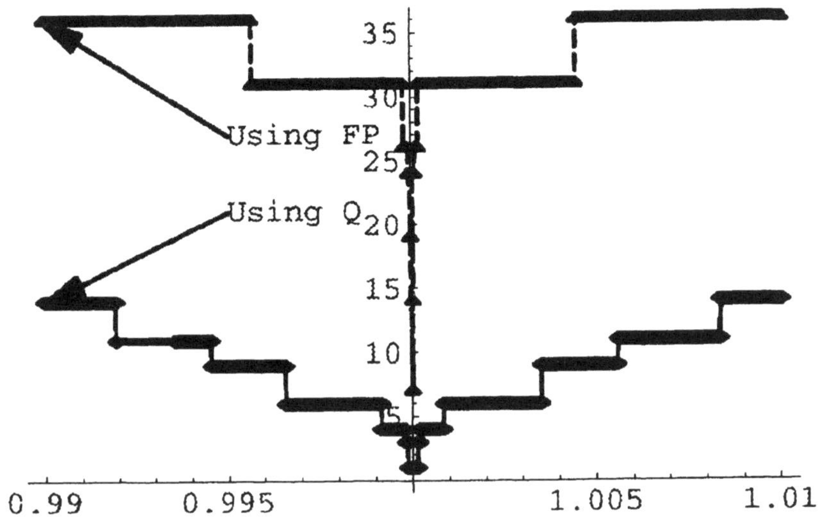

Figure 16: Horizon Length Versus Distance to Steady State

REFERENCES

Anderson, Gary, and Moore, George (1985), "A Linear Algebraic Procedure For Solving Linear Perfect Foresight Models", Economics Letters, Vol. 17.

Boucekkine, Raouf (1995), "An Alternative Methodology for Solving Nonlinear Forward-Looking Models", *Journal of Economic Dynamics and Control*, Vol. 19, pp. 711-734.

Fair, Ray, and Taylor, John (1983), "Solution and Maximum Likelihood Estimation of Dynamic Rational Expectations Models", *Econometrica*, Vol. 51.

Fuhrer, Jeffrey C, and Bleakley, C Hoyt (1996), "Computationally Efficient Solution and Maximum Likelihood Estimation of Nonlinear Rational Expectations Models", Tech. report, Federal Reserve Bank of Boston.

Guckenheimer, John, and Holmes, Philip (1983), "Nonlinear Oscillations, Dynamical Systems, and Bifurcations of Vector Fields", Springer-Verlag.

Numerical Algorithms Group (1995), C05PCF- NAG Fortran Library Routine Document, 14th edition.

A AIM Bootstrap Example

For $T^0 = 0$ we can use Equation 12 to compute $\hat{x}_0, \hat{x}_1 \ldots$ for arbitrary initial conditions:

$$\hat{x}_0 = B_1 \begin{bmatrix} (\bar{m}_{-1} - x^*) \\ (\bar{p}_{-1} - p^*) \\ (\bar{s}_{-1} - s^*) \end{bmatrix} = \begin{bmatrix} (1+\gamma)(\bar{m}_{-1} - m^*) + \delta(\bar{s}_{-1} - s^*)\lambda(1-2s^*) \\ \frac{(1+\gamma)(\bar{m}_{-1} - m^*)p^*\rho}{m^*(\beta\gamma+\rho)} + \frac{\delta(\bar{s}_{-1} - s^*)\lambda(1-2s^*)p^*\rho(\rho-\beta)}{m^*(\beta\gamma+\rho)(\beta-\beta\lambda-\rho+2\beta\lambda s^*)} \\ (\bar{s}_{-1} - s^*)\lambda(1-2s^*) \end{bmatrix}$$

$$\hat{x}_1 = B \begin{bmatrix} \hat{m}_0 \\ \hat{p}_0 \\ \hat{s}_0 \end{bmatrix} = \begin{bmatrix} (1+\gamma)(\hat{m}_0 - m^*) + \delta(\hat{s}_0 - s^*)\lambda(1-2s^*) \\ \frac{(1+\gamma)(\hat{m}_0 - m^*)p^*\rho}{m^*(\beta\gamma+\rho)} + \frac{\delta(\hat{s}_0 - s^*)\lambda(1-2s^*)p^*\rho(\rho-\beta)}{m^*(\beta\gamma+\rho)(\beta-\beta\lambda-\rho+2\beta\lambda s^*)} \\ (\hat{s}_0 - s^*)\lambda(1-2s^*) \end{bmatrix}$$

$$\vdots$$

Since the eigenvalues of B_{-1} are $(1+\gamma)$ and $\lambda\ (1-2s^*)$ the bootstrap path ultimately converges to the steady state. The bootstrap path approximation to the non linear solution improves as the solution approaches the steady state.

For $T^0 = 1$ after substituting the initial conditions and the AIM bootstrap path, we must find m_0; p_0; s_0 satisfying the system

$$-\alpha + \log\left(\frac{m_0}{p_0}\right) - \beta \log\left(\rho + \frac{\frac{(1+\gamma)p^*\rho m_0}{m^*(\beta\gamma+\rho)} - p_0 + \frac{\delta\lambda p^*\rho(\rho-\beta)(2s^*-1)s_0}{m^*(\beta\gamma+\rho)(\beta-\beta\lambda-\rho+2\beta\lambda s^*)}}{p_0}\right) = 0$$

$$-\bar{m}_{-1} - \gamma\bar{m}_{-1} + \gamma\mu + m_0 - \delta s_0 = 0$$

$$-(\bar{s}_{-1}\lambda) + \bar{s}_{-1}\lambda + s_0 = 0$$

B Transition Matrix Details

0	0	0	0	0	0	1.	0	0	0	0	0	0	0	0
0	0	0	0	0	0	0	1.	0	0	0	0	0	0	0
0	0	0	0	0	0	0	0	1.	0	0	0	0	0	0
0	0	0	0	0	0	0	0	0	1.	0	0	0	0	0
0	0	0	0	0	0	0	0	0	0	1.	0	0	0	0
0	0	0	0	0	0	0	0	0	0	0	1.	0	0	0
0	0	0	0	0	0	0	0	0	0	0	0	1.	0	0
0	0	0	0	0	0	0	0	0	0	0	0	0	1.	0
0	0	0	0	0	0	0	0	0	0	0	0	0	0	1.
0	0	0	0	0	0	0	0	0	0	0	0	0	0	0
0	0	0	0	0	0	0	0	0	0	0	0	0	0	0
0	0	0	0	0	0	0	0	0	0	0	0	0	0	0
0	0	0	0	0	0	0	0	0	0	0	0	0	0	0
0	0	0	0	0	0	0	0	0	0	0	0	0	0	0
0	0	0	0	0	0	0	0	0	0	0	0	0	0	0
0	0	0	0	0	0	0	0	0	0	0	0	0	0	0
0	0	0	0	0	0	0	0	0	0	0	0	0	0	0
0	0	0	0	0	0	0	0	0	0	0	0	0	0	0
0	0	0	0	0	0	0	0	0	0	0	0	0	0	0
−1.61089	0	0	0	0	0	−1.23801	0	0	0	0	0	0	0.436880	[illegible]
$-0.548794\, y1(d)$	0	0	0	0	0	0	0	0	0	0	0	0	$0.148434\, y1(d)$	0
$-0.666667\, y1(d)$	0	0	0	0	0	0	0	0	0	0	0	0	$0.180961\, y1(d)$	[illegible]
1.77162	0	0	0	0	0	0	0	0	0	0	0	0	−0.372115	0
[illegible]	0	0	0	0	0	[illegible]	0	0	0	0	0	0	[illegible]	[illegible]

0	0	0	0	0	0	0	0	0
0	0	0	0	0	0	0	0	0
0	0	0	0	0	0	0	0	0
0	0	0	0	0	0	0	0	0
0	0	0	0	0	0	0	0	0
0	0	0	0	0	0	0	0	0
0	0	0	0	0	0	0	0	0
0	0	0	0	0	0	0	0	0
0	0	0	0	0	0	0	0	0
1.	0	0	0	0	0	0	0	0
0	1.	0	0	0	0	0	0	0
0	0	1.	0	0	0	0	0	0
0	0	0	1.	0	0	0	0	0
0	0	0	0	1.	0	0	0	0
0	0	0	0	0	1.	0	0	0
0	0	0	0	0	0	1.	0	0
0	0	0	0	0	0	0	1.	0
0	0	0	0	0	0	0	0	1.
0	0	0	0	0	0	0	0	0
0	0	0	0	0.333333	[illegible]	[illegible]	−1.94504	0
0	0	0	0	0	0	0.546796	$-0.657775\, y1(d)$	0
0	0	0	0	0	0	0.666667	$-0.402071\, y1(d)$	0
0	0	0	0	0	0	0	1.65	0
0	0	0	0	[illegible]	[illegible]	[illegible]	[illegible]	0

Table 6: State Space Transition Matrix

$$
Aux(R) =
$$

$$
\left[\begin{array}{cccccccccccccccccccccccc}
0 & 0 & 0 & 0 & 0 & 0 & 0 & 0 & 0 & 0 & 0 & 0 & 0 & 0 & 0 & 0 & 0 & 0 & 0 & \text{[illegible]} & 0 & \text{[illegible]} & 0 & 1 \\
\text{[illegible]} & 0 & 0 & 0 & 0 & 0 & 0 & 0 & 0 & 0 & 0 & 0 & 0 & \text{[illegible]} & \text{[illegible]} & 0 & 0 & 0 & 0 & \text{[illegible]} & 0 & \text{[illegible]} & \text{[illegible]} & 0 \\
0 & 0 & 0 & 0 & 0 & 0 & 0 & 0 & 0 & 0 & 0 & 0 & 0 & 0 & 0 & \text{[illegible]} & 0 & 0 & 0 & 0 & 1 & 0 & \text{[illegible]} & 0 \\
0 & 0 & 0 & 0 & 0 & 0 & 0 & 0 & 0 & 0 & 0 & 0 & 0 & 0 & 0 & 0 & 0 & 0 & 1 & 0 & 0 & 0 & 0 & 0
\end{array}\right]
$$

Table 7: Auxiliary Initial Conditions Dimension

PART TWO

RATIONAL EXPECTATIONS AND LEARNING

CHAPTER 4

MODIFYING THE RATIONAL EXPECTATIONS ASSUMPTION IN A LARGE WORLD MODEL

Stephen Hall and Steven Symansky

1. INTRODUCTION

Many of the large econometric models in use around the world have introduced rational expectations(RE) as their main operating assumption over the last ten years, largely because of the issues raised by Lucas(1976). These include the Fair model, Minford's Liverpool model, the quarterly models of the National Institute of Economic and Social Research, the London Business School and HM Treasury model in the UK, Multimod at the IMF, the Global Econometric Model (GEM) and a number of others. A considerable amount of effort has been spent in the academic literature on attempting to test the relevance of the RE assumption in the real world, we will not attempt to survey this literature here, a good introduction is the book by Pesaran(1987). This literature has not found overwhelming support for the RE assumption, but on the whole it has not fared too badly. We want however to make a clear distinction between these tests and the implementation of RE in an econometric model. Most of the standard tests of RE are attempting to test if agents use all available information in an efficient way. The model under study is usually not either complete or detailed and so forcing variables are often generated through unrestricted VARs or in some other, non-structural, way such as instrumental variable estimation. These tests may then be viewed as a test of a weak form of rational expectations. When the large econometric models make the RE assumption they are imposing a much stronger assumption, one which we feel is of a quite different nature. They are assuming that agents actually use that particular model to form their expectations. That is, to take an example, agents have full knowledge of the London Business School model; they believe it to be the true model of the economy and that they use it to form full model consistent expectations. Such an assumption has never been tested before it has been imposed on a model.

In this paper we propose a test of the relevance of this strong form of the RE assumption in a large econometric model (note this is not a test of the relevance of RE on the part of real world agents). If the model fails such a test the question then arises as to what should replace the full RE assumption. The alternative used in this paper is an expectations rule based on the learning literature. Some researchers have already begun to adopt this course; see Hall and Garratt(1992a, 1992b) or Barrell, Caporale, Hall and Garratt(1993). This has been partly motivated by the widespread realisation that the introduction of RE into the large forecasting models has made them almost unusable in a forecasting context. We will examine this option by introducing learning-based expectations into a single country sector of MULTIMOD and assessing how important the economic implications of the present RE assumption are. Learning based purely on past information is in a sense the opposite extreme to RE as it is essentially abandoning all the future information contained in the structure of the model. So this option represents a move from a complete belief in the structure of MULTIMOD to a total lack of belief in its structure. We therefore propose a form of learning which incorporates the structure of the model as one element in the learning rule but which has other element which allow the relaxation of the total belief assumption of full RE.

The plan of the paper is as follows: Section 2 will briefly discuss the implications of the RE assumption in a large model and the way learning has so far been implemented. Section 3 will outline the test for RE in a model and the way the standard learning rules can be modified to include information about the structure of the model. Section 4 will then introduce some standard learning procedures into MULTIMOD to asses the economic importance of the various alternative assumptions. Section 5 will apply the test of rationality to MULTIMOD. Section 6 will then illustrate the effect of introducing the modified expectations assumption which mixes both RE and learning into MULTIMOD and section 7 will conclude.

2. RATIONAL EXPECTATIONS (RE) AND LEARNING

The implications of RE in an econometric model have been discussed widely but it is worth restating the basic principals here as the test proposed in the next section will rest on a precise understanding of the implications of implementing RE in a complete model.

State the model we are using as

$$Y_t = f(X_t, \Omega, Y^e_{t+i}) \tag{1}$$

where Ω is the parameter vector. In obvious notation. The expectations variables have been treated in various ways over the years. Adaptive expectations and its generalization to extrapolative expectations generally sets up some explicit model of expectations formation of the form,

$$Y^e_{t+i} = k(X_1, \ldots, X_t, Y_1, \ldots, Y_{t-1}, \beta) \tag{2}$$

This may be specified either explicitly in the model or perhaps more usually an implicit rule of this type is used to substitute the expectations out of the structural equations (1). Expectations then simply disappear into the dynamics of the model. Under RE we replace this assumption with the following one,

$$Y^e_{t+i} = Y_{t+i} \tag{3}$$

where the future values for Y are given by the models own forecast, (3) can of course be rewritten in final form as,

$$Y^e_{t+i} = Y_{t+i} = g(X_1,\ldots,X_T,\Omega,Y_1,\ldots,Y_{t-1})$$

In this case, where g represents the fully restricted final form of the structural model implied by (1) and (3). If our macro models were fully specified [that is to say, if the processes generating X were made explicit] then we could further simplify (4) to give,

$$g(X_1,\ldots X_T,\Omega,Y_1,\ldots,Y_{t-1}) = h(X_1,\ldots,X_t,\Omega,Y_1,\ldots,Y_{t-1}) \quad (5)$$

This is simply a restricted form of (2) where the restrictions implicit in the function h come from the full structural model (1) and the expectations assumption (3). The advantages of (5) over the unrestricted expectations rule (2) is that any regime change which is implemented in (1) will automatically be reflected in the RE expectations rule (5) where as (2) will be unaffected by the regime change and so will be misspecified. This is, of course, the Lucas(1976) point that a model which relies on extrapolative, fixed parameter, rules will not be structurally stable in the face of regime changes.

Given the obvious presence of policy regime changes in the real world the Lucas critique provided considerable motivation for modellers to incorporate the rational expectations rule (3) or (4) into their models. It has long been recognized however that this involves a very strong assumption about both the degree of knowledge which agents have and the way they process it. An alternative, less stringent assumption which has received increasing attention in the theoretical literature and some recent attention in applied work is learning. Essentially the problem with (2) as an expectations model is that the coefficients of the expectations process are fixed. So, when a regime change occurs there is no way for the expectations mechanism to adjust to this change. This will, in general, lead to the possibility that the expectations rule will make systematic errors and be quite untenable as an appropriate rule for an intelligent agent to use. This has lead to the learning literature where agents specify an expectations rule such as (2) but then proceed to revise and learn about the parameters of the system so that (2) then takes on the general form of,

$$Y^e_{t+i} = k(X_1,\ldots,X_t,Y_1,\ldots,Y_{t-1},\beta_{t|t-1}) \quad (6)$$

In this model the parameters change over time, and agents form a view of these parameters based on the current information set. Variants of this learning procedure have been examined by Bray(1983), Bray and Kreps(1984), Bray and Savin(1986), Evans(1983, 1985, 1986a. 1986b), Woodford(1990), Townsend(1978, 1983) and Marcet and Sargent(1988, 1989a, 1989b) amongst others and a recent survey may be found in Evans and Honkapokja(1992). Marcet and Sargent(1988) summarize much of the main results of this literature, the concept of learning is characterized as a mapping in the parameter space, $\beta_{t|t-1} = S(\beta_{t-1|t-2})$, where, if this mapping achieves a fixed point, learning has ceased. This fixed point is referred to as an expectations equilibria (or E-equilibria) and it can be demonstrated under fairly weak assumptions that this equilibria is actually a RE equilibrium. So the learning approach has the attraction that it does not require the stringent informational assumptions of the full

RE assumption, but also that it is able to cope with regime changes and will not generally produce implausible expectations rules.

In small models it is fairly easy to specify learning rules which are adequate and uncontroversial as the full reduced form of the system can be used as a suitable specification. In large econometric models this is not possible and a restricted information set must be used simply because of the size of the unrestricted reduced form. This raises two questions. First how should we choose this restricted equation and how crucial is this choice to the final model properties? Second, how can we allow this restricted model to allow us the flexibility of analysing a broad range of policy questions? One of the great advantages of the RE model is that it uses the fully restricted reduced form of the model so that all exogenous processes are part of the expectations process. The model is therefore adequate to investigate the effect of changes in any future exogenous variable. Take, for example, a proposed future tax change, this will have immediate impact effects in the RE model. The learning model can be specified to deal with this if the announcement of future tax policies is included in the information set of the learning rule, but this has to be done explicitly. We cannot put all possible variables into the learning rule because there are too many and we cannot anticipate all future simulation needs. So the restricted information set of the learning rule represents a limitation on the practical usefulness of the model.

We therefore have a conflict of objectives. RE gives the sophistication of model properties that we want for many purposes; but it does so at the cost of what may appear an unreasonable informational assumption. Learning has a much more intuitively appealing informational base, but it does not offer the flexibility and richness of analysis which is sometimes required. In the next section we address this conflict by proposing the following methodology: first, test the RE assumption within the context of a large model. If it is found to be a reasonable assumption, supported by the data, then we may stay with the established RE procedures. Second, if as we suspect, RE is found to be an unrealistic assumption then the expectation rule may be augmented to allow for both rational components and for learning. This allows a much more complete analysis of future expectations, credibility, and speed of learning effects than either pure backward looking learning or pure RE.

The next section will address the question of how to perform such a test.

3. A TEST FOR RE IN A MODEL

The standard approach of testing the RE assumption in many settings is to take some measure of the expectation of a series, such as the forward exchange rate as a measure of the expected future spot rate, and then to see if any information available in the information set is able to add explanatory power. Under the RE assumption all available information should be analysed in the most efficient possible way, so nothing in the information set can add any extra explanatory power over the RE expectation itself(see for example Hoderick(1987). We propose to proceed in exactly the same fashion.

Equation (5) is the fully restricted reduced form forecast of the model, based only on information available at time t. We set up the null hypothesis that h is the true RE forecast of Y_{t+I} and therefore the expectations error should be a white noise innovation which is impossible to predict from the available information set. This may be tested simply by estimating a model of the following form,

$$Y_{t+i} = B(L)X_t + \Gamma h(X_1,\ldots,X_t,\Omega,Y_1,\ldots,Y_{t-1}) \tag{8}$$

Under the null hypothesis, that we have the true model and agents know and use this model we expect B=0 and the coefficient on h to be unity. If however we do not have the true model, or if there is some real world departure from rationality, then this may be captured in the model by some of the parameters in the B vector being non-zero. This is an explicit test of the restrictions imposed in the h formulation.

One complication is that for most econometric models we cannot solve the model for the formulation h in (5), but only for g in the same equation, as the model driving the exogenous process is not generally made explicit. But remember that h in (5) is simply equal to the models own conditional forecast based on information up to t, from (4). Hence, in place of h in (5) we could simply use $Y_{t+i|t-1}$ That is the model's own forecast of Y in t+i constructed only from information available at t.

We propose constructing a time series of forecasts from a given model and using these in a formal test such as (7). This test is however a rather weak one as we are limiting the way the information set is being used rather severely; the alternative to the RE assumption is a simple fixed parameter extrapolative rule and we know that if the data period has contained important regime changes this rule may not perform well. We also propose setting up a more general form of this test where the alternative is an explicit learning model. This would have the form of,

$$Y_{t+i} = B_{t|t-1}(L)X_t + \Gamma h(X_1,\ldots,X_t,\Omega,Y_1,\ldots,Y_{t-1}) \tag{9}$$

If a test such as (8) rejects the RE assumption, how should we then proceed to deal with expectations in the model. Our suggestion is to work directly with the information set which has proved to be superior in our formal testing. That is, if both parts of (8) hold some explanatory power then we should use both of them in the model to form expectations. In effect (8) will become the expectations generating equation in the model. This would then nest the standard RE solution within it as a special case. It would however modify the jump properties of the simple RE model if the estimation found the non RE parts of the model to be important. It would also retain the basic property of the RE model that a change in any future exogenous variable would potentially have a big impact on the present.

We need a way to estimate the time varying parameters in (8) and to simulate them in the full model solution if that should prove necessary. We will use the Kalman Filter for both purposes, following Cuthbertson Hall and Taylor(1992).

Let

$$Y_t = \delta' z_t + \varepsilon_t$$

be the measurement equation, where y_t is a measured variable, z_t is the state vector of unobserved variables, δ is a vector of parameters, and $\varepsilon_t \sim NID(0,\Gamma_t)$. The state equation is then given as:

$$z_t = \Psi z_{t-1} + \psi \tag{11}$$

where Ψ are parameters and $\psi \sim NID(0,Q_t)$. Q_t is sometimes referred to as a set of hyper parameters.

The appropriate Kalman filter prediction equations are then given by defining z^*_t as the best estimate of z_t based on information up to t, and P_t as the covariance matrix of the estimate z^*_t, and stating:

$$z^*_{t|t-1} = \Psi z^*_{t-1} \tag{12}$$

and

$$P_{t|t-1} = \Psi P_{t-1} \Psi' + Q_t \tag{13}$$

Once the current observation on y_t becomes available, we can update these estimates using the following equations:

$$z^*_t = z^*_{t|t-1} + P_{t|t-1}\delta(Y_t - \delta' z^*_{t|t-1}) / (\delta' P_{t|t-1}\delta + \Gamma_t) \tag{14}$$

and

$$P_t = P_{t|t-1} - P_{t|t-1}\delta\delta' P_{t|t-1} / (\delta' P_{t|t-1}\delta + \Gamma_t) \tag{15}$$

Equations (12)-(15) then represent jointly the Kalman filter equations.

If we then define the one-step-ahead prediction errors as,

$$v_t = y_t - \delta' z^*_{t|t-1}$$

then the concentrated log likelihood function can be shown to be proportional to

$$\log(l) = \sum_{t=k}^{T} \log(f_t) + N\log\left(\sum_{t=k}^{T} v_t^2 / N f_t\right) \tag{17}$$

where $f_t = \delta' P_{t/t-1}\delta + \varepsilon_t$ and N=T-k, where k is the number of periods needed to derive estimates of the state vector; that is, the likelihood function can be expressed as a function of the one-step-ahead prediction errors, suitably weighted. This allows us the estimate the hyper parameters and to derive standard likelihood function-based test procedures for the tests outlined in (8).

4. LEARNING IN MULTIMOD

In this section we examine two questions; what is the quantitative effect of replacing the RE assumption with learning in MULTIMOD?[1] And, how sensitive will the results are to the choice of the learning rule? We address these questions by taking a representative country block from the model and conducting our experiments on this prototype country in isolation from the rest of the model. This simplifies the computational burden of the following experiments at the cost of cutting of some of the feedbacks which would come from the rest of the world in response to a domestic shock. As these responses are relatively small and constant across the different experiments, we do not believe that this simplification will have a qualitative effect on the results to be reported.

In MULTIMOD the exchange rate is approximately determined by a standard open arbitrage equation under rational expectations, and that the expected exchange rate is taken as the next periods actual model solution for the exchange rate. In our experiments with learning we have replaced this assumption with an explicit learning rule for the expected exchange rate.[2] This rule takes the following form.

$$E^e_{t+1} = a_{1t} + a_{2t}E_{t-1} + a_{3t}RP_t + a_{4t}(r^f - r^{us}) \tag{18}$$

where E is the log of the exchange rate; RP is the log of the domestic to US price ratio (in domestic currency); and r^f and r^{US} are the French and US short term interest rates respectively. This equation was estimated using annual data over the period 1966-1993 using the Kalman Filter and this provided estimates of Q and P (the covariance matrix of the state equations and the uncertainty of the initial parameter estimates).[3] The following diagnostics describe the properties of the one-step-ahead

---

[1] For a detailed description of MULTIMOD see Masson et al (1990).

[2] In MULTIMOD there are several expected variables that are determined using RE, such as expected income, the expected short term interest rate and expected prices. In this paper we have only focused on the exchange rate.

[3] Data of a higher frequency would have provided better estimates, we have chosen to restrict the data frequency to that used by MULTIMOD to ensure compatibility with the model.

residuals,[4] Skewness=0.03, Kurtosis=-1.6, BJ=4.0, BP(1)=0.03, BP(4)=6.9, BP(8)=9.6.

In order to asses the sensitivity of our results to the specification of this equation we also considered three simplifications of this general learning rule.

rule 2: which contained only the time varying constant.
rule 3: which contained a time varying constant and a lagged dependent variable.
rule 4: which contained the time varying constant, the lagged dependent variable and the interest rate differential.

The initial experiment carried out was a simulation involving a reduction in the money supply of 10% for 60 periods (years). Under RE the expected result is that in the long run the price level will fall by 10%, the nominal exchange rate will rise by 10% and there will be no real consequences. In the short run we would expect the exchange rate to initially overshoot its long run equilibrium that is it would rise by more than 10% and then fall over time.

Figure 1 reports the change in the exchange rate from base for the rational model and for the four variants with learning. The long run equilibrium for all five simulations is nearly identical (given the size of the dynamic fluctuations) but the response of the model over the first 25 years is quite different. Under RE we see the expected overshoot in the exchange rate followed by a fairly rapidly damped cycle back to the long run equilibrium. In all cases the learning models have a much smaller initial change in the exchange rate but then show a much slower, and in some cases more erratic movement towards the equilibrium. So both the immediate impact and the medium term solution to the model are significantly affected by the introduction of learning.

It is interesting to note that the exchange rate response under the general rule tended to move the least amount, took longer to reach equilibrium and exhibited less cycling. This appears to be the result of the relative price term and is not necessarily a general result. The learning coefficient on the relative price term has the 'wrong' sign[5] in the base at this point in time, and this tends to depreciate rather than appreciate the exchange rate[6] However, over time the coefficient changes sign. In general the inclusion of this variable in the learning rule tends to damp the exchange rate movement in this scenario.

---

[4] BJ is the Bera-Jarque test for normality, distributed as $\chi^2(2)$ and BP(I) is the Box-Pierse test for serial correlation distributed as $\chi^2(\text{i})$.

[5] The notion of the 'wrong' sign is a little difficult here as we are dealing with a complete reduced form of the system and so we can not unambiguously sign any of the parameters. None the less we acknowledge the intuitive problem which exists here, we report these results as intellectually honest, but recognise that in a practical policy analysis we may wish to intervene here.

[6] Since the learning properties are not independent of time and the estimated relative price tends to change sign over the estimation period. If we had started the estimation during a period with the 'correct' sign , the exchange rate change would likely have been larger. This illustrates a general property of learning models, that the short rune response of the system will vary with the current state of the learning process.

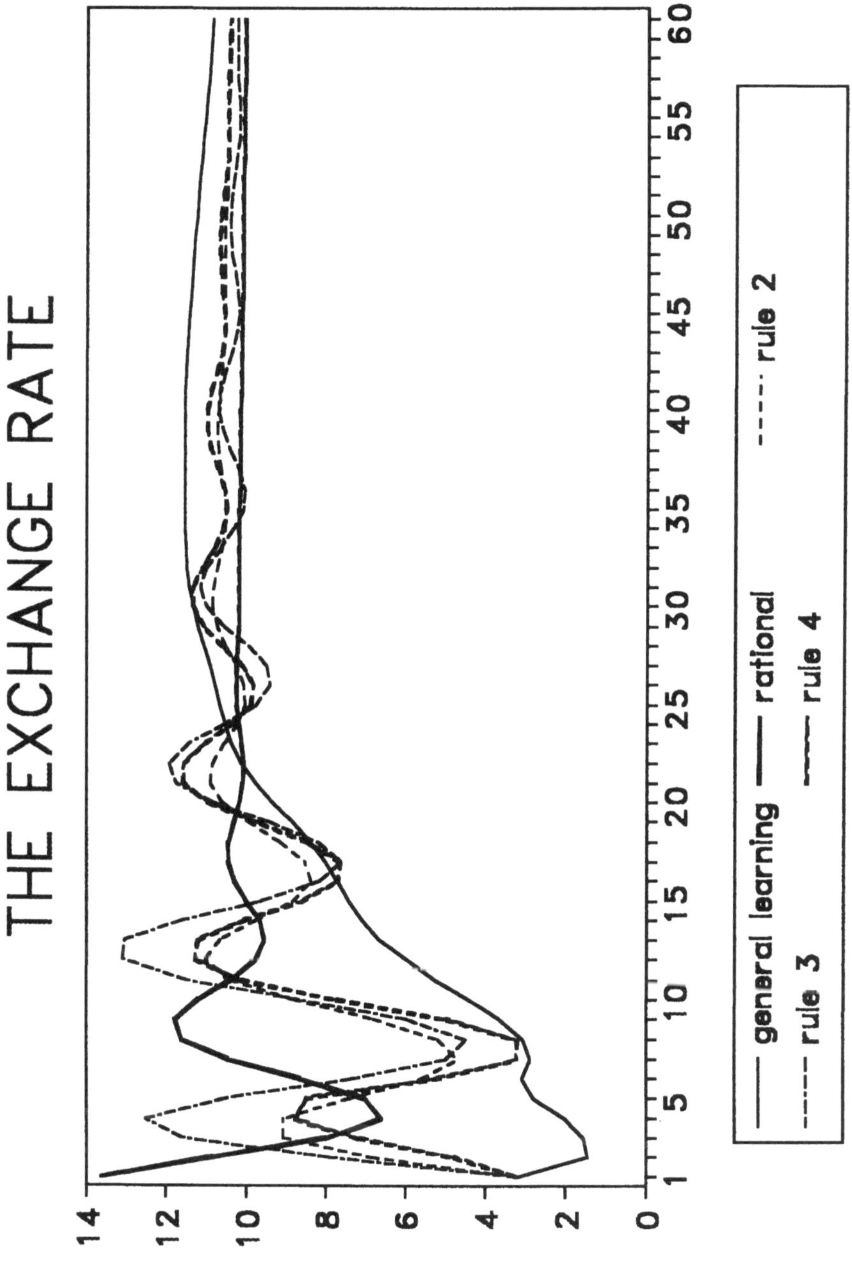
THE EXCHANGE RATE
0
2
4
6
8
10
12
14
1
5
10
15
20
25
30
35
40
45
50
55
60
general learning
rational
rule 2
rule 3
rule 4

Given that the model under all the learning rules still achieves the same equilibrium, it is to be expected that the learning procedures have all reached an expectations equilibria by the end of the period. This is confirmed by examining the change in the parameters for the learning rules which in all cases have stabilised by the end. The absolute change can however give a misleading impression as to the relative importance of the changes in the parameters as it does not take any account of the scaling of the variable which the parameter is affecting. We propose the following decomposition to illustrate the relative importance of the changes in the parameters. If the expectations rule is

$$Y_t^e = B_t X_t \tag{19}$$

and in the simulation this becomes

$$Y_t^{e*} = B_t^* X_t^* \tag{20}$$

then by construction

$$\begin{aligned} Y_t^e - Y_t^{e*} &= B_t X_t - B_t^* X_t^* \\ &= B_t^*(X_t - X_t^*) + X_t(B_t - B_t^*) \end{aligned} \tag{21}$$

Thus the total change in expectations may be divided into two parts; the change in the variables scaled by the new parameters, and the change in the parameters scaled by the base values of the variables. [This is not a unique decomposition but other alternatives give very similar answers.] Consequently it is appropriate to scale the change in the parameters by the value of the variables in each period. Figure 2 shows the scaled changes in the parameters. The importance of the change in three of the parameters is of a similar magnitude in the long run with the total effect explaining slightly more than half the total change in the expected exchange rate.

Figure 3,4 and 5 show the response of the rest of the economy (in terms of the change in the price level, GDP and interest rates) to the assumption about expectations formation in the exchange rate sector. Broadly the picture is as expected; the long run solution to the model is unaffected by the various assumptions about expectations formation and interestingly enough the immediate impact effect is also very similar. The real difference lies in the adjustment path. Here we see much longer lasting temporary effects on both real activities and prices. Under RE the real GDP effect is less than 0.5% after about 10 years while the general learning model takes about three times as long to reach this point. A very similar picture is also true for the price level. It should be remembered that learning only replaced RE in the formation of exchange rate expectations. The differences in output, prices and GDP would have been likely greater if learning replaced RE for all of the forward looking variables.

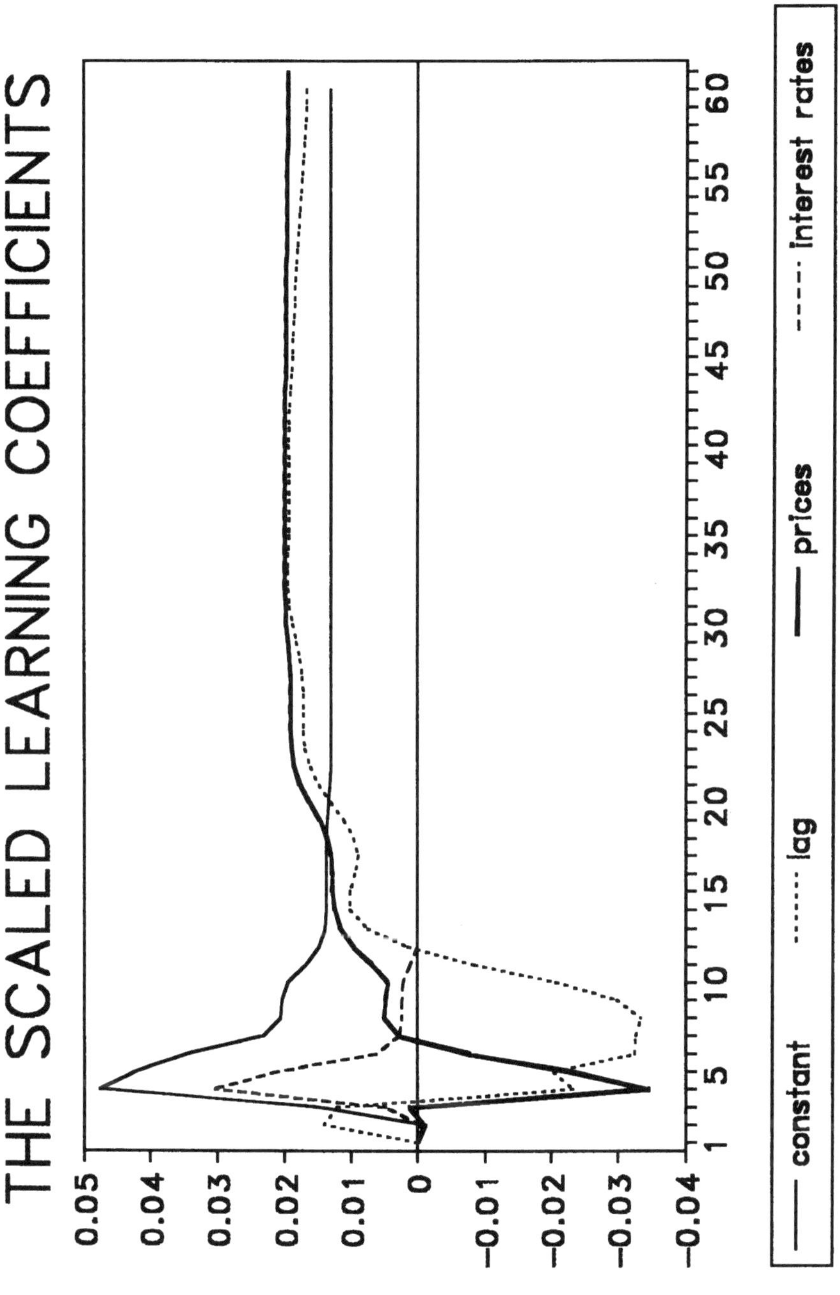
THE SCALED LEARNING COEFFICIENTS
0.05
0.04
0.03
0.02
0.01
0
-0.01
-0.02
-0.03
-0.04
1
5
10
15
20
25
30
35
40
45
50
55
60
constant
lag
prices
interest rates

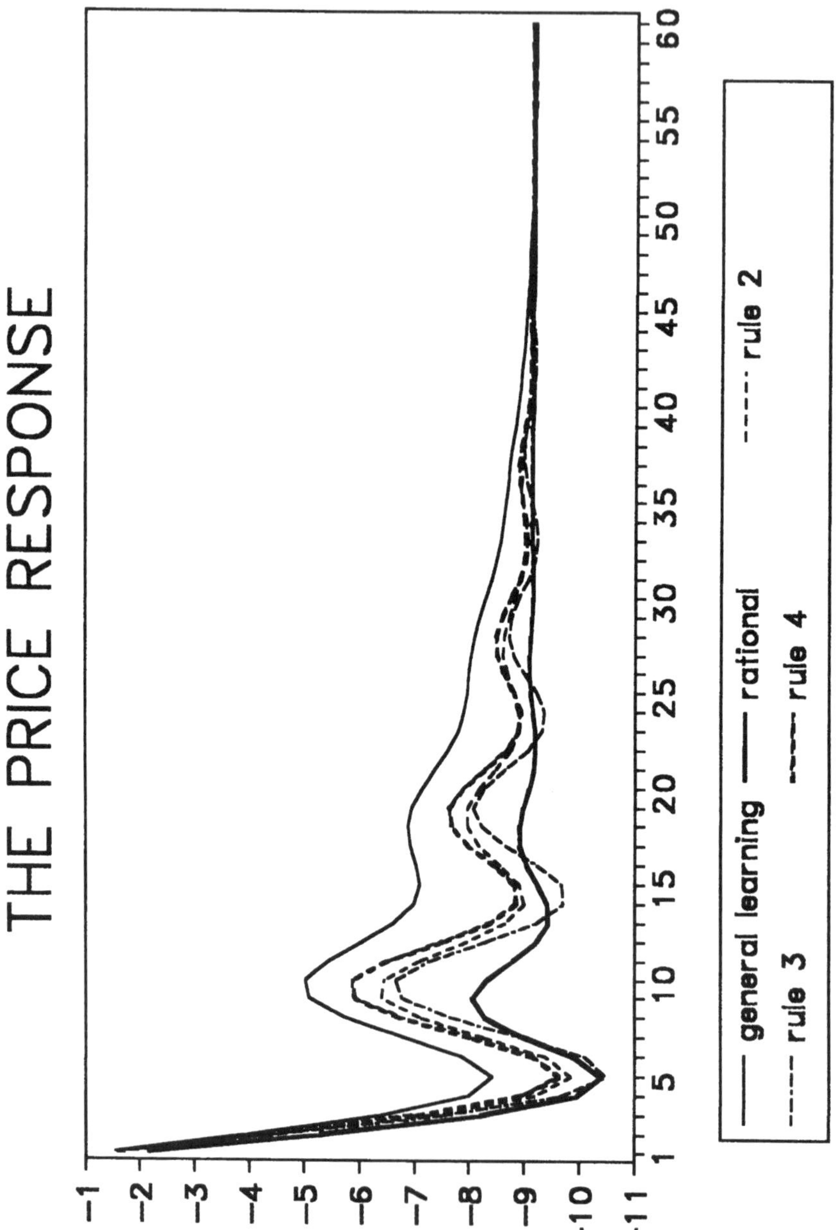
THE PRICE RESPONSE
-1
-2
-3
-4
-5
-6
-7
-8
-9
-10
-11
1
5
10
15
20
25
30
35
40
45
50
55
60
general learning
rational
rule 2
rule 3
rule 4

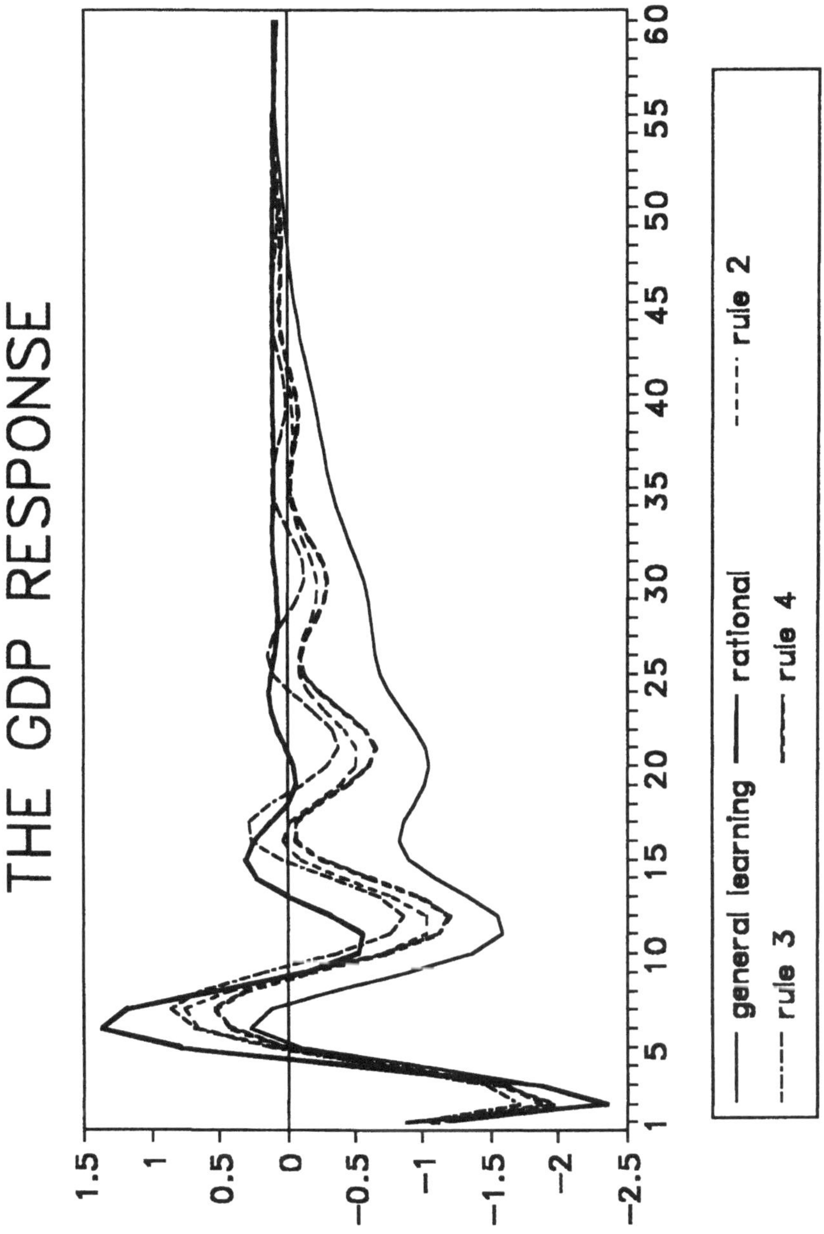
THE GDP RESPONSE
1.5
1
0.5
0
−0.5
−1
−1.5
−2
−2.5
1
5
10
15
20
25
30
35
40
45
50
55
60
general learning
rational
rule 2
rule 3
rule 4

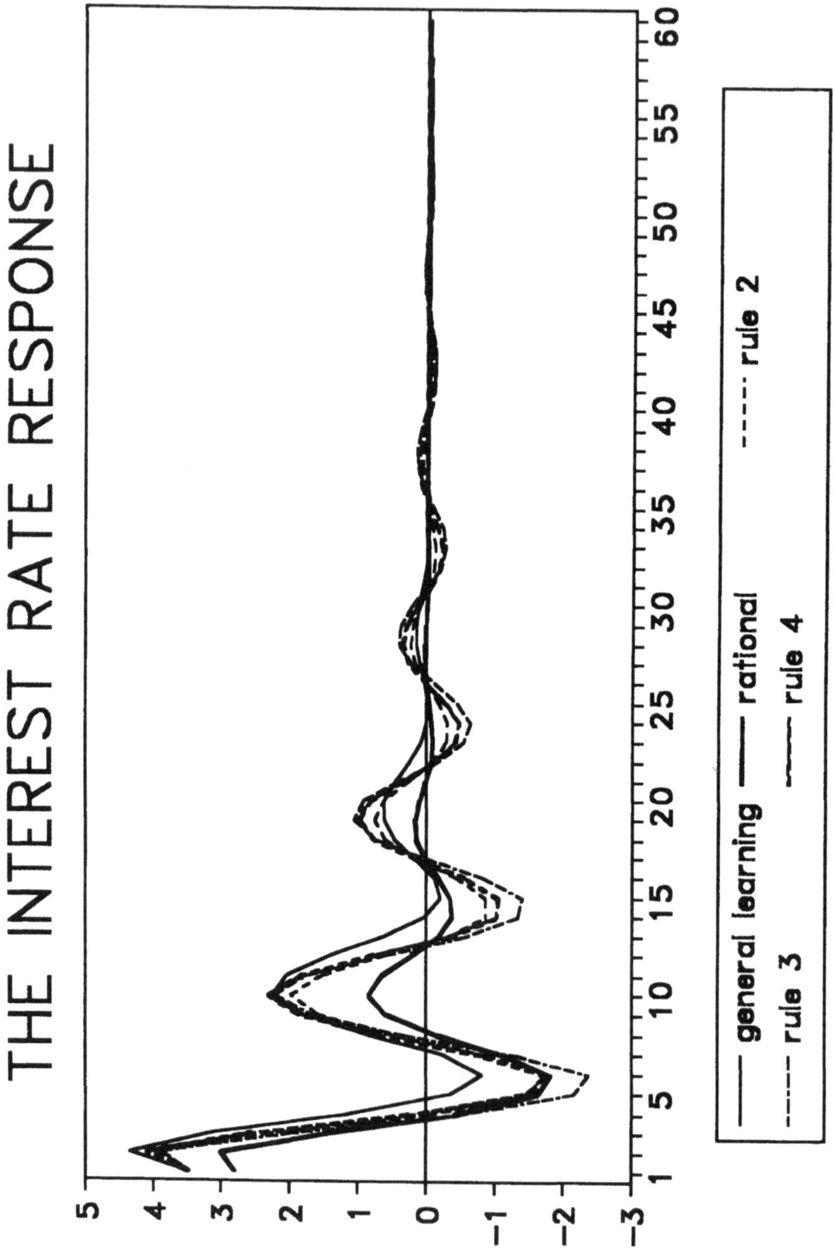
THE INTEREST RATE RESPONSE
5
4
3
2
1
0
−1
−2
−3
1
5
10
15
20
25
30
35
40
45
50
55
60
general learning
rational
rule 2
rule 3
rule 4

Figures 6 and 7 show a similar set of experiments for a fiscal policy change. Figure 6 shows the change in the exchange rate as a result of a fiscal stimulus equal to 5% of GDP. The impact effect of the learning models and the RE model are again quite different and this difference persists over the first 10 years of the simulation. In the longer run the two forms of expectations formation provides broadly similar results with the exception that the learning models tend to be somewhat more volatile. The various learning rules also yield a very similar path for the exchange rate, confirming that the choice of specification of these rules does not strongly affect the model's properties, at least when learning is only applied to the exchange rate. Note that the sharp movement at the end of the simulation period under RE is the result of the terminal condition which has been imposed on the model. This jump is not economically meaningful.[7]

Figure 7 shows the GDP response in the model and here the different expectations assumptions yield a remarkably similar profile, although the short run composition of GDP is altered somewhat under learning and rational expectations due to the very different exchange rate profile and hence different trade and investment patterns.

Figure 8 shows the change in the scaled parameters in the learning rule, this again confirms that an expectations equilibrium has been reached as the parameters have clearly converged on constant values.

The broad conclusions of these two sets of experiments are that learning converges on the RE solution fairly convincingly but that fairly substantial deviations exist in both the short and medium term between the implications of RE and learning. As expected the initial movement of the exchange rate under learning is much more moderate than under RE but often the response of the learning models are more dynamically complex and also more volatile. This can delay the approach to equilibrium considerably, perhaps from 10 years under RE to 30 years under learning, and it can give rise to substantially different economic consequences over this period.

[7] In general, most MULTIMOD simulations involve changes in the endpoint. However this was not done in this experiment, but it has little quantitative effects on the results.

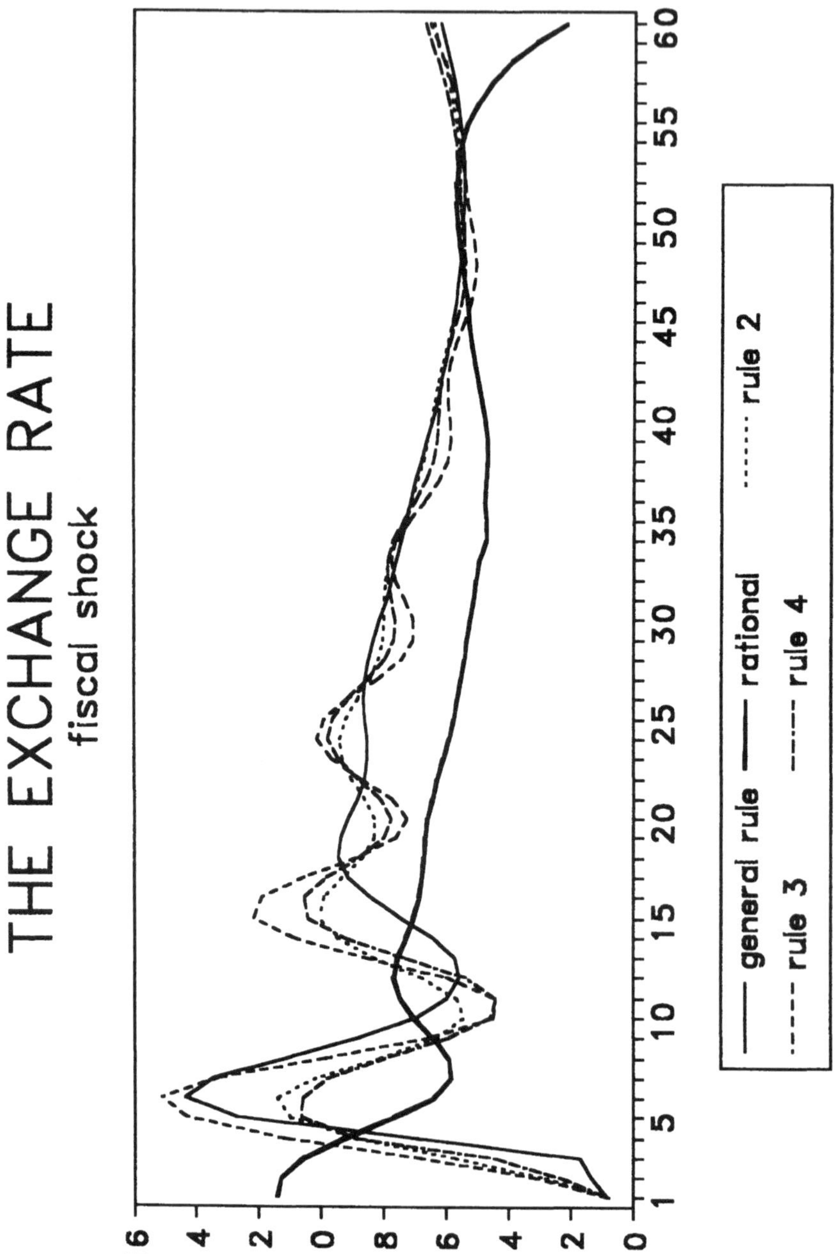
THE EXCHANGE RATE
fiscal shock
16
14
12
10
8
6
4
2
0
1
5
10
15
20
25
30
35
40
45
50
55
60
general rule
rational
rule 2
rule 3
rule 4

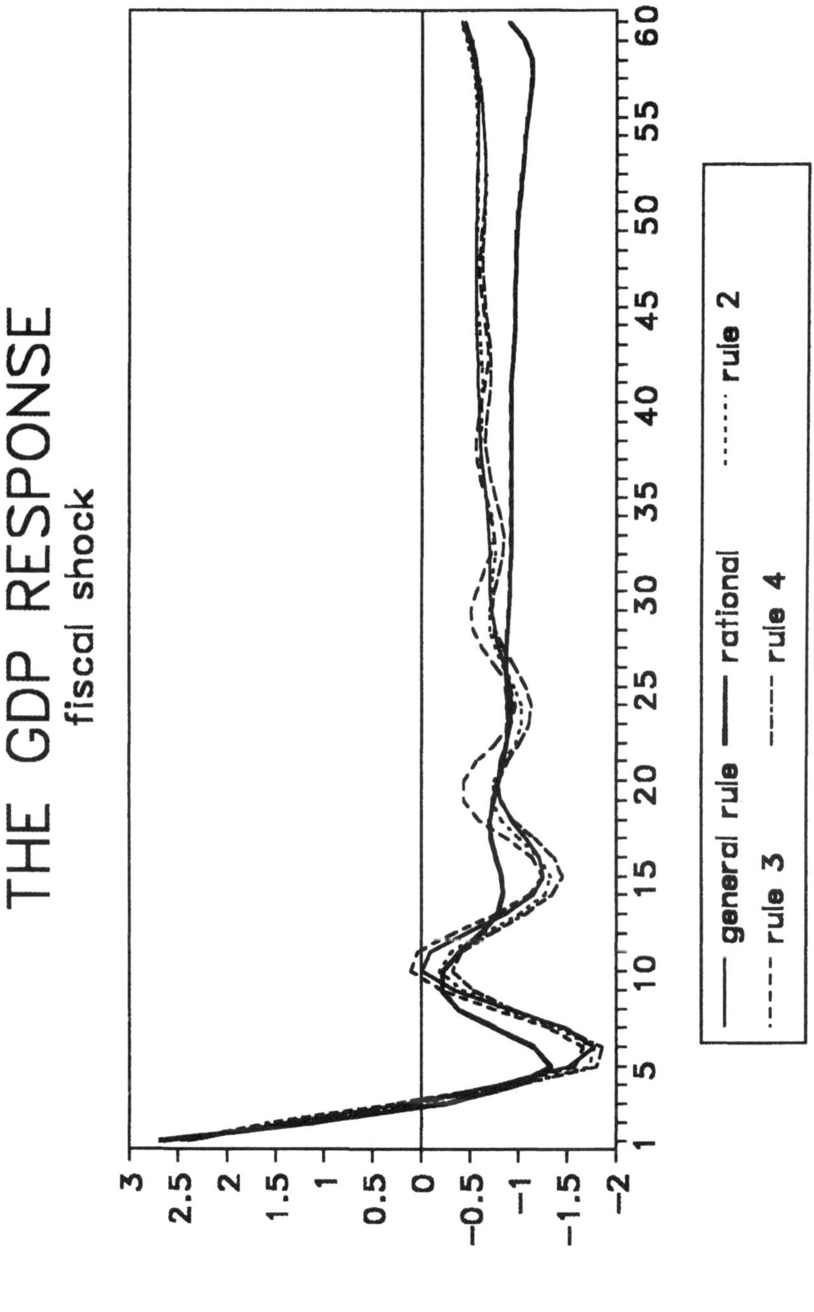
THE GDP RESPONSE
fiscal shock
3
2.5
2
1.5
1
0.5
0
-0.5
-1
-1.5
-2
1
5
10
15
20
25
30
35
40
45
50
55
60
general rule
rational
rule 2
rule 3
rule 4

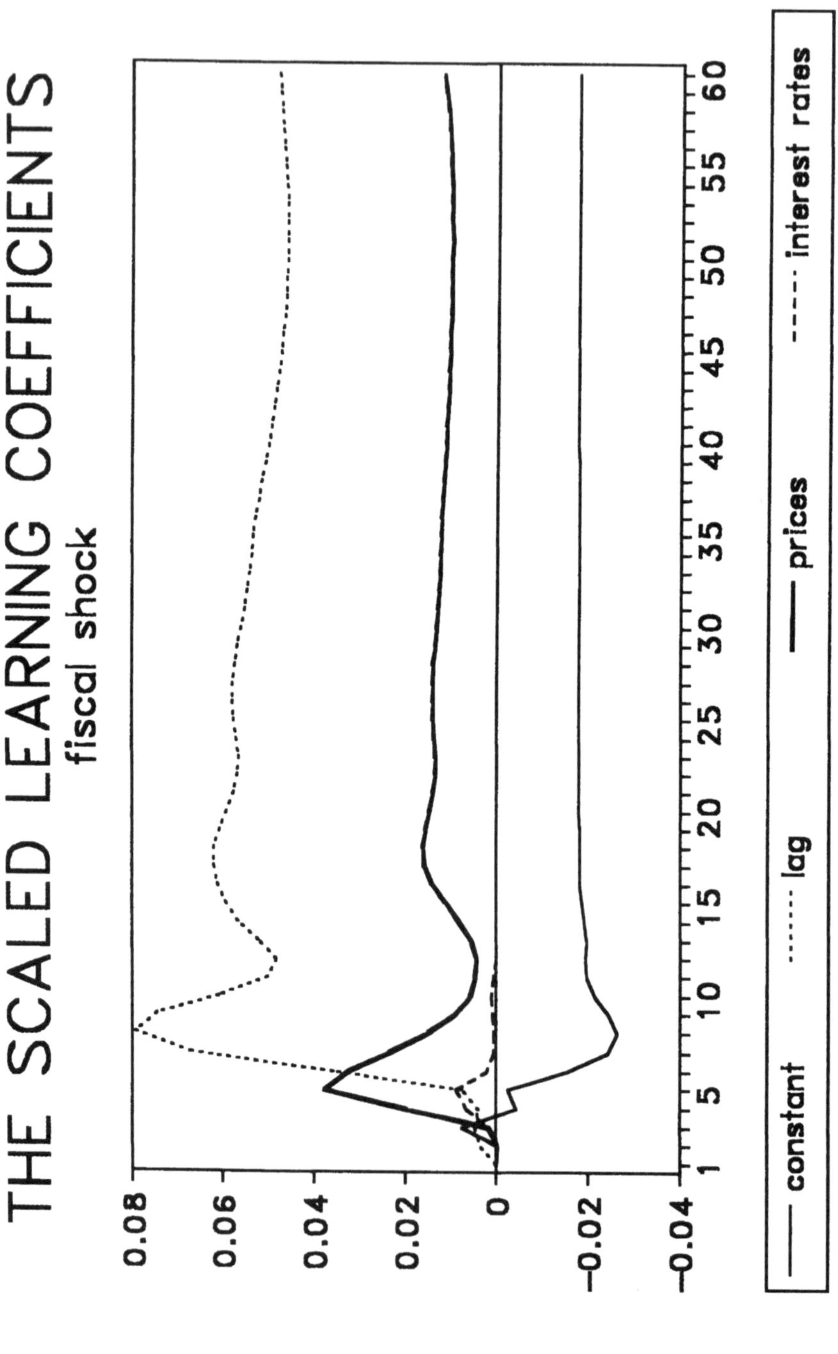
THE SCALED LEARNING COEFFICIENTS
fiscal shock
0.08
0.06
0.04
0.02
0
-0.02
-0.04
1
5
10
15
20
25
30
35
40
45
50
55
60
constant
lag
prices
interest rates

5. APPLYING THE TEST TO MULTIMOD

In this section we apply the testing procedure outlined in section (3) above. We can consider testing the RE hypothesis at two levels, the weak and strong form. The weak form test would be effectively testing the presence of RE in the real world but would not make the assumption that agents use a particular model to form their expectations. The strong form test would follow (8) in testing the validity of the hypothesis that expectations ore formed using a particular model.

A WEAK FORM TEST

We begin by asking the question, how relevant is RE to the real world? We address this in the following equation,

$$E_t - (r^f - r^{US}) = b_1 E^{RE}_{t+1} + b_2 E^L_{t+1} \tag{22}$$

This equation is a transformation of the open arbitrage equation which imposes the unit coefficient on the interest rate term and breaks the expected exchange rate term into two parts, a rational expectation term and a learning term. If the weak RE assumption is correct, we should expect $b_1=1$ and $b_2=0$. If however there is information contained in the learning rule which is useful in explaining the determination of the exchange rate - over and above that contained in the next period's outcome - then we would expect b_2 to be non-zero. The RE term is defined as the next periods actual exchange rate, which is instrumented in the test to allow for the measurement error bias generated under RE (following Wickens(1982)). The learning expectations term is derived as the forecast of the general time varying parameter rule. Note that these two procedures use the information sets in a very different way; the RE term is instrumented using the whole sample information, so at any point it contains information about the future, but it is constrained to use a constant parameterisation. The learning rule at any point in time uses only past information as the parameters are not influenced by future out turns for the exchange rate but the parameterisation is more flexible as the parameters are allowed to change over time. The instrumenting system for the RE expectations was a fourth order VAR in the exchange rate and interest rate differentials, Given that we only have some 29 annual observations to work with this was felt to give a reasonable balance between consistency and efficiency. This test then produced the following results,[8]

$$E_t - (r^f - r^{US}) = \underset{(2.6)}{0.42} E^{RE}_{t+1} + \underset{(3.7)}{0.59} E^L_{t+1}$$

$$\text{ARCH}(1) = 0.01 \quad \text{LM}(1) = 2.1 \quad \text{LM}(4) = 5.5 \tag{23}$$

$$\text{BJ}(2) = 0.49 \quad \text{RESET}(4) = 2.0$$

---

[8] 't' statistics in parenthesis, based on Newey-West corrected standard errors.

This equation shows that both b_1 and b_2 are significantly different from zero and that the slightly larger weight is on the learning expectations term. So this suggests that even the weak form of RE can be rejected in this instance.

THE STRONG FORM TEST

In order to implement the strong form test we need to produce a series of one-step-ahead forecasts of the exchange rate under full model consistent expectations. This amounts to a series of 'pure model' forecasts starting in successive periods. In principal all the future values for the exogenous variables should be generated endogenously using time series processes and the equations residuals should be set to zero. In practice it is often not wise to set the models residuals to zero as the historical behaviour of the models residuals may be a long way from white noise. If so the model's forecast can be substantially improved by generating residuals for the forecast period from a set of simple auto-regressive rules (these might be as simple as an average over the past or they are more complex time series models). The error terms in MULTIMOD are not even approximately white noise for several reasons; MULTIMOD was intended to be used in policy analysis and not for forecasting. The auto-regressive errors were not explicitly added into the model and constants were omitted and lumped into the error terms. In addition there have been the usual revisions to the historical data. Our initial intention therefore was to generate a series of one step ahead forecast from the model under full RE where both the exogenous variables and the residuals from the model equations were generated from a set of simple time series rules. In practice this turned out not to be feasible as the model failed to solve for a number of periods when this full set of rules was included. RE models have not been used for forecasting since practitioners have found that the forecasts are very poor, especially in terms of the first period forecast which is most heavily influenced by the RE jumping property. A backward looking model generally provides small short term forecast errors which tend to build up over time. With an RE model all the future movements in variables (including the forecast errors) affect the first forecast period. We believe that it would have been possible to implement this procedure fully by searching for rules that were suitably stable but the time and resource constraint limited the scope of this search and a full set of satisfactory rules could not be obtained. The procedure we adopted therefore was to set a small but key group of residuals to those needed to actually generate the true outcome. This probably has the effect of biassing the test in favour of the RE assumption as we are providing it with data which was not available at the time. A further limitation of the test is that the sample for the test was limited by the length of the MULTIMOD data base which only allows us to run the model from 1975, so that the test could only be carried out over the period 1975-1992. We therefore perform the formal test in the light of the likely bias towards RE and the relatively small sample available. The equivalent strong form RE test (22) is then,

$$E_t - (r^f - r^{US}) = \underset{(5.2)}{0.15} E^{RE}_{t+1} + \underset{(0.8)}{0.87} E^{L}_{t+1}$$

$$ARCH(1) = 1.0 \quad LM(1) = 5.4 \quad LM(4) = 6.1 \tag{24}$$

$$BJ(2) = 0.6 \quad RESET(4) = 2.0$$

Despite the bias in the informational assumption used to generate the full RE solution this test finds that the strong form assumption is significantly rejected and that the weight on the RE term is not significantly different from zero.

A COMPARISON OF THE TWO

In (23) we rejected the weak form of the RE assumption. This makes it unlikely that we would actually accept the strong form of the RE assumption. It is however possible that the strong form expectations series contains the same information as the weak form series. That is if only some agents are fully rational but they actually do use this model to form their expectations then we might expect to find that b_1 in (23) was identical to that in (24). In other words, although we have rejected the assumption that all agents are fully rational we might not reject the assumption that the forward looking part of the expectations process is actually well modelled by a particular model. This can be tested formally by asking if the two estimates of b_1 significantly different from each other. Because of the limitations surrounding the MULTIMOD RE forecasts and since the two estimates are so different, the formal test is unnecessary.

6. MODIFYING THE EXPECTATIONS RULE

In this section we will consider how the modified expectations rule can be incorporated into an econometric model. As in the testing case, there is basically two possible approaches resting on the two assumptions of weak and strong RE. If we make the strong assumption, that agents do indeed use this model to form expectations then we have a direct estimate from (23) of the relative weights that agents place on the RE and learning terms in (8). We can then incorporate this mixture of RE and learning quite simply by using (8) directly as an equation in the model which generates the expectations variables. (8) can be given a slightly different interpretation by reparameterising it as follows,

$$Y_{t+i} = (1-\Gamma)\zeta_{t|t-1}(L) X_t + \Gamma h(X_1,\ldots,X_t,\Omega,Y_1,\ldots,Y_{t-1}) \tag{25}$$

where $(1-\Gamma)\zeta_{t|t-1}(L) = B_{t|t-1}(L)$. This then weights together two parts, the standard RE solution given by h and the learning expectation given by the time varying parameter model.

If the tests in section 5 suggests that the strong form of the RE assumption is not valid then clearly we would want to give the RE assumption a much lower weight. We can do this by taking the estimated weight from (8) but there is however a further complication which rests in the fact that h is the reduced form of the model (1) while the expectations rule is taken to be (3) under RE. If we replace (3) with (8) this will actually change h. There are three ways to proceed. The first is to use the following algorithm to build up a solution, for the period t...T. First set I=0.

Then 1. set $\Gamma = 1$, solve the model for periods j=t+I...T, and define Y^{RE} as the solution and set it equal to h.

Next 2. set $\Gamma = \Gamma^*$, the estimated value. Then with $h(Y^{RE})$ fixed, solve the model for periods j=t+I...T.

3. Step 2 gives the solution for period t+I. If t+I=T stop; otherwise set I=I+1 and go to 1.

Second, a much easier alternative is to solve the model with the new expectations rule in it, although this will not be a true reflection of the dynamics of the rationality test because h will be modified by the new learning rule.

A third and final alternative is to recognize that the learning rule should be part of the model structure once we have rejected the simple RE assumption; but that it should have a different weighting pattern from that derived in (8). The way to estimate this weighting pattern is to derive a time series of forward model solutions based on an arbitrary Γ and then to estimate an equation of the form of (8) to derive a new value for Γ, and then to iterate over this procedure to convergence.

In general our preferred procedure is to use (8) to test the RE assumption and then to use the final of the three options above to estimate a parameter based on a combination of learning and model consistent expectations. However given that our test of the strong form RE assumption gave virtually an insignificant weight to the RE term there is little interest in performing simulations which would only replicate those of section 4. To illustrate the effect of the mixed rule on the models simulation properties we therefore performed a simulation based on the weak form parameter weightings given in (22), that is 0.6 on the learning term and 0.4 on the RE term. The equivalent simulation on monetary policy to figure 1 was then carried out under this mixture of RE and learning assumptions. The effect on the exchange rate is shown in Figure 9, under this mixed assumption the initial jump in the exchange rate is almost twice what it was under pure learning and the model reaches approximately the right level of the exchange rate almost as rapidly as under RE. It is however much more volatile and the cycles in the system take much longer to damp down to the full long run equilibrium. Again the medium term (say 10 years) implications of the model under this mixed assumption are very different from the full RE model.

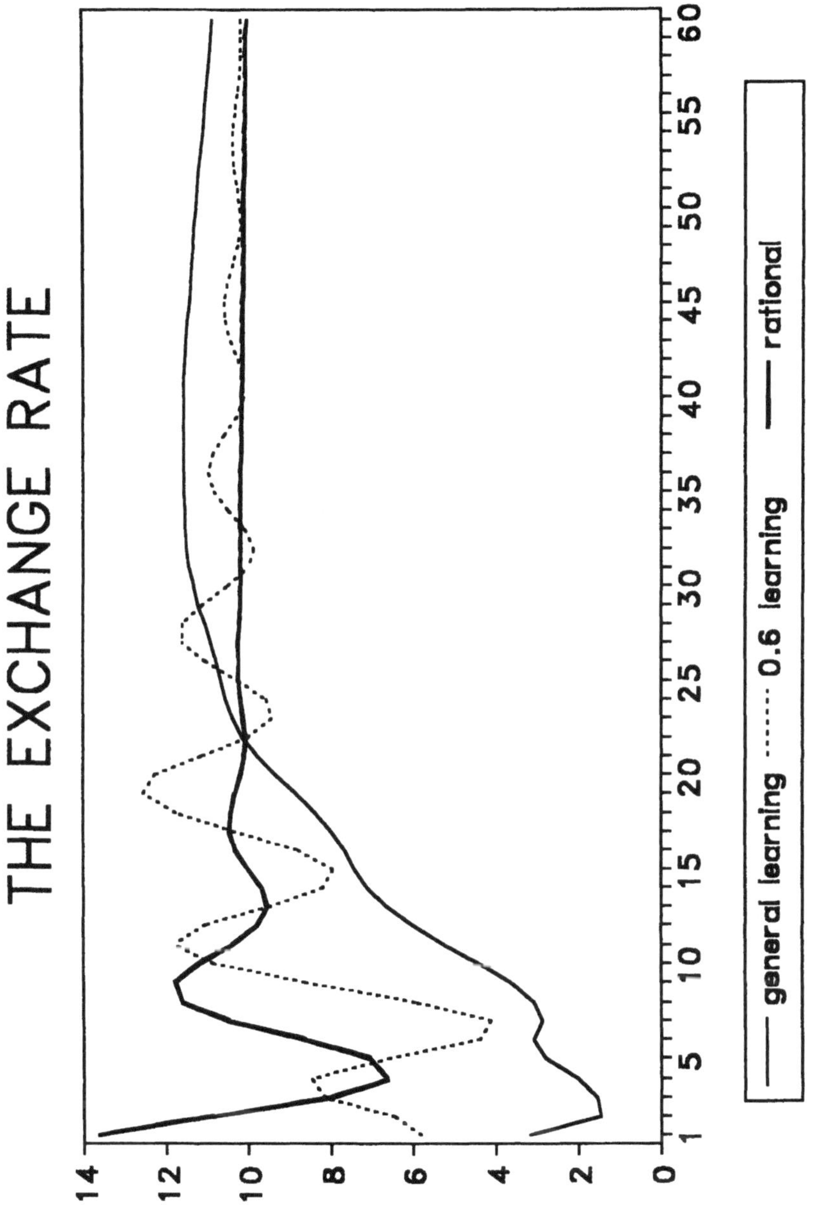
THE EXCHANGE RATE
14
12
10
8
6
4
2
0
1
5
10
15
20
25
30
35
40
45
50
55
60
general learning
0.6 learning
rational

7. CONCLUSIONS

This paper has argued that the RE assumption is an extreme and unrealistic one when it is applied to the context of a large econometric model. We have proposed a test of this assumption in a full model context and illustrated that one major model does not meet this test. We have then gone on to propose an expectations rule which mixes learning and model consistent expectations so that we make use of the restrictions on the full information set implied by the large model but we do not fully accept the rigour of these restrictions. We illustrate the effect of this new style learning rule with a range of simulation exercises.

REFERENCES

Barrell R, Caporale G M, Garratt A and Hall S G (1993), "Learning About Monetary Union: An Analysis of Boundedly Rational Learning In European Labor Markets", in Hall, S G (ed) "Applied Economic Forecasting Techniques". Simon and Schuster, New York.

Bray, M M (1983), "Convergence to Rational Expectations Equilibrium", in Frydman, R and Phelps, E S (eds) "Industrial Forecasting and aggregate Outcomes". Cambridge University Press, Cambridge.

Bray, M M and Kreps, C (1984), "Rational Learning and Rational Expectation", mimeo Cambridge University.

Bray, M M and Savin, N E (1986), "Rational Expectations Equilibria, Learning and Model Specification" *Econometrica*, Vol. 54, pp. 1129-60.

Cuthbertson K, Hall, S G and Taylor, M P (1992), "Applied Econometric Techniques", Michigan University Press.

Evans, G W (1983), "The Stability of Rational Expectations in Macroeconomic Models", in Frydman, R and Phelps, E S (eds) "Individual Forecasting and Aggregate Outcomes" Cambridge University Press, Cambridge.

Evans G W (1985), "Expectational Stability and the Multiple Equilibria Problem in RE Models", *Quarterly Journal of Economics*, Vol. 100, pp. 1217-1233.

Evans, G W (1986a), "Expectational Stability and the Multiple Equilibria Problem in Linear Rational Expectations Models", *Quarterly Journal Of Economics*, Vol. 101, pp. 1217-1233.

Evans, G W (1986b), "Selection Criteria for Models with Non-Uniqueness", *Journal of Monetary Economics*, Vol. 15, pp. 147-157.

Evans, G W and Honkapohja, S (1992), "Adaptive Learning and Expectational Stability: An Introduction", in Kirman, A and Salmon, M (eds) Learning and Rationality in Economics, Basil Blackwell, Oxford.

Hall, S G and Garratt, A (1992a), "Model Consistent Learning: The Sterling Deutschmark Rate in the London Business School Model", LBS-CEF Discussion Paper No. 92-02.

Hall, S G and Garratt, A (1992b), "Expectations and Learning in Economic Models", *Economic Outlook* Vol. 16, pp. 52-53.

Hoderick, R J (1987), "The Empirical Evidence on the Efficiency of Forward and Future Exchange Markets", Harwood Academic Publishers, London.

Lucas, R E Jr. (1975), "An Equilibrium Model of the Business Cycle", *Journal of Political Economy*, Vol. 83, pp. 1113-1144.

Marcet, A and Sargent, T J (1988), "The fate of Systems with Adaptive Expectations", *American Economic Review*, pp. 168-171

Marcet, A and Sargent, T J (1989a), "Convergence of Least-Squares Learning in Environment with Hidden State Variables and Private Information", *Journal of Political Economy*, Vol. 97, pp. 1306-1322.

Marcet, A and Sargent, T J (1989b), "Least Squares Learning and the Dynamics of Hyper inflation", in W A Barnett, J Geweke and K Shell (eds) "Economic Complexity, Chaos, Sunspots Bubbles and Nonlinearity" Cambridge University Press, Cambridge.

Masson, P R, Symansky, S, Meredith, M (1990) "Multimod: A Multi Region Econometric Model", Working Paper No. 88/23 , IMF, Washington DC.

Pesaran, M H (1987), "The Limits of Rational Expectations", Basil Blackwell, Oxford.

Townsend, R M (1978), "Market Anticipation, Rational Expectation and Bayesian Analysis", *International Economic Review*, Vol. 19, pp. 481-94.

Townsend, R M (1983), "Forecasting the Forecast of Others", *Journal of Political Economy*, Vol. 91, pp. 546-88.

Wickens, M R (1982), "The Efficient Estimation of Econometric Models with Rational Expectations", *Review of Economic Studies*, Vol. 49, 55-67.

Woodford, M (1990), "Learning to Believe in Sunspots", *Econometrica*, Vol. 58, pp. 277-308.

CHAPTER 5

BOUNDEDLY *VERSUS* PROCEDURALLY RATIONAL EXPECTATIONS

Scott Moss and Esther-Mirjam Sent

Some economists who have relied on the rational expectations hypothesis are now seeking to demonstrate that rational expectations equilibria can emerge in models with agents who are artificially intelligent. They typically model agents' intelligence through the use of genetic algorithms. However, these algorithms misrepresent current understanding of human cognition as well as well-known and long-standing evidence from business history and the history of technology. This paper implements a well-validated representation of human cognition in SDML, a logic-based programming language that is optimised for representations of interactions among agents. Within that software environment, a model of a transition economy is developed with three production sectors and a household sector. The numerical outputs from that model are broadly in accord with the statistical evidence from the Russian economy. The model itself is developed explicitly to incorporate qualitatively specified characteristics of entrepreneurial behaviour in that economy. Unlike conventional economic models, transactions are negotiated and effected explicitly — there are no unspecified or under-specified "markets".

BOUNDEDLY RATIONAL EXPECTATIONS

Adaptive expectations models contain an asymmetry in the sense that in those models econometricians, who are presumed to be fully knowledgeable, forecast better than agents, who are presumed to rely on mechanistic backward-looking extrapolative rules. One explanation for the rise of rational expectations economics is that it eliminates this asymmetry by placing econometricians and agents on an equal footing (see Sent (1998) for further explanations). Hence, rational and consistent expectations in macroeconometric models are often justified on the grounds that it would be wrong to assume that econometric modelers were smarter than the agents who make the decisions that generate the time-series data used to specify and estimate the model. If those agents are really as smart as the econometricians, and if the econometricians' model of the economy is correct, then the agents will also have specified the correct model of the economy and it will be the same as that of the econometricians.

One consequence of this line of reasoning is that, if all agents know the correct (econometricians') model of the economy, they therefore have the same model. By using this model to form their expectations, they must all have the same expectations and there is nothing analytically to distinguish one agent from another. The point can be put in two ways. Either there is a single representative agent or agents are homogeneous. This consequence is not only logical, but also desirable from the perspective of rational expectations economics. The reason is that many rational expectations models seek to derive macro results from general equilibrium models. Yet, the Sonnenschein (1972), Mantel (1976) and Debreu (1974) results illustrate the precarious nature of this endeavour. It shows that under standard assumptions on the individual consumers, such as strict convexity and monotonicity of preferences, so that each agent is characterised by textbook indifference curves and a positive bundle of endowments of all goods, we can derive an excess demand curve for each individual. Summing over all individuals, of whom it is assumed that there are only a finite number, gives the excess demand curve for society as a whole. Under certain not-very-restrictive conditions, three properties will carry over from the individual's excess demand curve to the aggregate demand curve: continuity, a value of total excess demand equal to zero at all prices, and excess demand being homogeneous of degree zero. However, these three properties turn out to be the only properties that carry over from the individual to the aggregate demand function. In particular, the Weak Axiom of Revealed Preference (WARP) may not be satisfied at the aggregate level. Yet, if we are to obtain uniqueness and stability of equilibria, some such restrictions must be imposed. Now, if the behaviour of the economy could be represented as that of a representative agent or a number of identical agents, the situation might be saved, since textbook individual excess demand functions do have unique and stable equilibria (Kirman (1972) and Sent (1998) for further discussions of this).

One rational expectations economist who has openly worried about such consequences of the rational expectations assumption is Thomas Sargent. For him, one undesirable consequence is the no-trade theorem for rational expectations models, which indicates that even if homogenous agents have different information, they will still not be willing to trade with each other. Consider a purely speculative market, meaning that the aggregate monetary gain is zero and that insurance plays no role. When it is common knowledge that traders are risk averse, rational, have the same prior, and that the market clears, then it is also common knowledge that a trader's expectation of monetary gain, based on given information, must be positive in order for that trader to be willing to trade. In other words, if one agent has information that induces willingness to trade at the current asset price, then other rational agents would be unwilling to trade with that agent, because they realise that that agent must have superior information. The equilibrium market price fully reveals everybody's private information at zero trades for all traders. According to Sargent (1993, p. 113): "The remarkable no-trade outcome works the rational expectations hypothesis very hard."

Sargent further discovered that rational expectations models are unable to place agents and econometricians on an equal footing. When implemented numerically or econometrically, rational expectations models impute more knowledge to the agents within the model (who use the equilibrium probability distributions in evaluating their Euler equations) than is possessed by an econometrician (who faces estimation and inference problems that the agents in the model have somehow solved). The reason is that close scrutiny of the justification of error terms reveals that identification and estimation of the models require the econometrician to know less than the agents. Whereas agents' decision rules are exact (non-stochastic) functions of the information they possess, the econometrician must resort to some device to convert the exact equations delivered by economic theory into inexact (stochastic) equations susceptible to econometric analysis, Sargent (1993, p. 21) therefore acknowledges: "The idea of rational expectations is ... sometimes said to embody the idea that economists and the agents they are modeling should be placed on an equal footing.... These ways of explaining things are suggestive, but misleading."

In an attempt to solve these problems, Sargent has joined the ranks of economists who are using algorithms from artificial intelligence and artificial life programs to represent heterogeneous agents. Sargent (1993, pp. 2-3) justifies this move as follows:

> I interpret a proposal to build models with boundedly `rational agents' as a call to retreat from the second piece of rational expectations (mutual consistence of expectations) by expelling rational agents from our model environments and replacing them with `artificially intelligent' agents who behave like econometricians. These `econometricians' theorize, estimate and adapt in attempting to learn about probability distributions which, under rational expectations, they already know.

In particular, Sargent seeks to demonstrate that it is not necessary to impose mutual consistency of expectations on all agents in order to get simulation results that approximate the rational expectations outcomes. He suggests that, in general, rational expectations equilibria can emerge from computational models in which "heterogeneous" agents develop models endogenously. Therefore, Sargent remains unwilling to relinquish rational expectations completely. Instead, he tries to reinforce rational expectations by focusing on convergence to this equilibrium (Marcet and Sargent 1992, p. 140; Sargent 1993, p. 133). Furthermore, he seeks to solve some of the problems associated with rational expectations such as multiple equilibria and no-trade theorems (1993, pp. 25, 133-134). Moreover, he desires to deal with some discrepancies in rational expectations (1993, p. 27). Finally, he hopes algorithms from artificial intelligence and artificial life could assist in the computation of equilibria (1993, pp. 106, 152).

Though inspired by the algorithms from artificial intelligence and artificial life developed by researchers associated with the Santa Fe institute, Sargent adopted a restricted interpretation of these algorithms as a result of his reluctance to relinquish expectations. Rather than using algorithms to think about populations as endorsed by many Santa Fe scientists, Sargent saw them as models of the neurons of an individual's brain (1993, p. 76). Rather than relinquishing the notion of an equilibrium as advocated by many Santa Fe researchers, he focused on convergence to equilibrium (1993, p. 153; Marimon and others 1990, p. 372).

There is nothing in the assumption of heterogeneous agents or artificial intelligence or artificial life to make convergence to equilibrium an obvious or, even more emphatically, a necessary outcome. Palmer, Arthur, Holland, LeBaron, and Tayler 1994, for example, did not find convergence to rational expectations in their first model of an artificial stock market. They conjectured that in on-off situations that are never going to happen again or in complicated situations where the agents have to do a lot of computing, establishing convergence to rational expectations requires loading almost impossible conditions onto these agents. Whereas prices in

Sargent's experiments fluctuate around the fundamental value, Palmer et al. observe speculative bubbles and crashes. Whereas markets in Sargent's simulations settle down to a stationary state, Palmer et al. find that their markets do not do this.

In a later paper (Arthur et al, 1996) however, the same authors found that essentially the same model will converge to rational expectations equilibrium provided that learning takes place at a rate which is sufficiently slow. Faster rates of learning generate a market regime in which psychological behaviour emerges, there are significant deviations from the rational expectations benchmark, and statistical "signatures" of real financial markets are observed.

Darley and Kaufman find two similar regimes in dynamic non-cooperative games in which agents learn from more or less local interaction with their neighbours. States resembling rational expectations equilibria (with shared agent perceptions) arise when prediction is easy (because each agent looks at the behaviour of a small number of neighbours so there is not much feedback) but not when prediction is difficult (because each agent notices the behaviour of a lot of other agents and, so there is a lot of feedback). When the model does not generate rational expectations equilibria marketed by mutually consistent models or perceptions, then the output is meta-stable in the sense that it is marked by periods of stasis interspersed with periods of turbulence.

Slow learning and local learning seemingly can support convergence of mutually consistent expectations. Both entail limited inputs of information to the learning process. This result is consistent with the findings of Moss and his colleagues in a number of simulation studies (Moss et al, 1998, for example) that local learning in a stable and relatively simple environment leads to agents to hold very similar or identical models of the environment and appropriate actions for achieving their aspirations. However, environments can sometimes become too complicated for the agents' conventional models to provide guides to action and then some exceptional means must be found to limit and focus the information presented to decision-makers.

We have now seen that the use of a particular range of artificial intelligence algorithms, those associated with Holland classifiers, can be used to represent agents who learn to specify mutually consistent mental models of their environments but who need not do so. In order to choose among these models, we require some criteria. The criteria of Sargent and his colleagues appears to be convergence to rational expectations equilibrium. We infer this criterion from Sargent's own methods. In several published works, Sargent tweaks the standard classifiers to establish optimisation and convergence.[1] For example, he imposes the same classifier systems on every agent of a given type. Hence, despite the claim that artificial intelligence algorithms allow the incorporation of heterogeneous agents, Sargent's models retain a high degree of homogeneity. Moreover, instead of adopting classifiers to model markets, he simulates single agents by the interaction of two autonomous classifiers. This leaves him with the awkward corollary that his agents make virtual bids (to themselves?) and transactions (with themselves?) to gain control of their own actions. Finally, rather than using genetic algorithms to provide

[1] Sargent (1993), Marimon et al (1990).

the environmental flexibility that other artificial intelligence techniques lack, Sargent diminishes their role. In fact, Marimon, McGrattan, and Sargent (1990, p. 358) acknowledge: "More standard Holland algorithms were first tried without much success, prompting us to produce the modified algorithm."

We conclude that the representations of cognition used by Sargent are arbitrary in the sense that there is no reason independent of his own models to devise and use such representations. They are certainly motivated by a wish to give his models an appearance of plausibility but there is no effort to demonstrate either that these representations are descriptively accurate or that the models in which they are incorporated yield outputs which are empirically verified. The only criterion seems to be that the model outputs should conform to the predictions of rational-expectations theory which, Sargent admits, rests on representations of cognition that are implausible in the extreme.

These analyses are sometimes seen as part of a bounded-rationality research program. However, Herbert Simon, the inventor of the notion of bounded rationality, would certainly reject the Sargent view. Sent, 1997, describes the difference between the Sargent and Simon approaches to representations of cognition as one that turns on the descriptive accuracy of the representation of cognition as behaviour. Whereas Sargent justifies the use of genetic algorithms to represent cognition on their effective parallelism in computation, Simon argues that cognition depends on serial symbol processing. In effect, Sargent appeals to current views of the physiological basis of all mental activity while Simon appeals to experimental evidence about the epiphenomena of decision-making and learning as observed by experimental psychologists. Furthermore, whereas Sargent sees bounded rationality as a means for strengthening mainstream economics, Simon seeks to develop an alternative to mainstream economics through bounded rationality.

Though Simon was the originator of the bounded rationality concept, he was not in complete control of it. Recognising this, Simon wrote in a letter to Sargent on 11 July 1995: "I could complain and say: 'I invented it and have a right to decide how it should be defined,' but as I failed to apply for trademark rights, I guess I have no standing in court." However, we would like to present some arguments to the jury in the remainder of this paper. Our defence is based on the criticism that Sargent-type results are generated by computational models with unknown analytical properties. Moreover, the learning procedures assumed for agents are arbitrary in the sense that there is no reason to believe that actual decision makers learn in a manner that is described by those assumptions. Building on this criticism, our defence further presents an alternative approach. The difference between the approaches outlined in this introduction and our proposal is important for economists if either (a) the two approaches imply different theoretical and modeling structures yielding different relationships between actions such as policy measures, on the one hand, and the consequences of those actions, on the other, or (b) one approach more usefully supports policy analyses than does the other. In the remainder of this paper, we consider only the second of these criteria.

Procedurally rational expectations

Although the phrase "bounded rationality" was originated by Herbert Simon, it has been taken over by more conventional economists and redefined to cohere with mainstream economic theory. For Simon, bounded rationality involves limited information-processing and computational capacities. For the more conventional economist Williamson (1975), in contrast, bounded rationality implies limited access to information. The difference is that, for Simon, bounded rationality entails the availability of more information than can be taken into account by decision makers while for economists such as Williamson bounded rationality entails the paucity of information which is therefore a constraint in optimisation procedures. Whereas Williamson is reluctant to accept the notion of satisficing, mainly because he thinks it would denote irrational behaviour, Simon himself considers satisficing to be a direct implication of bounded rationality.

The effect of redefinitions of bounded rationality such as Williamson's is to leave in tact the underlying precept of mainstream economic theory that agent behaviour can be represented by some constrained optimisation algorithm. The compulsion of economists to adhere to constrained optimisation as the defining characteristic of human behaviour is also manifest in, for example, Sargent's specification of artificially intelligent agents. The genetic algorithms and classifier systems he employs to represent behaviour are different but remain optimising algorithms that arguably misspecify the nature of human cognition.

Genetic algorithms and classifier systems

Classifier systems are parallel, message-passing, rule-based systems that model their environments by activating appropriate clusters of rules. This structure allows them to model complicated, changing environments, to interpret the internal states of agents in the theory so that the agents seem to progressively "model" their world, to make agents able to build up behavioural repertoires that include chains of actions that are initiated long before the agent obtains the reward, and to make agents able to develop the capacity to plan future actions on the basis of their expectations of what the consequences of those actions will be. In particular, classifier systems have two especially desirable efficiency properties. First, they do not impose heavy memory requirements on the system. Second, much of the information processing can be carried out in parallel.

In classifier systems, the agent is modeled as a collection of basic cognitive units, called classifiers. In contrast to standard economic theory, there are no consistency requirements on the classifiers of which an agent is comprised. In fact, there are some advantages to the notion of an agent as a bundle of possibly inconsistent behavioural propensities. First, requiring consistency imposes great computational costs on the system, as it entails a lot of internal structure and frequent consistency checking amongst different structural components. Second, since the world is always more complicated that our personal experience, maintaining consistency in an agent's behavioural or conceptual system almost necessarily requires a reduction in the agent's range of possible action, in particular in response to novel situations. Finally, evidence seems to suggest that we humans do in fact maintain overlapping and inconsistent conceptual systems and associated behavioural propensities.

An agent that maintains inconsistent behavioural propensities has to have some mechanism that determined on which of these propensities it would actually act. This is where competition enters the stage. There might be more than one winner of the competition at any given time, and as a result a cluster of rules could react to external situations. The competition mechanism in classifier systems depends on a number that is associated with each of the agent's classifiers, its strength, which registers the "memory" of how well the classifier has served in the past in the agent's quest for reward. A classifier's strength is modified over time by one of the system's learning algorithms.

A classifier system adapts or learns through the application of two well-defined machine learning algorithms. The first one, the bucket brigade algorithm, changes classifier strengths by identifying actions that lead to rewards — not just those that produce reward directly, but also those that "set the stage." It changes the strength associated with each classifier with experience in two ways. First, any classifiers whose action is implemented pass some of their strength to their immediate predecessors. Second, the strength of classifiers whose action is implemented when the agent receives an externally specified reward is increased as a function of the reward received. The system can be started off with a set of totally random classifiers. And then, as the environment reinforces certain behaviours and as the bucket brigade does its work, the classifiers organise themselves into coherent sequences that produce at least a semblance of the desired behaviour.

Even if the bucket-brigade credit assignment algorithm works perfectly, it could only rank the rules already present. By itself, it can only lead the system into highly optimised mediocrity. Two mechanisms are required to carry out the operation of replacing old classifiers with new ones. The first determines when replacements take place. It has to recognise situations in which the agent "needs" new classifiers. The second type of mechanism constructs new classifiers, which would probably improve the prospect for the agent to obtain a reward. This is a job for the genetic algorithm, which explores the immense space of possible new classifiers. Genetic algorithms carry out a subtle search for tested, above-average "building blocks" and build new classifiers by combining parts of existing high-strength classifiers. The idea is that useful classifiers work because they are composed of good building blocks, either in the features of the world that trigger them or in the actions they recommend. Trying out new combinations of these building blocks is more likely to produce useful new classifiers than is any kind of random search through the space of possible classifiers.

The genetic algorithm solves the problem of how to set the dial of rationality. The needle can be put at zero initially and then the genetic algorithm decides through mutation and recombination how far up the dial it goes. By adding the genetic algorithm as a third layer on top of the bucket brigade and the basic rule-based system, an adaptive agent not only learns from experience but can also be spontaneous and creative.

Classifier systems have been applied to economics in several ways. Instead of assuming that agents are perfectly rational, they can be modelled with classifier systems and learn from experience like real economic agents. Instead of modeling the economy as a Walrasian general equilibrium, societies of classifier systems can organise a set of interacting economic agents into an economy.

The argument that these implementations of genetic algorithms and classifier systems misspecify human cognition starts from the implication from cognitive science that cognition takes the form of exploitation of what we know and a highly directed exploration of our environment that is focused by our knowledge. This inference follows from the distinction in cognitive science between procedural and declarative knowledge (see, e.g., Anderson, 1993).

Procedural and declarative knowledge

Procedural knowledge is knowledge about how to do something and this knowledge is held by individuals in a way that does not allow it to be communicated directly to other individuals. Declarative knowledge is knowledge of what is true and can be communicated directly to other individuals. For example, an Englishman may have both procedural and declarative knowledge about the game of cricket. He can explain the rules of the game and describe or show a novice how to stand at the wicket or where to stand if he is to play off-stump or what to do if he is the wicket-keeper or the necessity of keeping the bowling arm straight at the elbow. All of this knowledge is declarative. To hit the ball successfully and place it where the batsman wants the ball to land or to spin-bowl so that the ball hits the ground and bounces so as to hit the wicket without coming into the range of the bat require abilities that can only be attained by practice. However well a person might know the rules and be able to describe the practices of cricket, that person will not be able actually to play cricket without acquiring substantial procedural knowledge.

Independently, this same distinction has been made by historians of business, the organisation and technological change who demonstrate its relevance to these areas of economic activity. For example, Edith Penrose (1959) calls the two types of knowledge objective and subjective in her seminal analysis of the direction of the growth of the firm. Yet, her differentiation between the two is couched in the same terms as Anderson's (1993) discussion of the difference between procedural and declarative knowledge. Similar distinctions — though not quite so explicit as in Penrose — are found in Chandler's (1975) work on the development of organisational structures and Rosenberg's (1975, 1980) discussions of the determinants of the direction of technical change.

Since we cannot know everything, a reasonable assumption is that the declarative knowledge we do have comes from the activities in which we engage. How we use this declarative knowledge follows from our experience and, to the extent that experience is necessary to use declarative knowledge effectively, its use is governed by procedural knowledge. In other words, we start from what we know and develop new ideas and perceptions only by extending our experience.

Genetic algorithms and classifier systems, by contrast, search the whole of the environmental information-space randomly and, if well constructed, evenly at the outset and concentrate increasingly on the parts of the information space that yield the best results. In the language of the field, genetic algorithms explore the search space and then exploit the subspaces described by classifiers that yield the greatest fitnesses. For cognitive scientists, human cognition takes the form of exploitation of what we know and a highly directed exploration that is focused by our procedural knowledge.

The difference has significant implications for economics. Either agents are global optimisers in which case genetic algorithms and classifiers can be used to represent that optimisation in conditions of constrained information-processing and computational capacities or they can at best exploit their existing procedural and declarative knowledge in the hope of gaining some local (though possibly large) improvement in their circumstances. Hence, the assumption of global optimisation can evidently support the construction of models with no concern for the procedures by means of which agents actually go about collecting declarative knowledge and then developing their procedural knowledge.

Implications for representations of cognition

Much of the work in the development of computational cognitive science stems from Simon's work and, in particular, Newell and Simon (1972). The later work in cognitive science, focused as we shall see on computer software architectures to represent cognitive processes, informs the approach taken here.

Indeed, Simon himself is critical of genetic algorithms and classifier systems to represent cognitive processes.

In his distinction between substantive and procedural rationality, Simon (1976) stresses the importance of the procedural aspects of cognitive behaviour that are left out by genetic algorithms and classifiers. Procedural rationality concerns the choice or development of procedures for making decisions when the decision maker has effectively limited capacities to process information and calculate appropriate outcomes. Certainly, procedural rationality entails satisficing. Our concern here is to find a representation of satisficing that uses artificial intelligence and supports models of decision making in a macroeconomic environment.

The particular representation reported in this paper is drawn from several cognitive theories that have been implemented as computer software architectures designed to replicate data from psychological experiments. These architectures are Soar (Laird et al, 1987) and ACT-R (Anderson, 1993). Both of these architectures are based on the concept of a problem-space architecture that itself is a tree structure of goals and subgoals. The original specification of this goal and subgoal structure was developed by Newell and Simon (1972) as a planning algorithm. The sort of situation in which it might be used in the Newell-Simon version was planning a trip from an office at MIT to an office at Berkeley. If the goal were to make that journey, a subgoal would be to fly from the nearest airport to MIT to the nearest airport to Berkeley. The subgoal of making that flight would be to get from the MIT office to the airport, which would be undertaken by (say) car or taxi. To take the car would entail the subgoal of getting from the MIT office to the car by walking.

A classic problem on which to test artificial-intelligence algorithms is the Tower of Hanoi problem. This involves moving a set of discs of graded size from one peg to another, using a third peg as an intermediate step. The five-disc Tower of Hanoi problem is illustrated below. The discs can be moved one at a time and it is not permitted to place a larger on a smaller disc. The problem-space architecture for this problem, as specified by Simon (1975) is to specify a subgoal of getting the top four discs onto peg B so that the largest disk and be placed on peg C and then to execute the next subgoal of moving the four discs on peg B to peg C. That move entails a subgoal of moving the top three discs to peg A so that the remaining disc cam be placed on the largest disc that is already on peg C. There is then a similar subgoal to get the three-disc tower onto peg A, and so on. Anderson (1993) developed a program in ACT-R to learn to solve the Tower of Hanoi problem and compared the results of that program with the results of experiments with human subjects. He found that the students did indeed learn to use a goal stack in the same way as ACT-R. The actual movements of the discs and the setting of goals and subgoals were accomplished in ACT-R by production (if-then) rules, see Figure 1.

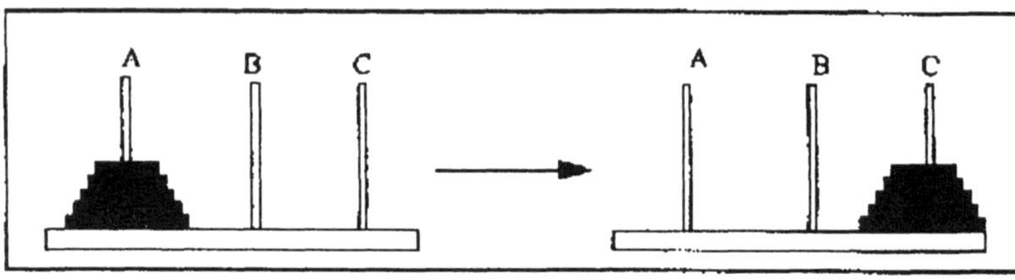

Figure 1: The Tower of Hanoi Problem

Three points about the ACT-R representation of cognition are relevant here. The first is that the results obtained from ACT-R programs can be compared with the results of psychological experiments to verify the accuracy of a program as a representation of cognitive behaviour in particular circumstances. Secondly, ACT-R is an encoding of an underlying theory of cognition. Thirdly, the representation of the problem-space architecture as rules for moving up and down the goal tree and the rules for performing tasks to achieve each goal can, in principle, be obtained by the standard knowledge-elicitation techniques used for building expert systems.

Taking the first two of these points together, we have a means of encoding procedural knowledge about how agents learn that is informed and justified by a particular theoretical structure and discipline that is independent of the domain of application in economics or the management sciences. Discussions or arguments about the appropriateness of that particular encoding are not likely to be influenced by the results desired for economics models. The third point allows us to develop independent evidence to support a particular encoding of agents' procedural and declarative knowledge.

As mentioned before, we believe that the difference between models such as Sargent's and ours is important if one approach more usefully supports policy analyses than does the other. Therefore, we will report a pilot model of a transition economy in the remainder of this paper. This model will be used to investigate the characteristics of procedures for learning and decision making that are validated in relation to cognitive science and verified in relation to economic time-series data. These procedures take for granted bounded rationality in the sense of Simon. These limitations preclude the assumption of optimising behaviour. Encoding the process of goal formation, learning and declarative knowledge about the environment in a manner that corresponds to encodings in the cognitive sciences, we are able to determine whether procedures for forming expectations and perceptions about the environment are rational in the sense that action based on those perceptions is increasingly likely or, in any case, not less likely to further the attainment of agents' goals.

An emerging-market model

The model reported here was developed to capture certain stylized descriptions of the commercial environment faced by newly- privatised and state-owned enterprises in the Russian Federation. One such fact of particular importance is the sharp increase in inter-enterprise arrears that was not being repaid during the first half of 1992 — an episode known as "the arrears crisis". As shown by Alfandari and Schaffer (1995), the volume of arrears peaked in the summer of 1992 at some 23 per cent of Russian GNP. The volume of arrears soon subsided to an average of about 5% for the period after 1992. Some experts find this figure to be not out of line with what is a normal amount of overdue trade credit by international standards. A straightforward statistical comparison, however, can be misleading because enterprise arrears in Russia represent a different type of economic relation. In many cases the credit is forced, bears negative real interest and has no fixed repayment period or agreed repayment schedule. To a degree, these peculiar features were conditioned by the shortage of working capital, a drastic fall in demand and other economic consequences of a government's attempt to put an end to the regime of soft budget constraints by lifting price control and removing state subsidies to producers.

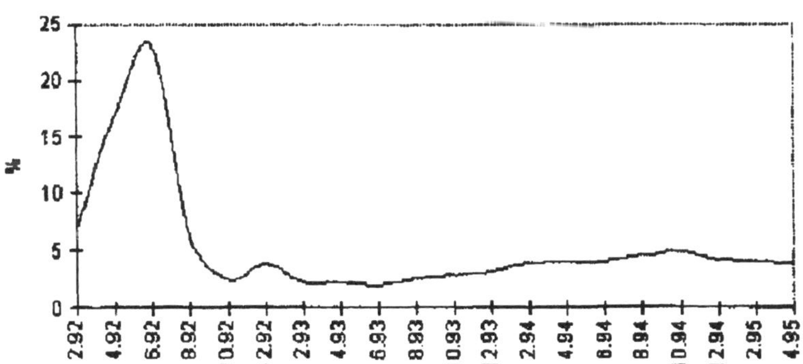

Figure 2: Arrears in the industrial sectors as shares of GDP 1992-1995

Source: The Monthly Bulletin of the Working Centre on Economic Reform of the Government of the Russian Federation, no., June 1995, p. 2.

Moss and Kuznetsova (1996) argue that the evolution of the arrears crisis provides a clear example of how enterprises cope with situations characterised by significant uncertainty. In the Russian case, enterprises were forced to adopt a survival strategy giving priority to existing, recognised constraints. There was no possibility to maximise anything in the framework of those constraints. Indeed, the scale of the accumulated debt and its persistence suggest that debt reduction was not a high priority. For one thing, both the liquid assets of enterprises and their debts have been growing simultaneously. The debt became an element of enterprises' survival strategy and was instrumental in prolonging the existence of a business environment to which they were accustomed, i.e., one governed by soft budget-constraints. Because the accumulated bad debt grew out of proportion on the national scale and became commonplace in all industrial sectors, this important business indicator ceased to be seen as a symptom of poor management efficiency. By the autumn of 1992, 95% of enterprises had bad debts enough to be proclaimed bankrupt on legal grounds. Debt performance had become separated from the business performance of a firm.

The Russian arrears crisis provides us with sufficiently clear stylized facts that we can use to assess whether the outputs from simulations conform to those facts or not. The stylized facts we want to capture, in addition to the arrears increases, are a high average and widely fluctuating rate of price inflation and volatile but trendless outputs. The point is to capture these stylized facts using a credible and validated specification of the processes agents use to develop their own models of their environments.

The modelling language

The model reported here was implemented in SDML, a strictly declarative modeling language that corresponds to strongly grounded autoepistemic logic (SGAL) (Edmonds et al (1996), Moss et al (1997). This means that any model that runs under SDML is formally sound and consistent with respect to the axioms and rules of inference of SGAL. Consequently, models written in SDML can entail qualitative as well as numerical relationships without loss of formal clarity and rigour. This is an important issue that is taken up in some detail below.

SDML has a number of object-oriented features that make it particularly useful for modelling cognition along the lines described at the start. The particular object-oriented features supporting the model reported here are the type (or class) hierarchy and the container hierarchy.

The type hierarchy is similar to the class hierarchy of, say, C++ but whereas C++ has simple inheritance (each class inherits the methods and instances of one superclass), SDML has multiple inheritance. The basic inheritance class is reproduced as Figure 3 from Moss *et. al.* (1998).

The user adds further subtypes, in particular, subtypes of Object, Agent and SDML's predefined Agent subtypes. The type Agent is distinguished from Object in that it has rulebases associated with it. The number of such rulebases varies with the time levels defined by the user. Time levels are discussed in several contexts below.

Agent is the principal type of interest here. Models are specified in terms of instances of agents but these will not normally be instances of the type Agent but of a user-defined subtype of Agent or one of its predefined subtypes (or of more than one of these). Clause definitions and rules are specified in types and are inherited from them by their instances. In this way, the rules for a number of identical agents can be defined in a shared type. Similarly, agents who are not identical may nevertheless share certain rules by means of a common supertype.

Abstract supertypes such as ParallelCompositeAgent or LoopingAgent add particular functionality to agents. The instances of every subtype of CompositeAgent can contain other agents (its subagents). Instances of subtypes of ParallelCompositeAgent contain subagents the rulebases of whom fire in parallel. Instances inheriting from type SerialCompositeAgent fire their rulebases in a previously specified order. LoopingAgents loop over time periods and there can be an arbitrary number of such time levels.

Finally, any agent can contain an instance of a subtype of type Meta-agent. Meta-agents can assert statements to, and retrieve statements from, their containers' rulebases in the same way that all agents assert to and retrieve from databases. The main difference is that meta-agents can only write rules to and read rules from their containers' rulebases whereas they and all other agents can read and write statements conforming to any previously defined clause definition when these statements are held on databases. Meta-agents are used to devise the sort of agent routines discussed by Nelson and Winter (1982) but to do so as a result of some representation of cognitive activity. These routines represent procedures that are the best the agents and their meta agents have so far found in their attempt to meet their current aspirations.

We will use the type and container hierarchies to put together a model in which enterprises learn about each other in the course of finding enterprise routines that support their goals and aspirations.

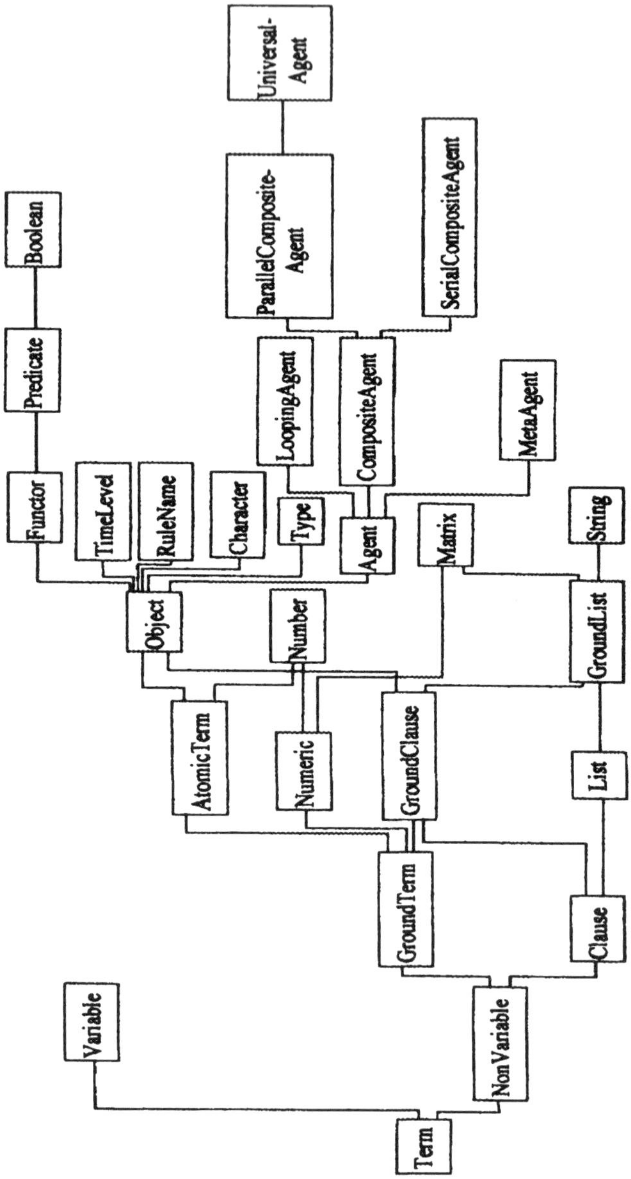

Figure 3: The Basic SDML Type Hierarchy

The type hierarchy defined for the Russian transition model is reproduced in Figure 4 and the container hierarchy in Figure 5 and Figure 6. The type symbols in boldface in Figure 4 are user defined.

All of the common features of agents that engage in transactions are implemented in the TradingAgent type. In the main, type TradingAgent defines clauses that are used to effect transactions. These clauses include "Order Placed With <ProductGroup> <TradingAgent> <Number>" and "Order Received From <ProductGroup> <TradingAgent> <Number>". The symbol <Type> indicates an instance of that type. If a household (say household-18) decides to purchase 12 units of corn from a farm (say farm-3), it would write "Order Received From corn household-18 12" to the database of farm-3. At the same time, it would write to its own database "Order Placed With corn farm-3 12". Similarly, if farm-3 decided to accept the order, it would write to the database of household-18 "Purchased From corn farm-3 1.305 12" where the price is 1.395 and the quantity 12 units of corn. In order to remember the sale itself, farm-3 would write to its own database "saleTo corn household-181.305 12". In this way the transaction would have been proposed and agreed by all of the different types of agent using the same language. However, households and enterprises behave differently in a number of ways in the model so that those clause definitions and rules that govern the behaviour of each of these subtypes of trading agents separately are implemented in their respective types.

In order to understand the nature of the subtypes of CompositeAgent and of LoopingAgent, it is necessary also to consider the container hierarchy of the model. The outermost container is debtArrearsModel, an instance of type ArrearsInflationModel. The type ArrearsInflationModel is a subtype of LoopingAgent from which it inherits all of the rules and clause definitions required to enable the model to loop over the time levels defined for instances of ArrearsInflationModel in the computational model. Type ArrearsInflationModel is also a subtype of type SerialCompositeAgent from which it inherits the rules and clause definitions to support subagents who fire their rules in a sequence determined by the agent. In this case, the agent environment fires its rules before the agent economy. The agent environment fires its rules once at each date. It is a simple agent the function of which is to introduce representations of environmental changes such as natural disasters into the simulations.

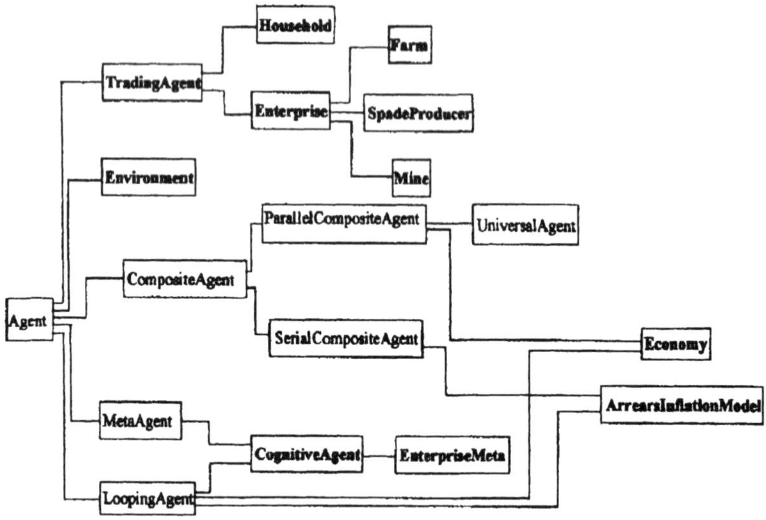

Figure 4: Hierarchy of agent types

The agent economy is an instance of type Economy that itself is a subtype of ParallelCompositeAgent and of LoopingAgent. As an instance of ParallelCompositeAgent, it contains agents who fire their rules effectively in parallel. This is an important feature in a model that represents transactions as the outcomes of communication among agents and where communication is represented by the assertion of clauses to the databases of other agents or some other database that is common to both. Since the agents are active at the same time, we have to represent the fact that a communication can be received only after it is sent. This means, in terms of any computational model, that an agent can retrieve any message written by another agent only at a time period subsequent to the period in which it was written. So, in order to effect a transaction, agent-1 will assert an order for goods to the database of agent-2 at time t; agent-2 will retrieve that assertion at time t+1 and

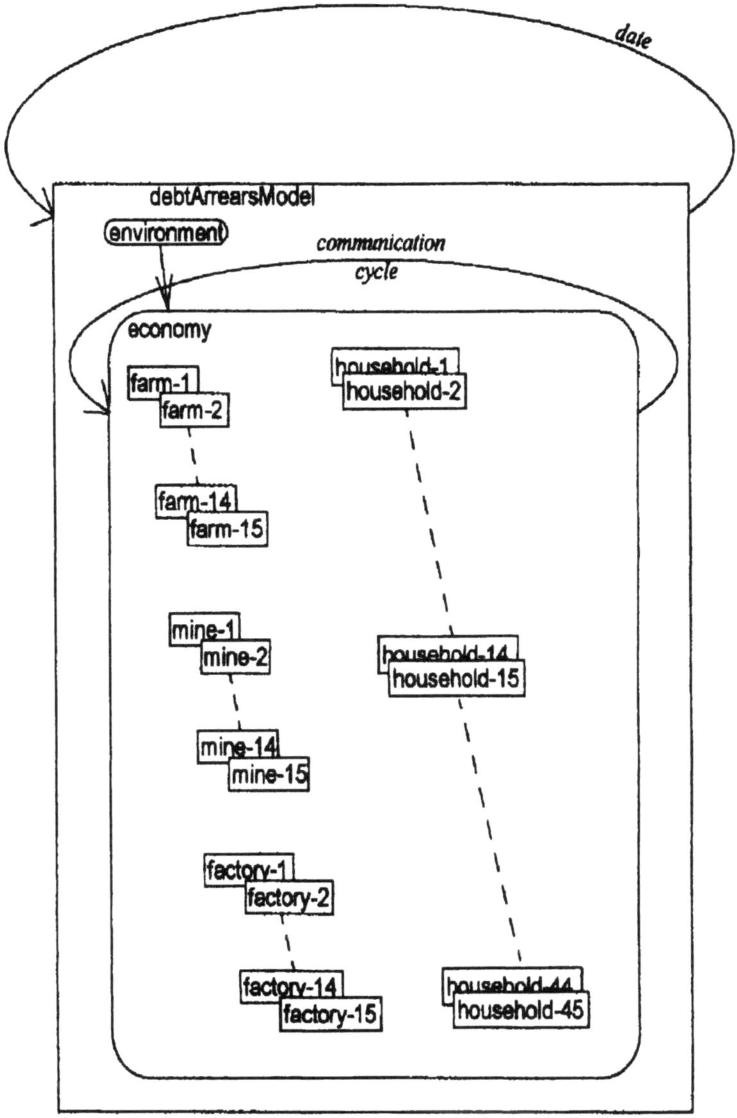

Figure 5: The Macro Container Structure

assert its acceptance of the offer to the database of agent-1. This acceptance will be

retrieved by agent-1 and time t+2 and the agreement to transact has been concluded.

In this model, transactions take place each date but the negotiations required to effect them we now see will take more than a single time period. For this reason, several communication cycles are allowed each date. The clauses shared by instances of TradingAgent include, for example, "purchased from" and "sold to", each of which has arguments to identify the product, the price, the amount and the trading partner.

Instances of type Enterprise represent cognitive agents. In this model, cognition takes the form of the building of mental models that are used to create rules for guiding the decisions of the enterprise. These decision rules are what Nelson and Winter (1992) call "routines".

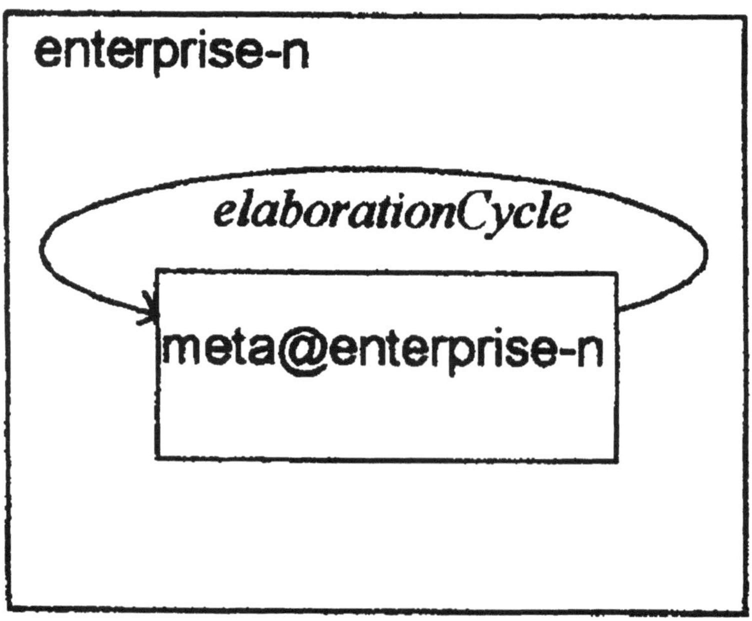

Figure 6: The enterprise container structure

The building and assessment of the mental models are undertaken by subagents of the enterprises. These subagents are instances of type EnterpriseMeta that is a subtype of Meta-agent. Meta-agents can use the rulebases of their containers and other subagents of their containers as databases. In this model, each instance inheriting from type Enterprise contains a meta-agent of type EnterpriseMeta. All instances of EnterpriseMeta build mental models in a procedure derived from computational cognitive science. This involves identifying goals and subgoals and the tasks needed to achieve those goals over a number of time periods called elaboration cycles. One of the tasks to be completed in this process is the writing of decision rules to the rulebase of the containing enterprise. For this reason, type EnterpriseMeta is itself a subtype of LoopingAgent as well as MetaAgent and it loops over time level elaborationCycle. The articulation of instance of type Enterprise, expanded from Figure 5, is given in Figure 6.

The model setup

In order to capture the essential elements of the position of Russian enterprises, we assume the decision variables of the enterprises to be planned output, output price, the wage rate, the offer of employment, orders placed with suppliers and payments to creditors. In addition, the enterprises choose the suppliers with whom they place their orders and the customers whose orders they will fill in whole or in part. Each enterprise notes at each date whether its suppliers have filled the orders placed with them and whether its customers have paid for the goods previously supplied to them. These notes take the form of endorsements attached to the enterprises records of its customers and suppliers. Orders are allocated among known suppliers in proportion to their records of reliability. Sales are allocated first to orders from known customers with the best records of payment. In effect, each enterprise builds up models of the enterprises with which it trades.

These endorsements are also used by enterprises to formulate views about which other firms are the most successful. It is natural to assume that those suppliers who are best at supplying orders and those customers who pay most quickly are also the strongest enterprises. On this basis, enterprises take into account any observable information they have about these trading partners and assume that their behaviour is highly functional. In the model reported here, the only information that one agent can observe about an enterprise is the output prices it sets, its employment of labour and information arising from the transactions in which they engage (supplies, orders and payments). Thus, if one enterprise observes its best trading partners lowering (or raising) prices, it will assume that to lower (or raise) prices increases the values of goal variables and, so, will conjecture a model to that effect.

The goals of the enterprises are sales volume and cash. There is no attempt at optimisation of these values but, rather, the agents seek strategies that will increase the value of one or the other of these goals. In the present setup, neither is given pride of place. In the event that changing the value of one decision variable is expected to increase the value of one goal value and diminish the other, then the action that is considered most likely to have the anticipated outcome will dominate the decision. If the agent has more confidence that the goal value diminution will occur then she will change the decision variable value to reduce or prevent the diminution. If she has more confidence that the other goal value will be increased, then she will change the value of the decision variable in the appropriate direction.

The pre-defined intermediate variables observed by the enterprises are their own purchases, their own sales, their current stocks of real goods (inputs and unsold outputs), their current financial asset holdings (only cash, so far), and the wage bill (the product of the wage rate paid and employment by the enterprise).

The wage bill is the only intermediate variable to be calculated from other variables observed by the enterprise. It gets this special treatment because we assume that it is paid in the same period as the employment it covers. This assumption itself seems appropriate because of the relatively insignificant incidence of delayed wage payments and also because, in inflationary conditions, the impact of delayed wage payments is much the same as offering a lower wage rate. A rather more elaborate setup would be required directly to capture the effects of wage arrears. If such a model were thought likely to be useful, it would be a straightforward extension of the model reported here.

In general terms, the setup reported here was devised only to capture a coarse-grained account of the development of Russian enterprises and to demonstrate how our modelling techniques perform on problems relating to the emergence of new markets and market institutions.

Results

Our first simulation setup included a specification of the input-output relations and the inclusion as model variables of inter-enterprise debts as well as payments and the usual economic variables of employment, prices, wage rates, production decisions, actual outputs and sales. The Russian experience is of steady, even rising, employment, rapidly rising prices, growing debt and declining output and sales.

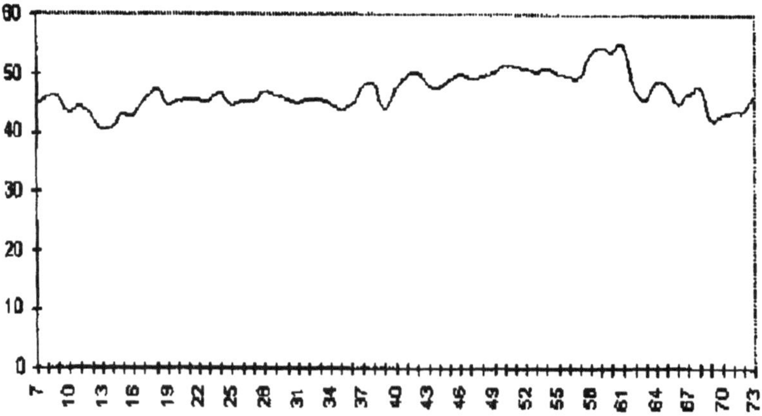

Figure 7: Total employment (simulated)

We have run the setup for 73 periods. What we get is not too dissimilar to what we observe. Employment, for example, does not show any dramatic changes at all although, reflecting variations in production activities over the whole of the simulation, it has not been stable. The time path of employment is given in Figure 7.

In production we observed a collapse after an initial surge (probably due to initial simulation conditions) but starting from date 7 production trends varied from sector to sector. The production of corn remained remarkably stable because corn has at least one relatively stable source of demand in the form of households. The production of both spades and iron shows considerable oscillation but it develops accordingly with the picture of unit sales that demonstrates a certain cyclical pattern. Series for production is shown in Figure 8 and for unit sales in Figure 9.

A key result in the development of the simulation setup was the price series. The series, reproduced as Figure 10, now reflects the stylized facts of the Russian experience. However, earlier models generated trendless, though moderately volatile, price series. The achievement of the price series of Figure 10 was obtained by specifying credible information sources.

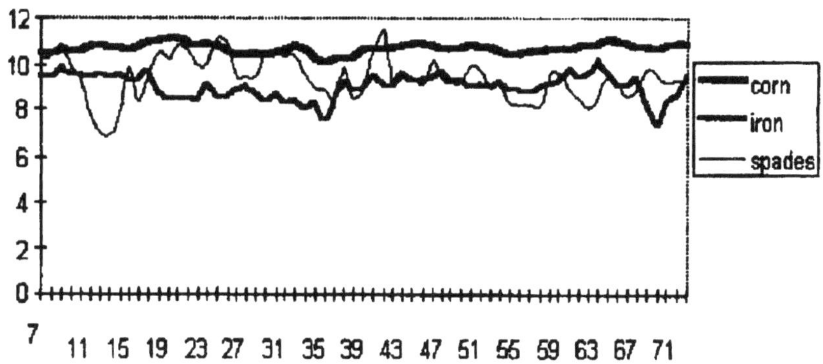

Figure 8: Sectoral production (simulated)

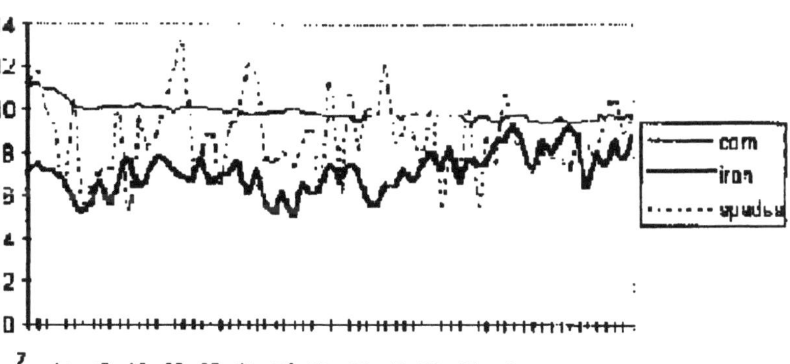

Figure 9: Unit sales (simulated)

Procedural rationality as modelling

The goals of the enterprises are sales volume and cash. The numerical controls are price, wage rate, employment, input demands and debt payments. In addition, each enterprise has to determine the allocation of its orders for inputs and the allocation of its debt repayments.

Agent cognition is represented by a process of model building that has more in common with the cognitive sciences than with genetic algorithms and classifiers as used by Sargent and others in the economics community. The modelling strategy of each enterprise in the simulation model is to formulate its own models relating selected control variables to at least one goal variable. Initially, following Moss (1995), control variables and goal variables were combined at random and the control variable was either increased or decreased with equal probability. There was a standard generate-and-test procedure so that enterprises kept those of their models that yielded improved goal variable values and abandoned those that did not. Agents kept track of how good their models were by a process of endorsement first suggested by Cohen (1995) and implemented by Moss. In general terms, models were endorsed as successful at a date when they were used to formulate an action undertaken in the same period that a goal variable value was improved. They were endorsed as being unsuccessful when the goal value was not improved. Models that were usually successful or usually unsuccessful were endorsed as such. This would happen when four of the five most recent applications of a model earned the successful or unsuccessful endorsements, respectively. Collections of endorsements mapped into numerical values with positive endorsements increasing overall endorsement values and negative endorsements reducing overall endorsement values. The probability of applying a model is proportional to its overall endorsement value. Models with negative overall endorsement values are abandoned.

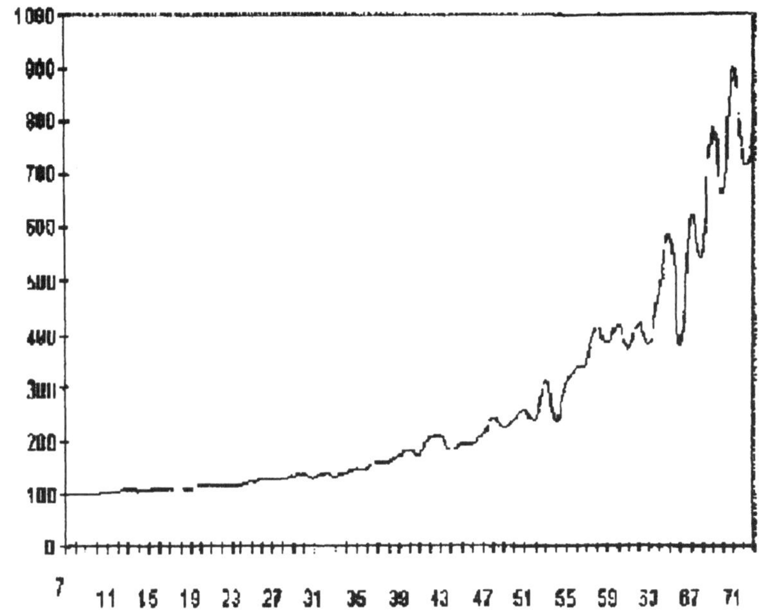

Figure 10: the Paasche Price Index (simulated)

Enterprises also endorsed other agents as being reliable or unreliable suppliers, reliable or unreliable debtors and so on. The resulting overall endorsement values attaching to these other agents were used to determine suppliers and, when orders exceeded stocks of outputs, the order in which to allocate outputs to customers. In this way, stable trading relationships were established among agents in the model.

An important feature of this model was the absence of any *deus ex machina*. There was no auctioneer, no bulletin board on which to post prices, supplies or demands for all agents to see. All information was communicated directly by one agent to another. Learning and expectations about the behaviour of other agents and the system as a whole resulted from an explicit cognitive mechanism that gains its credibility from disciplines outside economics. Procedural rationality entails the selection of information when more is available than an agent can process. It also involves identifying relations from that data without relying on it being correct in some fundamental sense. If the relationships suggest actions that improve on an agent's present position, then they constitute a good model. Otherwise, the model needs to be abandoned or revised. An important means of understanding for humans is the forming of analogies. The analogy in the simulation environment reported here took the form of applying behaviour by agents who appear to be successful to one's own behaviour. If, for example, we know that the farmer to whom we sell our spades pays her bills immediately and is raising the price of corn, then she must be doing well enough to pay her bills so we will try raising the price of our spades in order to do well ourselves.

What did not work (i.e., did not conform to the stylized facts) in the simulation experiments that led to this model was random generation and testing. Classifiers rely on a generate-and-test algorithm, too, but on a much larger scale since a population of models would be generated, mutated, crossed-over and tested at each date rather than just the one model selected by the agent in our simulations. We know that such models can yield outputs that converge towards rational-expectations equilibria. This issue of the relationship between simulation outputs and rational expectations equilibrium is clearly of some importance to economists. It is, therefore, addressed in the following section.

Model validation and verification

The validation of a computer program is the process of applying formal methods to ensure that a program design will achieve what is expected of it in appropriate conditions and, in particular, will not get into a confused or illegal state. If a program runs without error in any computer programming language, then that program is consistent and sound relative to that language. That is, the program does not generate or entail mutually contradictory statements and it does not generate statements that the language does not support. Consequently, program validation entails ascertaining that the program is consistent and sound relative to a formal statement of the properties of the programming language.

In this section, we argue that validation should be an important issue in the specification of economic models in general and economic cognition in particular. Two aspects of validation are considered: validation with respect to logical formalisms and validation with respect to cognitive theories.

Logical validation

The virtue of validating the consistency and soundness of a model relative to a logical formalism is that it removes ambiguity from the specified relationships comprising the model. The particular formalisms that economists rely on are mathematical systems that are well-suited to optimising functions subject to well-specified constraints. Such mathematical bases are inappropriate for the model above because of its strong reliance on qualitatively defined variables such as endorsements and because there is no element of optimisation in the model. Nonetheless, the model is consistent and sound relative to at least one logical formalism (and, though unproved, probably many such formalisms).

The logical formalism under which the transition model is consistent and sound is a fragment of strongly grounded autoepistemic logic (FOSGAL). The proof of the consistency and soundness of the model relative to FOSGAL runs as follows:

If a programming language corresponds to a logical formalism, then any program viewed as a set of statements or sentences that runs in that language will necessarily be sound and consistent relative to that logical formalism. One such language, implemented precisely to capture this feature of programs, is SDML which corresponds to FOSGAL. This particular logical formalism of SDML has emerged as one that supports the kind of multi-agent, strictly declarative modelling favoured by the SDML user community. It is by no means the only possible or appropriate logical formalism for modelling organisations. Indeed, the choice of logical formalisms for different classes of problems is already a fruitful field of enquiry in the artificial intelligence literature. A natural extension of the work described in this paper is the explication of the properties of appropriate logics to underpin a language of discourse for the management and economic sciences.

In SDML, and therefore in the model reported here, each agent is defined on a rulebase and database for each period of time. Every rule in the rulebases and every clause asserted to the databases is sound and consistent relative to strongly grounded autoepistemic logic. If any were not, then the model would not run and inconsistency error would be reported.

FOSGAL emerged as a good logical basis for modelling agent behaviour and interaction because of its encoding of negative knowledge. Such encodings are well- recognised to be difficult simply because it is not possible in practice to store all the facts that are not true. For this reason, SDML follows the conventional practice of storing only positive knowledge and dealing with negation by allowing rules that have `not inferred' operators in their antecedents.

SDML was designed principally as a forward-chaining language because drawing inferences from a set of beliefs and facts and then remembering those inferences by asserting them to a database seemed a more natural representation of agent reasoning than backward chaining, in which the implication is stated and then the antecedents evaluated to see if the assertion can be justified. In order to perform forward chaining efficiently, SDML will fire rules but keep track of any assumptions it had to make on the way. This helps to minimise any back-tracking to try alternative assumptions in the more commonly occurring situations. Thus SDML sometimes needs to make inferences from its own lack of inference of certain facts, just as in SGAL one can infer from one's own lack of belief.

Theoretical validation

The position we have now reached is that a model written in SDML is consistent and sound relative to a particular formal logic that is well-suited to the development of computational models involving interaction among agents that takes the form of direct communication of information. Genetic algorithm and classifier representations of agents are doubtless consistent and sound relative to the mathematics underlying these representations. Hence, we have two, alternative representations of cognition that have equal claim to logical rigour. How then do we choose between them?

It seems likely that the appeal of genetic algorithms to economists such as Sargent is that they are optimising algorithms. However, not all problems are well conditioned to be optimised using genetic algorithms in general and Holland classifiers in particular. In fact, Sargent (1993) and Marimon et al (1990) imposed many restrictions on standard genetic algorithms. Rather than using the standard one-point crossover reproduction mechanism, he included a two-point method of recombination. Rather than adopting classifiers to model markets, he simulated single agents by the interaction of two autonomous classifier systems. Rather than using genetic algorithms to provide the environmental flexibility that traditional artificial intelligence techniques lacked, he diminished their role. Hence, he moved away from standard interpretations of classifier systems in his desire to salvage methodological individualism and neoclassical equilibrium. First, standard genetic algorithm methods differed from methodological individualism in that they simultaneously involved a parallel search involving hundreds or thousands of points in the search space. Second, convergence to a globally suboptimal result was a major concern with genetic algorithms.

We are not aware of any independent argument that Holland classifiers are accurate representations of human cognition. In fact, as discussed before, Simon (1993) opposes this interpretation. Hence, their main virtue seems to be that, under some circumstances at least, computational models representing agents as Holland-type classifiers yield outputs that converge over simulated time towards rational expectations equilibria.

To find that a result can be achieved in a variety of different ways and, in particular, using a variety of distinct approaches is a standard means in the natural and mathematical sciences of building confidence in the result. The fact that genetic algorithms can be used to generate rational expectations equilibria in computational models thus enhances confidence in the importance of the rational expectations hypothesis. If the attempt to generate the same result with different techniques sometimes leads to the intended result and sometimes does not, then the failure can itself lead to a deepening of our understanding of the phenomena under investigation. One possibility is that a number of different approaches to the investigation yield a similar set of conditions under which the original result can be expected. In this way, we begin to identify the conditions of application of, in this case, the rational expectations hypothesis.

One such development looks to be emerging from the papers by Arthur *et. al.* (1996) and by Darley and Kaufman (1997) as cited earlier. These papers follow Sargent in relying on classifiers to represent key aspects of cognition. A complementary approach in the investigation of the conditions in which we might expect rational expectations equilibria to arise is suggested by computational cognitive science. Both Soar and ACT-R offer points of departure for this approach. Although we do not yet have complete results, we can exhibit the key features of and some early results from an implementation of key ideas from cognitive science into the transition model reported above.

The core concept drawn from both Soar and ACT-R (and originally from Newell and Simon, 1972) is the problem-space architecture (PSA). The PSA rests on the experimentally verified idea that, in undertaking complex decisions, we engage in a process of sub-goaling. What is involved here is readily seen from the PSA devised for a new version of the model reported in Section 0.

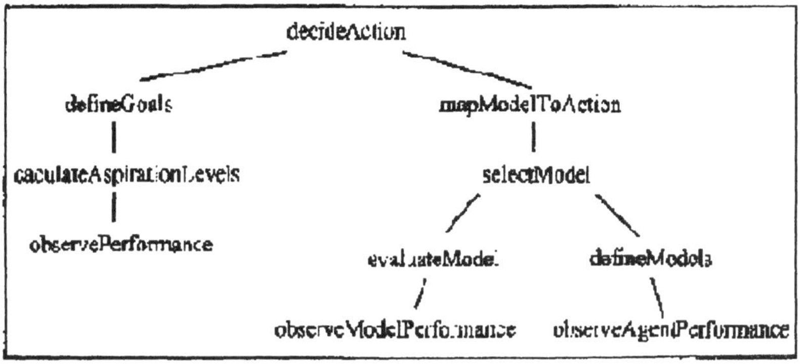

Figure 11: Transition enterprise problem-space architecture

The label of each problem space in Figure 11 indicates a task to be completed. The top-level task (decideAction) that must be completed at each date is to decide what actions to take. Examples of the actions to be decided upon are price levels, wage rate, planned output, input demands and how much of current cash resources to pay out. Actions are predicated upon goals so that, before deciding on an action, the agent must determine what the action is meant to achieve. In this model, aspiration levels are set for the various goal variables and this is done on the basis of the enterprise's observation of its own performance. Once the goals are defined, it is necessary to translate perceptions of the environment into some action. Since these perceptions are represented by mental models of the agents, an appropriate model must be selected. The selection will be from existing models and new models. The existing models are evaluated as they are used and the evaluations are remembered as endorsements. New models are defined on the basis of observations of the behaviour of the most successful (best endorsed) of the enterprise's trading partners. Consequently, the performance of these trading partners must be observed and evaluated.

Declarative knowledge is composed of facts that can be retrieved from one database or another by the agent and some relationships encoded as mental models. Procedural knowledge is composed of the means of mapping models into rules of action. There is also some common knowledge such as the impossibility of increasing outputs without increasing inputs that is declarative in the sense that agents could in principle communicate such knowledge to one another. Such knowledge is encoded as models that cannot be eliminated from the databases of an agent.

Models (apart from the common-knowledge models) and the memory of trading relations can be retrieved by agents with a probability related to their importance and the length of time since they were last retrieved. The scheme used to determine the probability of retrieval at need is taken from Anderson (1993). In particular, the odds in favour of retrieval are

$$\sum_{i=1}^{n} a\, t_i^d$$

where the t_j are the lags since the jth prior retrieval of the endorsement; d is a positive parameter determining the half-life of the influence of a prior retrieval on current retrieval. The value of a is determined in the simulation model by the endorsement values of models and the agents.

One virtue of this formula is its consistency with experimental data about memory. The choice of the d and a parameters is not determined by that experimental literature. Setting those values is an empirical issue to be considered presently. The precise specification of the PSA is also an empirical issue. In terms of validation, however, it seems much more robust to develop representations of cognition that, like this one, can be assessed on a basis that is independent of the application rather than to assess an arbitrary representation of cognition on the basis of its convergence to a rational expectations equilibrium.

Verification

While the PSA specified above conforms to similar models developed for social simulations (see, for example, Ye and Carley, 1995; Moss et al, 1998), we have not yet sought independent evidence of its descriptive accuracy. The source of such evidence would naturally come from knowledge-elicitation exercises with enterprise managers in the Russian Federation. Such an exercise would also inform our assumptions about goals and goal-conflict resolution.

Parameterising the model is computationally expensive and requires reliable data series. Previous models produced by the Centre for Policy Modeling have been parameterised using genetic programming algorithms. These extend genetic algorithms by representing data as tree structures that are subject to mutation and cross-over at points where usable programs result. Edmonds and Moss, 1997, report this technique in detail. The fitness functions are typically related inversely to root mean-squared errors and are also biased in favour of parameters that look reasonable to domain experts. In this way, we not only get results from application to hold-out data sets that are at least as good as ordinary regression methods applied to the same data but also results that reflect at the same time-domain expertise.

Conclusion

A necessary but not sufficient condition for simulation models to converge towards a rational expectations equilibrium is that agent perceptions converge so that mean expectations are close to model outcomes. The Sargent research programme seeks to demonstrate that non-homogeneous agents who search the whole possibility space will converge on perceptions that are effectively consistent with the outputs of the system model. The transition models described in this paper generate convergence in behaviour — specifically in price-setting behaviour — by local exploitation of declarative knowledge. These models were not implemented with rational expectations equilibria in mind. They were implemented to demonstrate that models that are well-validated with respect to both formal logics and independent theoretical structures relating to learning and decision making also lead to verifiably accurate model outputs.

We conjecture that any cognitive behaviour that entails the convergence of individuals' perceptions while these perceptions are changed when systematically wrong will also entail convergence towards expectations that are not wrong in any biased way. If so, then ultimate convergence towards a rational expectations equilibrium or something similar is a weak condition in the absence of structural change in the economy. However, the process of learning by global search and the process of learning by local exploitation might well yield very different results in relation to the effects of economic and social policies that are intended to effect particular structural changes. Before implementing policies based on either of these approaches, it would be important to look for reasons to believe in one or the other. Validation with respect to formalisms — mathematics or predicate or propositional logics — ensures rigour in the sense of a lack of ambiguity in specifications and implementations of models. Validation with respect to independent, experimentally or otherwise verifiable theories gives us confidence that our own models are better than just data-mining. We can see no reason to have confidence in the encoding of human cognition as genetic algorithms and classifiers simply because the resulting models converge to something that is not too different from conventional rational-expectations-type results. This scepticism stems from the absence of any independent reason to believe that agents learn by global search and the plethora of evidence that they learn by local exploitation of declarative knowledge conditioned by their procedural knowledge. Since procedural knowledge can only be acquired by experience, the identification and use of declarative knowledge must always be based on the experience of what the agent has done and this is itself an inherently local processing of declarative knowledge.

Experience indicates that economists are unlikely to be influenced by the very different style of process-centred disciplines such as cognitive science. Nonetheless, we have shown the feasibility of implementing models using concepts that have arisen independently in analyses of business history, the economic history of technical change and in the cognitive sciences to explain with empirical verification how learning and decision making actually take place.

REFERENCES

Alfandari G, Schaffer, M (1995), "On 'Arrears' in Russia", Paper presented at the Joint Conference of the World Bank and the Ministry of Economy of the Russian Federation, St.Petersburg, June 12-13.

Anderson, J R (1993), *Rules of the Mind* (Hillsdale NJ: Lawrence Erlbaum Associates).

Arthur, W B, J Holland, B LeBaron, R Palmer and P Tayler (1996), "Asset Pricing under Endogenous Expectations in an Artificial Stock Market", University of Wisconsin-Madison, Social Systems Research Institute Discussion Paper 9625.

Aukutsionek, S (1995), "Market Reform and Transitional Crisis", *The Russian Economic Barometer*, Vol. 4, pp. 22-41.

Belianova E. (1995) "Motivation and Behaviour of Russian Enterprises" [in Russian], *Voprosy ekonomiki*, Vol. 6, pp. 15-21.

Chandler, A (1975), The Visible Hand, (Cambridge MA: Harvard University Press).

Cohen, P R (1985), Heuristic Reasoning: An Artificial Intelligence Approach, (Boston: Pitman Advanced Publishing Program).

Darley, V and S Kaufman (1997), "Natural Rationality" in W B Arthur, et al (eds), Economy as a Complex Evolving System II (Reading, MA: Addison-Wesley).

Debreu, G (1974), "Excess Demand Functions", Journal of Mathematical Economics, Vol. 1, pp. 15-23.

Edmonds, B and S Moss (1997), A Formal Preference State Model with Qualitative Market Judgements, OMEGA - the International Journal of Management Science, Vol. 25(2), pp. 155-169.

Edmonds, B, S Moss and S Wallis (1996), "Logic, reasoning and a programming language for simulating economic and business processes with artificially intelligent agents" in Ein-Dor, Phillip (ed) Artificial Intelligence in Economics and Management (Boston: Kluwer Academic Publishers).

Kirman, A P (1992), "Whom or What Does the Representative Individual Represent?", *Journal of Economic Perspectives*, Vol. 6, pp. 117-136.

Konolige, K (1988), "On the relation between default and autoepistemic logic", *Artificial Intelligence*, Vol. 35, pp. 343-382.

Laird, J E, A Newell and P S Rosenbloom (1987), "Soar: An architecture for general intelligence", *Artificial Intelligence*, Vol. 33, pp. 1-64.

Mantel, R R (1976), "Homothetic Preferences and Community Excess Demand Functions", *Journal of Economic Theory*, Vol. 12, pp. 197-201.

Marcet, A and T J Sargent (1992), "The Convergence of Vector Autoregressions to Rational Expectations Equilibrium" in Vercelli, A. et al. (eds), Macroeconomics: A Strategic Survey (Oxford: Oxford University Press).

Marimon, Ramon, Ellen McGrattan, and Thomas J Sargent (1990), "Money as a Medium of Exchange in an Economy with Artificially Intelligent Agents", *Journal of Economic Dynamics and Control*, Vol. 14, pp. 329-374.

Moss, Scott and Edmonds (1998), "Modelling economic learning as modelling", *Cybernetics and Systems*, Vol. 29, pp. 215-247.

Moss, Scott, Helen Gaylard, Steve Wallis and Bruce Edmonds (1998), "SDML: A multi-agent language for organisational modelling", *Computational and Mathematical Organization Theory*, Vol. 4, pp. 43-69.

Moss, Scott (1995), "Control Metaphors in The Modelling of Decision-Making Behaviour", *Computational Economics*, Vol. 8, pp. 283-301.

Moss, Scott and Olga Kuznetsova (1996), "Modelling the Process of Market Emergence". In Owsinski, J. W. and Nahorski, Z. (eds.), Modelling and Analysing Economies in Transition, (Warsaw: MODEST).

Nelson, R and S Winter (1982), An Evolutionary Theory of Economic Change (Cambridge, MA: Harvard University Press).

Newell, A and H Simon (1972), Human Problem Solving, (Englewood Cliffs: Prentice-Hall).

Palmer, G R G, W B Arthur, J H Holland, B LeBaron and P Tayler (1994), "Artificial Economic Life: A Simple Model of a Market", *Physica D*, Vol. 75, pp. 264-274.

Penrose, E (1959), The Theory of the Growth of the Firm (Oxford: Basil Blackwell).

Rosenberg, N (1975), Perspectives on Technology (Cambridge: Cambridge University Press).

Rosenberg, N (1980), Inside the Black Box (Cambridge: Cambridge University Press).

Sargent, T J (1993), Bounded Rationality in Macroeconomics (Oxford: Clarendon Press).

Sent, E-M (1997) , "Sargent versus Simon: Bounded Rationality Unbound", *Cambridge Journal of Economics*, Vol. 21, pp. 323-338.

Sent, E-M (forthcoming), The Evolving Rationality of Rational Expectations: An Assessment of Thomas Sargent's Achievements (Cambridge: Cambridge University Press).

Simon, H A (1975), "The Functional Equivalent of Problem-Solving Skills", *Cognitive Psychology*, Vol. 8, pp. 268-288.

Simon, H A (1976), "From Substantive to Procedural Rationality", in Latsis, S J (ed), Method and Appraisal in Economics. (Cambridge: Cambridge University Press).

Simon, H A (1993), "The Human Mind: The Symbolic Level", *Proceedings of the American Philosophical Society*, Vol. 137, pp. 638-647.

Sonnenschein, H (1972), "Market Excess Demand Functions", *Econometrica*, Vol. 40, pp. 549-563.

Tambe, M and P S Rosenbloom (1996), "Architectures for Agents that Track Other Agents in Multi-agent Worlds", Intelligent Agents, II, Springer Verlag Lecture Notes in Artificial Intelligence (LNAI 1037).

Williamson, O E (1975), Markets and Hierarchies (New York: Macmillan).

Yavlinsky G (1994), "The Lessons of the Economic Reform" [in Russian], Oktiabr', Vol. 9, pp. 136-149.

Ye, M and K E Carley (1995), "Radar Soar: Towards an Artificial Organization Composed of Intelligent Agents", *Journal of Mathematical Sociology*, Vol. 20, pp. 219-246.

CHAPTER 6

INSTRUMENT RULES, INFLATION FORECAST RULES AND OPTIMAL CONTROL RULES WHEN EXPECTATIONS ARE RATIONAL

Sean Holly and Paul Turner

1. INTRODUCTION

Over the last decade, as a number of industrialised countries[1] have gone over to the use of explicit inflation targets, there has been a resurgence of interest in the use of feedback rules to characterise monetary policy. In this paper we consider how the type of rule suggested by the methods of optimal control can be derived when the model we have of an economy is non-linear and the model contains forward-looking expectations. Although the literature in this area is voluminous, there is still considerable interest in seeking computational improvements to existing algorithms[2] and in deriving methods that can be applied to the highly non-linear, and analytically intractable, dynamic, stochastic general equilibrium models that have grown out of the original real business cycle methodology. Although the methods we describe in this paper could be applied to this class of model, we confine our attention here to non-linear models more in the Cowles Foundation tradition.[3] One approach to the problem of dealing with non-linear, rational expectations models is to apply direct methods such as the Penalty Function method of Holly and Zarrop (1983), or the extended path methods associated with Anderson, Fair and Taylor used for solution and estimation, or for computing time consistent solutions (see Hall, 1986). The disadvantage of this approach, in the context of this paper, is that the solutions are in open-loop form; there is no explicit control rule that can be compared directly to other forms of rule existing in the literature.

There is also another reason for concentrating on the derivation of an explicit control rule. A striking feature of the way in which the inflation-targeting regime is operated concerns the use of an *inflation forecast.* Because it is believed that changes in monetary policy take some time to appear in changes to the rate of inflation, the monetary policy stance, it is argued, should be set with respect to the expected inflation rate 18 months to two years ahead (Svensson, 1997a, 1997b, Haldane, 1998). To quote Svensson (1998):

---

[1] Since 1990 New Zealand, Canada, UK, Sweden, Finland, Australia and Spain have adopted explicit targets for the rate of inflation.

[2] For recent contributions see Sims (1996), Anderson (1998), and Amman and Kendrick (1998).

[3] At this stage in their evolution dynamic stochastic general equilibrium models do not have too much to say about the policy problem of inflation targeting in a world in which monetary impulses take some time to show up in the rate of inflation.

> In order to implement inflation targeting efficiently, an inflation-targeting central bank must have a forward-looking perspective, and must construct conditional inflation forecasts in order to decide upon the current instrument setting.
>
> The above operating procedure implies that all relevant information is used in conducting monetary policy. It also implies that there is no explicit instrument rule; that is, the current instrument setting is not a prescribed explicit function of current information. Nevertheless, the procedure results in an endogenous reaction function, which expresses the instrument as a function of the relevant information. The reaction function will, in general, not be a Taylor-type rule (where a Taylor-type rule denotes a reaction function rule that is a linear function of current inflation and output only), except in the special case when current inflation and output are sufficient statistics for the state of the economy. Typically, it will depend on much more information; indeed on anything affecting the central bank's conditional inflation forecast. Especially for an open economy, the reaction function will also depend on foreign variables, for instance foreign inflation, output and interest rates, since these have domestic effects. (Svensson, 1998, pp 1-2)

Rudebusch and Svensson (1998) provide considerable evidence that what they call *instrument rules* such as the Taylor rule and its many variants[4] are very inefficient compared to what they call *targeting rules*. An instrument rule in the spirit of Taylor can be written for the instrument x, as a function of current or lagged deviations of targets from their desired path:

$$x_t = \lambda x_{t-1} + \gamma(y_{t-i} - y^d) \tag{1.1}$$

while the targeting rule would be:

$$x_t = \lambda x_{t-1} + \gamma(y_{t+j} - y^d) \tag{1.2}$$

So while under an instrument rule, the instrument, x, only responds to current or lagged information, the targeting rule looks forward. The choice of i and j is then largely an empirical matter. Rudebusch and Svensson also solve for the optimal feedback rule, where the instruments feed off the lagged state, minimising a loss function quadratic in deviations of targets from desired paths. Obviously the optimal rule dominates all other rules.[5]

Given the clear advantages of the forward-looking targeting rule over the backward looking instrument rule, at first glance the superiority of the optimal feedback rule may appear odd. In fact, the terminology is misleading because in the standard linear, quadratic gaussian case, the optimal rule contains both forward-looking and backward looking elements. There are certain conditions under which

---

[4] The use of feedback or instrument rules in economic policymaking was originally proposed by Tustin (1953) and Phillips (1954). For recent applications see Westaway (1986) and Blake and Westaway (1996). The inefficiency of instrument rules, compared to target rules, was also noted by Ghosh et al (1987), Chapter 10.

[5] For applications to a simple output-inflation model of the UK similar to that of Rudebusch and Svensson see Bean (1998) and Holly and Turner (1998).

the feedback component of the optimal rule becomes a *constant* function of the lagged state, but even in this case there will still remain a forward-looking element that comes through the so-called tracking gain of the control rule (Holly and Corker, 1984). This of course quite separate from the forward-looking element that arises when private agents formulate expectations rationally.

In principle there are clear advantages to having monetary policy expressed as a rule – at least formally- since in a forward-looking world building credibility through the transparency of the decision-making process, may make the process of inflation targeting more effective. What we propose to do in this paper is to describe some methods for computing the 'optimal' control rule using dynamic programming while also allowing expectations to be forward-looking. For this to be entirely convincing as a feasible solution we must assume that there is a sufficient commitment technology in place to prevent the issue of time inconsistency raising its head. Given that Central Bank independence is an important element in the conduct of inflation control, it seems unlikely that the Central Bank would play hard and fast with the expectations of the public.[6] Added to which the dynamic programming solution is straightforward to calculate and provides a natural benchmark against which to compare other 'handcrafted' rules of the instrument or targeting variety.

In this paper we bring together a number of approaches to the design of feedback rules for inflation targeting. We adopt a stochastic linearisation approach[7] (Kim et al, 1975, Holly et al,1978 and Zarrop et al, 1979) in order to produce a linear reduced form version of CUSUM (the Cambridge University Small UK Model). We use the method of Christodolakis (1987) in order to take into account the presence of forward-looking expectations. We then solve for the dynamic programming optimal control rule and use the method of Amman(1996) in order to ensure that the saddlepoint features of a forward looking uncovered interest parity condition are satisfied along with the dynamic programming solution. We then explore how these methods perform when there are shocks to the economy that drive the inflation rate away from its desired path.

2. THE METHOD

In this section we describe the steps we go through in order to (1) linearise a non-linear rational expectations model, (2) estimate a reduced form, (3) convert it into state space form and (4) compute the optimal control solution while satisfying the saddlepoint requirements of the rational expectations solution.

2.1 The Linearisation

Assume we can write our non-linear model as:

$$F_i(y_t, y_{t-1},\ldots,y_{t-s}, x_t, x_{t-1},\ldots, x_{t-r}) = 0 \quad (2.1)$$
$$i = 1,m,;\ t = 1, T$$

---

[6] See Blinder (1997) for an academic's perspective on the US monetary policymaking process.

[7] What we do has many similarities to the balanced realisation method of Maciejowski, and Vines (1984) with the difference that they fit a low order polynomial to the impulse response function for a deterministic shock whereas we fit a regression model to a series generated by a white noise process.

There are m endogenous variables, y, with a maximum lag of s and a maximum of r lagged values of n exogenous variables, x. We can expand (2.1) about some initial path to give:

$$\sum_{j=0}^{s}\left[\frac{\delta F_i}{\delta t_{t-j}}\right]\tilde{y}_{t-j}+\sum_{j=0}^{r}\left[\frac{\delta F_i}{\delta x_{t-j}}\right]_0\tilde{x}_{t-j} \tag{2.2}$$

$i = 1,..,m,. t = 1,..,T.$

The perturbations to the initial path are defined as:

$$\tilde{y}_t = y_t - y_{0t}, \quad \tilde{x}_t = x_t - x_{0t} \tag{2.3}$$

$i = 1,..,T.$

In general (2.2) is time-varying. However, we want to obtain an approximation to this time-varying representation. We will also only be interested in some subset of the endogenous variables, the targets and a subset of the exogenous variables, among which will be the policy instruments.. We can write this representation in vector polynomial form in the lag operator L, as:

$$A(L)y_t + B(L)x_t = 0 \tag{2.4}$$

In order to derive a constant coefficient, linear representation we do the following. We perturb the chosen instrument by a discrete white noise sequence. The use of a white noise sequence is one way of making sure that we obtain a good estimate of the relationship between the target and the instrument. The white noise sequence, since it contains all frequencies, will excite all of the dynamic modes of the non-linear system (Hannan, 1971, Zarrop, 1981). We then obtain a time series for each of the targets which in general will not be a white noise process because of the dynamic structure of the model being perturbed.

We can then write the relationship between a perturbed instrument and a perturbed target as a rational function:

$$\tilde{y}_{ti} = \frac{\alpha_i(L)}{\beta_i(L)}\tilde{x}_{ti}$$

$i = 1,n, j = 1,m.$

We could estimate the relationship between the each instrument and each target separately. However, it is equally convenient to perturb each of the instruments at the same time using a sequence of iid random disturbances and then estimate by ordinary least squares the reduced form. The estimated reduced form is:

$$y_t = A_1 y_{t-1}+\ldots+A_s y_{t-s} + B_1 x_t +\ldots+B_r x_{t-r} \tag{2.5}$$

2.2 Allowing for Rational Expectations

Since the non-linear model may contain forward-looking expectations we need to take this into account when linearising. To do this we follow the approach of Christodolakis (1987). This involves first 'exogenising' any equations involving jump variables and then perturbing the jump variables with a white noise sequence in the same way that the set of policy instruments is perturbed.[8] Once we have approximated the relationship between the targets and the instruments augmented by the endogenous jump variables, we can write the linearisation as:

$$A_0 y_t = A_1 y_{t-1} + \ldots + A_s y_{t-s} + D_1 y_{t+1} + B_1 x_t + \ldots + B_r x_{t-r} \tag{2.6}$$

Where now the jump variables appear on the left hand side, and y_{t+1} is the vector of expected endogenous variables. Since A_0 is no longer an identity matrix, we invert A_0 and multiply through to obtain the reduced form.

$$y_t = \Pi_1 y_{t-1} + \ldots + \Pi_s y_{t-s} + \Gamma_1 y_{t+1} + \Omega_1 x_t + \ldots + \Omega_r x_{t-r} \tag{2.7}$$

2.3 State Space Form

The state vector is simply defined as:

$$z'_t = (y_t, \ldots, y_{t-s-1}, x_{t-1}, \ldots x_{t-r-1}) \tag{2.8}$$

and the state transition matrix:

$$z_t = Az_{t-1} + Bx_t + Dz_{t+1}$$

where:

$$A = \begin{bmatrix} \Pi_1 & \Pi_2 & \ldots & \Pi_s & \Omega_2 & \ldots & \Omega_r \\ I & 0 & \ldots & & & & 0 \\ 0 & I & & & & & \vdots \\ \vdots & 0\vdots & I & & & & \\ & \vdots & 0 & I & & & \\ & & \vdots & 0 & I & & \\ 0 & 0 & 0 & 0 & \ldots & I & 0 \end{bmatrix}, B = \begin{bmatrix} \Omega_1 \\ 0 \\ \vdots \\ \\ \\ \\ 0 \end{bmatrix}, D = \begin{bmatrix} \Gamma_1 \\ 0 \\ \vdots \\ \\ \\ \\ 0 \end{bmatrix}$$

z is a f=nx(s+r-1) dimensional vector, x is an m-dimensional vector. The transition matrix A is fxf, B is fxm, D is fxf,

Since the state space form contains forward-looking expectations, and in general D is not invertible, we could follow the approach of Blanchard and Kahn

---

[8] If wished other exogenous, non-instrument variables can be perturbed and included in the linearisation also.

(1980), Sims (1996), Amman and Kendrick (1998), Anderson (1998), among others, and solve explicitly for the rational expectations solution. Instead we follow the suggestion of Amman and Kendrick (1992) and solve for the saddlepoint path iteratively using the extended path methods of Anderson (1979), Fair and Taylor (1983) and Fisher et al(1986). We rewrite the state transition equation as:

$$z_t = Az_{t-1} + Bx_t + Ce_t \tag{2.9}$$

The vector e subsumes the expected values, and in general could also include any other 'exogenous' variables.

2.4 The Optimal Control Solution

To solve for the optimal control rule we define a loss function for the monetary authorities in terms of the state variables and the control or instrument variables, x.

$$L_t = 1/2\sum_{t=0}^{n}(z_t - z_t^d)'Q(z_t - z_t^d) + (x_t - x_t^d)'N(x_t - x_t^d) \tag{2.10}$$

where the superscript defines desired values for the state variables and the policy instruments. Q is a symmetric, semi-positive definite fxf matrix, and N is a symmetric mxm positive definite matrix.

To minimise (2.10) subject to the state transition equation (2.9) we can apply the well-known method of dynamic programming to compute a optimal control rule of the form:

$$x_t = K_t z_{t-1} + k_t \tag{2.11}$$

where K_t (t = 1, ... , T) are a sequence of feedback control matrices and k_t (t = 1, ... T) represents what is known as the *tracking gain* in the control literature. These are solved for recursively by first solving the period T problem to obtain a solution for x_T conditional on x_{T-1}. This is used to write a value function for period T which depends on x_{T-1} and which in turn forms part of the objective function for the period T-1 problem. Using this procedure, along with the terminal conditions $H_T = Q$ and $k_T = h_T = Qz^d_T$ we can solve for the sequence of feedback control matrices and tracking gains as:

$$K_T = -(N+B'H_TB)^{-1}(B'H_TA) \tag{2.12.a}$$
$$k_T = -(N+B'H_TB)^{-1}B'(H_TCe_T-h_T -Nx^d_T) \tag{2.12.b}$$
$$H_{T-1} = Q + (A+BK_T)'H_T(A+BK_T) \tag{2.12.c}$$
$$h_{T-1} = k_{T-1} + (A+BK_T)'(h_T-H_TCe_T + Nx^d_T) \tag{2.12.d}$$

These are solved recursively to obtain the control rule: Note that the feedback gains, K_i , for i = 1...T, depend only on the (constant) matrices of the transition equation and the loss function. The feedback part of the control rule then feeds only off the lagged state vector z_{t-1}. By contrast the tracking gains, vary over time depending upon the current and future values of the exogenous variables and expectations in the vector e. This is the feedforward part of the control rule.

2.5 Incorporating Rational Expectations

The solution in (2.12) is the well known regulator problem for a non-rational expectational model. However, in the vector e, which appears in the recursion for the tracking gain, we have an expectation of the state in the next period.

There is a large class of methods for solving this problem. However, there is in principle a difficulty with the computation of an optimal control solution in this case because of the time inconsistency problem first identified by Kydland and Prescott (1977). However, if we are willing to accept that there is a sufficient commitment to ensure that reneging is rules out (Holly and Hughes Hallett, 1989), we can use the extended path methods of Anderson (1979), Fair and Taylor (1983) and Fisher et al (1986), in the following procedure (Amman and Kendrick (1992):

Step 1: For initial assumptions about the expected path for the expectational state, z_{t+j}, j =1,T-1, and a terminal condition for T, compute the feedback and tracking gains. Store the feedback gains.

Step 2: Update the vectors $E^{j+1}z_{t+i}$, for i =1,T, where j is an iteration counter, using $E^{j+1}z_{t+i} = \lambda\, E^{j}z_{t+i} + (1-\lambda)^{j+1}z_{t+i}$, for i =1,T, where λ is the relaxation factor (Fisher et al, 1986).

Step 3: Recompute the tracking gain matrices.

Step 4: Test whether: $|E^{j+1}z_{t+i} - {}^{j+1}z_{t+i}| < \varepsilon$, for i =1, T, where ε is an arbitrarily small convergence criteria. If not true go to step 2.

Step 5: Stop.

This will compute a control rule for an expectationally consistent path.

3. AN APPLICATION

In this section we provide an application to the UK. We use a small non-linear model of the UK economy in order to generate a linearisation and then use the linearisation to examine a policy question in which the Bank of England uses the short term interest rate in order to pursue a target path for the rate of inflation. Expectations are forward looking in the foreign exchange rate market so the effective exchange rate is determined by an uncovered interest parity condition. The expected change in the exchange rate is equal to the risk adjusted interest rate differential.

3.1 The Cambridge University Small UK Model (CUSUM)

The model we use for the experiments is CUSUM a small, quarterly model of the UK economy which has been developed as a vehicle for exploring asymmetries over the business cycle (see Arden et al (1998) for an example). However, in this paper we confine ourselves to a symmetric version of the model. It has 15 behavioural equations, some 79 technical relationships and identities, and 8 exogenous variables. The profusion of technical relationships and identities arises from the need to link the income and expenditure accounts, model the balance of payments and the public sector borrowing requirement and generate sectoral flows. It has been kept small by working at the highest level of aggregation possible. The model has the following important features:

- The supply side is captured by a cost function approach to the determination of output, prices and employment. (See Arden et al, 1997.)
- The Cobb-Douglas, constant returns to scale form of the production function ensures that the share of labour income in national income is constant in the long run.
- The growth rate of the economy is endogenous through the capital accumulation process.
- Investment depends on Tobin's Q. But an important distinction is drawn between average and marginal Q. In imperfectly competitive markets the difference between the two depends on the present discounted value of the marginal revenue product of capital.
- There is nominal inertia in prices and wages. Presently there is no forward-looking element in wage and price setting.
- There are a number of forward expectations variables: - the expected effective exchange rate, the expected price of equity, the expected long term interest rate, expected personal sector income and personal sector real wealth. The exchange rate, the price of equity and long term interest rates (the inverse of bond prices) are jump variables. However, for the application in this paper we only assume rational expectations in the foreign exchange rate market.

3.2 The Linearised Model

The linearisation was obtained by passing white noise through both the short term interest rate and the (exogenised) exchange rate for 92 periods and storing the effect of these stochastic perturbations on inflation (RPIX) = π, and output growth = g. In order to smooth the use of the interest rate, r, as an instrument we also included as an endogenous variable, the first difference of the interest rate, Δr. The vector y in (2.4) is now y' = (π, g, eer, Δr). We then estimated distributed lag model of inflation and output growth on the interest rate and the exchange rate, eer, with five lags in inflation and output growth, and eight I the interest rate and the exchange rate. We use an uncovered interest parity condition that the expected change in the exchange rate is equal to the interest rate differential between the domestic interest rate and the overseas interest rate, rw. We also want to allow for the possibility of independent shocks to inflation and output growth. So the vector of exogenous variables, is now defined as $e' = (eer_{t+1}, rw_t, \xi_{\pi t}, \xi_{gt})$, where the last two elements are designed to allow for shocks to inflation and output growth, and eer_{t+1} is the expected exchange rate. This means our linearisation takes the structural form:

$$A_0 y_t = A_1 y_{t-1} + \ldots + A_5 y_{t-5} + D_1 e_t + B_1 x_t + \ldots + B_8 x_{t-8} \tag{3.1}$$

where:

$$A_0 = \begin{bmatrix} 1 & 0 & \alpha_{13} & 0 \\ 0 & 1 & \alpha_{23} & 0 \\ 0 & 0 & 1 & 0 \\ 0 & 0 & 0 & 1 \end{bmatrix}, D_1 = \begin{bmatrix} 0 & 0 & 1 & 0 \\ 0 & 0 & 0 & 1 \\ 1 & -1 & 0 & 0 \\ 0 & 0 & 0 & 0 \end{bmatrix}, B_1 = \begin{bmatrix} \beta_1 \\ \beta_2 \\ 1 \\ 1 \end{bmatrix}$$

$$\sum_{i=1}^{5} A_i = \begin{bmatrix} \alpha_{i11} & 0 & \alpha_{i13} & 0 \\ 0 & \alpha_{i22} & \alpha_{i23} & 0 \\ 0 & 0 & 0 & 0 \\ 0 & 0 & 0 & 0 \end{bmatrix}, \sum_{i=6}^{8} A_i = \begin{bmatrix} 0 & 0 & \alpha_{i13} & 0 \\ 0 & 0 & \alpha_{i23} & 0 \\ 0 & 0 & 0 & 0 \\ 0 & 0 & 0 & 0 \end{bmatrix}, \sum_{j=2}^{8} B_j = \begin{bmatrix} \beta_{j1} \\ \beta_{j2} \\ 0 \\ 0 \end{bmatrix}$$

and $B_2(4)$=-1. This then produces a 39 dimensioned state vector.

3.3 Some Illustrative Simulations

The state space is of quite a high order, however, it is not out of line with the annual models in Bean(1998) and Holly and Turner (1998) which suggest that it takes some time for interest rate changes to affect the rate of inflation. For the purposes of the simulations in this section we attach a weight on inflation in the loss function twenty times that on output growth and on the change in the interest rate. The weight on inflation is four times that on the level of the interest rate. If we sum the coefficients in the feedback gain, K, for the first period we have:

$$r_t = 0.341\pi_{t-1} + 0.136\pi_{t-2} + 0.0003y_{t-1} + 0.0649e_{t-1} - 0.007e_{t-2} - 0.060\Delta r_{t-1} \quad (3.2)$$

So, in annual terms, the feedback rule is very simple.

One of the perceived drawbacks of a feedback rule is that it appears to be invariant to changes in expected shocks to the economy emanating from exogenous variables. For example, if there is a well founded expectation that there will be a downturn in world economic activity or that energy prices will rise sharply in the near future, a feedback rule will not produce a change in monetary policy until the effects of the exogenous events show up in the lagged state vector. While it is true that the feedback rule only works off the lagged state, it is not true that the optimal control rule is not forward-looking and capable of responding in anticipation of future shocks. This forward-looking role is provided by the tracking gain, the second part of the control rule.

In this section we report some simulations designed to illustrate the forward-looking nature of the optimal control rule. We are particularly interested in the relative roles of the feedback and tracking gains when shocks to inflation are anticipated and when they are not. However, there is a complication because the expected exchange rate appears in the tracking gain when expectations are rational. In order to disentangle the forward looking part of the control rule from the forward-looking exchange rate, we first examine a version of the model in which the exchange rate does not appear.

We examine two types of shock. First there is an unanticipated shock to the initial state. Inflation turns out to be 5 percentage points higher than expected. In the absence of any monetary response the effect on the path for inflation *relative* to the base inflation rate, is shown in Figure 1. There is considerable persistence in the inflation rate. When the optimal control rule is used the path for inflation in Figure 1 does return to base more quickly, but much of the inflationary spurt is unavoidable, even though interest rates are raised by 5 percentage points. Note, that there is no forward-looking element to the interest rate jump (Figure 2). Once the shock occurs there is nothing else to anticipate.

The second shock we consider is an anticipated shock to inflation. This time the inflation rate is expected to receive a 2 percentage point shock in each of periods 3 and four, so the shock is expected (with certainty) to occur in 6 months time. In this case the forward looking nature of the optimal control rule becomes clear. In Table 1 we show the response of inflation and interest rates to the expected shock. Because of the tracking gain component of the optimal control rule, interest rates jump immediately in response to the expected rise in inflation. Once the shock has passed, the tracking gain term drops back to zero.

Table 1.

	Inflation	Interest Rate	Tracking gain
Initial State	0	0	0
1	0.00	3.33	3.33
2	0.00	6.20	3.07
3	2.00	5.79	2.76
4	3.83	5.34	1.27
5	3.88	4.56	0.00
6	4.16	3.97	0.00
7	3.59	3.44	0.00
8	2.84	3.02	0.00

In Figures 7 onwards we show the effect of re-introducing the exchange rate. Once we have an additional channel by which interest rates affect the rate of inflation we obtain a considerable increase in the ability to offset even the unanticipated shock. The monetary contraction triggers an immediate jump in the exchange rate which bears down on inflation. However, this is also associated with larger, and more volatile, output losses. In Figure 8 we show the interest rate outcome. What is particularly striking is that the tracking gain contribution is negative. This is because the tracking gain includes a term in the expected exchange rate. Essentially the tracking gain leans against the jump in the exchange rate and provides a measure of the extent to which monetary policy would have to be tighter in order to achieve the same inflation path without the help of the exchange rate appreciation.

In Figures 11 to 14 we show the outcome when the inflation shock is anticipated. The inclusion of the exchange rate channel enhances the effectiveness of monetary policy considerably. As before, the forward-looking part of the control rule triggers a monetary tightening in anticipation of the future shock. This actually reduces inflation prior to the shock as the exchange rate appreciates.

4. DISCUSSION AND CONCLUSIONS

We have sought to show in this paper that a properly specified control rule derived by the method of dynamic programming has both a forward and a backward looking dimension. The feedback part of the rule responds to the lagged state, but the forward-looking tracking gain allows monetary policy to respond in anticipation of future shocks.

Clearly the approach of this paper encompasses the instrument rules approach. For a given loss function the feedback rule derived by dynamic programming will always dominate any arbitrary, handcrafted rule. Moreover, we describe a computationally simple method for calculating the feedback rule under rational expectations.

Our approach also addresses in a straightforward way the concerns of Svensson and others that monetary policy needs a forward-looking dimension. If it is felt that there is information about appertaining to the future path for inflation *over and above* that captured by the lagged state then the approach of this paper allows that information to be reflected in the current stance of monetary policy. For example, in this paper we have been working at the quarterly frequency. So the feedback part of the control rule responds to information three months old. However, there is usually a plethora of information available at monthly frequencies which can provide information about the current state. By including this information in the calculation of the tracking gain, the stance of monetary policy can be made consistent with all relevant information.

Needless to say there are numerous other issues that one would wish to take into account in the design of policy. It is well understood that rules which are optimal for one model may not be very robust across other models. However, given the ease with which the methods of this paper can be applied,[9] calculating optimal policies across a suite of models should be feasible.

REFERENCES

Amman, H (1996), "Numerical Methods for Linear-Quadratic Models", chapter 13 of Amman, H M, Kendrick, D A and Rust, J (eds) *Handbook of Computational Economics: Volume 1*, Amsterdam: North Holland.

Amman, H and Kendrick, D (1992), "Forward Looking Variables in Deterministic Control", *Annals of Operational Research*, Vol. 68, pp. 141-60.

Amman, H and Kendrick, D (1999), "Linear Quadratic Optimisation for Models with Rational Expectations", Mimeo, *Macroeconomic Dynamics* (forthcoming).

9 All of the calculations in this paper were carried out in EViews, the windows version of TSP.

Anderson, P A (1979), "Rational Expectations Forecasts from Nonrational Models", *Journal of Monetary Economics*, Vol. 5, pp. 67-80.

Anderson, G (1998), "A Reliable and Computationally Efficient Algorithm for Imposing the Saddlepoint Property in Dynamic Models", Mimeo, Federal Reserve Board.

Arden, R A , Cook, S Holly, S and Turner, P (1998), "The Asymmetric Effects of Monetary Policy: Some Results from a Macroeconometric Model", Mimeo, University of Cambridge.

Arden, R, Holly, S, and Turner, P, (1997c), "Asymmetric Adjustment Costs, Asymmetric Pricing And Employment: Evidence From The UK", Department of Applied Economics Discussion Paper No. 9717, University of Cambridge.

Ball, Laurence (1994), "What Determines the Sacrifice Ratio?" in N Gregory Mankiw, ed, Monetary Policy, University of Chicago Press, 155-182.

Bean, C (1998), "The New UK Monetary Arrangements: A View from the Literature", paper presented at the 1998 Royal Economic Society conference, University of Warwick.

Bernanke, B S, and Mishkin, F S (1997), "Inflation Targeting: A New Framework for Monetary Policy?" *Journal of Economic Perspectives*, Vol. 11, pp. 97-116.

Bernanke, B S, and Woodford, M (1997), "Inflation Forecasts and Monetary Policy", *Journal of Money, Credit, and Banking*, Vol. 29, pp. 653-684.

Blake, A P, and Westaway, P F (1996), "Credibility and the Effectiveness of Inflation Targeting Regimes", *Manchester School Supplement*, pp. 20-50.

Blanchard, O J and Kahn, C M (1980), "The Solution of Linear Difference Models under Rational Expectations", *Econometrica*, Vol. 48, pp. 1305-1311.

Blinder, A S (1997), Central Banking in Theory and Practice: The 1996 Robbins Lectures, MIT Press, Cambridge, MA.

Chow, G C (1970), Analysis and Control of Dynamic Economic Systems, John Wiley and Sons, New York.

Christodoulakis, N (1989), "Extensions of Linearisation to Large Econometric Models with Rational Expectations", *Computers and Mathematics with Applications.*

Cook, S, Holly, S and Turner, P (1999), "The Conduct of Monetary Policy when the Business Cycle is Non-Linear", *Econometric Modelling: Techniques and Applications*, edited by S Holly and M Weale, Cambridge University Press, Cambridge.

Currie, D., and Levine, P. (1984), 'Simple Macropolicy Rules for the Open Economy,' *Economic Journal*, Vol. 95 (Supplement), 60-70.

Currie, David, and Paul Levine (1993), *Rules, Reputation and Macroeconomic Policy Co-ordination*, Cambridge University Press, Cambridge.

Fair, R C (1997), "A Fiscal-Policy Rule for Stabilization", Cowles Foundation, Yale University, Mimeo.

Fair, R C and Taylor, J B (1983), "Solution and maximum likelihood estimation of dynamic nonlinear rational expectations models", *Econometrica*, Vol. 51, pp. 1169-86.

Federal Reserve Bank of Kansas City (1996), Achieving Price Stability, Federal Reserve Bank of Kansas City.

Fisher, P G, Holly, S and Hughes Hallett, A J (1986), "Efficient solution techniques for dynamic rational expectations models", *Journal of Economic Dynamics and Control*, Vol. 10, pp. 137-45.

Ghosh, S, Gilbert C L and Hughes Hallett A J (1987), "Stabilising Speculative Commodity Markets", Oxford University Press, Oxford.

Haldane, A G (1997a), "Designing Inflation Targets," in Philip Lowe, ed., Monetary Policy and Inflation Targeting, Reserve Bank of Australia, Sidney, 74-112.

Haldane, A G, and Batini, N (1998), "Forward-Looking Rules for Monetary Policy", Working Paper, Bank of England, London.

Haldane, A G, ed (1995), "Targeting Inflation", Bank of England, London.

Haldane, Andrew G, (1998), "On Inflation-Targeting in the United Kingdom", *Scottish Journal of Political Economy*, Vol. 45, pp. 1-32.

Hall, S G (1986), "An Investigation of Time Inconsistency and Optimal Policy Formulation in the Presence of Rational Expectations", *Journal of Economic Dynamics and Control*, Vol. 10, pp. 323-26.

Hannan, E J (1971), "The Identification Problem for Multiple Equation Systems with moving Average Errors", *Econometrica*, Vol. 39, pp. 751-65.

Holly, S, Zarrop, M B and Westcott, J (1978), "Near optimal stabilisation policies with large nonlinear economic models: an application to the LBS econometric model of the UK economy", *Programme of Research on Economic Methods* Discussion Paper no. 23, Imperial College London.

Holly, S and M B Zarrop, (1983), On optimality and time consistency when expectations are rational. *European Economic Review*, Vol. 20, pp. 23-40.

Holly, S and Corker, R (1984), "Optimal feedback and feedforward stabilisation of exchange rates, money, prices and output under rational expectations", in *Applied Decision Analysis* (Edited by Andrew Hughes Hallet), Dordrecht , Kluwer.

Holly, S and Hughes Hallett, A (1989), *Optimal Control, Expectations and Uncertainty*, Cambridge: Cambridge University Press.

Holly, S and Turner, P (1998), "Interest Rates, Optimal Control and Current Monetary Policy", University of Cambridge Mimeo.

Kim, H K L, Goreaux, M and Kendrick, D A (1975), "Feedback control rules for cocoa market stabilisation", in W.C Labys (ed) *Quantitative Models for Commodity Markets*, Cambridge, Mass., Ballinger.

King, M (1996), "How should Central Banks Reduce Inflation? - Conceptual Issues", in *Achieving Price Stability*, Federal Reserve Bank of Kansas City.

King, M A (1994), "Monetary Policy in the UK", *Fiscal Studies*, Vol. 15, pp. 109–128.

King, M, (1997), "The Inflation Target Five Year on", Lecture given at the London School of Economics, 29th October, 1997.

Kydland, F and Prescott, E (1977), "Rules rather than Discretion: the inconsistency of optimal plans", *Journal of Political Economy*, Vol. 85, pp. 473-92.

Leiderman, L, and Lars E O Svensson, eds (1995), *Inflation Targets*, Centre of Econonomic Policy Research, London.

Lowe, Philip, ed, (1997), Monetary Policy and In‡ation Targeting, Reserve Bank of Australia.

Maciejowski, J and Vines, D (1984), "Decoupled control of a Macroeconomic Model using Frequency-Domain Methods", *Journal of Economic Dynamics and Control*, Vol. 7, pp. 55-77.

McCallum, Bennett T (1988), "Robustness Properties of a Rule for Monetary Policy", *Carnegie-Rochester Conference Series on Public Policy*, Vol. 29, pp. 173-204.

Phillips, A W (1954), "Stabilisation Policy in a Closed Economy", *Economic Journal*, Vol. 64, pp. 290-323.

Rogoff, K (1985), "The Optimal Degree of Commitment to an Intermediate Monetary Target", *Quarterly Journal of Economics*, Vol. 100, 1169–1190.

Rudebusch, G D and Svenson, L E O (1998), "Policy Rules for Inflation Targeting", NBER Discussion Paper 6512, NBER, Cambridge, MA.

Sims, C A (1982), "Policy Analysis with Econometric Models", Brookings Papers on Economic Activity (1), 107-152.

Sims, C A (1996), "Solving Linear Rational Expectations Models", Mimeo, Yale University.

Stevens, G, and Debelle, G. (1995), "Monetary Policy Goals for Inflation in Australia", in Haldane, op cit.

Svensson, Lars E O (1996), "Commentary: How Should Monetary Policy Respond to Shocks while Maintaining Long-Run Price Stability?—Conceptual Issues", in Federal Reserve Bank of Kansas City , op cit.

Svensson, Lars E O (1997a), "Inflation Forecast Targeting: Implementing and Monitoring Inflation Targets", *European Economic Review*, Vol. 41, pp. 1111-1146.

Svensson, Lars E O (1997b), "Inflation Targeting in an Open Economy: Strict vs. Inflation Targeting", Public Lecture at Victoria University of Wellington, Reserve Bank of New Zealand Discussion Paper, forthcoming.

Svensson, Lars E O (1998), "Open-Economy Inflation Targeting", Working Paper.

Tustin, A (1953), The Mechanism of Economic Systems: an approach to the problem of economic stabilisation from the point of view of control-system engineering, Cambridge, Mass: Harvard University Press.

Westaway, P (1986), "Some Experiments with Simple Feedback Rules on the Treasury Model", *Journal of Economic Dynamics and Control*, Vol. 10, pp. 239-48.

Williams, John C (1997), "Simple Rules for Monetary Policy", Working Paper, Board of Governors of the Federal Reserve System.

Zarrop, M B (1981), *Optimal Experimental Design for Dynamic System Identification*, no. 21, Berlin, Springer Verlag.

Zarrop, M, Holly, S, Rustem, B and Westcott, J H (1979), "The Design of Economic Stabilisation Policies with Large, Nonlinear Econometric Models: Two Possible Approaches", in P Ormerod (Editor) *Economic Modelling*, London, Heinemann.

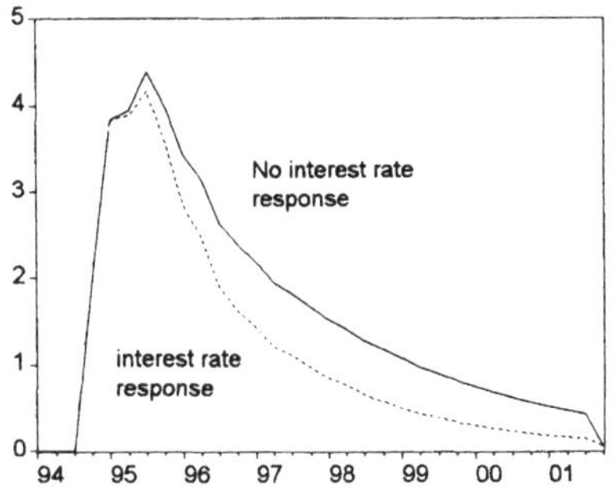

Figure 1. Inflation.
The effect on inflation of an unanticipated shock to inflation. No exchange rate channel.

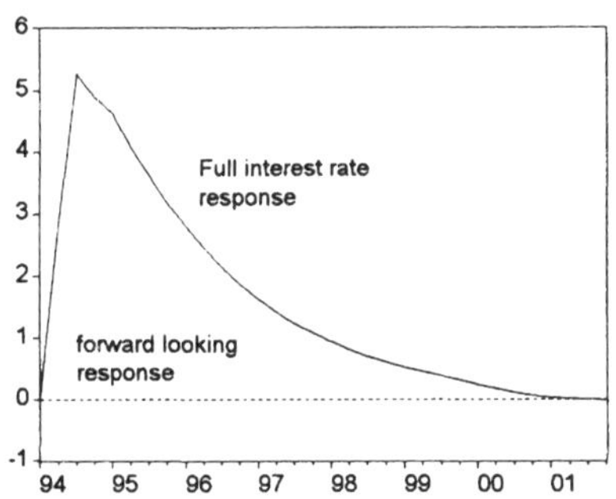

Figure 2. Interest rate.
The interest rate response to an unanticipated shock to inflation. No exchange rate channel.

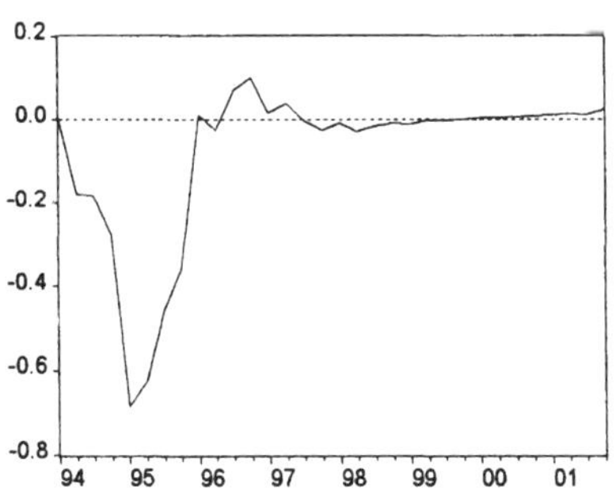

Figure 3. Output growth.
Effect on output growth of monetary response to unanticipated shock to inflation. No exchange rate channel.

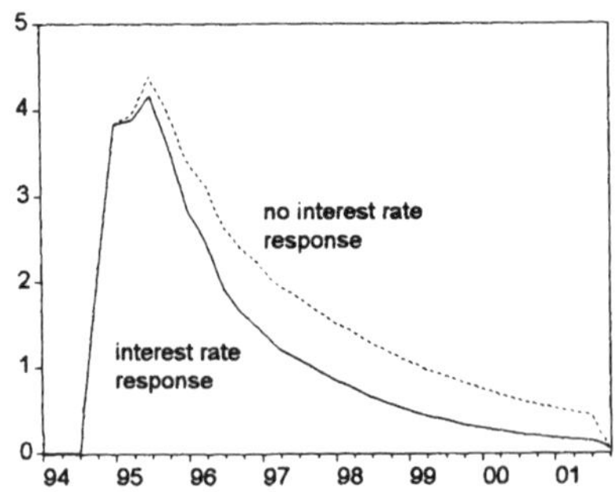

Figure 4. Inflation.
Response of inflation to an anticipated shock to inflation rate 6 months ahead. With and without monetary response. No exchange rate channel.

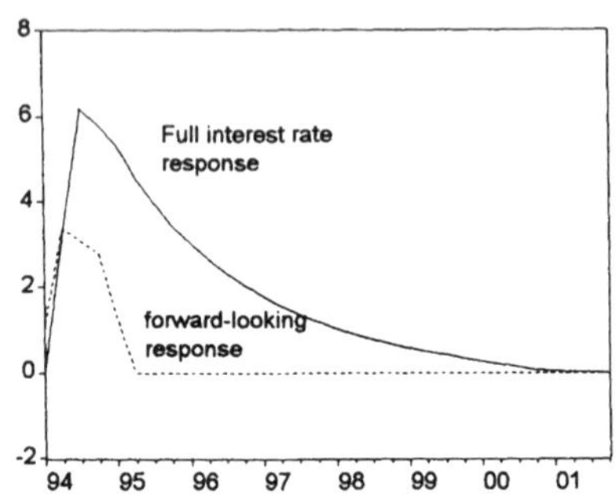

Figure 5. Interest rate.
The optimal response of the interest rate to an anticipated shock to inflation rate 6 months ahead. No exchange rate channel.

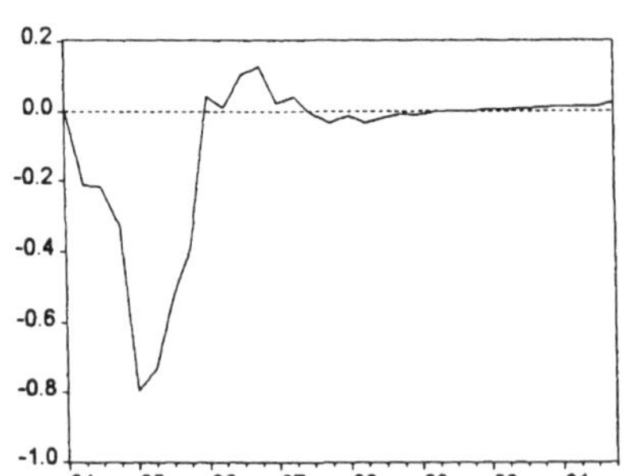

Figure 6. Output growth.

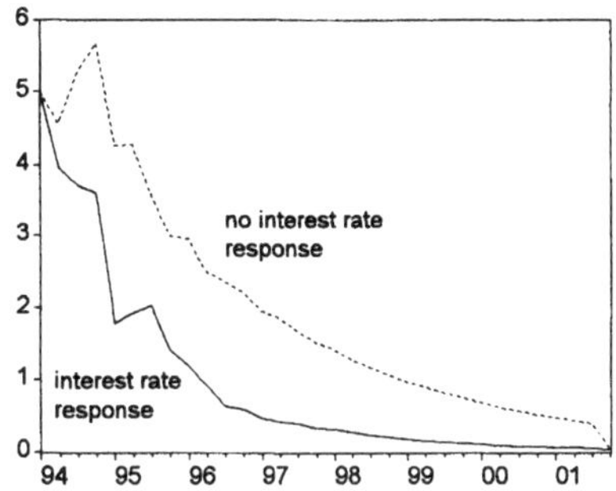

Figure 7. Inflation.
Inflation response to an unanticipated inflation shock. With and without a monetary response. Exchange rate channel.

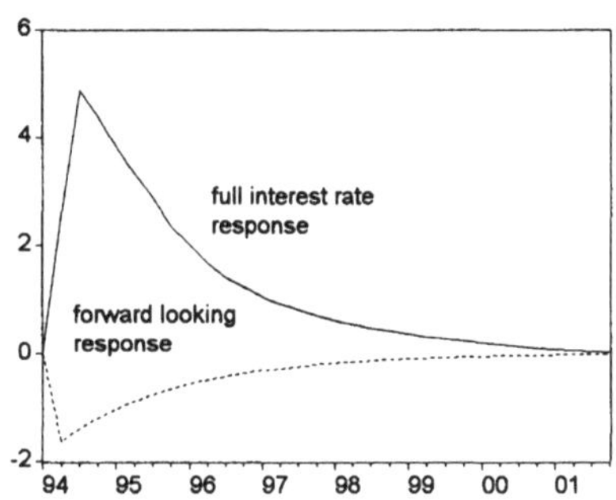

Figure 8. Interest rate.
Optimal interest rate response to an unanticipated inflation shock. Exchange rate channel.

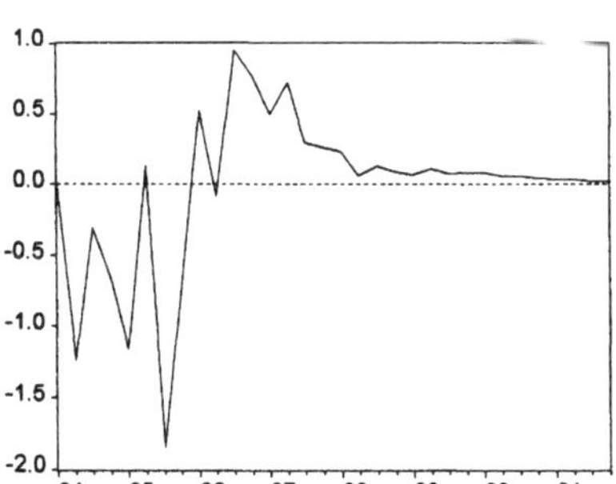

Figure 9. Output growth.
Response of output growth to monetary response to an unanticipated inflation shock. Exchange rate channel.

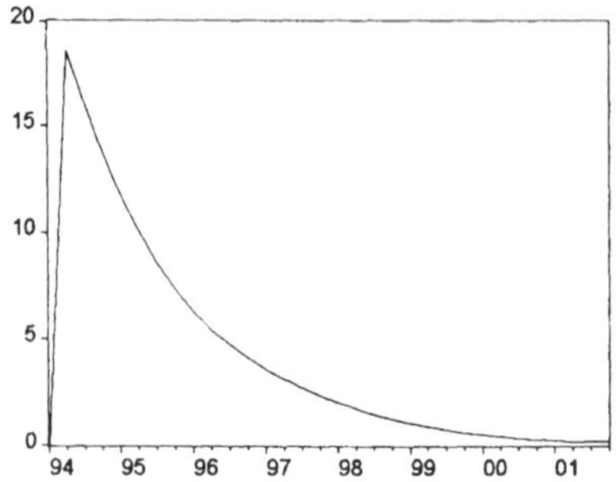

Figure 10. Exchange rate.
Response of exchange rate to monetary response to an unanticipated inflation shock.

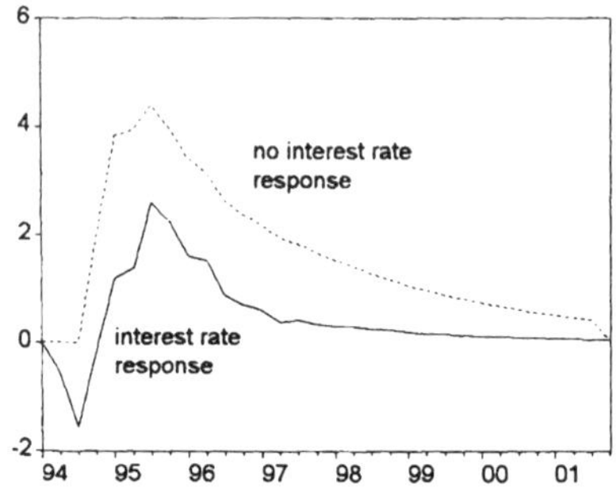

Figure 11. Inflation.
Inflation response to an anticipated inflation shock. With and without a monetary response. Exchange rate channel.

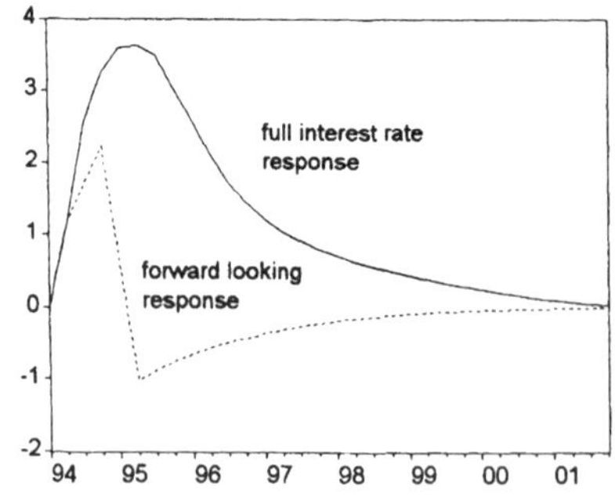

Figure 12. Interest rate.
Optimal interest rate response to an unanticipated inflation shock. Exchange rate channel.

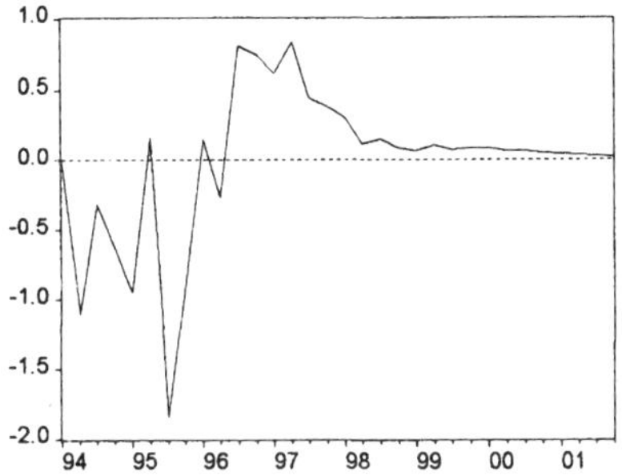

Figure 13. Output growth.
Response of output growth to monetary response to an unanticipated inflation shock. Exchange rate channel.

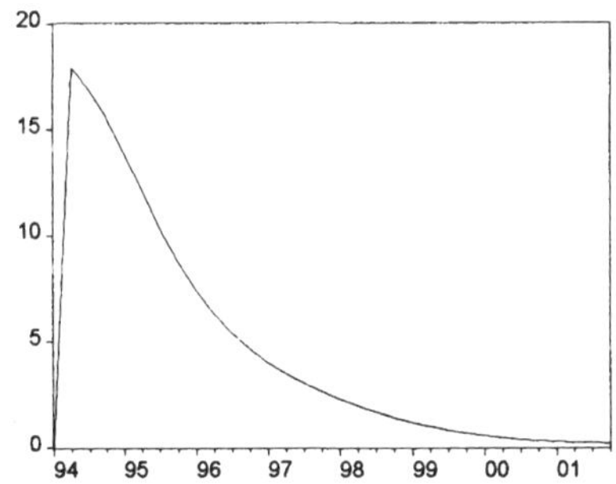

Figure 14. Exchange rate.
Response of exchange rate to monetary response to an anticipated inflation shock.

PART THREE

MACRODYNAMICS

CHAPTER 7

ASYMPTOTIC HIERARCHIES IN AN ECONOMIC MODEL

Cuong Le Van and Pierre Malgrange[1]

INTRODUCTION

The dynamic specification of the various equations of an economic model and the numerical results associated with their estimation imply varying sluggishness of the different variables involved. This feature has extremely important outcomes on the dynamic evolution of the macroeconomic system. This problem is generally studied through the computation of the eigenvalues of the system under review, approximated by its linear-stationary state space correspondent. The dynamical behavior of some variables is mainly described in the short to medium run by their autoregressive structure. More generally, this is the well-known problem of assignment of eigenvalues to variables (see for instance Kuh et al (1985), Malgrange (1989), or Schoonbeek (1984)). One can also study the system in terms of blocks. The relevant concept is that of "near decomposability" investigated by depth by Ando et al (1963) for linear systems. They showed that, if the system is undecomposable, but can be decomposed into blocks with links between blocks "weak" relatively to links within blocks, then each block behaves, up to a certain horizon T1, "almost" independently of each other. Furthermore, after T1 and before T2, each block can be described by one representative variable, the behaviour of which is driven by the largest eigenvalue of the block. At last, after T2, all variables of the model are driven by the largest eigenvalue.

In the present contribution, we undertake a methodological investigation on the asymptotic, long run, time hierarchies which are implicit in a given macroeconomic model. The proposed technique aims at analysing the strong trends of the system, leaving aside short run fluctuations. We show that the time hierarchies between the endogenous variables, reflecting their "convergence speed", can be determined in a simple way through the computation of the eigenvalues and eigenvectors of the system and, in many cases, are independent of initial conditions.

The first section develops the methodology, which is applied in the second section to a quarterly RBC like small model of the French economy.

[1] We are most grateful to Michel Juillard for his help in interpreting the numerical computations done with the software DYNARE, see Juillard (1996).

I. METHODOLOGY

We first develop the case of a traditional backward-looking model, before dealing with the case of a forward-looking system, which is not fundamentally different.

1.1. The case of a purely backward-looking model

Starting from a given macroeconomic model possessing a well-defined steady-state growth path, it is standard to transform it into a stationary model evolving around a constant equilibrium steady state, by an adequate change of variables (division of each variable of the model by its (constant) growth trend, i.e. putting variables in "intensive form"). Then, by linearization around its steady state, and by a standard redefinition of the variables of the system, we can write it in terms of a model in state space form.

Let us then consider the following linear stationary model:

$$x_t = Ax_{t-1} + Bz_t, \tag{1}$$

where x is the n-vector of endogenous state variables and z the p-vector of the exogenous shocks of the model. We will write, for the moment, $u_t = Bz_t$, of the same dimension n as x.

Let us assume that the matrix A is diagonalizable and that (I-A) is invertible. We will suppose that the greatest eigenvalue of A is less than one in modulus and real and that $\lambda_1,\ldots, \lambda_n$ verify:

$$1>|\lambda_n|>|\lambda_{n-1}|>\ldots>|\lambda_1|.$$

Then one has:

$$A = P\Lambda P^{-1} \tag{2}$$

where P is the matrix of (right) eigenvectors, and $\Lambda=(\lambda_i)$, a is a diagonal matrix of the n eigenvalues.

Corresponding to the assumption that $u_t = \overline{u}$, for every t, the system (1) has a unique long term $\overline{x}$:

$$\overline{x} = (I-A)^{-1}\overline{u}. \tag{3}$$

Let us suppose that the system is at equilibrium at t = -1, and consider a temporary shock u_0 at date 0.

The dynamics of x around $\overline{x}$, are given by:

$$x_0 - \overline{x} = u_0 - \overline{u} \tag{4}$$

$$x_t - \bar{x} = A(x_{t-1} - \bar{x}) \qquad \text{for } t \geq 1. \tag{5}$$

We will consider variables x_i for which $\bar{x}^i \neq 0$.

<u>Definition</u>

An endogenous variables x^i is said to converge more quickly to its steady state than an endogenous variables x^j if there exists T such that for every t≥T,

$$\left|\left(x_t^i - \bar{x}^i\right)/\bar{x}^i\right| < \left|\left(x_t^j - \bar{x}^j\right)/\bar{x}^j\right| \tag{6}$$

In other words, we are concerned with the comparison of the relative distances to the steady state of the different variables of the system.

Let us define $y_t = x_t - \bar{x}, v_0 = u_0 - \bar{u}$ and $Q = P^{-1}$ (matrix of left eigenvectors).

The explicitation of (4)-(5) yields:

$$y_t^i = \sum_j p_{ij}\lambda_j^t \sum_k q_{jk} v_0^k \qquad \text{for } t \geq 1 \tag{7}$$

Let us consider a "pure" temporary shock on the mth component of v_0:

$$v_0^m \neq 0 \text{ and } v_0^k = 0 \qquad \text{for } k \neq m.$$

Then (7) becomes:

$$y_t^i = v_0^m \sum_{j=1}^n p_{ij} q_{jm} \lambda_j^t \tag{8}$$

Hence the asymptotic behaviour of yi;t is given by the expression:

$$y_t^i \sim v_0^m p_{in} q_{nm} \lambda_n^t \tag{9}$$

Assume $q_{nm} \neq 0$. Then from our definition - formula (6) - and from the assumption made on the eigenvalues (λ_1, ..., λ_n), under a shock on u^m, x^i will converge more quickly (relatively to its steady state) than x^j iff

$$\left|p_{in}/\bar{x}^i\right| < \left|p_{jn}/\bar{x}^j\right| \tag{10}$$

Properties

(i) The hierarchy is indeed independent of the magnitude of the shock v_0^m, but may depend on the component itself, m, of the shock vector. However, in the case where the property $q_{nk} \neq 0$ holds true for every k (i.e. n^{th} left eigenvector strictly different from zero), then the hierarchy will be independent of the component of v_0 also, and is easily computed from the components of the right eigenvector associated with λ_n.

(ii) The case $q_{nm}=0$ for some m means that the weight of λ_n is null when we consider a shock on v_0^m. In that case formula (8) shows that the relevant eigenvalue governing the asymptotic response of the system is the greatest one in modulus, λ_1, for which qlm≠0.

(iii) Considering back the form (1), the argument for the study of structural shocks z must be transposed from Q to Q B. In other words, we have simply to consider the components of the vector $q_n B$.

(iv) Symmetrically, other variables of interest linked to the model, by static or dynamic relations can be ordered in the hierarchy. Indeed, let a variable y_h write (in reduced-linearized-difference form):

$$y_t^h = \sum c_i(L) y_t^i \qquad \text{with } c_i(L) \text{ a lag polynomial.}$$

Then, by application of (9), we have:

$$y_t^h \sim v_0^m \left(\sum c_i(1/\lambda_n) p_{in} \right) q_{nm} \lambda_n^t. \tag{11}$$

1.2 The case of a forward-looking model

It is straightforward to extend our previous argumentation to the case of a model containing forward-looking variables and admitting a Blanchard-Kahn representation, that is of the form (see Blanchard and Kahn (1980)):

$$\begin{pmatrix} y_{t+1} \\ x_t \end{pmatrix} = A \begin{pmatrix} y_t \\ x_{t-1} \end{pmatrix} + v_t \begin{cases} t \geq 0 \\ x_{-1} \text{ given} \end{cases}$$

where y is now the m-vector of non-predetermined variables, x is the (n-m)-vector of predetermined variables, and v is the vector of exogenous shocks. System (12) is completely determined as soon as we know y_0. Again, let us suppose that y_t and x_t are expressed as differences with respect to the steady state values. Let us assume that the system (12) verifies the Blanchard-Kahn condition, i.e. admits m eigenvalues with modulus strictly larger than one, and n-m eigenvalues with modulus less than one. In that case system (12) possesses a stable manifold.

Under a regularity condition on the stable manifold, there exists a unique $y_0 = Rx_{-1} + S\ v_0$, where R and S are matrices depending on A, such that system (12) with (x_{-1}, y_0) as initial conditions will converge to the steady state. Moreover for $t \geq 1$, one has $y_t = Rx_{t-1}$, and (12) becomes, with some matrix B depending on A:

$$x_t = Bx_{t-1} \quad t \geq 1$$

Furthermore, the eigenvalues of B are the stable eigenvalues of A (for more details see e.g. Boucekkine and Le Van (1996)).

We are formally back to the case of a purely backward-looking model.

II. NUMERICAL ILLUSTRATION

The previous methodology has been applied to a quarterly RBC like small model of the French economy called PLM (for more details see Lafargue et al (1992) or Laffargue (1995)). The main 13 equations of this model, written in intensive form, are given in the following Table 1:

TABLE 1: MAIN EQUATIONS OF THE CORE MODEL PLM

(M1)	$\ln(L) = \alpha \ln(L^*)+(1-\alpha)\ln(L(-1))$
(M2)	$Q = (\beta(K(-1)/g)^{-\omega}+\beta' L^{-\omega})^{-1/\omega}+AI^2 g/K(-1)+ \upsilon$
(M3)	$I = K-(\mu/g)K(-1)$
(M4)	$Q = V+S-S(-1)/g$
(M5)	$P = (\pi/r)P(+1)(1+\eta 2/\eta 1 gV(+1)/S)$
(M6)	$Pd+2\eta P\ A\ g\ I/K(-1) = (\pi/r)(\mu Pd(+1)+\eta 1\ P(+1)\ (\beta(\beta+\beta'(g(L(+1)/K^{-\omega})^{(-1-1/\omega)}$
(M7)	$C^{-\lambda}/Pd = \gamma(r/\pi)C(+1)^{-\lambda}/Pd(+1)$
(M8)	$Pd = (a\ P^{(1-\sigma)} +(1-a)P^{*(1-\sigma)})^{1/(1-\sigma)}$
(M9)	$V = a(P/Pd)^{-\sigma}(C+I+G)+X$
(M10)	$M = (1-a)(P^*/Pd)^{-\sigma}(C+I+G)$
(M11)	$X=x_0 Y^{*x1}(P/P^*)^{x2}$
(M12)	$U = r(U(-1)/g\pi)+P^*M-PX+N)$
(M13)	$r = \phi_0(U/\pi PX)-U^*)^{\phi 1}+r^*$

Let us describe briefly the equations:

The model aims at describing a small open economy under imperfect competition on both labor and goods markets. We suppose that the economy evolves around a well defined steady state growth path (with g, growth index of quantities, π, growth index of prices, and no trend on labor). As explained above, equations are written in intensive form so that the reference path becomes a steady state, constant through time. The first equation formalizes a dynamical behavior of employment L consistent with the insider-outsider theory, as presented for instance in Blanchard and Summers (1986). L* is the long run employment level. The technology is supposed to be of the constant return to scale CES type with quadratic adjustment costs on capital K -eq M2. The depreciation rate of capital is μ, eq M3. The inventories S are built up from the cumulation of the difference between output Q and sales V, eq M4. The global intertemporal optimisation of production factors, prices and inventories, leads both to an optimal choice of the inventories-sales ratio, function of inflation P(+1)/P and real interest rate r/π, eq M5, and an optimal choice of technique (L(+1)/K, as shown in eq M6. Eq. M7 results from the standard intertemporal substitution of consumption based on an isoelastic utility function. This consumption demand, as well as all final demands, is shared between the home-produced aggregate good and the imported good in relation to their relative price P/P*, with a constant elasticity of substitution. The price of the aggregate demand, Pd, is itself computed by the conventional duality property. Hence the four equations M8 to M11. The cumulation of net nominal foreign debt U obtains through the sum of trade balance (P* M - P X) and net nominal -exogenous- transfers N, eq M12. At last, eq M13 formalizes the idea that -nominal- interest rate differential (r-r*) increases with the debt-exports ratio.

This model, put in linear stationary form, includes six variables forwarded: C, I, L, P, Pd, V, four variables predetermined: K, L, S, U, and four static variables: M, Q, r, X. However, the forward variables are not independent. L(+1) and Pd(+1) can be substituted in equations M6 and M7 by their expressions, given respectively by the equations M1 and M8 forwarded. V may be also expressed as a function of the only endogenous variables, P, C, I, and various exogenous. Then forwarded, V can be eliminated of equation M5. At this stage there is the problem of the equilibrium value of U which is zero. We then express U by its value in function of r in equation M13 and put it in equation M12. Hence the system admits a Blanchard-Kahn representation of the form (12), with 3 non predetermined variables, C, I, P, and the 4 predetermined variables K, L, r and S.

Computed around its steady state, the values of the 7 roots of the system are:

(.843, .942, .950, .977, 1.025, 1.068, 1.209).

Hence, the system contains as many stable roots as there are predetermined variables. In other words, the Blanchard-Kahn condition holds true.

If we take the right eigenvector associated with the greatest stable root .977, compute the expressions $|p_{in} / \overline{x}^i|$, and normalize the first component to 1, we find the following values:

Variable:	K	L	r	S	C	I	P
Eigenvector Component:	1	0	.080	4.553	2.854	.287	2.537

It can be verified that all the components of the left eigenvector associated with the root .977 are different from 0.

We can also compute the asymptotical component of the other variables from formula (11).

Hence in response to any temporary shock, the asymptotic relative hierarchy is: labour L, the quickest variable, interest rate r, output Q, investment I, sales V, capital K, demand price Pd, exports X, output price P, inventories S, consumption C, and the slowest, imports M.

The graphs I and II illustrate the dynamic reaction after 100 periods of selected variables to a temporary shock on productivity and public expenditures respectively.

REFERENCES

Ando, A, F M Fisher and H A Simon, (1963), *Essays on the Structure of Social Science Models*, MIT Press, Cambridge.

Blanchard, O J and C M Kahn (1980), "The Solution of Linear Difference Models under Rational Expectations", *Econometrica*, Vol. 48, pp. 1305-1311.

Blanchard, O J and L Summers (1986), "Hysteresis and the European Unemployment Problem", *NBER Macroeconomics Annual*, pp. 15-77.

Boucekkine, R (1995), "An Alternative Methodology for Solving Nonlinear Forward-Looking Models", *Journal of Economic Dynamics and Control*, Vol. 19, pp. 711-734.

Boucekkine, R and Le Van C (1996), "Checking for Saddlepoint Stability: An Easy Test", *Computational Economics*, Vol. 9, pp. 317-330.

Juillard, M (1996), "DYNARE: A Program for the Resolution and Simulation of Dynamic Models with Forward Variables Through the Use of a Relaxation Algorithm", *Working Paper, CEPREMAP n° 9602.*

Kuh, E, J Neese and P Hollinger (1985), *Structural Sentivity in Econometric Models*, Wiley, New-York.

Laffargue J-P (1995), "A Dynamic Model of the French Economy with Rational Expectations, Monopolistic Competition and Labour Market Bargaining", *Annales d'Economie et de Statistique*, Vol. 37-38, pp. 465-530.

Laffargue J-P, Malgrange P et Pujol T (1992), "Une maquette trimestrielle de l'économie française avec anticipations rationnelles et concurrence monopolistique", *Actualité Economique*, Vol. 92, pp. 225-261.

Malgrange, P (1989), "The Structure of Dynamic Macroeconomic Models", in *Contributions to Operations Research and Economics: The Twentieth Anniversary of CORE*, B. Cornet, H. Tulkens Eds., M.I.T. Press.

Schoonbeek, L (1984), "Coefficient Value and Dynamic Properties of Econometric Models", *Economic Letters*, Vol. 16, pp. 303-308.

GRAPH I: PRODUCTIVITY SHOCK

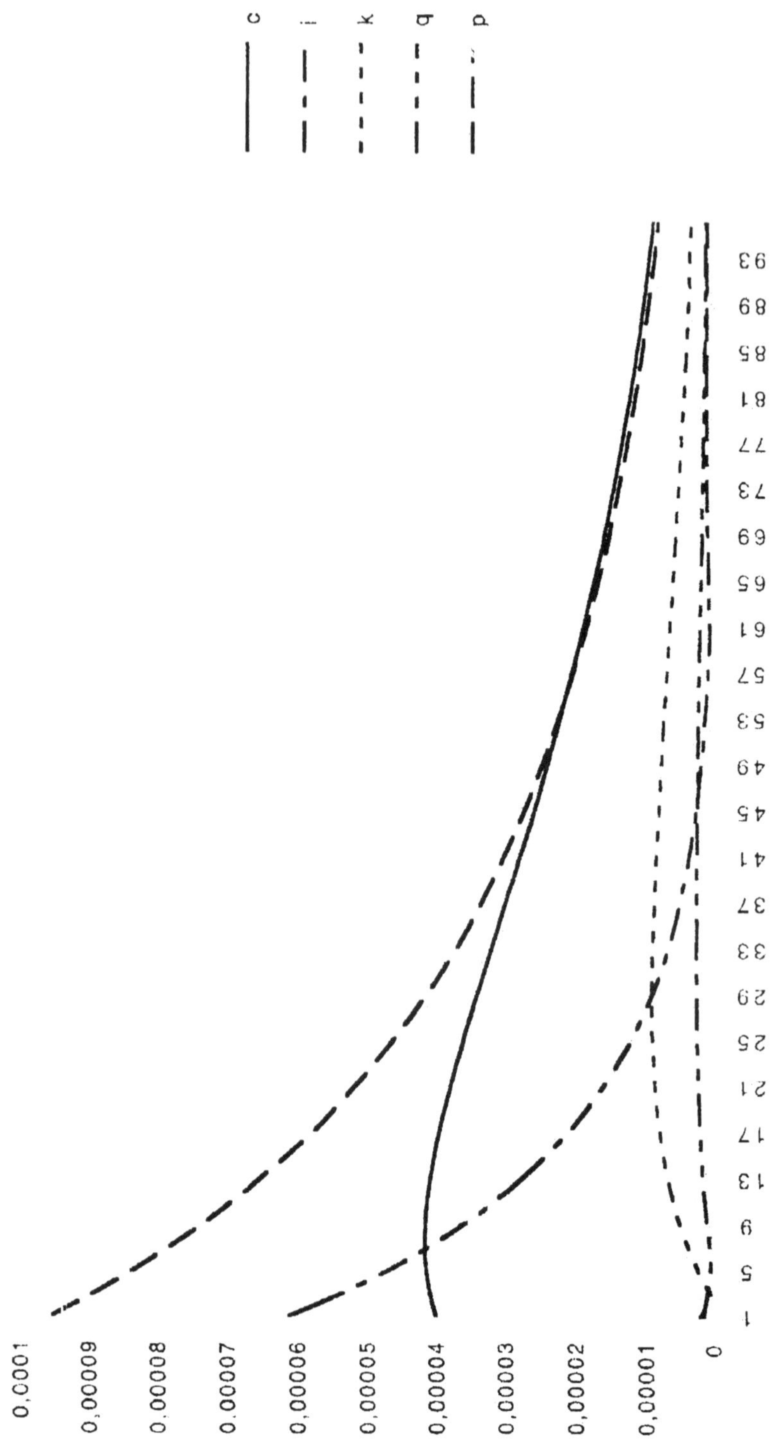

GRAPH II: GOVERNMENT EXPENDITURES SHOCK

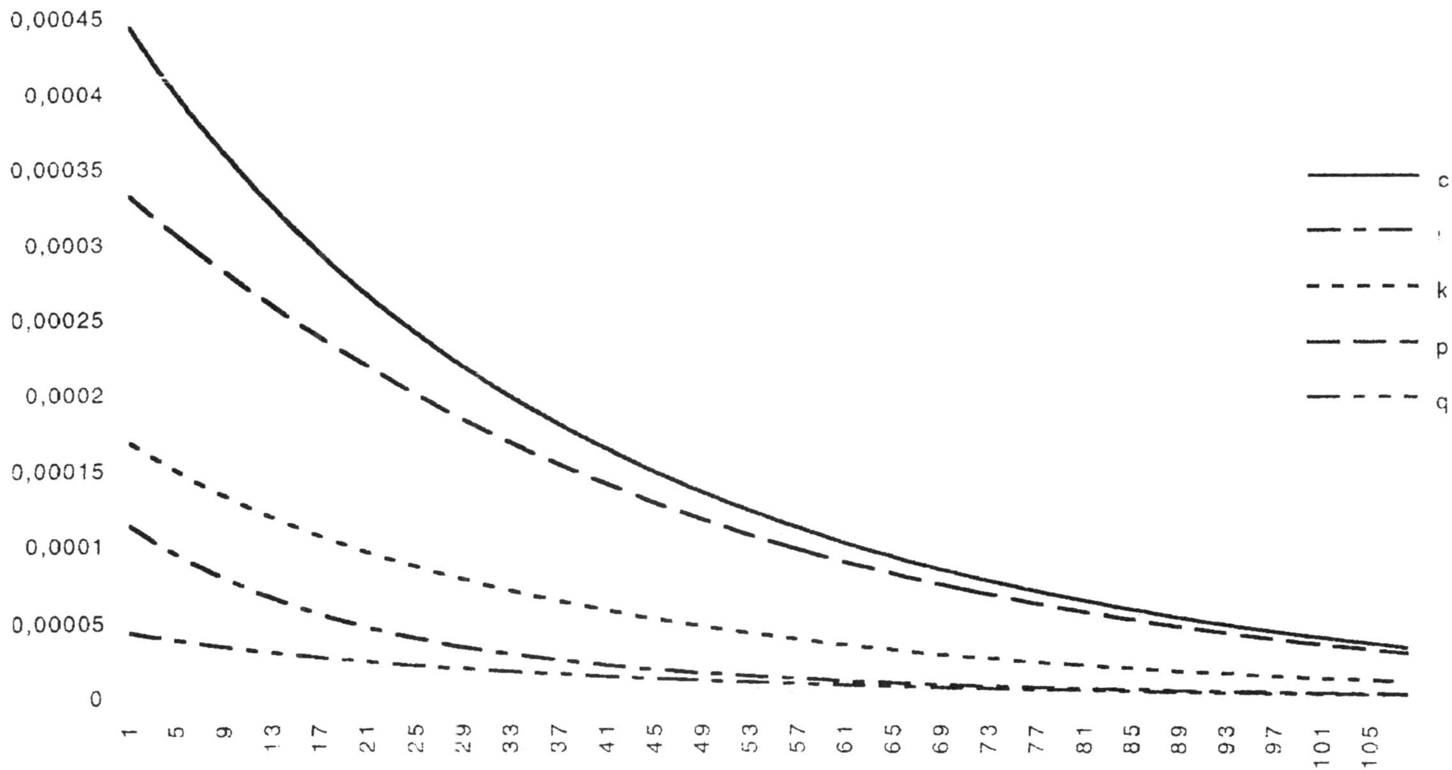

CHAPTER 8

COMPUTATIONAL METHODS FOR MACRO POLICY ANALYSIS: HALL AND TAYLOR'S MODEL IN DUALI

P Ruben Mercado and David A Kendrick

1. INTRODUCTION

This, and its sibling paper (Mercado and Kendrick (1997c)), provide a practical introduction to macroeconomic policy analysis methods and show how to obtain in DUALI deterministic and stochastic control solutions with standard and rational expectations models. In the sibling paper we focus on models with rational expectations and forward variables. In this paper we confine ourselves to standard models without forward variables.

The analysis of the *general properties of dynamic economic systems* is a complex task, facilitated by the application of some theoretical results and relatively simple simulation techniques. *Dynamic optimal policy* analysis is more demanding, usually requiring specialized software. DUALI[1] is an optimal control software which is able to generate deterministic and stochastic simulation environments and to compute, among other things, the optimal feedback rule and the implied optimal paths for target variables and policy tools.

Our general goals here are:

a) to introduce the use of some concepts for the analysis of dynamic properties of economic systems

b) to introduce the use of DUALI to perform deterministic and stochastic dynamic optimal policy analysis.

As an illustration of solution concepts and computational techniques, we use a linearized version of Robert Hall and John Taylor's open economy-flexible exchange rate model.[2]

2. HALL AND TAYLOR'S OPEN ECONOMY MODEL

This is a twelve-equation nonlinear dynamic model for an open economy with flexible exchange rates which generates interesting and realistic patterns of macroeconomic behavior.

---

[1] Amman and Kendrick (1996) and (1997b).

[2] Hall and Taylor (1993). Though its building blocks are developed throughout the book, the whole model is presented only in MACROSOLVE, the software accompanying Hall and Taylor's book.

Hall and Taylor's model contains the equations, variables and parameters listed below. Equations i-v and ix-x can be seen as a standard IS-LM-Open Economy sub-model for aggregate demand. Equations vi-viii define an "expectations augmented" Phillips Curve, that is, aggregate supply. Finally, equations xi and xii are definitions for the government deficit and the unemployment rate. The parameters are taken from the 1993 edition of the Hall and Taylor text. They explain that the parameters were chosen in such a way as to provide consistent numerical values so as to give a sense of the magnitudes involved.

The model is dynamic - all variables without subscripts correspond to time "t", those with a "-1" subscript correspond to "t-1", and so on. Also the model is nonlinear - nonlinearities appear in equations v, viii, ix and x. Its dynamic behavior displays the "natural rate" property: nominal shocks may affect real variables in the short-run, but not in the long run.

Equations

i)	GDP identity	$Y = C + I + G + X$
ii)	Disposable Income	$Y^d = (1-t)\,Y$
iii)	Consumption	$C = a + b\,Y^d$
iv)	Investment	$I = e - d\,R$
v)	Money Demand	$M/P = k\,Y - h\,R$
vi)	Expected Inflation	$\pi^e = \alpha\,\pi_{-1} + \beta\,\pi_{-2}$
vii)	Inflation Rate	$\pi = \pi^e + f\,\{(Y_{-1} - Y_N)/Y_N\}$
viii)	Price Level	$P = P_{-1}\,(1 + \pi)$
ix)	Real Exchange Rate	$E\,P/P_w = q + v\,R$
x)	Net Exports	$X = g - m\,Y - n\,E\,P/P_w$
xi)	Government Deficit	$G_d = G - t\,Y$
xii)	Unemployment Rate	$U = U_N - \mu\{(Y - Y_N)/Y_N\}$

Parameters

$a = 220$; $b = 0.7754$; $d = 2000$; $e = 1000$; $f = 0.8$; $g = 600$; $h = 1000$; $k = 0.1583$; $m = 0.1$; $n = 100$; $q = 0.75$; $t = 0.1875$; $v = 5$; $\alpha = 0.4$; $\beta = 0.2$; $\mu = 0.33$;

Endogenous Variables	Policy Variables
C : Consumption	G : Government Expenditure
E : Nominal Exchange Rate	M : Money Stock
G_d : Government Deficit	
I : Investment	
P : Domestic Price Level	**Exogenous Variables**
R : Real Interest Rate	
U : Unemployment Rate	P_w : Foreign Price Level
X : Net Exports	U_N : "Natural" Rate of Unemployment
Y : GDP	Y_N : Potential GDP
Y^d : Disposable Income	
π : Inflation Rate	
π^e : Expected Inflation	

To make use of theoretical results from the analysis of dynamic systems and from the optimal control literature, and to be able to perform policy analysis with DUALI, we need to obtain the state-space representation of Hall and Taylor's model, that is, to transform the model into a system of first order difference equations. To do this, we first linearize the model, then obtain its reduce form representation, and finally transform the reduce form into the state-space form.

Detailed steps to transform Hall and Taylor's nonlinear model into its state-space representation are in Mercado and Kendrick (1997a). The linearization technique chosen is a variant of the Johansen's method, in which all the variables in the model are expressed as percent deviations from the model's steady-state solution. Without loss of generality, and to make the analytical and computational work easier, the original twelve-endogenous variables model was collapsed into a four-endogenous variables model involving (1) GDP, the real interest rate, the nominal exchange rate and the price level as endogenous variables, (2) the money supply and government expenditure as policy variables, and (3) potential GDP and foreign prices as exogenous variables.

The state-space representation of Hall and Taylor's model when collapsed into a four-endogenous variables model in which all the variables are percent deviations from the steady-state is given below.[3, 4]

---

[3] The steady-state solution for Hall and Taylor's original nonlinear model in levels is: Y = 6000, R = 0.05, plev = 1 and E =1. These steady-state values correspond to the following values for policy and exogenous variables: M = 900, G = 1200, YN = 6000 and plevw = 1. Since in the linearized state-space representation all variables are in percent deviations, their steady-state values are all zeroes.

[4] In Hall and Taylor's model, the policy variables contemporaneously affect the model's endogenous variables, and this is also true for its "state-space" representation. In order to obtain a proper state-state representation, that is, one in which the control variables also appear with one lag, we have to assume that there is one lag of delay between a policy decision and its implementation (see Kendrick (1981), p. 10). Then, we can substitute M_{-1}^* for M^*, and G_{-1}^* for G^*. We will also assume that the exogenous variables YN^* and $plevw^*$ affect the system with one lag instead of contemporaneously. Expressing the model in this way, we can make use of many results from the optimal control literature, which works with models with one-lag controls. Also, the DUALI software works in this way.

$$Y^* = A_{11} Y^*_{-1} + A_{13}\, plev^*_{-1} + A_{17}\, xlplev^*_{-1} + A_{1.11}\, xllplev^*_{-1} + B_{11} M^*_{-1} + B_{12}\, G^*_{-1} + C_{11} YN^*_{-1} + C_{12}\, plevw^*_{-1} \quad (1.1)$$

$$R^* = A_{21} Y^*_{-1} + A_{23}\, plev^*_{-1} + A_{27}\, xlplev^*_{-1} + A_{2.11}\, xllplev^*_{-1} + B_{21} M^*_{-1} + B_{22}\, G^*_{-1} + C_{21} YN^*_{-1} + C_{22}\, plevw^*_{-1} \quad (1.2)$$

$$plev^* = A_{31}\, Y^*_{-1} + A_{33}\, plev^*_{-1} + A_{37}\, xlplev^*_{-1} + A_{3.11}\, xllplev^*_{-1} + C_{31}\, YN^*_{-1} \quad (1.3)$$

$$E^* = A_{41} Y^*_{-1} + A_{43}\, plev^*_{-1} + A_{47}\, xlplev^*_{-1} + A_{4.11}\, xllplev^*_{-1} + B_{41} M^*_{-1} + B_{42}\, G^*_{-1} + C_{41} YN^*_{-1} + C_{42}\, plevw^*_{-1} \quad (1.4)$$

$$xlY^* = Y^*_{-1} \quad (1.5)$$

$$xlR^* = R^*_{-1} \quad (1.6)$$

$$xlplev^* = plev^*_{-1} \quad (1.7)$$

$$xlE^* = E^*_{-1} \quad (1.8)$$

$$xllY^* = xlY^*_{-1} \quad (1.9)$$

$$xllR^* = xlR^*_{-1} \quad (1.10)$$

$$xllplev^* = xlplev^*_{-1} \quad (1.11)$$

$$xllE^* = xlE^*_{-1} \quad (1.12)$$

where:

Endogenous Variables

Y^* = GDP
R^* = Real Interest Rate
$plev^*$ = Domestic Price Level

Policy Variables

M^* = Money Stock
G^* = Government Expenditure
E^* = Nominal Exchange Rate

Exogenous Variables

$plevw^*$ = foreign Price Level
YN^* = Potential GDP

where the remaining "xl…" and "xll…" variables come from the re-labeling of the endogenous variables with lags greater than one, and where:

A_{11} = -0.346, A_{13} = -0.606, A_{17} = 0.087, $A_{1.11}$ = 0.087,
A_{21} = 7.811, A_{23} = 13.669, A_{27} = -1.953, $A_{2.11}$ = -1.953,
A_{31} = 0.800, A_{33} = 1.400, A_{37} = -0.200, $A_{3.11}$ = -0.200,
A_{41} = 1.154, A_{43} = 2.019, A_{47} = -0.288, $A_{4.11}$ = -0.288,

B_{11} = 0.433, B_{12} = 0.231, B_{21} = -9.763, B_{22} = 4.386,
B_{41} = -2.442, B_{42} = 1.097,

C_{11} = 0.346, C_{12} = 0.000, C_{21} = -7.811, C_{22} = 0.000,

$$C_{31} = -0.800, \quad C_{41} = -1.154, \quad C_{42} = 1.000.$$

In matrix notation, the state-space representation of Hall and Taylor's model can be written as:

$$x = A\,x_{-1} + B\,u_{-1} + C\,z_{-1} \tag{1.13}$$

where x is an augmented state vector defined as:

$$x = \begin{bmatrix} X \\ XL \\ XLL \end{bmatrix}, \tag{1.14}$$

where:

$$X = \begin{bmatrix} Y^* \\ R^* \\ plev^* \\ E^* \end{bmatrix} \qquad XL = X_{-1} \qquad XLL = X_{-2} \tag{1.15}$$

$$u = \begin{bmatrix} M^*_{-1} \\ G^*_{-1} \end{bmatrix}, \quad z = \begin{bmatrix} YN^*_{-1} \\ plevw^*_{-1} \end{bmatrix}, \tag{1.16}$$

and where:

$$A = \begin{bmatrix} -0.346 & 0 & -0.606 & 0 & 0 & 0 & 0.087 & 0 & 0 & 0 & 0.087 & 0 \\ 7.811 & 0 & 13.669 & 0 & 0 & 0 & -1.953 & 0 & 0 & 0 & -1.953 & 0 \\ 0.8 & 0 & 1.4 & 0 & 0 & 0 & -0.2 & 0 & 0 & 0 & -0.2 & 0 \\ 1.154 & 0 & 2.019 & 0 & 0 & 0 & -0.288 & 0 & 0 & 0 & -0.288 & 0 \\ 1 & 0 & 0 & 0 & 0 & 0 & 0 & 0 & 0 & 0 & 0 & 0 \\ 0 & 1 & 0 & 0 & 0 & 0 & 0 & 0 & 0 & 0 & 0 & 0 \\ 0 & 0 & 1 & 0 & 0 & 0 & 0 & 0 & 0 & 0 & 0 & 0 \\ 0 & 0 & 0 & 1 & 0 & 0 & 0 & 0 & 0 & 0 & 0 & 0 \\ 0 & 0 & 0 & 0 & 1 & 0 & 0 & 0 & 0 & 0 & 0 & 0 \\ 0 & 0 & 0 & 0 & 0 & 1 & 0 & 0 & 0 & 0 & 0 & 0 \\ 0 & 0 & 0 & 0 & 0 & 0 & 1 & 0 & 0 & 0 & 0 & 0 \\ 0 & 0 & 0 & 0 & 0 & 0 & 0 & 1 & 0 & 0 & 0 & 0 \end{bmatrix}, \tag{1.17}$$

$$B = \begin{bmatrix} 0.433 & 0.231 \\ -9.763 & 4.386 \\ 0 & 0 \\ -2.442 & 1.097 \\ 0 & 0 \\ 0 & 0 \\ 0 & 0 \\ 0 & 0 \\ 0 & 0 \\ 0 & 0 \\ 0 & 0 \\ 0 & 0 \end{bmatrix}, C = \begin{bmatrix} 0.346 & 0 \\ -7.811 & 0 \\ -0.8 & 0 \\ -1.154 & 1 \\ 0 & 0 \\ 0 & 0 \\ 0 & 0 \\ 0 & 0 \\ 0 & 0 \\ 0 & 0 \\ 0 & 0 \\ 0 & 0 \end{bmatrix} \quad (1.18)$$

3. INTRODUCTION TO DYNAMIC ANALYSIS METHODS

Before performing optimal policy experiments with a given model, it is useful to analyze its basic dynamic behavior. Here, we will introduce the most common theoretical results and simulation procedures to that end.

3.a Eigenvalues: Computation and Use

The eigenvalues of matrix A convey useful information about the dynamic properties of the model.[5] They can be easily computed with specialized software such as Matlab, Mathematica, etc.

Let's assume that the model has a steady-state. Then, depending on the magnitude of those eigenvalues, the system will be stable, unstable, or it will display the saddle-point property:

.. if they all lie within the unit circle,[6] the model is globally stable. It will converge to its steady-state from any initial conditions

.. if they all lie outside the unit circle, the model is dynamically unstable. Unless it starts from the steady-state itself, it will diverge from it for any other set of initial conditions

.. if some lie within the unit circle, while others lie outside the unit circle, the steady-state is a saddle point. The system will converge towards the steady-state from some initial conditions, and will diverge from other.

---

[5] For an extended treatment of the analysis of dynamic systems related to economics, see Chiang (1984), and Azariadis (1993).

[6] If the eigenvalues are complex numbers, this means that their modulus is smaller than 1. If they are real number, it means that their absolute value is smaller than one.

The speed of convergence or divergence is also determined by the magnitude of the eigenvalues. For instance, a modulus smaller than one but near one will indicate a slow adjustment towards the steady-state, while a modulus near zero will imply a faster convergence. A modulus greater than one but near one will indicate that anticipated changes in exogenous variables that will take place in the future can have large effects today. Finally, the presence of complex eigenvalues will imply cyclical behavior for some or all of the system variables.

For the linearized version of Hall and Taylor's model, we have the following eigenvalues:[7]

$\lambda_1 = 0.68431+0.4042i$
$\lambda_2 = 0.68431-0.4042i$
$\lambda_3 = -0.31663$
$\lambda_4 = 0.002$
λ_5 to λ_{12} = all near zero

There are two complex eigenvalues, with modulus less than one. The remaining eigenvalues are all real and smaller than one in absolute value. Thus, Hall and Taylor's linearized model is stable and has cyclical behavior. That is, its convergence toward the steady-state will be in the form of damped oscillations.

3.b Dynamic Paths

In the following it is important to distinguish between two ways of describing the steady state solution of the model. The first is the *steady state levels.* For example the steady state levels for the Hall and Taylor model are

Y = 6000	i.e. 6000 billion or 6 trillion dollars
R = 0.05	i.e. 5 percent
plev = 1	i.e. a price index of 100
E = 1	i.e. a nominal exchange rate index of 100

This values come from a solution in which the policy variables are set to

M = 900	i.e. a money stock of 900 billion
G = 1200	i.e. government expenditures of 1200 billion

and of exogenous variables of

YN = 6000	i.e. a potential GDP of 6 trillion dollars
plevw = 1	i.e. a foreign price level index of 100

[7] There are many software packages capable of computing eigenvalues. These were computed with Matlab (see the Appendix).

The second way is the steady state *in percentage deviations from the steady state levels.* Thus in the model in use here all the variables are in percentage deviations from steady state levels, so the steady state solution to that model will sometimes be zero meaning that those values are at their steady state levels. For example in time period one we may obtain a solution of 0.04 which means that Y is 4 percent above its steady state level so it is at 6024. Then in the long run the values of Y may return to 0.00 meaning that it is zero percent above its steady state level so it is at 6000. (Notice that 0.04 does *not* mean "a 4% increase with respect to the previous period".) To learn more about this way of representing a model see Mercado and Kendrick (1997a).

This can be confusing since a statement that the steady state solution of the model for GDP was zero means that GDP is at a steady state level of 6000 billion, i.e. 6 trillion dollars.

With this background, the next step in the analysis of the model is to visualize its dynamic evolution for given changes in policy variables, as a way of detecting implausible patterns of behavior.[8,9] The graphs below shows the results of two experiments: a one time and permanent 10% increase in the money supply (M) and a one time and permanent 10% increase in government expenditure (G).[10] Thus in the first experiment M is set to 0.1 for all time periods. This can be thought of as the money stock increasing from its steady state value to a level ten percent higher in the first time period and then remaining at that level throughout the run. This has the effect of giving a shock to the economy in the first time period and the effects of this shock then dissipate slowly over time. The same is true for G in the second experiment, i.e. it has a value of 0.1 in all time periods. This means that it increases from it steady state level by 10 percent in the first time period and then stays at that level throughout the run. In the engineering literature these types of policy changes are sometimes called "step" functions because the policy steps up from one level to another and remains at that higher level.

In the following graphs the percent deviations from steady-state values are on the vertical axes (e.g.: a value of 0.02 means 2% above steady-state) and the time periods on the horizontal axes. Since all variables (endogenous, policy and exogenous) are in percent deviations, their steady-state solution values in the model are all zeroes.

---

[8] These simulations can be easily implemented in software with standard simulation capabilities, such as, for example, GAMS (see Mercado, Kendrick and Amman (1997), and Mercado and Kendrick (1997a)). Though DUALI is a software oriented toward deterministic and stochastic control applications, it can also handle standard simulations. To do so, set to zero the weights on the state variables (W matrix) and set to the maximum possible value the weights on the controls (Lambda matrix). Then, define the desired path for the controls as equal to the policy change to be introduced, and solve as a Deterministic QLP problem (see Amman and Kendrick (1996), Chapter 1). Simulations of shocks to the exogenous variables and to the initial values for the endogenous variables can be implemented in an analogous way.

[9] To run these simulations, use program htdua01.dui (making the appropriate changes. See the "Description" section in the "Data" menu).

[10] To simplify the notation, from now on we will not use the " * " on the model's variables, but it should be clear that we will still be making reference to percent deviations from baseline.

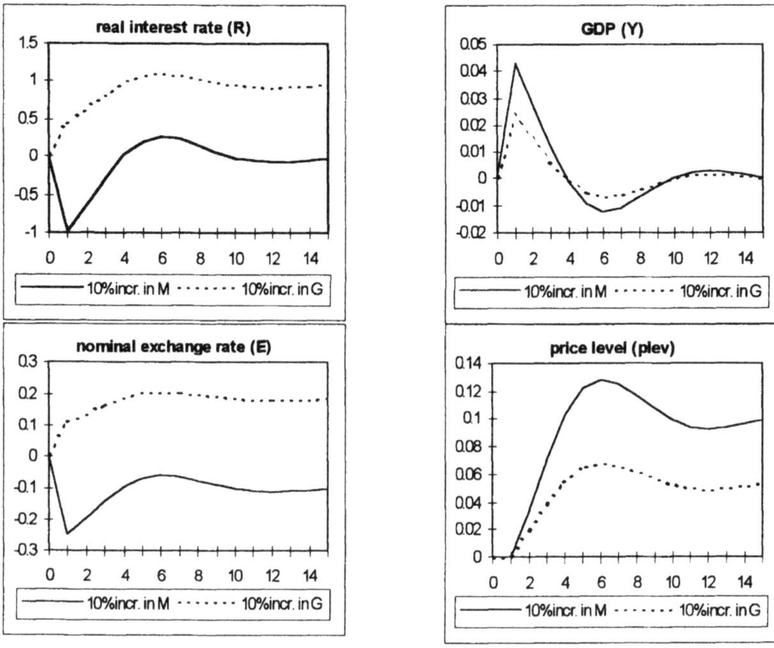

Figure 1. Responses to One Time Policy Changes.

As expected, the increase in M causes a significant drop in R and thus an increase in Y during the first periods. The value of -1 in the graph for the real interest rate means that R has fallen by 100% (i.e. from, say, 5% to 2.5%), while the value of 0.04 on the vertical axes of the GDP graph means that Y went up by 4% in the first quarter from say 6000 to 6024. However, in the long-run, the real variables (Y and R) come back to their steady-state values, while nominal variables experience permanent changes (plev increases 10%, the same amount as M, while E decreases 10%) of equal magnitude to the change in M. Thus the price level is ten percent higher at the end of the experiment than at the beginning, moving from an index level of say 140 to 154. Also, the exchange rate is ten percent lower, changing from say 120 yen per dollar to 108 yen per dollar.

The increase in G has a smaller effect on Y, which is also neutral in the long-run. However, there is a strong impact on R, which after five periods increases by more than 100% with respect to its previous steady-state value, due to the crowding-out effect of government expenditure on private expenditure. Meanwhile, plev and E both increase and then stabilize on a new and higher steady-state value (around 6% higher for plev and almost 20% higher for E).

3.c Dynamic Controllability: Computation and Use

Once we have studied the dynamic properties of the model, the next step is analyze its controllability, that is, the power of the available policy tools to drive the system towards pre-specified desired paths. Jan Tinbergen[11] established the conditions for static controllability. In order to hit a number "n" of targets, we need at least an equal number of independent policy instruments. However, this condition can be overcome in a dynamic context.[12]

We may start by asking if it is possible to transfer the system from any given state at time "0" to any other state at time "0 + t" through a suitable choice of values of the policy tools. This is the condition of dynamic controllability. For a system to be dynamically controllable, it has to be true that:

$$\text{rank}(R_1, \ldots, R_m) = m \tag{2.1}$$

where "m" is the number of target variables, where "t" (the time horizon) is greater than "m", where:

$$R_i = S\, A^{i-1}\, B \tag{2.2}$$

and where A and B are respectively the state and control matrices of the model, and S is a matrix to select, from the set of state variables, those that will be the targets of policy. That is:

$$S\, Z = Y \tag{2.3}$$

where Z is the vector of state variables and Y is the vector of target variables.

For the state-state representation of Hall and Taylor's model, we know that A is a (12 x 12) matrix. However, 8 out of the 12 state variables are in fact lagged endogenous variables re-defined for convenience. Thus, for instance, we may be interested in controlling 4 variables only (Y, R, plev and E), or even a smaller subset. Assuming that we want to control all the four variables, we will have:

$$S = \begin{bmatrix} 1 & 0 & . & . & . & . & . & . & . & . & . & 0 \\ 0 & 1 & 0 & . & . & . & . & . & . & . & . & 0 \\ 0 & 0 & 1 & 0 & . & . & . & . & . & . & . & 0 \\ 0 & 0 & 0 & 1 & 0 & . & . & . & . & . & . & 0 \end{bmatrix} \tag{2.4}$$

Thus, the dynamic controllability condition is:

---

[11] See Tinbergen (1956).

[12] See Hughes Hallett (1989) who makes the point that it may be easier to control just the targets of policy rather than the whole model.

$$\text{rank}(R_1, \ldots, R_4) = 4 \tag{2.5}$$

which is effectively met by the linearized Hall and Taylor's model (see Appendix A.2).

There are many more theoretical results in connection with the controllability properties of a system in both deterministic and stochastic settings. The one presented here is one of the most intuitive and relatively easy to check.[13]

4. INTRODUCTION TO OPTIMAL POLICY ANALYSIS METHODS WITH DUALI

In the previous section, we presented the responses of Hall and Taylor's model to changes in the policy variables. Optimal policy analysis is interested in a sort of "reverse" analysis. It begins by posing this question: how should policy variables be set in order for the target variables to follow pre-specified paths?[14]

The most popular way of stating this problem is as a Quadratic Linear Problem (QLP). In formal terms, the problem is expressed as one of finding the controls $(u)_{t=0}^{N}$ to minimize a quadratic "tracking" criterion function J of the form:

$$J = E\left\{\frac{1}{2}\left[x_N - x_N^{\#}\right]' W_N\left[x_N - x_N^{\#}\right]\right.$$

$$\left. + \frac{1}{2}\sum_{t=0}^{N-1}\left(\left[x_t - x_t^{\#}\right]' W_t\left[x_t - x_t^{\#}\right] + \left[u_t - u_t^{\#}\right]' \Lambda_t\left[u_t - u_t^{\#}\right]\right)\right\} \tag{3.1}$$

subject, as a constraint, to the state-state representation of the economic model:

$$x_t = A\,x_{t-1} + B\,u_{t-1} + C\,z_{t-1} + \varepsilon_{t-1} \tag{3.2}$$

where E is the expectation operator, $x^{\#}$ and $u^{\#}$ are desired paths for the state and controls variables respectively, W and Λ are weighting matrices for states and controls respectively, ε is a vector of random disturbances, and where all the other variables were defined above.

The quadratic nature of the criterion function implies that deviations above and below target are penalized equally, and that large deviations are more than

---

[13] For example, there are also uniqueness, stabilizability and instrument stability conditions for a dynamic system when it is put, as we will see below, within a control framework. For an introductory presentation of these conditions, see Turnovsky (1977) and Holly and Hughes Hallett (1989). For an advanced treatment, see Aoki (1976).

[14] For an introductory presentation of optimal control for economic models, see Turnovsky (1977). For a more advanced treatment, see Chow (1975), Holly and Hughes Hallett (1989), and Kendrick (1981).

proportionally penalized than small deviations. This particular form of the criterion function is not the only possible one, but is the most popular.[15]

The way in which we treat uncertainty has important implications for the solution methods of this problem, as well as on the simulation techniques. If we completely ignore the presence of uncertainty - which may arise, for example, from additive noise, parameter uncertainty or measurement error - we are left with a deterministic control problem. If we account for some or all of the possible forms of uncertainty, we face a stochastic control problem.

The solution of deterministic or stochastic control problems, even when they are of the Quadratic Linear form, quickly becomes very involved. Thus, to make our task feasible, we have to rely on computational methods and specialized software.

DUALI is a specialized software that can receive as inputs the desired paths for target and control variables, weighting matrices, and the state-space representation of the economic model with or without its stochastic specifications, and which is able to generate sophisticated simulation environments and to compute, among other things, the optimal feedback rule and the solution paths for states and controls.[16]

In what follows, we will use DUALI to perform deterministic and stochastic experiments with the state-space representation of Hall and Taylor's model. We will assume that the policy goal is to stabilize Y, R, plev and E around steady-state values (that is, around zero). High and equal weights[17] will be put on stabilizing Y and plev, lower and equal on R and E, and even lower and equal on the policy variables M and G. Neither the desired paths nor the weighting matrices (shown below) will vary with time.

---

[15] For a discussion of the properties of different criterion functions, see Blanchard and Fischer (1989), Chapter 11.

[16] See Amman and Kendrick (1996) and (1997b).

[17] There is a conceptual difference between "weights" and "priorities" which arises when the variables of interest are in levels and also expressed in different units of measurement. For instance, if GDP is measured in dollars and prices are measured by an arbitrary price index, equal weights on these two variables will probably imply different policy priorities and vice versa. Since all variables in the state-space representation of Hall and Taylor's model are in percent deviations from steady-state, weighs and priorities can be considered as equivalent within certain limits. However, it should be clear that, for example, an interest rate 50% below steady-state values is something feasible, while a level of GDP 50% below steady-state is not. In such a case, there is not an analogy between weights and priorities. See Park (1997).

$$W = \begin{bmatrix} 100 &&&&&&&&&&& \\ & 50 &&&&&&&&&& \\ && 100 &&&&&&&&& \\ &&& 50 &&&&&&&& \\ &&&& 0 &&&&&&& \\ &&&&& 0 &&&&&& \\ &&&&&& 0 &&&&& \\ &&&&&&& 0 &&&& \\ &&&&&&&& 0 &&& \\ &&&&&&&&& 0 && \\ &&&&&&&&&& 0 & \\ &&&&&&&&&&& 0 \end{bmatrix}, \quad \Lambda = \begin{bmatrix} 25 & \\ & 25 \end{bmatrix}. \tag{3.3}$$

4.a Deterministic Control

In this section, we will ignore all possible sources of uncertainty. Assume, for example, that the economy is going through a recession provoked by a temporary adverse shock to net exports which causes Y to be 4% below its steady-state value. Given the weight structure adopted in the previous section, what would be the optimal paths for government expenditure (G) and the money supply (M) in order to bring the economy back to its steady-state? How do the optimal paths for the state variables compare against what would be the autonomous response of the system to that kind of shock?

To implement this experiment in DUALI, we have to

(1) set the problem complexity to deterministic,
(2) set all the desired paths for states and controls equal to zero,
(3) impose the corresponding weights on states and controls as indicated above,
(4) set an initial value for Y equal to -0.04, and
(5) chose the option "Solve: QLP" or "Solve:QLP Print".[18]

To obtain the autonomous path of the system, we have to proceed in an analogous way as we did in the previous section to simulate the effects of changes in policy variables. That is, we have to

(1) impose zero weights on the state variables,
(2) place high and equal weights on the controls and,
(3) as above, set an initial value for Y equal to -0.04.

The results for the main four state variables are shown in Figure 2.[19]

[18] See Amman and Kendrick (1996), Chapter 1. Use the program htdua01.dui.

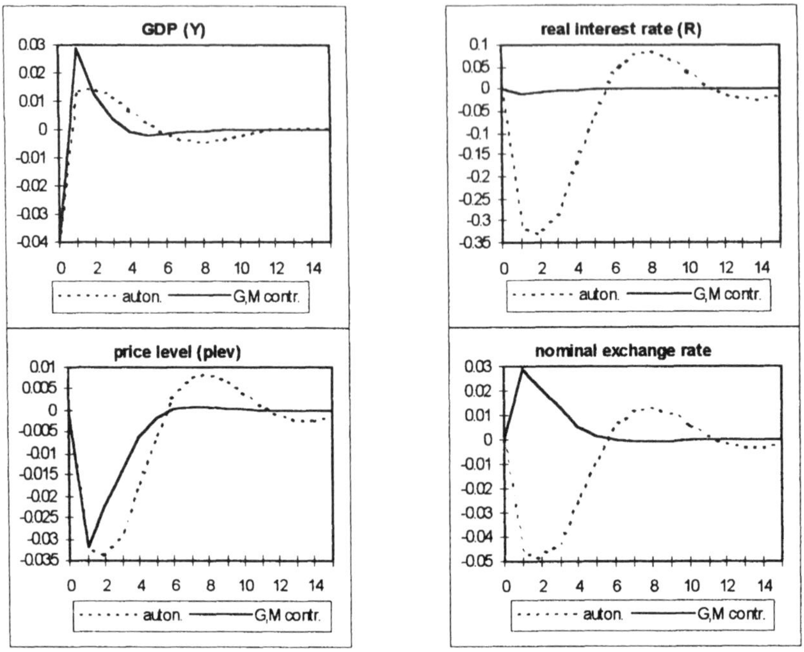

Figure 2. Autonomous Solution Versus Optimal Control Solution: State Variables.

The optimal solution paths for the states outperform the autonomous responses of the system for all the four target variables. This is true even for GDP where the optimal output stays closer to the desired path of zero than does the autonomous output path over most of the period covered by the model. This comes as no surprise, though it may not always be the case. Indeed, remember that the optimal solutions are obtained from the minimization of an overall loss function. On some occasions, depending on the weight structure, it may be better to do worse than the autonomous response for some targets in order to obtain more valuable gains from others.

Why does the autonomous path of the economy display the observed behavior? Here is how Hall and Taylor explain it:

"With real GDP below potential GDP after the drop in net exports, the price level will begin to fall. Firms have found that the demand for their products has fallen off and they will start to cut their prices (...). The lower price level causes the interest rate to fall.[20] With a lower interest rate, investment spending and net exports

[19] To run this simulations, use program htdua01.dui (making the appropriate changes. See the "Description" section in the "Data" menu).

[20] Since less money is demanded by people for transactions purposes. See Hall and Taylor (1993), Chapter 8.3.

will increase.[21] The increase in investment and net exports will tend to offset the original decline in net exports. This process of gradual price adjustment will continue as long as real GDP is below potential GDP."[22]

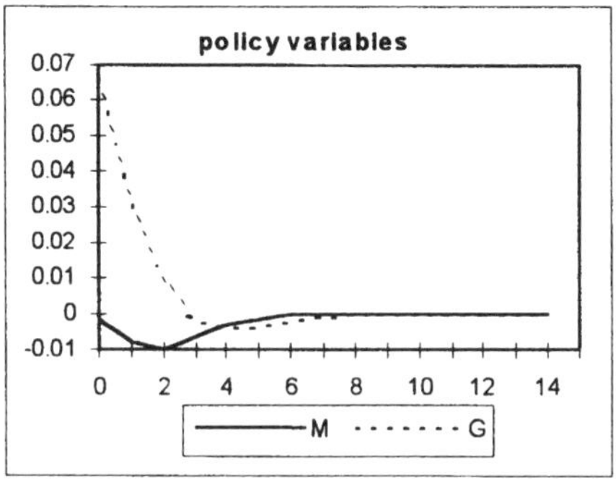

Figure 3. Autonomous Solution Versus Optimal Control Solution: Policy Variables

What explains the observed optimal path of the four variables of interest? Y was brought up very quickly, going from 4% below steady-state to 3% above steady-state, to then decay slowly to its steady-state value. This performance can be attributed to the more than 6% increase in G that can be observed in the policy variables' graph in Figure 3. Meanwhile, R experiences almost no variation when compared to the big drop - almost 35% - implied by the autonomous behavior of the system. This happens in the optimal control solution because, the increase in G puts an upward pressure on the interest rate, thus keeping it from falling. Finally, the nominal exchange rate has to go up to compensate for the fall in prices, given that the real interest rate does not change much.

We can also see that monetary policy plays a minor role when compared with fiscal policy.[23] Even though we put the same weights on both variables, government expenditure appears to be more effective to bring the economy out of its recession given the weight structure we put on the target variables.

The kind of optimal control experiments done above lend themselves well to tradeoff analysis. A curve of this sort is known as the policy frontier.[24] For instance, we may want to depict the trade-off between the standard deviations of Y and plev in Hall and Taylor's model when, as above, Y is shocked by a negative 4% in period zero. To obtain the corresponding policy frontier, we vary the relative

[21] Since the price level falls much less than the real interest rate during the first periods of the adjustment, the nominal exchange rate has to fall too, as can be derived from equation "ix" in the original Hall and Taylor's model. This implies that the real exchange rate will fall, then causing net exports (see equation "x") to raise.

[22] Hall and Taylor (1993), page 232.

[23] Notice that the optimal values for the policy variables are computed for periods 0 to 14 only. Given that we are working with a state-space representation of the model, policy variables can only influence the next period state variables. That is, the controls at period 0 are chosen, with a feedback-rule, as a function of period 0 states, but they determine period 1 states, and so on. See Kendrick (1981).

[24] See Hall and Taylor (1993), Chapter 18.

weights on Y and plev, perform one simulation for each weight combination and compute the corresponding standard deviations. The results of six experiments, keeping the same weights on the remaining states and controls as in the above simulation, are shown in Table 1 and Figure 4.[25]

Table 1. Weights and Tradeoff.

Experiment	Weight on Y	Weight on plev	STD (y)	STD (plev)
1	100	0	0.0479	0.0500
2	80	20	0.0489	0.0466
3	60	40	0.0499	0.0440
4	40	60	0.0509	0.0419
5	20	80	0.0520	0.0401
6	0	100	0.0531	0.0386

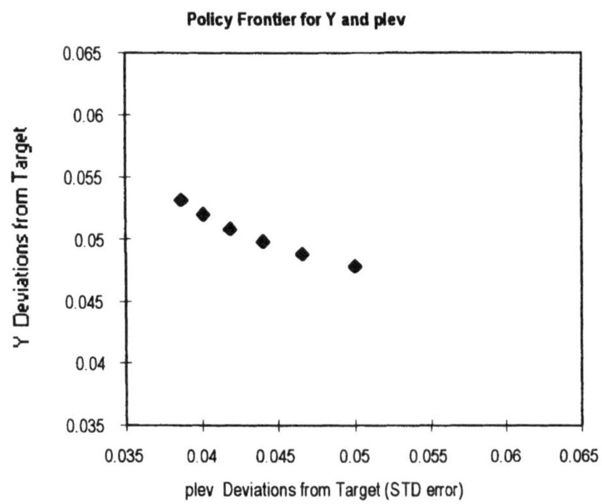

Figure 4. Policy Frontier for Y and plev.

The policy frontier for Y and plev is clearly shown in the graph above, where each diamond represents the result of an experiment. The higher the weight on Y relative to that of plev, the lower its standard deviation, and vice versa. The flatness of the curve indicates that it is easier to achieve a reduction in the percent deviation from target for plev than for Y. Of course, shape and location of this particular policy frontier are conditional on the weight structure imposed on the other variables. For example, if we increase the weight on the policy variables, the policy frontier will shift up and to the right, farther away from the origin (the (0,0) point of

[25] To run these simulations, use program htdua01.dui, changing the weights on Y and plev.

zero deviations for Y and plev). This will be due to the more restricted possibilities for actively using the policy variables to reach the targets for Y and plev.

4.b Stochastic Control

In this section, we will begin to take uncertainty into account. Indeed, macroeconomic models are only empirical approximations to reality. Thus, we have to consider that there are random shocks frequently hitting the economy (additive uncertainty), that the model parameters are just estimated values with associates variances and covariances (multiplicative uncertainty), and that the actual values of the model's variables and initial conditions are never known with certainty (measurement error).[26]

Stochastic control methods artificially generate a dynamic stochastic environment through random shocks generation. They use specific procedures for choosing the optimal values for each period policy variables: Certainty Equivalence (CE) when only additive uncertainty is considered, Open Loop Feedback (OLF) when parameter uncertainty is considered with passive learning, and DUAL when parameter uncertainty is considered and there is active learning. Also, there are specific mechanisms of projection-updating of parameters and variables. Thus these methods allow us to perform sophisticated simulations.

In what follows, we will perform experiments incorporating some forms of additive and parameter uncertainty into Hall and Taylor's model. We will proceed in two steps. First, we will analyze the differences in qualitative behavior of the policy variables when different procedures for choosing their optimal values are used (specifically, (CE) versus (OLF)). This will be done at first in an environment in which there is no updating of parameter estimates. Second, we will compare the quantitative performances of CE and OLF using Monte Carlo procedures and including passive learning with Kalman filters for updating parameter estimates.

4.b.1 Qualitative comparison between CE and OLF: control without parameter updating

Some years ago, William Brainard[27] showed that, for a static model, the existence of parameter uncertainty causes the optimal policy variables to be used in a more conservative way as compared to the case of no parameter uncertainty. However, this finding could not be completely translated into a dynamic setting. The existence of dynamics implies considerable changes, and at the same time opens new possibilities for policy management.

The procedure for choosing the controls in the presence of parameter uncertainty (OLF) differs from the standard deterministic QLP procedure or its

---

[26] See Kendrick (1981).

[27] See Brainard (1969).

"certainty equivalent" (CE).[28] Some analytical results have been provided by Franklin Shupp[29] in connection with the qualitative behavior of the policy variables when the OLF procedure is used in a model with one state and one control. He found that when uncertainty concerns the control parameters only, Brainard's result still holds: a more conservative use of the controls will be the optimal policy. However, he also found that the reverse is true when the uncertainty is in the state parameters only. Finally, he found that when uncertainty is in both the control and the state parameters, no general results can be obtained.

There are not straightforward theoretical results for the case of models with several states and controls. To illustrate some possible outcomes, and to show a first contrast between patterns of behavior generated by CE and OLF procedures, we will perform an experiment with Hall and Taylor's model. As in the previous section, we will assume that Y is 4% below its steady-state value at time zero and we will keep the same weight structure and desired paths. We will also assume that there is uncertainty in connection with six out of the parameters in the B matrix, and that the standard deviation of each of these parameters is equal to 20%. The vector of the initial values of uncertain parameters (TH0), the matrix that indicates which parameters in the model are treated as uncertain (ITHN), and the variance-covariance matrix of uncertain parameters (SITT0) will be as follows:

$$\mathrm{TH0} = \begin{bmatrix} b_{11} = 0.433 \\ b_{12} = 0.231 \\ b_{21} = -9.763 \\ b_{22} = 4.386 \\ b_{41} = -2.442 \\ b_{42} = 1.097 \end{bmatrix}, \quad \mathrm{ITHN} = \begin{bmatrix} 1 & 1 & 1 \\ 1 & 1 & 2 \\ 1 & 2 & 1 \\ 1 & 2 & 2 \\ 1 & 4 & 1 \\ 1 & 4 & 2 \end{bmatrix}, \tag{3.4}$$

$$\mathrm{SITT0} = \begin{bmatrix} 0.00749 & & & & & \\ & 0.00213 & & & & \\ & & 3.81264 & & & \\ & & & 0.76947 & & \\ & & & & 0.23853 & \\ & & & & & 0.04813 \end{bmatrix},$$

All three matrices will remain constant during the simulation. The elements in SITT0 are computed by taking 20% of the corresponding element in TH0 and then squaring the result. Thus, for the b_{11} coefficient this is

[28] See Kendrick (1981). CE presupposes additive uncertainty only, while QLP is deterministic (no uncertainty). However, the presence of additive uncertainty does not affect the form of the solution procedure for choosing the optimal controls (of course, it implies a different simulation method in order to generate additive uncertainty). In this sense, QLP and CE are equivalent.

[29] See Shupp (1976).

$[(0.2)\ (0.433)]^2 = 0.00749.$

To carry out the experiment, we will select the following DUALI options: *complexity*: stochastic without measurement error; *model size*: 6 uncertain parameters; *Monte Carlo runs*: 1; *options stochastic*: read in random terms, but set them (i.e. the XSIS) all equal to zero.[30]

The graphs below show the results for both the CE[31] solution obtained with "Solve: QLP" and the OLF solution obtained with "Solve: OLF".[32]

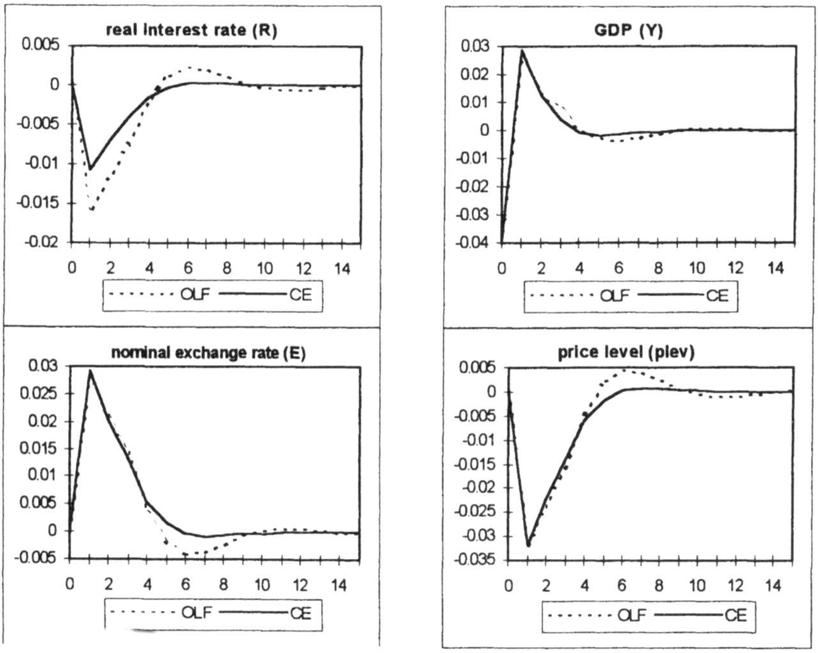

[30] See Amman and Kendrick (1996), Chapter 2.

[31] Since the only disturbance is the off-steady state initial Y value (equal to -0.04), the CE solution and the deterministic solution are completely equivalent.

[32] To run these simulations, use program htdua01.dui for the CE procedure (making the appropriate changes as described in the "Description" section in the "Data" menu) and, for the OLF procedure, use program htdua02.dui.

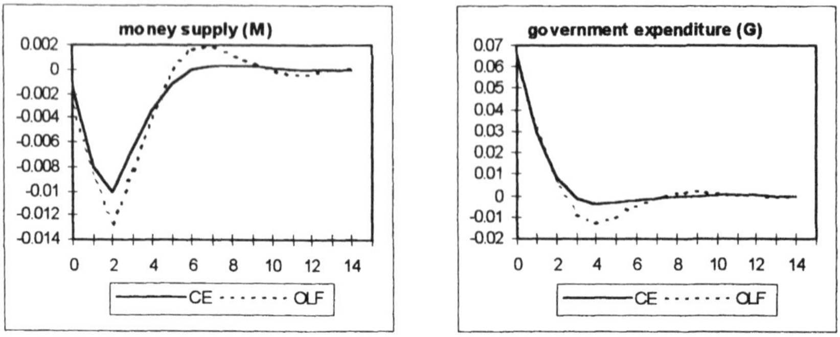

Figure 5. CE versus OLF: State and Control Variables.

Qualitatively, the patterns of behavior for both the state and policy variables appear quite similar under the two methods, though overall results are worse in the OLF case. This is not surprising, since the "quasi-deterministic" environment within which we performed the experiment does not allow the exploitation of the knowledge of the variance-covariance parameter matrix through a learning process.[33] In fact, the interest of this experiment resides in the comparison between the behavior of the policy variables across different procedures.

As can be seen in the graphs above, the use of government expenditure is slightly "more cautious" with the OLF procedure and for the first periods. This seems to be in line with the Brainard-Shupp results mentioned before. However, the reverse is true for the case of the money supply, which is used "more aggressively" with OLF. Thus, we can see how going from a univariate to a multivariate setting may have important consequences, as is also the case of a change from static to dynamic models.

It is interesting to explore the consequences of increasing the level of uncertainty of the model parameters corresponding to one of the policy variables. For example, we double the standard deviation of the parameters corresponding to government expenditure (parameters b_{12}, b_{22} and b_{42}) from 20% to 40%. Then, the SITT0 matrix becomes:

$$\text{SITT0} = \begin{bmatrix} 0.00749 & & & & & \\ & 0.00853 & & & & \\ & & 3.81264 & & & \\ & & & 3.07791 & & \\ & & & & 0.23853 & \\ & & & & & 0.19254 \end{bmatrix} \tag{3.5}$$

[33] This point will become more clear in the next section, when we compare CE versus OLF across Monte Carlo simulations with a projection-updating mechanism

The graphs below contrast the behavior of the policy variables for this experiment[34] (named OLF-B) against their behavior showed by the same variables in the experiment analyzed above (named, as above, OLF).

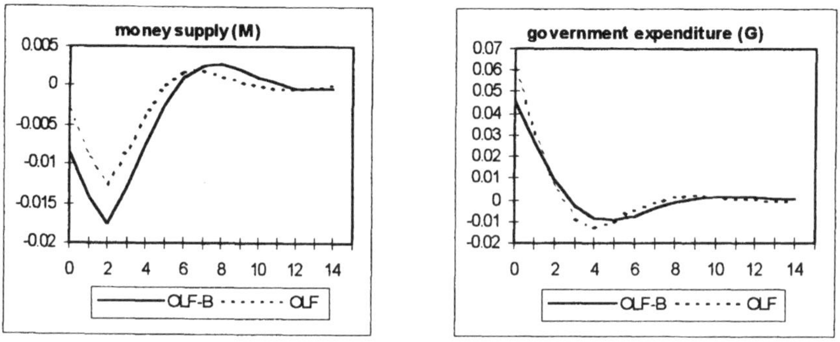

Figure 6. OLF-B versus OLF : Policy Variables.

As one could expect, the increase in the relative uncertainty of government expenditure parameters induces a more cautious use of that policy. At the same time the money supply, now with a relatively lower associated uncertainty, is used more actively. Though these findings seem plausible, they do not reflect any theoretical result, since such results are not yet available for this kind of problem. As with the previous experiments, we could perhaps find different results for a different model.

4.b.2 Quantitative Performance Comparison between CE and OLF: Control with Parameter Updating

We will now move towards a more complex stochastic environment. As in the previous section, we will assume that some of the model parameters are uncertain, but now we will also assume that the model is constantly shocked by additive noise, that the true model is not known to the policy maker, and also that a passive-learning process takes place. We will perform several Monte Carlo runs for each of the procedures (CE and OLF).[35]

The general structure of each Monte Carlo run will be as follows. At time zero, a vector of model parameters will be drawn from a normal distribution whose mean and variances are those of matrices TH0 and SITT0. Then, at each time "t", we will have:

1) random generation of a vector of an additive shocks
2) computation of the optimal controls for periods t to N (terminal period)

---

[34] To run this experiment, use program htdua02.dui, introducing the corresponding changes in the SITT0 matrix.

[35] See Amman and Kendrick (1996), Chapter 4.

3) propagation of the system one period forward (from period t to period t+1) applying the vector of controls (for period t only) computed in step 2.
4) projection-updating of next period parameters and variance-covariance matrix

For choosing the optimal control at each period (step 2) we will use either a Certainty Equivalence (CE) procedure or, alternatively, an Open Loop Feedback procedure (OLF). For the projection-updating mechanism (step 4) we will use a Kalman filter.

Thus, each Monte Carlo run begins with a vector of parameter estimates which is different from their "true" value. Using this parameter vector, the policy maker computes (with a CE or an OLF procedure) the optimal values of the controls, and then she "applies" those values corresponding to time "t" only. However, the response of the economic system (its forward movement from time "t "to time "t+1") will be generated by "the computer" using the "true" parameter values which are unknown to the policy maker. Then, at period "t+1" a new observation is made of the state vector, which is used to compute updated parameter estimates with a Kalman filter. After a number of time periods, the sequence of updated estimates will hopefully begin to converge to their "true" value.

As in the previous section, we will assume that there is uncertainty in connection with six out of the parameters in the B matrix, and that the standard deviation of each of these parameters is equal to 20%. Then, matrices TH0, SITT0 and ITHN will be the same as in Eq. 3.5. We will also assume that GDP (Y) and the price level (plev) are hit by additive shocks of 2% the standard deviation, while the real interest rate (R) and the nominal exchange rate (E) experience shocks of 5% of their standard deviations. Thus, the variance-covariance matrix of additive noises (Q), will be as follows:[36]

[36] We want the shocks to affect contemporaneous variables only, and not their lagged values. However, if we set to zero the elements of the Q matrix corresponding to lagged variables, DUALI will give us an error message. That is why we set those elements equal to the minimum possible value (0.000000001).

$$Q=\begin{bmatrix} 0.0004 \\ & 0.0025 \\ && 0.0004 \\ &&& 0.0025 \\ &&&& 0.1^{(-9)} \\ &&&&& 0.1^{(-9)} \\ &&&&&& 0.1^{(-9)} \\ &&&&&&& 0.1^{(-9)} \\ &&&&&&&& 0.1^{(-9)} \\ &&&&&&&&& 0.1^{(-9)} \\ &&&&&&&&&& 0.1^{(-9)} \\ &&&&&&&&&&& 0.1^{(-9)} \end{bmatrix} \quad (3.6)$$

The results of 100 Monte Carlo runs are shown in the table below.[37]

	CE	OLF
Average Criterion Value	5.60	5.59
Runs with Lowest Criterion	47	53

The Open Loop Feedback procedure does slightly better than the Certainty Equivalence, not only in connection with the average criterion value, but also in terms of the number of Monte Carlo runs with the lowest criterion. As can be seen in the graph below, where each diamond represents the value of the criterion function for one Monte Carlo run, most of the diamonds are close to the 45 degree line, indicating a similar performance for both procedures. There are no significant outliers that could be introducing a bias in the computed average criterion values.

[37] To run this simulation, use program htdua03.dui (see the "Description" section in the "Data" menu).

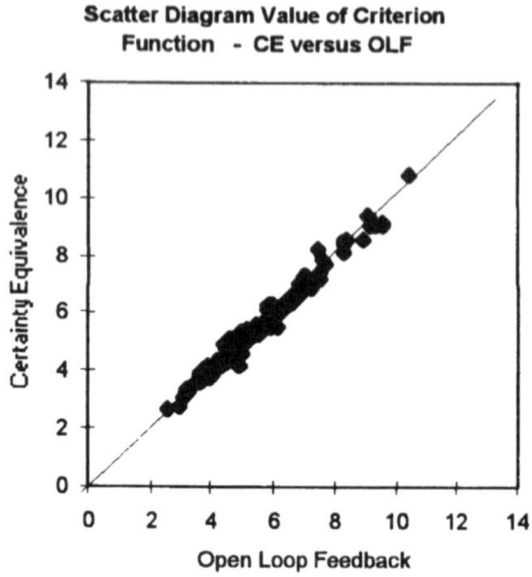

Figure 7. Scatter Diagram.

These results are against what one would intuitively expect, since in the presence of parameter uncertainty OLF should do better than CE. However, we have to mention that there are no theoretical results yet developed in connection with the relative performance of CE versus OLF. This experiment results are conditioned on the model structure, its parameter and parameter variances values, and may well change (in any direction) in a different context.[38]

5. EXTENSIONS

We presented here some basic approaches for analyzing properties of dynamic economic systems and for performing optimal policy analysis in deterministic and stochastic environments with passive learning. The next natural step would be to continue our sequence of experiments making use of active learning methods (DUAL), that is, not only using the policy variables to control the economic system but also to gain information about its structure as discussed in Kendrick (1981). Also, with suitable modifications, the analysis and experiments could be implemented using rational expectations models instead of the standard models used here as in discussed in the sibling to this paper, i.e. Mercado and Kendrick (1997c).

[38] See Amman and Kendrick (1997a). Working with a different model, they find a better performance for OLF with respect to CE.

Appendix

A.1) Matlab Program to Compute Eigenvalues

```
% Computes the eigenvalues for the A matrix for
% the linearized version of Hall and Taylor's (1993)
% macroeconomic model.

echo on;
clear;

A = [ -0.346 0 -0.606  0  0 0 0.087  0  0 0 0.087 0 ; ...
    7.811  0  13.669  0  0 0 -1.953  0  0 0 -1.953 0 ; ...
    0.8  0  1.4  0  0 0 -0.2  0  0 0 -0.2  0 ; ...
    1.154  0  2.019  0  0 0 -0.288  0  0 0 -0.288 0 ; ...
    1  0 0  0 0 0 0  0 0 0 0  0 ; ...
    0  1 0  0 0 0 0  0 0 0 0  0 ; ...
    0  0 1  0 0 0 0  0 0 0 0  0 ; ...
    0  0 0  1 0 0 0  0 0 0 0  0 ; ...
    0  0 0  0 1 0 0  0 0 0 0  0 ; ...
    0  0 0  0 0 1 0  0 0 0 0  0 ; ...
    0  0 0  0 0 0 1  0 0 0 0  0 ; ...
    0  0 0  0 0 0 0  1 0 0 0  0 ]

lambda = eig(A)
```

A.2) TSP Program to Compute Dynamic Controllabity Conditions

```
? Computes dynamic controllability for both the full
? state vector and a subset of target variables for
? the linearized version of Hall and Taylor's (1993)
?  macroeconomic model.

load (nrow=12, ncol=12,  type=general) A;
-0.346  0  -0.606  0  0  0  0.087   0  0  0  0.087   0
 7.811  0  13.669  0  0  0  -1.953  0  0  0  -1.953  0
0.8     0  1.4     0  0  0  -0.2    0  0  0  -0.2    0
1.154   0  2.019   0  0  0  -0.288  0  0  0  -0.288  0
1       0  0       0  0  0  0       0  0  0  0       0
0       1  0       0  0  0  0       0  0  0  0       0
0       0  1       0  0  0  0       0  0  0  0       0
0       0  0       1  0  0  0       0  0  0  0       0
0       0  0       0  1  0  0       0  0  0  0       0
0       0  0       0  0  1  0       0  0  0  0       0
0       0  0       0  0  0  1       0  0  0  0       0
0       0  0       0  0  0  0       1  0  0  0       0
```

```
load (nrow=12, ncol=2,type=general) B;
 0.433 0.231
-9.763 4.386
   0   0
-2.442 1.097
   0   0
   0   0
   0   0
   0   0
   0   0
   0   0
   0   0
   0   0


load (nrow=4, ncol=12, type=general) S;
   1  0  0  0  0  0  0  0  0  0  0  0
   0  1  0  0  0  0  0  0  0  0  0  0
   0  0  1  0  0  0  0  0  0  0  0  0
   0  0  0  1  0  0  0  0  0  0  0  0

print A, B, S;


mat AB = A*B;
mat A2B = (A**2)*B;
mat A3B = (A**3)*B;
mat A4B = (A**4)*B;
mat A5B = (A**5)*B;
mat A6B = (A**6)*B;
mat A7B = (A**7)*B;
mat A8B = (A**8)*B;
mat A9B = (A**9)*B;
mat A10B = (A**10)*B;
mat A11B = (A**11)*B;

mmake  P  B, AB, A2B, A3B, A4B,A5B,A6B,A7B,A8B,A9B,A10B,
A11B;

mat G = rank(P); print G;

mat R1 = S*B;
mat R2 = S*A*B;
mat R3 = S*(A**2)*B;
mat R4 = S*(A**3)*B;

mmake R  R1, R2, R3, R4;
```

```
mat M = rank(R); print M;

end;
```

REFERENCES

Amman, Hans M and David A Kendrick (1996), *The DUALI/DUALPC Software for Optimal Control Models: User's Guide*, Center for Applied Research in Economics, The University of Texas, TP 92-03, (revised September 1996).

Amman, Hans M and David A Kendrick (1997a), "Should Macroeconomic Policy Makers Consider Parameter Covariances?", Working Paper 9701, Center for Applied Research in Economics, The University of Texas, Austin, Texas.

Amman, Hans M and David A Kendrick (1997b), "The DUALI/DUALPC Software for Optimal Control Models: Introduction", in Amman, Hans M., Berc Rustem and Andrew Whinston, *Computational Approaches to Economic Problems*, Kluwer Academic Publishers, Dordrecht, The Netherlands, pp. 363-372.

Aoki, Masanao (1976), *Optimal Control and System Theory in Dynamic Economic Analysis*, North Holland.

Azariadis, Costas (1993), *Intertemporal Macroeconomics*, Blackwell Publishers Inc., Cambridge, MA.

Blanchard, Olivier and Stanley Fischer (1989), *Lectures on Macroeconomics*, The MIT Press.

Brainard, W (1969), "Uncertainty and the Effectiveness of Policy", *American Economic Review*, Vol. 57, pp. 411-425.

Chiang, A (1984), *Fundamental Methods of Mathematical Economics*, McGraw-Hill.

Chow, Gregory (1975), *Analysis and Control of Dynamic Economic Systems*, John Wiley & Sons.

Hall, Robert and John Taylor (1993), *Macroeconomics*, fourth edition, W.W. Norton & Company, New York.

Holly, Sean and Andrew Hughes Hallett, (1989), *Optimal Control, Expectations and Uncertainty*, Cambridge University Press.

Hughes Hallett, Andrew (1989), "Econometrics and the Theory of Economic Policy: the Tinbergen-Theil Contributions 40 Years On", *Oxford Economic Papers*, Vol. 41, pp. 189-214.

Kendrick, David A (1981), *Stochastic Control for Economic Models*, McGraw-Hill Book Company, New York.

Mercado, P Ruben and David A Kendrick (1997a), *HTGAMS: Hall and Taylor's Model in GAMS*, Working Paper 9704, Center for Applied Research in Economics, The University of Texas, Austin, Texas.

Mercado, P Ruben and David A Kendrick (1997b), *TAYGAMS: John Taylor's Two-Country Model in GAMS*, Working Paper 9703, Center for Applied Research in Economics, The University of Texas, Austin, Texas.

Mercado, P Ruben and David A Kendrick (1997c), *Computational Methods for Macro Policy Analysis: Taylor's Model in DUALI*, Department of Economics, The University of Texas, Austin, Texas.

Mercado, P Ruben, David A Kendrick and Hans M Amman (1997), "Teaching Macroeconomics with GAMS", *Computational Economics*, (forthcoming).

Park, Hyung Jin (1997), *A Control Theory Analysis of Macroeconomic Policy Coordination by the US, Japan and Korea*, Ph.D. Dissertation, Department of Economics, The University of Texas, Austin, Texas.

Shupp, Franklin (1976), "Uncertainty and Optimal Stabilization Policy", *Journal of Public Economics*, Vol. 6, pp. 243-253.

Tinbergen, Jan (1956), *Economic Policy: Principles and Design*, North-Holland Publishing Company, Amsterdam.

Turnovsky, Stephen J (1977), *Macroeconomic Analysis and Stabilization Policy*, Cambridge University Press.

CHAPTER 9

THE DYNAMIC ANALYSIS OF FORWARD-LOOKING MODELS[1]

Michel Juillard

This paper discusses the computation and interpretation of eigenvalues of forward-looking models. It expands results already present in Blanchard and Kahn (1980) to the case where there are singularities in the dynamics of the model. Anderson and Moore (1985) had proposed an iterative procedure based on successive singular value and QR decompositions. We introduce here a direct application of generalized eigenvalue methods.[2] Finally, the paper presents an application of this methodology to discuss monetary policy rules in the framework of Fuhrer and Moore (1995) model.

1. EIGENVALUES AND DYNAMIC PROPERTIES OF A MODEL

For linear models, it is well known that their dynamical properties are nicely summarized by the eigenvalues of the transition matrix of the system. For non-linear models, it is always possible to linearize them around some reference state (stationary or steady state, for example). The eigenvalues of the resulting linear model let us then characterize the dynamical properties of the original non-linear model locally, in the neighbourhood of the reference trajectory.

We will therefore pursue the discussion only for linear models. Furthermore, as any linear dynamical model of order greater than one can be transformed into a larger model of order one through the addition of suitable auxiliary variables and equations, we will only discuss linear dynamical models of order one.

Once it is established that the model has a reference state, the eigenvalues inform us of three aspects of the model dynamics:

- whether this reference state is stable;
- whether, after a shock away from the reference state of a stable model, the system goes back to the stationary state in a monotonic manner or with damped cycles;
- what is the speed of convergence back to stationary state.

---

[1] I thank Douglas Laxton and Pierre Malgrange for many suggestions in the preparation of this paper. I remain however sole responsible for any remaining errors.

[2] See Klein (1997) and Sims (1997) for other applications of generalized eigenvalues methods to rational expectations models.

At this point, it is necessary to make a distinction between traditional, backward looking, models and models with explicit expectations. In backward-looking models, shocks will only affect the future trajectory of the variables. In forward-looking models, the expectation of future shocks will alter agents' behavior and shocks will modify the trajectory of the variables before and after they occur.

In what follows, we will briefly discuss the eigenvalues of a backward looking model, then turn to forward-looking models.

1.1 Backward-looking Models

We consider models of the form

$$y_{t+1} = Ay_t + Bx_t \qquad t = t_0,\dots,\infty$$

where y is the vector of endogenous variables and x a vector of exogenous variables.[3] A and B are matrices of parameters. Because of formal resemblance with the state-space model representation one sometimes refers to A as the transition matrix.

When the exogenous variables have constant value, $x_t = \bar{x}$, a stationary state exists for this model if and only if (I-A) is non-singular. Let $\bar{y}$ be this stationary state:

$$\bar{y} = (I - A)^{-2} B\bar{x}$$

Given initial conditions y_{t_0}, the final form of the model is

$$y_t = A^t y_{t_0} + \sum_{i=t_0}^{t-1} A^{t-i-1} Bx_i$$

Let's imagine a single shock away from stationary state in period t':

$$x_t = \bar{x} \qquad t \neq t'$$
$$x_t = \bar{x} + \Delta x_{t'} \qquad t = t'$$

In this case, the deviation of stationary state, $\Delta y_t = y_t - \bar{y}$ is described by:

$$\Delta y_t = 0 \qquad t < t'$$
$$\Delta y_t = A^{t-t'-1} \Delta x_{t'} \qquad t \geq t'$$

---

[3] We could also consider lagged values of some exogenous variables, but it would only complicate the presentation without adding anything.

Obviously, this system will converge back to stationary state if and only if all the eigenvalues of A are inside the unit circle, so as $\lim_{t\to\infty} A^t = 0$.

It is also evident that the shock will have effects only at the time of the shock and thereafter, but that there will be no anticipation of it. The nature of the response to this shock depends on the shock itself, $\Delta x_{t'}$, and on the eigenvalues of A.

To see how, let's consider the Jordan decomposition of matrix A:

$$A = C^{-1}JC$$

When matrix A is nondefective, the matrix $P = C^{-1}$ contains its eigenvectors that make a basis for R^n and the vector $B\Delta x_{t'}$ can be expressed as a linear combination of these eigenvectors.

$$B\Delta x_{t'} = P\gamma$$

where γ is the vector of coefficients of $B\Delta x_{t'}$ expressed in basis P.

The shock response is therefore function of some or all of the eigenvalues of A.

$$\begin{aligned} A^{t-t'-1}B\Delta x_{t'} &= PJ^{t-t'-1}P^{-1}P\gamma \\ &= \sum_{i=1}^{n} \lambda_i^{t-t'-1}\gamma_i P_i \end{aligned}$$

Whether the dynamics of the model depends on eigenvalue λ_i is determined by whether eigenvector P_i contributes to $\Delta x_{t'}$.

A real positive eigenvalue generates a monotonic component to the trajectory of y_t, a real negative eigenvalue generates saw like oscillations changing sign every period and a pair of complex eigenvalues make for sinusoidal damped cycles, as long as their modulus is smaller than one.

The speed of convergence depends on the eigenvalue with the largest modulus. For example, half of the shock effect generated through the leading eigenvalue will have dissipated in k periods:

$$k = 1 - \frac{\ln 2}{\ln \lambda_1}$$

1.2 Purely Forward-looking Models

In the previous model, agents react in adaptive manner to previous events and the variables at time t depends on their value at time t-1. We can however use the same type of model to represent anticipatory behavior where agents react to what they expect future events will be. If we assume perfect foresight, variables at time t will depend on their value at time t+1. We can just use the previous model backwards:

$$y_t = A^{-1} (y_{t+1} - Bx_t)$$

In such a model, the past has no influence on the future: there is no inertia. Expected future shocks have effects on the present until they are realized, but none thereafter. Let's assume, as in the previous section, that the exogenous variables x_t are constant through time, except for a shock in period t'. As before, the equilibrium position is

$$\bar{y} = (I - A)^{-1} B\bar{x}$$

As the shock is fully anticipated, the system will immediately go back to equilibrium after it. For the periods before the shock, the trajectory of the system is given by

$$\begin{aligned} \Delta y_t &= A^{t-t'-1} B \Delta x_{t'} & \quad t \le t' \\ \Delta y_t &= 0 & \quad t > t' \end{aligned}$$

If we consider that the future shock has not always been known, but that it is learned at some date t_0 previous to its realization at date t' and that the system was in equilibrium until then, then the variables y will show a discrete jump at date t_0:

$$\begin{aligned} \Delta y_t &= 0 & \quad t < t_0 \\ \Delta y_t &= A^{t-t'-1} B \Delta x_{t'} & \quad t_0 \le t \le t' \\ \Delta y_t &= 0 & \quad t' < t \end{aligned}$$

Note that once the future shock is known, the trajectory is always the same, independently of when the shock has been known. In particular, if the shock is unexpected (t_0 = t') the agents will instantaneously react in such a way as to bring back the system in equilibrium in the next period (t'+1).

In the above formula, t-t'-1 is always negative. Therefore, if the eigenvalues of A are larger than one in modulus, the anticipatory reaction will be smaller the further away in the future the shock is expected. On the contrary, if some roots of A are smaller than one, the anticipatory reaction will be larger and larger as the shock is further away in the future, which is obviously not a stable characteristic. The conditions for stability are reversed in the forward-looking and in the backward-looking case.

1.3 Backward and Forward-looking Models

In forward-looking models, the behavioral equations take into account agents' expectations about the future values of some of the variables. In the spirit of rational expectation models, we assume that agents' expectations are model consistent. In the deterministic set up, which is used in this paper, it is equivalent to perfect foresight models.

In complete models with both backward and forward dynamics, inertia and anticipatory mechanisms discussed above are at work.

A generic structural form of such a model, limited to one period forward and one period backward,[4] is:

$$F_+ y^*_{t+1} + F_0 y_t + F\_ y^*_{t-1} + F_x x_t = 0$$

The dynamics of variables y_t depend here on adjustment mechanisms transmitted through lagged variables y_{t-1} and on expectations about the future expressed by y_{t+1}. In most models, only some variables will appear with lag, we will note them as the subvector y*, or with lead, noted y**. Of course a given variable can be common to both subvectors or not appear in either set. In the latter case, we will call it a static variable, as it will not affect the dynamics of the model.

To study the dynamics of such a model, it is helpful to rewrite it as a system of difference equations of the first order. As it is shown in Appendix A, this model can easily be rearranged in the form

$$Dz_{t+1} = Ez_t + Bx_t$$

where

$$z_t = \begin{bmatrix} y^*_{t-1} \\ y^{**}_t \end{bmatrix}$$

and y* represents the variables in y actually present in the model at lag t-1 and y**, the variables present in the model at lead t+1.

Again, for a given level of the exogenous variables, a unique stationary state exists if (D-E) is non-singular:

$$\bar{z} = (D - E)^{-1} B\bar{x}$$

The eigenvalues of the above system, λ_i, must satisfy $\lambda_i D x_i = E x_i$. It is a generalized eigenvalue problem (see, for example, Golub and Van Loah, 1989, ch. 7.7). When D is not singular, λ_i is simply eigenvalue of $A = D^{-1}E$, as in the previous section. When D is singular, the effective dynamical order is less than the order of D and E. It is the case, when one uses forward variables that are linked through static relationships elsewhere in the model. This redundant use of forward variables is very frequent in macroeconometric models, as it permits a much clearer writing of structural relationships.

---

[4] There is no loss of generality in considering only second order difference models can be written in lower order difference form with the introduction of auxiliary variables.

A deeper understanding of the problem is obtained from the generalized real Schur decomposition (Golub and Van Loan, 1989, p. 396): if D and E are in $R^{n\times n}$ then there exist orthogonal matrices Q and Z such that Q'EZ = S and Q'DZ = T are upper triangular. Then the generalized eigenvalues are defined as $\lambda_i = S_{ii}/T_{ii}$. If for some i, $T_{ii} = S_{ii} = 0$, then any complex number is a generalized eigenvalue. Otherwise, $T_{ii} = 0$ and $S_{ii} \neq 0$ corresponds to an infinite eigenvalue.

When D is singular, some of the T_{ii} will be equal to zero and will correspond to infinite eigenvalues. Remember now from the previous section that eigenvalues larger than one control the anticipatory reactions to a future shock. An infinite eigenvalue describes an instantaneous anticipatory reaction, as a null eigenvalue describes an instantaneous adjustment towards the future. Neither of them affects the dynamics of the model.

In light of the previous development, the Blanchard and Kahn (1980) condition for the existence and unicity of trajectory in such model must be expressed as the equality between the number of eigenvalues larger than one in modulus and the number of *independent* forward variables.[5] Alternatively, when compared to the number of forward variables appearing in the model, infinite eigenvalues should be counted with the eigenvalues larger than one in modulus.

Furthermore, even when matrix D is singular, it is possible, using the generalized Schur form, to rewrite the model in canonical form (see Appendix B).

$$z_{t+1} = Az_t + \sum_{i=0}^{k} B_{(i)} x_{t+1}$$

where k is the dimension of the null space of D. This transformation is possible for all models with a unique equilibrium and for models with unit roots in the dynamics. We can then proceed to the discussion of stability conditions as in the previous cases.

As this model is a mixture of backward and forward-looking processes, it is necessary to partition the model to put them in evidence. Following Blanchard and Kahn (1980) we use a Jordan decomposition of matrix A:

$$A = C^{-1} J C$$

where matrix J contains on its main diagonal the eigenvalues of A in increasing order. Let's also consider the following partition of vector $z_t = \lfloor y^{*}_{t-1}{}' \; y^{**}_t{}' \rfloor$ where y^{*}_{t-1} represents the predetermined variables in z_t (the ones with an initial condition) and y^{**}_t, the forward-looking variables (with a terminal condition). Matrix A is also partitioned accordingly:

[5] There is a numerical accuracy problem in deciding how small a S_{ii} must be considered as null. Note that this does not affect the evaluation of the Blanchard and Kahn condition as for each eigenvalue that we consider infinite we reduce the number of independent forward variables by one.

$$\begin{bmatrix} A_{11} & A_{12} \\ A_{21} & A_{22} \end{bmatrix} = \begin{bmatrix} C_{11} & C_{12} \\ C_{21} & C_{22} \end{bmatrix}^{-1} \begin{bmatrix} J_1 & 0 \\ 0 & J_2 \end{bmatrix} \begin{bmatrix} C_{11} & C_{12} \\ C_{21} & C_{22} \end{bmatrix}$$

where J_1 contains the eigenvalues of A smaller than 1 in modulus and J_2, the eigenvalues larger[6] than 1. In addition, the two blocks in the first column of C corresponds to the predetermined variables y^*_{t-1} and the second column to the forward-looking variables y^{**}_t. Let's also define

$$C^{-1} = P = \begin{bmatrix} P_{11} & P_{12} \\ P_{21} & P_{22} \end{bmatrix}$$

As Blanchard and Khan (1980) have shown there exists a unique solution path for this model if and only if there are as many forward-looking variables as there are eigenvalues larger than one in modulus and sub-matrix P_{11} is invertible.

Several cases should be considered here, depending on the horizon of the simulation and the date of learning of the future shock. The simplest case mathematically is when the future shock has always been known since the beginning of times ($t_0 \to -\infty$) and the simulation has an infinite horizon. Next, we consider the case where the shock is learned a finite number of periods before its realization, but the simulation still has an infinite horizon. Finally, we discuss what happens with a finite simulation horizon.

1.3.1 Shock always known and infinite simulation horizon

The shock $\Delta x_{t'}$ occurs in period t' and the trajectory for Δy^*_t and Δy^{**}_t is[7]

$$\Delta y^*_t = -P_{12} \sum_{i=0}^{k} J_2^{t-t'-k} C_{2\bullet} B_{(i)} \Delta x_{t'} \qquad t \le t'$$

$$\Delta y^{**}_t = -P_{22} \sum_{i=0}^{k} J_2^{t-t'-k-1} C_{2\bullet} B_{(i)} \Delta x_{t'}$$

$$\Delta y^*_t = -P_{11} \sum_{i=0}^{k} J_1^{t-t'-k} C_{1\bullet} B_{(i)} \Delta x_{t'} \qquad t > t'$$

$$\Delta y^{**}_t = -P_{22} \sum_{i=0}^{k} J_1^{t-t'-k-1} C_{1\bullet} B_{(i)} \Delta x_{t'}$$

---

[6] As we are going to use this decomposition to discuss stability, we exclude the case of eigenvalues equal to one which would obviously preclude stability.

[7] The derivation of these properties is available from the author upon request.

In this case, the trajectory of the system before the shock is only driven by the eigenvalues larger than one and by the eigenvalues smaller than one after the shock.

1.3.2 The future shock is learned sometime before its realization and there is an infinite simulation horizon

Let's assume as before that the shock $\Delta x_{t'}$ occurs in period t', but now it is only known at period t_0. Until then the system was at equilibrium. The trajectory is then

$$M1_t = P_{11} J_1^{t-t_0+1} P_{11}^{-1} P_{12} \sum_{i=0}^{k} J_2^{t_0-t'-k-1} C_{2\bullet} B_{(i)} \Delta x_{t'}$$

$$M2_t = P_{21} J_1^{t-t_0} P_{11}^{-1} P_{12} \sum_{i=0}^{k} J_2^{t_0-t'-k-1} C_{2\bullet} B_{(i)} \Delta x_{t'}$$

$$\Delta y_t^{*} = -P_{12} \sum_{i=0}^{k} J_2^{t-t'-k} C_{2\bullet} B_{(i)} \Delta x_{t'} + M1_t \qquad t \le t'$$

$$\Delta y_t^{**} = -P_{22} \sum_{i=0}^{k} J_2^{t-t'-k-1} C_{2\bullet} B_{(i)} \Delta x_{t'} + M2_t$$

$$\Delta y_t^{*} = -P_{11} \sum_{i=0}^{k} J_1^{t-t'-k} C_{1\bullet} B_{(i)} \Delta x_{t'} + M1_t \qquad t > t'$$

$$\Delta y_t^{**} = -P_{21} \sum_{i=0}^{k} J_1^{t-t'-k} C_{1\bullet} B_{(i)} \Delta x_{t'} + M2_t$$

The terms $M1_t$ and $M2_t$ express the jump in behavior when the future shock is known and its consequences in following periods because of inertia.

One case see from the above formulas that as the interval between the news of the future shock and its realization increases, one tends towards the trajectory of the first case. At the date when the shock is learned, there is a sudden anticipatory reaction, which will have consequences in future periods.

1.3.3 The future shock is learned some time before its realization and the simulation horizon is finite

In practical work, it is not possible to compute a simulation on an infinite horizon. We assume here that we constrain the system to be back to equilibrium in period T, the trajectories are then as follows:

$$M = \left((_{11} - P_{12} J_2^{t_0-T} P_{22}^{-1} P_{21} J_1^{T-t_0}\right)^{-1}$$

$$M1_t = \left(P_{11} J_1^{t-t_0+1} - P_{12} J_2^{t-T+1} P_{22}^{-1} P_{21} J_1^{T-t_0}\right) M P_{12} \sum_{i=0}^{k} J_2^{t_0-t'-k-1} C_{2\bullet} B_{(i)} \Delta x_{t'}$$

$$M2_t = \left(P_{21} J_1^{t-t_0} - P_{22} J_2^{t-T+1} P_{22}^{-1} P_{21} J_1^{T-t_0}\right) M P_{12} \sum_{i=0}^{k} J_2^{t_0-t'-k-1} C_{2\bullet} B_{(i)} \Delta x_{t'}$$

$$N1_t = \left[P_{12} J_2^{t-T+1} - \left(P_{11} J_1^{t-t_0+1} - P_{12} J_2^{t-T+1} P_{22}^{-1} P_{21} J_1^{T-t_0}\right) M P_{12} J_2^{t_0-T}\right] P_{22}^{-1} P_{21} \sum_{i=0}^{k} J_1^{t'-t_0-k} C_{1\bullet} B_{(i)} \Delta x_{t'}$$

$$N2_t = \left[P_{22} J_2^{t-T} - \left(P_{21} J_1^{t-t_0} - P_{22} J_2^{t-T} P_{22}^{-1} P_{21} J_1^{T-t_0}\right) M P_{12} J_2^{t_0-T}\right] P_{22}^{-1} P_{21} \sum_{i=0}^{k} J_1^{t'-t_0-k} C_{1\bullet} B_{(i)} \Delta x_{t'}$$

$$\Delta y_t^{*} = -P_{12} \sum_{i=0}^{k} J_2^{t-t'-k} C_{2\bullet} B_{(i)} \Delta x_{t'} + M1_t - N1_t \qquad t_0 < t \le t'$$

$$\Delta y_t^{**} = -P_{22} \sum_{i=0}^{k} J_2^{t-t'-k-1} C_{2\bullet} B_{(i)} \Delta x_{t'} + M2_t - N2_t$$

$$\Delta y_t^{*} = -P_{11} \sum_{i=0}^{k} J_1^{t-t'-k} C_{1\bullet} B_{(i)} \Delta x_{t'} + M1_t - N1_t \qquad t' < t \le T$$

$$\Delta y_t^{**} = -P_{21} \sum_{i=0}^{k} J_1^{t-t'-k-1} C_{1\bullet} B_{(i)} \Delta x_{t'} + M2_t - N2_t$$

The basic mechanisms is still at work: eigenvalues with modulus larger than one determines the anticipatory dynamics in the system between the time the shock is realized and eigenvalues with modulus smaller than one dictates the inertia after the shock. In addition fixing initial conditions and terminal conditions to be at the stationary state influence now the dynamics. Close examination of the above formulas reveals that this influence decreases with the delay between the news and the realization of the shock ($t'-t_0$) and with the horizon of simulation after the shock ($T-t'$).

In the following section, I apply this methodology to discuss the dynamic properties of a simple monetary policy model with various policy rules.

2. THE FUHRER-MOORE MODEL

Fuhrer and Moore (1995) suggest a simple structural model on a quarterly basis to discuss monetary policy and provide the following estimation. The output gap between actual and potential output, $\tilde{y}_t$, depends on its past values and long-term interest rate, ρ_t, lagged one period.

$$\tilde{y}_t = .008 + 1.34\tilde{y}_{t-1} - .372\tilde{y}_{t-2} - .36\rho_{t-1}$$

The persistence of inflation in the economy is explained through the existence of overlapping nominal contracts. By assumption, these contracts remain in effect four quarters. The aggregate log price index in quarter t, p_t, is a weighted average of the log contract prices, x_t, which were negotiated in the current and the previous three periods:

$$p_t = \sum_{i=0}^{3} f_i x_{t-i}$$

with weights

$$f_0 = .3715 \quad f_1 = .2905 \quad f_2 = .2095 \quad f_3 = .1285$$

The index of real contract prices, v_t, is given by

$$v_t = \sum_{i=0}^{3} f_i (x_{t-i} - p_{t-i})$$

Agents negotiate nominal contract prices so that the current real contract price is equal to the average expected in the future and adjusted for excess demand conditions:

$$x_t - p_t = \sum_{i=0}^{3} f_i E_t (v_{t+i} + .008\tilde{y}_{t+i})$$

The relation between the long-term and the short-term rates of interest is given by the intertemporal arbitrage condition where one assumes that the bond duration is 40 quarters.

$$\rho_t - 40\,[E_t(\rho_{t+1}) - \rho_t] = r_t - E_t\,(\pi_{t+1})$$

where r_t is the short-term nominal rate of interest and π_t is the annual rate of inflation.

$$\pi_t = 4(p_t - p_{t-1})$$

A monetary policy rule closes the model by representing the way monetary authorities set the short-term interest rate in reaction to changes in inflation and output gap. In the following section, the dynamic properties of the model are studied for various policy rules. For each type of rule, the eigenvalues of the model are computed and stability is discussed.

2.1 The Policy Rule Estimated by Fuhrer and Moore

In their article, Fuhrer and Moore provide also the estimated parameters of the policy rule followed by the Federal Reserve Bank:

$$\Delta r_t = .003 + .126\Delta r_{t-1} - .397\Delta r_{t-2} + .060\pi_{t-2} - .116\pi_{t-3} + .102\tilde{y}_t$$

It contains an interest smoothing mechanism and represents a *lean against the wind* policy as it raises short term nominal interest rate when inflation or the output gap is above target. The eigenvalues of this model are reported in the table below.

Table 1. Eigenvalues of the Model with the Estimated Rule.[8]

Real	Imaginary	Magnitude	Period
-2.010	2.492	3.201	2.8
1.145	0.000	1.145	
1.000	0.000	1.000	
0.956	0.141	0.967	42.9
0.862	0.000	0.862	
0.063	0.627	0.630	4.3
-0.269	0.364	0.452	2.8
0.393	0.000	0.393	
-0.196	0.243	0.312	2.8

In addition to the four eigenvalues larger than one reported in Table 1, there are four infinite eigenvalues that make eight eigenvalues with a modulus larger than one. As there are eight forward variables $(v_{t+1}\ v_{t+2}\ v_{t+3}\ \tilde{y}_{t+1}\ \tilde{y}_{t+2}\ \tilde{y}_{t+3}\ \pi_{t+1}\ \rho_{t+1})$, the condition of Blanchard and Kahn is verified: there is a unique stable trajectory. The presence of a unit root in the system means that the price variables do not go back to their original level, as it is inflation which is controlled for in the policy rule, not the price level.

2.2 The Taylor Rule

Monetary authorities modify the interest rate so as to bring back the economy to targeted inflation, paying attention to the output gap:

$$r_t = \pi_t^* + \bar{\rho} + .5(\pi_t^* - \bar{\pi}) + .5\tilde{y}_t$$

where π_t^* is the observed inflation rate over the previous four quarters, $\bar{\pi}$, the target inflation rate, and $\bar{\rho}$, an "equilibrium" real interest rate compatible with the steady state.[9]

---

[8] Only one of the two conjugate complex eigenvalues is reported in the table.

Table 2. Eigenvalues of the Model with a Taylor Rule.

Real	Imaginary	Magnitude	Period
-2.010	2.492	3.201	2.8
1.090	0.051	1.091	133.6
1.000	0.000	1.000	
0.895	0.088	0.899	64.1
-0.269	0.364	0.452	2.8
0.396	0.000	0.396	
-0.196	0.243	0.312	2.8

In addition to the ones reported in Table 2, there are four infinite eigenvalues that make eight eigenvalues with a modulus larger than one. As before there are eight forward variables and the condition of Blanchard and Kahn is verified.

The rule estimated by Fuhrer and Moore and the Taylor rules differ only by the form of the function of reaction to inflation and the output gap. The former supposes a richer dynamical response with more parameters. If we compare the size of the eigenvalue immediately below one, one can see that with the Taylor rule it is smaller, $|\lambda_1| = .899$, than with the estimated rule, $|\lambda_1| = .967$. As this eigenvalue controls the speed of return to equilibrium after a shock, one can conclude that the Taylor rule, which implies a stronger reaction to inflation, generates a faster return to steady state than the estimated rule.

2.3 Constant Nominal Interest Rate

What will be the behavior of the model, if the monetary authorities keep the nominal interest rate constant without considerations for inflation or real output? In this case the monetary rule is simply to set the nominal interest rate exogenous.

Table 3. Eigenvalues of a Model with a Constant Nominal Interest Rate.

Real	Imaginary	Magnitude	Period
-2.010	2.492	3.201	2.8
1.147	0.000	1.147	
1.000	0.000	1.000	
0.984	0.137	0.993	45.4
0.857	0.000	0.857	
0.269	0.363	0.452	2.8
0.393	0.000	0.393	
-0.196	0.243	0.312	2.8

[9] As the model is linear in its variables, its dynamic properties do not depend on the value of the target variables. Therefore they have been set for zero for the computation of the eigenvalues.

The model still has four infinite eigenvalues, but, as Table 3 indicates, there are only three other eigenvalues with modulus larger than one. With four independent forward-looking variables, the Blanchard-Kahn condition is not met. There are more forward-looking variables than eigenvalues outside the unit circle, therefore there is an infinity of stable trajectories. One possible interpretation of this result is to consider that a pegged interest rate policy does not anchor agent's expectations regarding future inflation.

2.4 Constant Long Term Real Rate

For the sake of argument, one can go one step further and imagine that the monetary authorities somehow manage to keep the long-term interest rate constant. Then, there is no more feedback of the monetary conditions on the real economy.

Table 4. Eigenvalues of a Model with a Constant Long-term Real Interest Rate

Real	Imaginary	Magnitude	Period
-2.010	2.492	3.202	2.8
1.000	0.000	1.000	
1.000	0.000	1.000	
1.000	0.000	1.000	
0.947	0.000	0.947	
-0.269	0.364	0.452	2.8
0.393	0.000	0.393	
-0.196	0.243	0.312	2.8

Table 4 reports only two eigenvalues are larger than one, for three independent forward-looking variables and four redundancies. As with a constant nominal interest rate, there is an infinity of stable trajectories. In addition, because of the separation between the real and nominal spheres, there are now three unit roots in the nominal variables.

3. CONCLUSION

In this paper, we use generalized eigenvalues to solve perfect foresight linear models. This approach delivers direct solutions even when there are singularities in the dynamics, an occurrence very frequent in applied work. In addition, it provides us with algorithms, which can be readily implemented[10] in simulation programs.

As was illustrated with the discussion of various monetary rules, looking at eigenvalues permits a broad characterization of the dynamics of a given model before resorting to actual simulation.

---

[10] The methodology described in this paper is used to compute eigenvalues in TROLL and DYNARE (Juillard, 1996).

REFERENCES

Anderson, G and G Moore (1985), "A Linear Algebraic Procedure for Solving Linear Perfect Foresight Models", *Economics Letters*, Vol. 17, pp. 247-252.

Blanchard, O and C Kahn (1980), "The Solution of Linear Difference Models under Rational Expectations", *Econometrica*, Vol. 48, pp. 1305-1311.

Golub, G and C Van Loan (1989), *Matrix Computations*. The John Hopkins University Press, Baltimore.

Fuhrer, J and G Moore (1995), "Monetary Policy Trade-offs and the Correlation between Nominal Interest Rates and Real Output", *American Economic Review*, Vol. 85 (1), pp. 219-39.

Juillard, M (1996), "DYNARE: A Program for the Resolution and Simulation of Dynamic Models with Forward Variables through the Use of a Relaxation Algorithm", CEPREMAP Working paper No. 9602, Paris.

Klein, P (1997), "Using the Generalized Schur Form to Solve a System of Linear Expectational Difference Equations", Institute for Economic Studies, Stockholm University.

Sims, C (1997), "Solving Linear Rational Expectations Models", Yale University.

APPENDIX A: THE STATE SPACE REPRESENTATION

In order to compute the eigenvalues of a model, it has first to be put in state space form. Let's consider the following model in structural form:

$$F_{+}y^{**}_{t+1} + F_{0}y_{t} + F^{*}_{t-1} + F_{x}x_{t} = 0$$

In general, not all variables appear at all leads or lags. Furthermore, some variables are static, meaning that they do not appear with leads or lags. These variables do not matter for the dynamic of the system and can be eliminated in the following manner.

Each equation of the original model can be normalized so as to have a different variable with a coefficient of one. It is possible to obtain such a renormalization of the model by premultiplying the system by the inverse of the matrix of coefficients on current variables, F_0,

$$F_0^{-1}F_{+}y^{**}_{t+1} + y_{t} + F_0^{-1}F^{*}_{t-1} + F_0^{-1}F_{x}x_{t} = 0$$

In the above system, static variables do not appear in the determination of dynamic variables. It is therefore possible to eliminate the equations pertaining to static variables. The selection of rows of the above system can be obtained by premultiplying the system with an appropriate rectangular matrix made of null and unit vectors and noted K.

To assume the state space representation, the model must be put in the following form:

$$Dz_{t+1} = Ez_{t} + Bx_{t}$$

with $x_t' = \lfloor y^{*}_{t-1}{}' \;\; y^{**}_{t}{}' \rfloor$, y^{**}_{t} contains all the variables appearing with a lead and y^{*}_{t-1}, all the variables appearing with a lag.

Having built the vector of state variables, the coefficient matrices are defined as

$$D = \begin{bmatrix} G \;\vdots\; KF_0^{-1}F_{+} \\ \hline M \end{bmatrix}, \quad E = \begin{bmatrix} -KF_0^{-1}F_{-} \;\vdots\; -H \\ \hline N \end{bmatrix} \text{ and } B = \begin{bmatrix} -KF_0^{-1}F_{x} \\ 0 \end{bmatrix}$$

where G and H are made of unit vectors corresponding to the current variables in z_{t+1} and z_t, respectively. Finally, M and N are the coefficients of the auxiliary equations specifying that some elements of z_{t+1} are equal to elements of z_t. This is the case when a variable appears in the model both with a lead and a lag.

APPENDIX B: TRANSFORMATION OF A MODEL WITH REDUNDANCIES

Let's consider the following model with forward-looking variables, written in space-state form:

$$Dz_{t+1} = Ez_t + Bx_t$$

According to the generalized Schur decomposition of the pencil <D, E>, it is always possible to find two orthogonal matrices Q and Z such that

$$D = QTZ' \text{ and } E = QSZ'$$

where S and T are triangular matrices. The generalized eigenvalues, $\lambda_i = S_{ii}/T_{ii}$, satisfy

$$\lambda_i l_i'D = l_i'E \text{ and } \lambda_i Dr_i = Er_i$$

where l_i and r_i are left, respectively right, generalized eigenvectors of D and E.

Consider the generalized Schur decomposition of the model:

$$\begin{aligned} QTZ'y_{t+1} &= QSZ'y_t + Bx_t \\ TZ'y_{t+1} &= SZ'y_t + Q'Bx_t \end{aligned}$$

If the D matrix is singular, there are some zeros on the diagonal of T. It is always possible to rearrange the system so as to put the zero diagonal elements on the bottom rows of T (see Golub and Van Loan, 1989, 7.7.5). We obtain

$$\begin{bmatrix} T_{11} & T_{12} \\ 0 & T_{22} \end{bmatrix} \begin{bmatrix} Z_1' \\ Z_2' \end{bmatrix} y_{t+1} = \begin{bmatrix} S_{11} & S_{12} \\ 0 & S_{22} \end{bmatrix} \begin{bmatrix} Z_1' \\ Z_2' \end{bmatrix} y_t + \begin{bmatrix} Q_1' \\ Q_2' \end{bmatrix} Bx_t$$

where T_{11} is a triangular matrix with non-zero elements on the diagonal and T_{22} with zeros on the diagonal. S_{11} and S_{22} are also triangular.

The second part of the system has k equations, corresponding to a null space of dimension k for D:

$$T_{22}Z_2'y_{t+1} = S_{22}Z_{22}'y_t + Q'Bx_t$$

As long as S_{22} is not singular, one can write:

$$Z_2'y_t = -\sum_{i=0}^{\infty} \left(s_{22}^{-1}T_{22}\right)^i S_{22}^{-1}Q_2'Bx_{t+i}$$

however, as $S_{22}^{-1}T_{22}$ is a matrix of order k with only zeros on the main diagonal, $\left(S_{22}^{-1}T_{22}\right)^i = 0$ for all i≥k. The singularity of D implies that the second part of the system can be solved independently of the first one:

$$Z_2'y_t = -\sum_{i=0}^{k-1}\left(S_{22}^{-1}T_{22}\right)^i S_{22}^{-1}Q_2'Bx_{t+i}$$

There exist k static relationships between the state variables. Therefore, the dynamical order of the model is less than the dimension of the state system.

With the partial solution for $Z_2'y_t$, and therefore for $Z_2'y_{t+1}$, it is possible to rewrite the original model in an equivalent form and to solve it for y_{t+1}:

$$\begin{bmatrix} T_{11} & T_{12} \\ 0 & I \end{bmatrix}\begin{bmatrix} Z_1' \\ Z_2' \end{bmatrix} y_{t+1} = \begin{bmatrix} S_{11} & S_{12} \\ 0 & 0 \end{bmatrix}\begin{bmatrix} Z_1' \\ Z_2' \end{bmatrix} y_t + \begin{bmatrix} Q_1'Bx_t \\ -\sum_{i=0}^{k-1}\left(S_{22}^{-1}T_{22}\right)^{-1} S_{22}^{-1}Q_2'Bx_{t+i+1} \end{bmatrix}$$

and

$$y_{t+1} = Z_1T_{11}^{-1}(S_{11}Z_1'+S_{12}Z_2')y_t + Z_1T_{11}^{-1}Q_1'Bx_t + \left(Z_1T_{11}^{-1}T_{12} - Z_2\right).$$
$$\sum_{i=0}^{k-1}\left(S_{22}^{-1}T_{22}\right)^i S_{22}^{-1}Q_2'Bx_{t+i+1}$$

So, even when matrix D is singular, it is possible to write the model in the canonical form:

$$y_{t+1} = Ay_t + \sum_{i=0}^{k-1} B_{(i)}x_{t+i}$$

with

$$A = Z_1T_{11}^{-1}(S_{11}Z_1'+S_{12}Z_2')$$
$$B_{(0)} = Z_1T_{11}^{-1}Q_1'B$$
$$B_{(i)} = \left(Z_1T_{11}^{-1}T_{12} - Z_2\right)\left(S_{22}^{-1}T_{22}\right)^i S_{22}^{-1}Q_2'B \quad i = 0,\ldots,k-1$$

This demonstration relies on the condition that S_{22} is non-singular. This excludes only degenerate cases: a model where S_{22} is singular does not have a unique equilibrium and this indeterminacy is not the result of a unit root in the dynamics. This results from the fact that if S_{22} is singular, so is (T-S) and the equation of the equilibrium,

$$(T - S)Z\bar{y} = Q'B\bar{x}$$

has an infinity of solutions.[11]

[11] In the case of a unit root, on the contrary, $S_{ii} = T_{ii} \neq 0$.

PART FOUR

LONG RUN AND CLOSURES IN MACRO MODELS

CHAPTER 10

THE LONG RUN IN MACRO-ECONOMIC MODELS: A GUIDE[1]

Peter McAdam

1. INTRODUCTION

Despite their relative fall from grace (Whitely, 1997) macro models still remain a common tool for policy makers in judging the relative desirability of various policy interventions and regimes. For example much of the work geared towards analysing monetary union in Europe (for example Hughes Hallett and McAdam, 1998a, b, Masson and Turtleboom, 1997) has been guided by the use of such models – both in policy and academic circles. Yet, there still remains much scepticism about their use given their relatively poor forecasting record and the confusion regarding the interpretation of the long run features of these models. Often, particularly among non-modellers, there is misunderstanding as to why for example increases in government expenditure or technical progress may not have long run implications for real variables. The purpose of this paper is to elucidate the long run properties of models, which are well, if implicitly, known by modelling teams but obscure to those outside the field.

We discuss therefore why modellers incorporate explicit long run properties into their models and the consequences and trade-offs such practises bring. The paper is organised as follows: in Section 2 we sketch the reasons why modellers are interested in solving their models over a long run; in Section 3 we define the algebraic concept of the long run; in Section 4 we specify the key decisions in constructing the extended base on which a model operates and discuss these in relation to an encompassing model in Section 5. Section 6 offers conclusions.[2]

2. THE REASONS FOR MODELLING THE LONG RUN

The reasons for specific attention to the long run may be roughly categorised as follows:

---

[1] With the usual disclaimer, I'm very grateful to Andy Dickerson, Andrew Hughes Hallett, Werner Roeger and Jan in 't Veld for helpful comments and suggestions.

[2] Throughout this paper, I use the terms 'steady state' and 'long run' interchangeably. To illustrate, the long run of the model presented later in the text would involve either collapsing its dynamics (solving for the steady state version) or solving the full dynamic model over an extended simulation horizon (long run); the two methods need not be equivalent. However though model builders may not keep a separate steady-state version they will be aware of and refine its long run properties of their full model; hence the words highlight the same objective.

(1) Often modellers seek to contribute to the *policy debate*. Thus models are geared towards examination both of the immediate and long run consequences of alternative scenarios – e.g. whether chosen policy innovations permanently affect growth or foreign indebtedness or exchange rates etc. Indeed a model which, say, does not incorporate the Government Budget constraint, reaction functions to maintain fiscal solvency, homogeneity restrictions or various identities would generate what might be regarded as fundamentally unsound policy advice. In that respect, modellers' attention to long run concerns have made clear the inherent instability of permanent bond finance, the need to finance higher steady state debt via a trade surplus, or the inability to target real interest rates etc.

(2) Examining the long run can often be a good *diagnostic* device. For example, models which are stable and plausible over a "short" horizon may not exhibit such properties over a longer run. Possible instabilities in the model might be drowned out in short run but not so in the long run; this may necessarily limit their relevance for short-run examination but will invalidate their long run use. For example, Wallis and Whitely (1987) found difficulty solving the steady state version of the City University Business School model which required, amongst other things, changes in the long run deficit financing pattern and a re-modelling of the production function. Similarly, Masson (1987) reports that, when constructing the steady state of MiniMod, finding the 'correct' marginal propensity to consume out of wealth was crucial to building a stable steady state version.

Solving and constructing a model's steady state can illuminate inconsistencies, as would be the case if various homogeneity restrictions do not hold. For example, lack of price homogeneity would imply that money has real long-term effects - a proposition that the model-builder might not support or intend.

(3) This concentration on long run issues itself reflects *dissatisfaction with older models* which typically focused on short run or demand features. Brayton *et al.* (1997) discuss the greater concentration on the supply side of the Federal Reserve's models after events like the first oil shock and the 'breakdown' of the Phillips curve (see also Whitely, 1997). This refocus has prompted more work on theoretical foundations such as microeconomic life cycle features, a greater awareness of policy issues/closures and the inclusion of Rational Expectations to avoid systematic errors in agents' forecasts etc.

(4) The derivation of a model's long run characteristics facilitates *comparison between other models*, smaller (or single) equation studies or economic theory in general. This is particularly so if that comparison is over certain key parameters; for example one might expect models to have long run unit elasticities in their money demand-income and their consumption-wealth relationships. Models, which generated non-standard results, would therefore be forced to explain and rationalise those differences. For example, in deriving the long run of the Bank Of England's small Monetary Model, Currie (1982) comments on the fact that in the long run, money

demand depends positively on long run inflation (rather than negatively as theory implies) and that the demand for public sector debt is inconsistent with a long-run stock/flow equilibrium.

(5) The construction of a model's steady state facilitates the setting of *terminal conditions* for the full dynamic model. The model is shocked and the resulting long run path of the jump variables is examined. Subsequent simulations can then be set with the 'correct' terminal conditions in place.

The inclusion of Rational Expectations (RE) itself has contributed towards a better understanding and modelling of the long run. RE models tend to advance the effect of long run shocks - since lead variables jump onto the saddle path which thereafter move the model to the equilibrium - and so it is important for RE models to have more sensible and identifiable long run properties than, say, backward looking models. To ensure a unique solution we know that models with forward looking variables - if in linear difference form - should have as many unstable roots (i.e. eigenvalues with roots outside the unit circle) as lead variables (Blanchard and Kahn, 1980). Moreover, a variable's terminal condition should be its steady state solution with the convergence to that steady state governed by the stable root of the system or equation. On a large (highly disaggregated) non-linear model however, it might not be possible to derive the analytical solution for the lead variables and steady state. In this case, arbitrary terminal conditions may be a substitute and the model solved over a sufficiently long horizon that the nature and specification of the terminal conditions do not unduly affect the initial jump in the lead variables.[3]

3. THE CONCEPT OF THE LONG RUN

In this Section, we review some well-known stability properties for single and multi equation models. Consider the general auto-regressive distributed lag (ADL) equation:

$$A(L)Y_t = B(L)X_t + V_t \tag{1}$$

Where A and B are finite polynomials in the lag operator L:

$$A(L) = 1 - \sum_{i=1}^{I} \alpha_i L^i \text{ and } \quad B(L) = \sum_{j=0}^{J} \gamma_j L^j .$$

and V_t are well-behaved residuals.

[3] However the popular Fair-Taylor (1983) algorithm provides a way of solving for the 'true' terminal conditions by iteratively extending the simulation horizon. A Type I iterative layer solves the model for fixed expectations terms and a second layer equates the expectations variables and the solution from the first layer. After these layers, the solution period is extended for a set period and solved. If the percentage difference between the latest solution and the previous one within the same solution period is below a prescribed tolerance then this solution procedure (or Type III iteration) is building up the true terminal conditions and solving the model consistently. The conditions for the last layer of iterations to converge, such that terminal conditions do not unduly affect the current solution, are given in Fisher and Hughes Hallett (1988).

Hendry *et al.* (1984) provide a number of testable restrictions on the ADL format to retrieve various economically meaningful relationships such as leading indicators, common factors and error correction mechanisms (ECM) etc. Considering the ECM in itself,[4] equation (1) can be rearranged as a difference equation:

$$A(L)\Delta Y_t = B(L)\Delta X_t - (1-\pi)[Y_{t-p} - \beta_1 X_{t-p}] + V_t$$

where,

$$A(L) = 1 - \sum_{i=1}^{p} \alpha_i L^i, \quad B(L) = \sum_{j=0}^{q} \gamma_j L^j$$

$$\pi = \sum_{i=1}^{p} \alpha_i, \ \beta_1 = \sum_{j=0}^{J} \gamma_j (1 - \sum_{i=1}^{I} \alpha_i)^{-1}$$

with the restriction,

$$(1 - \sum_{i=1}^{I} \alpha_i) \neq 0.$$

The parameter β_1 is the estimate of the long run elasticity between Y and X (given logarithmic specifications) and will be unity if there is a long run proportionate growth rate between the variables.

The **Static State** equilibrium (where $\Delta Y_t = \Delta X_t = 0$)[5] yields (for logarithmic-form models):

$$Y_t = \beta_1 X_t$$

By contrast, the **Steady State** equilibrium (where $\Delta Y_t = \Delta X_t = g$) yields

$$Y = ([B(L) - A(L)]g) / (1-\pi) + \beta_1 X$$

Using the same type of analysis, we can examine a full structural model:

$$A(L)Y_t = B(L)X_t + C(L)E_t + V_t$$

---

[4] The ECM has proved particularly popular since it generates a statistically meaningful regression (ensuring common orders of integration) and also explicitly defines long run relationships between variables and their short run dynamics.

[5] Notice of course that models defined purely in difference terms have no long run solution since the roots lie on the unit circle.

where Y represents endogenous elements, X policy variables, E other exogenous factors and V a vector of residuals. From this, we can derive the final form:

$$Y_t = [A(L)]^{-1}[B(L)X_t + C(L)E_t + V_t]$$

where the stability of the final form requires that the roots of the polynomial A(L) matrix lie within the unit circle. Stacking this yields:

$$Y_t = AY_{t-1} + BX_t + CE_t + V_t$$

Now let $\pi_1 = A; \pi_2 = B; \pi_3 = C$. In full matrix form, this equation becomes

$$\begin{bmatrix} Y_1 \\ . \\ . \\ . \\ Y_T \end{bmatrix} = \begin{bmatrix} \pi_2 & 0 & 0 & 0 & 0 \\ \pi_1\pi_2 & . & 0 & 0 & 0 \\ . & . & . & 0 & 0 \\ . & . & . & . & 0 \\ \pi_1^{T-1}\pi_2 & . & . & \pi_1\pi_2 & \pi_2 \end{bmatrix} \begin{bmatrix} X_1 \\ . \\ . \\ . \\ X_T \end{bmatrix} + \begin{bmatrix} \pi_3 & 0 & 0 & 0 & 0 \\ \pi_1\pi_3 & . & 0 & 0 & 0 \\ . & . & . & 0 & 0 \\ . & . & . & . & 0 \\ \pi_1^{T-1}\pi_3 & . & . & \pi_1\pi_3 & \pi_3 \end{bmatrix} \begin{bmatrix} E_1 \\ . \\ . \\ . \\ E_T \end{bmatrix}$$

$$+ \begin{bmatrix} I & 0 & 0 & 0 & 0 \\ \pi_1 & . & 0 & 0 & 0 \\ . & . & . & 0 & 0 \\ . & . & . & . & 0 \\ \pi_1^{T-1} & . & . & \pi_1 & I \end{bmatrix} \begin{bmatrix} V_1 \\ . \\ . \\ . \\ V_T \end{bmatrix} + \begin{bmatrix} \pi_1 \\ \pi_1^2 \\ . \\ . \\ \pi_1^T \end{bmatrix} Y_0$$

i.e. a model whose backward substitution to an arbitrary start yields:

$$Y_t = \pi_1^t Y_0 + \sum_{j=0}^{t-1} \pi_1^j \pi_2 X_{t-j} + \sum_{j=0}^{t-1} \pi_1^j \pi_3 E_{t-j} + \sum_{j=0}^{t-1} \pi_1^j V_{t-j}$$

From this, we can derive key multiplier relationships:

The Impact Multiplier is: $\dfrac{\partial Y_t}{\partial X_t} = \pi_2$

The Interim Multiplier is: $\dfrac{\partial Y_{t+j}}{\partial X_t} = \pi_1^j \pi_2$

The Dynamic multipliers, the total impact of a unit step change in a policy variable after T periods, are:

$$\sum_{\tau=t}^{T} \frac{\partial Y_{i\tau}}{\partial X_{jt}}.$$

For stability purposes, consider the interim multiplier. As $j \rightarrow \infty$, $\pi_1^j \rightarrow 0$ (of course, if this condition was not satisfied, history would have a cumulatively increasing effect on the present). Thus, stability may be redefined as: $\lim_{j\rightarrow\infty} \pi_1^j \pi_2 = 0$. Cumulating this is equivalent to

$$(I - \pi_1)^{-1} \pi_2,$$

this latter form being the final or long run multiplier. However, most models are non-linear to varying degrees and so yield no analytic reduced form solution since the multipliers are base and perturbation dependent. Other than linearising the model and examining its eigenvalue structure (see for example McAdam,1998b) checking for the stability, reliability and consistency of models requires forward simulation and the setting up of an extended base, which is examined in the next Section.

4. SETTING UP THE LONG RUN

A number of important decisions have to be made before the long run of a model can be constructed. These may be roughly categorised as in Table 1.

4.1 Closures

The closures for the labour and goods market are particularly important in generating different long run responses to shocks although they will be dealt with briefly here since their specification is entirely model specific. It is clear, however, that models incorporating goods markets with imperfect competition (i.e. P > MC; increasing returns to scale) will behave differently in the long run from competitive models (i.e. P = MC; constant returns to scale technology). For example, if a steady state mark up (over marginal costs) exists then steady state economic activity will be below that for a perfectly competitive economy. The same is true for labour market specifications; for example, fiscal injections have most impact under pure Keynesian closures (such as fixed nominal wages) since they imply an infinitely elastic labour supply passing on all of the demand expansion onto employment. Classical closures however equilibrate wages to their market clearing 'full employment' level whilst other closures such as sticky wages, mark-up, bargaining or real wage resistance have intermediate impacts. In our core model presented in Section 5 we apply a hybrid model which replicates staggered contracts in the short run.

TABLE ONE: Long Run Model Decision Map

Section	Sub-Section	Options
Closures	Labour Market	Competitive Keynesian Sticky Wages Real Wage Resistance Exog.Labour Supply Bargaining Hybrid
	Goods Market	Competitive Imperfect Competition Hybrid
Economic Growth	Population Growth Migration Technical Progress	 Harrod Neutral Hicks Neutral Solow Neutral
Technology	CES Cobb-Douglas Leontief	
Time Horizon	Short-term Long-term	Exogenous Choice General Closures
Policy Rules	Fiscal Monetary	Solvency Rule Balanced Finance Monetary Base Exchange Rate Inflation Targets
Terminal Conditions	General Consumption Exchange Rate	Growth or Differences Trade Balance/Assets

4.2 Economic Growth

The 'natural' rate of economic growth (g) is equal to the rate of growth of the effective labour force[6] (n) plus the rate of increase in technical progress (α). For example, if the labour force is growing at n and producing α then a full employment (or constant unemployment) equilibrium would require real output growth to equal

[6] The labour-force growth rate can be disaggregated into domestic and migration-induced components although migration specifications are more often found in General Equilibrium than traditional macro-models.

($n + \alpha$). All other (domestic) real variables grow at this rate. Since both n and α can be considered exogenous (and subject to off-model calibration) solving for a model's long run real growth rate is relatively straightforward.[7] Indeed, there are only three fundamental rates governing the long run of a model: n, α and μ (the rate of growth of the money supply). Thus, to ensure unique (exponential) growth rates for all real and nominal magnitudes we have:

$$(1+g) \approx (1+n)(1+\alpha) \tag{2}$$

$$(1+\Pi) \approx (1+g)^{-1}(1+\mu) \tag{3}$$

where Π is core inflation.

Moreover the technical progress element, α, can be modelled as Harrod-, Hicks- or Solow-Neutral. Harrod-Neutral technical progress implies a constant capital to output ratio (hence labour augmenting), Hicks-Neutral (a constant capital-to-labour ratio) and Solow-Neutral is where growth points in the steady state are defined along a constant labour-output ratio (and hence capital augmenting).

Solving for the long run requires post-historical simulation and so the construction of an extended base; this involves forecasts of key variables - e.g. output growth, population, factor prices - as well as policy-mix assumptions made explicit. Subsequently forecasts can be made or inferred for all endogenous variables conditional on assumptions about technical progress and growth in population and the monetary base. The residuals fit the behavioural and identity equations given these assumptions. This represents an extended simulation base - though it does not necessarily imply that the model exhibits well-defined long run properties such as financial neutrality or fiscal solvency since these depend on other factors such as the stability of the model, the specification of the individual equations, policy reaction functions, the level of disaggregation in the price/wage equations and so on.[8]

4.3 Technology

The choice of production function is not crucial to the long run of the model since, whatever the choice, steady state output usually coincides with full, potential or 'natural rate' output. Production functions tend to be Cobb-Douglas, Leontief, or Constant Elasticity of Substitution (CES):

---

[7] Policy interventions will not therefore affect the rate of steady state economic growth unless they affect technical progress, population growth and the rate of time preference. Of course, prior to the steady state, policy *can* affect the (growth) dynamics towards equilibrium. Policy however can affect the steady state level of output mainly from the choice of public debt holdings.

[8] Long run properties can also be examined with reference to a model's parameterisation - see Deleau et al (1981) and Malgrange (1983). The actual method of solving for the steady state will not be dealt with here but is achieved solving the model with standard iterative techniques with the steady state values as the starting guesses (Murphy, 1990). Having solved for the steady state, there involves the interesting issue of how one interpolates between the medium term projections imposed or forecasted from the dynamic model and this new steady state solution. Usually one imposes some (partial) convergence of national PPP-measured GDP per capita (the Solow unconditional convergence hypothesis) relative to, say, the US and then either a linear or a logarithmic interpolation. Usually if the current growth of an economy is large relative to trend one chooses the former.

$$Y = A\left[a(Ne^{\lambda Nt})^{-p} + b(Ke^{\lambda Kt})^{-p}\right]^{-1/p} \tag{4}$$

where: Y is output; A, a, b and p are constants; and λN and λK are labour and capital augmenting technical progress respectively. Invariably, we assume $b = 1 - a$ (constant returns). The elasticity of substitution between capital and labour is given by $\sigma = (1+p)^{-1}$, $\sigma \geq 0$. The special cases $p = 0$ $(\sigma = 1)$ and $p = -1$ $(\sigma = \infty)$ retrieve Cobb Douglas and Leontief forms respectively. The marginal productivity terms for labour and capital are:

$$MP_N = A^{-p} a e^{-p\lambda Nt} (Y / N)^{1+p}$$

$$MP_K = A^{-p} (1-a) e^{-p\lambda Kt} (Y / K)^{1+p}$$

Given perfectly competitive behaviour (which might be expected to hold in the long run) these equate respectively to the real wage and the opportunity cost of capital.

Technical progress can modelled as either embodied or disembodied. In the latter, technology enters as a constant while in the former it is captured by a time trend in the production function (although this often causes problems in generating long run balanced growth in capital and labour see Wallis and Whitely (1987)).

4.4 Policy Assumptions

The methodology on policy rules[9] stems mainly from that of optimal control theory. Given a dynamic linear reduced form,

$$Y_t = \Pi_1 Y_{t-1} + \Pi_2 X_t + \Pi_3 E_t \tag{5}$$

where the explanatory variables are lagged dependent variables, exogenous policy instruments and other exogenous variables, and an additively separate quadratic loss function:

$$L = \tfrac{1}{2} \sum_{t}^{T} \left[y_t' Q_Y y_t + x_t' Q_X x_t \right] \tag{6}$$

where $y = (Y - Y^d)$, $x = (X - X^d)$, and Y^d and X^d are the desired values for targets and instruments respectively. Q_Y and Q_X are diagonal penalty cost matrices (cross-variable deviations being usually unpunished) and are, respectively, symmetric positive semi-definite and symmetric positive definite implying that Q_Y might incorporate some zero penalty costs on target deviations in contrast to Q_X.

---

[9] For a more detailed discussion of how these policy rules may be computed, and their design, see Hughes Hallett (1989).

Substitution of model (5) into the loss function (6) and differentiating with respect to the instrument set yields an optimal feedback rule of the following general form:

$$X_t^* = F_t Y_{t-1} + T_t$$

where, removing time subscripts,

$$F = -[Q_X + \Pi_2' Q_Y \Pi_2]^{-1} [\Pi_1' Q_Y \Pi_2]$$

$$T = -[Q_X + \Pi_2' Q_Y \Pi_2]^{-1} [Q_Y \Pi_3 E - Q_X X^d - Q_Y \Pi_2 Y^d]$$

F and T are, respectively, the feedback and feed forward gain. Whilst the feedback gain is time *in*variant but recursive - being related to (known) model parameters and all penalty weights - the feed forward gain is time varying but forward looking - being related to present and future trends in the exogenous and bliss values. Thus policy interventions may be sequentially updated depending on the out-turn path for exogenous elements.

A distinction may be drawn between policy types. Open Loop rules - e.g. a fixed money supply growth - involve policies calculated at time t for periods t to t + i (i > 0). Alternatively, Closed Loop rules (as illustrated above) take the form of feedback rules sequentially updated in the light of unanticipated shocks and/or changes in the expected out-turn for exogenous variables. Of those rules which are of a feedback form we can identify three policy types: proportional, integral and derivative:

$$\text{Proportional: } X = \phi(Y^d - Y), \quad \phi > 0 \tag{7}$$

$$\text{Integral: } \Delta X = \phi(Y^d - Y), \quad \phi > 0 \tag{8}$$

$$\text{Derivative: } X = -\phi \Delta Y, \quad \phi > 0 \tag{9}$$

A proportional policy rule as in (7) links instrument interventions contemporaneously to target failures. However unless $\phi = \infty$ or the rule is supplemented by a term in the steady state instrument value (X^{SS}), target failures - i.e. $(Y^d - Y) \neq 0$ - continue in the steady state.[10] An integral control rule as in (8) relates policy interventions to both contemporaneous and past policy failures and achieves stabilisation with the higher ϕ, the more rapid the convergence. Finally, in a derivative policy rule (9) policy interventions respond purely to the rate of change

---

[10] An example of which would be the Taylor rule. There, interest rate react to return the economy to targeted inflation conditional on an output gap target: $r_t = \pi_t^* + r\_bar + \theta (\pi_t^* - \pi\_bar) + (1 - \theta) Y\_gap_t$ where π_t^* is the observed inflation rate over the previous year, , π_bar the target inflation rate, and r_bar, an "equilibrium" real interest rate compatible with the steady state. This therefore is an example of a Proportional Rule.

of the target. Such a rule again is not guaranteed to meet the final target since it is not specified.

The choice of such rules (commonly employed in tax and monetary reaction functions) have a direct bearing on the long run. For example an integral control rule ensures convergence to the target with the speed of convergence to that target given by the feedback behaviour from the rest of the model.

4.5 Monetary Policy

A number of interesting issues arise with monetary policy. For example the long run equilibrium of an economy is invariant to the price level; to remove this 'indeterminacy of the price level' outcome, monetary policy usually ties down the long run price level by, for example, reaction functions from *nominal* interest rates to other *nominal* targets such as inflation, monetary base or bilateral exchange rates. In the latter case inflation will be anchored by the monetary growth rate of the exchange rate hegemon. Similarly, it will not be possible to move nominal interest rates to target real rates since it again leaves the price level indeterminate.[11] Moreover leaving nominal interest rates as a policy instrument causes a number of problems in that it is inconsistent with the Uncovered Interest Parity (UIP) relationship and the construction of the yield curve.

4.6 Fiscal Policy

In the long run we would wish fiscal balances to be on a solvent or non-explosive trajectory since otherwise any policy advice derived thereof would not itself prove sustainable.[12] Strictly speaking, solvency implies that the outstanding present debt is less than or equal to the present value of the future expected deficits. More formally, the conventional public accounting identity in continuous time can be written as:

$$S + rb = \dot{b} + \dot{m} \tag{10}$$

where $S = (g + h - t)$ is the primary surplus, g is government expenditures, h is transfers, t is tax revenues, r is the discount rate, b is debt and $\dot{m}$ is the rate of growth of the monetary base. In discrete time, this can be expressed as:

$$b_t = (1 + r)b_{t-1} + S_t - \Delta m_t \tag{11}$$

Furthermore standard manipulation yields,

$$\Delta b_t = S_t + (r - k)b_{t-1} - \Delta m_t \tag{12}$$

---

[11] This is not *strictly speaking* true in a simulation since with appropriately chosen terminal conditions for the price level nominal interest targeting may be convergent.

[12] There is also the question of ensuring a convergent solution generally. Although with terminal conditions elsewhere many models will solve with unsustainable fiscal closures (Smith and Wallis, 1994) but yield no economically meaningful content.

Where k is the growth rate. If we solve (11) forward in the usual manner (setting $\Delta m_t = 0$ for simplicity), we obtain:

$$b_t = -\sum_{i=0}^{\infty} \varepsilon_t \prod_{j=0}^{i} (1+r_{t-j})^{-1} S_{t+1+i} + \lim_{i\to\infty} \varepsilon_t \prod_{j=0}^{i} (1+r_{t+j})^{-1} b_{t+1+i} \tag{13}$$

where ε_t denote expectations of future variables conditioned on the information set available at time t. Thus, we see that that discounted debt must be at least equal to terminal period debt and the discounted sum of (non-interest) balances.

If we transform the above into discounted debt, with a discount factor projected back to the base period:

$$q_i = \prod_{j=0}^{i} (1+r_j)^{-1}, \qquad q_{-1} = 1$$

we can write (13) in discounted terms:

$$b_t = -\sum_{i=0}^{\infty} \varepsilon_t [q_{t+i} / q_{t-1}] S_{t+1+i} + \lim_{i\to\infty} \varepsilon_t [q_{t+i} / q_{t-1}] b_{t+1+i} \tag{13'}$$

The terminal (or No Ponzi) condition that we impose on (13') to derive the solvency constraint is that the terminal debt term (or its expectation) goes to zero:

$$\lim_{i\to\infty} \varepsilon_t [q_{t+i} / q_{t-1}] b_{t+1+i} \le 0 \tag{14}$$

and hence

$$b_t = -\sum_{i=0}^{\infty} \varepsilon_t [q_{t+i} / q_{t-1}] S_{t+1+i} \tag{13''}$$

So solvency implies (13") that the discounted sum of primary deficits equals the initial debt given this terminal condition. With finite horizons, this simply means that public debt in the terminal period is zero; in infinite horizons, the debt must ultimately be serviced either by present and/or future primary surpluses and monetary creation.

Notice two things. First, in (14) we usually discard the inequality sign since we rule out the case of super solvency whereby, in the limit, Governments become net creditors. Second, note that this definition of solvency applies *only* to a dynamically efficient economy. If an economy is dynamically inefficient with growth rates exceeding real interest rates (i.e. $k > r$) in (12), then the debt would forever roll over without the question of solvency arising.[13]

---

[13] Dynamic inefficiency implies that the capital stock is greater than its golden rule level, which maximises steady state consumption per capita, and so the resource allocation is Pareto sub-optimal.

Fiscal solvency therefore requires more than the mere specification of the financing identity. Usually models specify government expenditure and transfers as exogenous; whilst tax rules are in integral control form and preclude debt explosions which are quite necessary since, in the long run, $(r - k) > 0$.[14] The method of financing fiscal innovations is thus an important element in setting up the long run. Monetary finance implies that monetary expansion accommodates the fiscal one leaving nominal interest rates constant. Under bond finance, monetary policy is not affected and so interest rates rise with increased debt. Invariably in the long run we assume balanced finance (i.e. $\dot{b}^{SS} = \dot{m}^{SS}$) such that the ratio of bonds to money is a constant in the steady state (i.e. portfolio balance).[15]

4.7 Time Horizon

The time horizon cannot be explicitly divided into a short, medium and long run in anything other than a model-specific way but there are qualitative ways in which we can differentiate time horizons. In the short run, certain variables - for example foreign interest rates, world oil prices, population growth, environmental and resource constraints - which might well normally be modelled can be legitimately considered exogenous over a short-term forecasting horizon. In collapsing a larger model into one suitable for forecasting purposes, the user has to isolate those variables to be exogenized. There is some cross-over in this: for example modellers may wish to use long run models, but in the short run to exogenize endogenous reactions such as the fiscal solvency rule to examine cases where necessary fiscal adjustments are postponed; see for example Smith and Wallis (1995).

Moreover, models designed for forecasting may not be suitable for policy analysis - for example short run models may not incorporate policy closures rules such as those required to preclude fiscal insolvency, or pay much regard to issues such as long run balanced debt finance of policy, financial neutrality etc. Indeed, there may be a trade-off between a model's theoretical specifications and its forecasting abilities - the implication being that forecasting should be done with small models or cheap time series methods and long run analysis with theoretically well specified (though often highly aggregated) macro-models (Wren-Lewis, 1993).[16] There is no consensus; whilst many model builders claim their models as purely policy oriented (e.g. Masson *et al.*, 1990,Roeger and In't Veld,1997), others

Therefore, the solvency question is predicated on the condition $(r - k) > 0$. Such a condition seems generally consistent with historical data, although there are clearly specific periods for which this condition did not hold. For example, in the 1970s many industrialised countries experienced negative real rates (and hence $k > r$) which made the debt easier to service whilst positive and high real rates ($k < r$) in the 1980s complicated solvency.

[14] This will hold and would also be the case for a permanent bond finance government expansion.

[15] We preclude a permanent increase in bond-financed government expenditures since the debt/gdp ratio would rise without limit requiring an ever increasing build up of foreign liability (as well as positive trade surpluses) which would be incompatible with stock equilibrium. It would also imply an infinite appreciation of the nominal exchange rate given an uncovered interest parity formulation.

[16] Similarly it is well known that price and wage homogeneity is less likely to hold in highly disaggregated (and hence more forecasting-type) models with the result that it tends to underestimate the monetary transmission mechanism compared to, say, smaller and theoretically tighter models or reduced-forms.

highlight both their forecasting record and theoretical modernity (e.g. Brayton *et al.*, 1997).

Dividing a model up, we might say that the short run is characterised by degrees of price and wage *in*flexibility: output is demand determined; incomplete stock adjustment; departures from long run growth; unemployment and output away from full utilisation rates; and the model possibly used for forecasting whilst the long run is characterised by: balanced growth; balanced finance of government debt; price and wage flexibility; flows fully adjusted to stocks; unemployment and output at 'normal' capacity rates; output supply determined; and the model used extensively for policy analysis.

4.8 Terminal Conditions

Terminal conditions tend to be set rather arbitrarily - at a constant value (of the prior period):

$$X^{e}_{t+1} = X_{t} \tag{15}$$

at a constant growth rate:

$$X^{e}_{t+1} = \dot{X}_{t} / X_{t-1} \tag{16}$$

or imposed in some way consistent with the priors of the model builder and/or the model's steady state:

$$X^{e}_{t+1} = X^{SS} \tag{17}$$

An example of the latter is often embodied in the treatment of the exchange rate. Despite its limited empirical support (see Messe and Rogoff, 1983) exchange rates are popularly modelled as uncovered interest parity (UIP) meaning the expected appreciation of the dollar exchange rate is set equal to the short-term interest differential in favour of the dollar; this is often modified to include a term in either net foreign assets (NFA) or current account to gdp ratios which proxy a risk premia:[17]

$$ER_{t} = ER^{e}_{t+1} + (r_{t} - r^{*}_{t}) + qNFA_{t}, \quad q \geq 0 \tag{18}$$

This equation (being forward looking) still however needs a terminal condition to ensure a unique solution; and an arbitrary terminal condition like

[17] The UIP equation caused - at least initially - persistent solution problems since we have a unit root in the forward expectation when we should have a root outside the unit circle to provide saddle-path stability (see, for example, Fisher, 1992). This precludes a unique solution unless the roots of the rest of the model are such as to provide sufficient feedback to obtain an overall solution - although equally endogeneity of either nominal interest rates or a risk premia element specified to tie down the terminal value of the exchange rate provides a stable solution to this equation and alters the system root away from unity. Often however it is still the case that the system root may be close to unity one, requiring a long solution horizon.

constant growth might be 'unsatisfactory' if it implies counter-intuitive movements in the exchange rate and trade variables. The typical constant growth terminal condition therefore is usually supplemented with a term in NFA deviations (from base).

Solving (18) for the first period:

$$ER_0 = ER_T + \sum_{t=0}^{T}(r_t - r_t^*) + \sum_{t=0}^{T} qNFA_t$$

This defines the exchange rate's initial jump defined by its terminal value and the sums of present and future interest rate differentials and net foreign asset ratios. After this initial jump the exchange rate evolves as

$$\Delta ER_t = -[(r_t - r_t^*) + qNFA_t]$$

for a given terminal condition

$$ER_{t|t+1} = \theta_1 \dot{E}R_t / ER_{t-1} + \theta_2(NFA_t - NFA_0)$$

Notice, therefore, that modelling exchange rates as modified uncovered interest parity implies:

(i) The exchange rate jumps in response to any change in exogenous instruments with that change sufficient to clear any effect on net foreign assets brought about by the shock.

(ii) The uncovered interest parity formulation implies that monetary policy has no long run output effect since nominal interest rates converge on those of the 'large' country - otherwise there would be constant expectations of currency movements which would be inconsistent with a long run *steady state* solution; a permanent interest rate would imply an infinite and hence explosive appreciation.

In this case therefore the choice and specification of terminal condition has a direct bearing on the model's steady state since it produces asset equilibrium in the long run (the NFA ratio stabilising).

5. A PROTOTYPE MODEL

Here we sketch out a small core (annual) macro-model (taken from McAdam,1998a) which mirrors the principle elements in a larger one. Its long run is supply determined, but the staggered contracts and rational expectations cause dis-equilibrium and overshooting results in the short run. Besides its (12 out of 22) identities this model has standard features - classical optimality in Investment, standard Consumption (as an ECM) and money demand formulations, a simple interest parity and term structure, basic trade equations and integral control policy rules - and so is intended as an uncontroversial approximation to larger models such as the European

Commission's *Quest*, the IMF's *Multimod* or the Federal Reserve's *MCM.* A parameterisation of the model is beyond the scope and motivation of this paper. Generally, the model is theory led - e.g. the Investment optimality closures -with the exception of two equations (s.4, s.5) which are simple pressure-of-demand indicators.

Aggregate Demand

S.1

$$Y = C + I + G_o + (X - M)$$

S.2

$$\Delta c = c_0 + c_1(\text{wealth}/c)_{-1} - c_2 RLR + c_3 \Delta(y(1 - TX))$$

S.3

$$\Delta k^d = \zeta((MP_K P_Y)/P_K - UCOC)$$

S.4

$$\Delta l^d = \mu(y - y^*)$$

S.5

$$\Delta \text{wages} =$$

$$a_1 + a_2 \Pi^e_{t+1} + a_3 \Pi_{t-1} + a_4(y - y^*) - a_5(w - p - pr)_{t-1}$$

S.6

$$\text{WEALTH} =$$

$$\sum_i \varphi_{1i} \text{WEALTH}_{t+i} + \varphi_2 Y(1 - TX) + K + B + M_o + NFA.E$$

Aggregate Supply

S.7

$$Y = \text{production function} \Rightarrow MP_L,\ MP_K$$

S.8

$$I = K + (\delta - 1)K_{-1}$$

S.9

$$UCOC = (RL + \delta - \Pi^e)(1 - f(TX))$$

S.10

$$P_K = zP + (1 - z)ER.PIM$$

S.11

$$P_Y = jP - (1 - j)ER.PIM$$

S.12

$$P = n(W / MP_L) + (1 - n)ER.PIM$$

Policy Sector

S.13

$$\Delta B + \Delta M = (G - T) + RL_{t-1} B_{t-1}$$

S.14

$$\Delta TX = f(DEBT / GDP, DEFICIT / GDP, \theta_{TX})$$

S.15

$$\Delta RS =$$

$$f(\text{MONETARY BASE, EXCHANGE RATES,}$$

$$Y - Y^d, \Pi - \Pi^d, \theta_{RS})$$

Demand For Liquidity and Overseas Sector

S.16

$$CA / Y =$$

$$\Delta NFA / Y = ((X.PX - IM.PIM) + RS^{**}.NFA_{t-1}) / Y$$

S.17

$$ER = ER_{t+1} + (RS - RS^{**}) + qNFA$$

S.18

$$RL / 100 = (\prod_{t=0}^{I-1}(1 + RS_{t+i} / 100)^{1/I}) - 1$$

S.19

$$m^d / p =$$

$$\beta_0 + \beta_1 y + \beta_2 y_{t-1} + \beta_3 (m^d / p)_{t-1} - \beta_4 RS - \beta_5 RS_{t-1}$$

S.20

$$im = \varepsilon_1 y - \varepsilon_2 (er.pim / p)$$

S.21

$$\Delta x = \phi_1 \Delta m^{**} + \phi_2 (ep^{**} / p) + \phi_3 \Delta(er.im.pim / p)$$

S.22

$$rlr = rl - \Pi^e$$

Notation: Capital letters symbolise variables in levels and lower-case variables in logarithms; starred (double starred) indicates full capacity (foreign) values; we omit time subscripts except lags and leads. Otherwise obvious notation applies: RL and RS are the long-term and short-term interest rates respectively; TX is the aggregate tax rate; l^d is labour demand, φ_2 ($\varphi_2 < 1$) is the parameter for labour's share from the production function (φ_1 incorporates the $(r + \rho + n)$ discount factors); UCOC is the user cost of capital; ER is the exchange rate; I = term structure length. The subscript o represents exogenous.

Equation S.1 defines goods market equilibrium. We have already discussed matters relating to the UIP formulation (S.17) and production functions (S.7). The tax and nominal interest rate (S.14; S.15) equations are of integral control type and achieve their specified targets. Equations S.10 to S.12 define respectively the investment and value-added deflator and the output price. We omit the 'other' country.

5.1 Consumption

The modelling of consumption reflects the Blanchard (1985) model whereby a single representative consumer maximises expected discounted utility subject to the constraint that the present value of consumption is less than or equal to the initial stock of human and non-human wealth and faces (in the perpetual youth variant) a constant probability of death. Human or labour wealth is simply the present value of disposable income discounted over time by the real equilibrium interest rate (r), the (constant) probability of death (ρ) and population growth (n):

$$\text{Labour Wealth} = \int_{t=0}^{\infty} Z_t e^{-(r+\rho+n)t} dt \tag{19}$$

where $Z_t = (Y_t - T_t)$ .Given a utility function with constant relative risk aversion, optimal consumption is proportional to wealth by a proportionality factor, α, determined by the three discount factors, the rate of time preference (tp) and the degree of relative risk aversion, viz:

$$\text{Consumption} = \alpha(r, \rho, n, tp)\text{Total Wealth} \tag{20}$$

where Total Wealth is the sum of labour and asset wealth,

$$\text{Total Wealth} = \text{Labour Wealth} + (K + B + M + NFA)$$

Asset wealth incorporates the capital stock value (K) and holdings of government bonds (B), high-powered money (M) and net foreign assets (NFA). We have therefore incomplete Ricardian Equivalence; human wealth is constrained to cover future tax liabilities, however, since human wealth is discounted at a rate *greater than* the real interest rate (because of positive death probability and population growth rates) the proposition does not fully hold.[18]

Furthermore, consumption (see equation S.2) is often modelled as an ECM ensuring that wealth and consumption are homogenous of degree one. In the medium term, consumption is also affected by disposable income (reflecting liquidity constraint considerations) and perhaps other demographic, banking and structural factors embodied in constant or dummy terms. In the long run we see the wealth/consumption ratio is determined by the real interest rate:

$$c = \Psi_0 + \text{wealth} - \Psi_1(RLR) \tag{21}$$

where $\Psi_0 = c_0 / c_1$ and $\Psi_1 = c_2 / c_1$. Thus shocks to human wealth only have a transitory effect on consumption since it has a long-run co-integrating relationship with wealth, with their ratio determined by the real interest rate. Hence consumption follows a life-cycle approach in that current income need not necessarily drive current spending decisions.

[18] ρ is the constant probability of death and $(1/\rho)$ effectively the horizon index. For $\rho>0(\rho=0)$, we have finite (infinite) horizons for consumers. Ricardian Equivalence holds for $\rho=0$ since consumers will live long enough to meet the implied future increase in taxes from previous debt issues.

5.2 Investment

The neo-classical model of investment derives investment demand from the firm's optimisation problem. We assume entrepreneurs maximise their profit function which is revenue (output times price) minus labour costs (real wage times labour) minus capital costs (the "user cost of capital" times capital).

$$P_Y.Y - w.L - r_K.K$$

The user cost of capital, r_K, represents the various costs to holding a unit of capital made up of three components: a foregone interest rate for the equivalent cash sum (usually proxied by the long term interest rate, RL), a depreciation rate (given that existing capital must be replaced and repaired), δ, the fact that the capital stock price might be changing (and so incurring capital losses for the entrepreneur) and the effects of taxation on capital holdings. In other words,

$$r_K = \left(RL + \delta - \Pi_K^e\right)\left(1 - t_K\right)$$

Maximisation of the profit function with respect to Capital yields the First Order Conditions:

$$MP_K P_Y = r_K P_K$$

Hence Investment expenditures will continue up until the point that the price adjusted marginal product of capital equals the price adjusted user cost of capital ; when the marginal product is above (below) its user costs there is a positive (negative) increment to the capital stock :

$$\Delta k^d = \zeta\left((MP_K P_Y)/P_K - r_K\right)$$

In the (static) steady state ,

$$\Delta k = 0 ,$$

and given the law of motion for the capital stock :

$$I = K + (\delta - 1)K_{-1}$$

we can derive the steady state optimal investment/capital ratio (given by the rate of depreciation):

$$\frac{I^{ss}}{K^{ss}} = \delta$$

If we further assume growth in both technical progress and population (i.e. capital and output both growth at this rate) then the optimal steady state ratio incorporates these two further elements :

$$\frac{I^{ss}}{K^{ss}} = \delta + g_{TP} + g_{POP}$$

5.3 Money Demand and Supply

Money Demand comes from the quantity-theory identity $M = aPY$ where a is the inverse of the velocity of money and represents its opportunity cost typically proxied by interest rates (RS) :

$$M^d = PYe^{-bRS} \tag{22}$$

Typically money demand functions are of the following ADL form:[19]

$$(m^d / p)_t =$$
$$\beta_0 + \beta_1 y_t + \beta_2 y_{t-1} + \beta_3 (m^d / p)_{t-1} - \beta_4 RS_t - \beta_5 RS_{t-1}$$

The Static long run solution is:

$$(m^d / p)^{SS} =$$
$$(1-\beta_3)^{-1}[\beta_0 + (\beta_1 + \beta_2)y^{SS} - (\beta_4 + \beta_5)RS^{SS}] = (m^s / p)^{SS}$$

In the steady state, therefore, money demand equals money supply, output reverts to its natural rate and interest rates equate money demand and supply and fulfil the Uncovered interest parity equation. The long-run demand for real balances therefore is invariant to the inflation rate. Moreover, the equilibrium or steady state price level can be solved as:

$$p^{ss} = (1-\beta_3)m^{s,ss} \times [\beta_0 + (\beta_1 + \beta_2)y^{ss} - (\beta_4 + \beta_5)RS^{ss}]^{-1} \tag{23}$$

If $(1-\beta_3)^{-1}(\beta_1 + \beta_2) = 1$, then this implies that real money demand was homogenous of degree one in real income - i.e. financial neutrality. Solving for the steady state equilibrium we differentiate (23) with respect to time and (given zero long run growth in the rate variables) we retrieve equation (3).

Short run nominal interest rates form part of an integral control rule around some nominal target but in the long term are determined by the UIP equation (and hence by the 'Large Country' monetary policy).We have a conventional term structure for long run nominal rates (S.18). In the steady state long run nominal rates converge on short rates after a lag determined by the length of the term structure:

---

[19] Variables are in natural logarithms except nominal interest rates since that would impose an unrealistic constant elasticity. Price homogeneity is imposed as above in order that the demand for money becomes the demand for *real* money balances. Interest rates are rationalised as the (opportunity) cost of holding real money balances but if the interest rate is a policy variable this equation may be reformulated with inflation acting as a substitute or supplement to interest rates.

$$RL^{SS} = RS^{SS} \tag{24}$$

The real interest rate (rlr) is given by (S.22) - in the long run Π^e converges on core or steady state Π, essentially derived out as in (3).[20] Essentially therefore the rlr is exogenous since it depends on nominal rates - set by large country monetary policy - and monetary base and economic growth both exogenously determined.

5.4 Labour Markets

We see that wage adjustments are sluggish on over-lapping contracts reasoning. The specification for wages implies imperfect adjustment to labour market equilibrium and expected inflation:

$$\begin{aligned} &\Delta \text{wages} = \\ &a_1 + a_2\Pi^e_{t+1} + a_3\Pi_{t-1} + a_4(y - y^*) - a_5(w - p - pr)_{t-1} \end{aligned} \tag{24}$$

where Π is inflation rate in consumption prices, PR a long run productivity trend and Y^* is full capacity output. Thus wages are a function of labour market dis-equilibrium, the real product wage and are assumed to adjust imperfectly to inflation. The interpretation of these parameters is straightforward: reducing a_1, a_2, a_4 or a_5 would increase market sensitivity by increasing market responsiveness to demand conditions, labour market dis-equilibria or conditions in the labour market itself. A fall in a_2 (a_4) implies greater real (nominal) wage rigidity.

If $a_2 = (1 - a_3)$ - as they would be if expectations were a weighted average of rational and backward looking components - then we could cancel the wage and price inflation terms which would be growing at the same rate. If output reverted to its 'natural' rate then we would expect the real product wage to equal the productivity terms and whatever structural factors are embodied in the intercept.

5.5 Trade Variables

The Current Account equation (S.16) is of particular interest If in the steady state $\Delta NFA = g$, then (S.16) can be re-expressed as:

$$\begin{aligned} &((X_t PX_t - M_t PIM_t) + r_t^{**} NFA_{t-1}) / Y_t = \\ &(NFA / Y).((g - r) / (1 + g)) \end{aligned} \tag{25}$$

This implies that steady state debtor countries (e.g. $NFA^{SS} / Y^{SS} < 0$) must run a positive trade surplus and *vice versa*; given that $g^{SS} - r^{SS} < 0$ and the stock of

---

[20] Inflationary expectations may be set in a model consistent manner or as some weighted sum of backward and consistent components.

NFA to income is a constant.[21] This has implications for fiscal policy; for example a permanent debt/income expansion increases consumption in the short run (through normal Keynesian channels) but - if financed by increases in foreign indebtedness - implies *lower* steady state consumption as the trade balance moves inevitably into surplus.[22]

Imports depend on domestic output and the relative price of domestic and import prices - the equilibrium of which is simply the replacement of the steady state value for each variable in the equation. Exports react to foreign imports, the gap between foreign and domestic prices and the change in the deflated value of imports. In the long run we would expect exports and imports to grow at a common rate (for $\phi_1 = 1$) and the price ratios to be constant in the steady state - the long run equilibrium for export demand ensures that imports respond to the foreign/domestic price ratio, a constant in the steady state.

6. CONCLUSIONS

This paper has attempted to briefly survey and motivate the incorporation of long run elements into macro economic models. We have suggested that, *inter alia*, modellers are interested in the long run for reasons of theory (for example, to ensure sustainable policy closures and tighter theoretical foundations) and also for algorithmic convenience (for example, in setting and resolving appropriate terminal conditions). We have ignored many related issues such as cointegration analysis in macro models and numerical issues in solving for the steady state etc but have suggested other more dominant themes common to supply-driven macro models.

These themes may be roughly listed as:

- **Balanced Growth**

- **Balanced Public Finance**

- **Homogeneity Restrictions**

For example in prices, wages, money demand, constant returns technology etc.

- **Money Neutrality**

- **Sustainable Policy Feedback Rules**

This implies not only that their parameterisation leads to robust and stable feedbacks but also that base fiscal projections are internally consistent.

- **Long Run Vertical Phillips Curves**

---

[21] This also depends on how and if the terminal condition on the exchange rate handles net foreign assets. Typically in macro models the roots associated with net foreign assets and the nominal exchange rates tend to be *just stable* implying that these are the variables driving the length of the model's steady state simulation horizon.

[22] This also implies a steady state depreciation of the exchange rate to produce the trade surplus.

Construction of a steady state model from a larger dynamic one yields several obvious benefits in terms of being numerically more straightforward to simulate ,providing appropriate terminal conditions for lead variables as well as forcing model builders to consider their overall model structure and its theoretical coherence. Indeed an "appropriate" long run specification is crucial to understand the full policy and stock-flow implications of certain permanent shocks .This is where such improvements have enriched our analysis over earlier mainly demand-driven models or simple text book flow tools like the Mundell-Fleming IS-LM-BP framework.

The trade-off that such practises bring might be that models with a large emphasis on theoretical and long run coherence might have a poor forecasting record. This is often of course to the immediate financial disadvantage of private-sector modelling groups who depend on the commercial saleability of their model.[23] It could well be argued however that forecasting could be done relatively cheaply with small reduced form models or time series approaches leaving policy analysis in the hands of models with some explicit theoretical long run foundation.[24]

REFERENCES

Armstrong, J, Black, R, Laxton, D and Rose, D (1995), "A Robust Method For Simulating Forward Looking Models", Technical Report No. 73, Bank Of Canada .

Blanchard, O (1985), "Debt, Deficits and Finite Horizons", *Journal of Political Economy*, Vol. 93, pp. 223-47.

Blanchard, O and Kahn, C (1980), "The Solution Of Linear Difference Equations Under Rational Expectations", *Econometrica*, Vol. 48, pp. 1305-11.

Brayton, F, Levin, A, Tyron, R and Williams, J (1997), "The Evolution Of Macro Models at the Federal Reserve Board", mimeo, Federal Reserve Board.

Bryant, R, Henderson, D W, Holtham, G and Symansky, S (1988), *Empirical Macroeconomics For Interdependent Economies*, Brookings Institution, Washington DC.

Bryant, R, Hooper and Mann C (1993), *Evaluating Policy Regimes: New Research in Empirical Macroeconomics*, Brookings Institution, Washington DC.

Correira, Isabel (1996), "Dynamic Optimal Taxation in Small Open Economies", *Journal of Economic Dynamics and Control*, Vol. 20, pp. 691-708.

Currie, D (1982), "The Long Run Of The Bank Of England's Monetary Model", mimeo, London Business School.

Deleau, M, Le Van, C, and Malgrange, P (1989), "The Long Run Of MacroEconometric Models", ESRC MacroEconomic Modelling Bureau, Discussion Paper No.21, University of Warwick, UK.

Fair, R C and Taylor, J B (1983), "Solution and Maximum Likelihood Estimation of Dynamic Non-Linear Rational Expectation Models", *Econometrica*, Vol. 51, pp. 1169-1186.

---

[23] It also tends to imply that such groups engage on substantial residual adjustment and judgmental assumptions which invariably goes un-reported to the final buyers of those "forecasts".

[24] Fisher and Whitely (1997), for example, look at the different models that the Bank of England uses for policy analysis.

Fisher, P G (1992), *Rational Expectations In Macro-economic Models*, Kluwer, Dordrecht and Boston.

Fisher, P G and Hughes Hallett A J (1988), "Efficient Solution Techniques For Linear and Non-Linear Rational Expectations Models", *Journal Of Economic Dynamics and Control*, Vol. 12, pp. 635-57.

Fisher, P G and Whitely, J (1997), "Macro Economic Models at the Bank Of England", mimeo.

Hendry, D, Pagan, A R and Sargan J D (1987), "Dynamic Specification", Chapter 18 in Griliches, Z and Intriligator, M D (eds), *Handbook of Econometrics: Volume II*, Amsterdam, North Holland.

Hughes Hallett, A J (1989), "Econometrics and the Theory of Economic Policy", *Oxford Economic Papers*, Vol. 41, pp. 189-214.

Hughes Hallett, A J and Peter McAdam, (1998a), "Fiscal Deficit Reductions in Line with the Maastricht Criteria: An Empirical Analysis", in Jeffry Frieden, Daniel Gros and Erik Jones, eds. *The New Political Economy of EMU*. Boulder: Rowman and Littlefield. pp. 83-123.

Hughes Hallett, A J and Peter McAdam, (1998b), "Implications of the Growth and Stability Pact: Why the Growth Element is Important", A J Hughes Hallett, Michael Hutchison, and Svend E Hougaard Jensen (eds), *Fiscal Aspects of European Monetary Integration*, Cambridge University Press, 1999.

Malgrange, P (1983), "Steady State Growth Path in a Short-Run Dynamic Model", CEPREMAP mimeo.

Masson, P (1987), "The Dynamics Of A Two-Country MiniMod under Rational Expectations", *Annales D'Economie et Statistique*, Avril-Septembre 1987, 6/7*, pp. 37-69.

Masson, P, Symansky, S and Meredith, G (1990), "MULTIMOD: Mark II: A Revised and Extended Model", IMF Occasional Paper 71.

Masson, P, and B.Turtleboom (1997), "Characteristics of the EURO, the demand for reserves, and Policy Co-ordination under EMU", IMF Working Paper Series, WP/97/58 (May).

McAdam, P (1998a), "A Pedagogical Note On The Long Run Of Macro Economic Models", University Of Kent Discussion Paper No. 98/7, Canterbury, UK.

McAdam, P (1998b), "Dynamical Analysis Of Economic Models", paper presented to the European Central Bank, Frankfurt, 8th December, 1998.

Meese, R and Rogoff, K (1983), "Empirical Exchange Rate Models of the seventies: do they fit out of sample?", *Journal of International Economics*, Vol. 14, pp. 3-24.

Mitchell, P R, Sault, J, Smith, P N, Wallis, K (1995), "Comparing Global Econometric Models", Discussion Paper No. 40, University of Warwick, UK.

Murphy, C (1990), "The Steady State Properties Of A Macro Model", mimeo.

Roeger, W and J in't Veld (1997), "QUEST II: A Multi-Country Business Cycle and Growth Model", European Community, Economic Papers No. 123.

Smith, P and Wallis, K (1995), "Policy simulations and long-run sustainability in forward-looking macroeconometric models", pp. 203-221 in Schoonbeek, L, Sterken, E and Kuipers, S K (eds.), *Methods and Applications of Economic Dynamics*, Amsterdam: North-Holland.

Wallis, K and Whitely, J (1987), "Long Run Properties Of Large Scale MacroEconometric Models", *Annales D'Economie et de Statistique*, Vol. 6/7, pp. 207-224.

Whitely, J (1997), "Economic models and Policy Making", *Bank Of England Quarterly Bulletin*, May.

Wren-Lewis, S (1993), "MacroEconomic Theory And UK Econometric Models", International Centre For MacroEconomic Modelling, Discussion Paper No. 9, University of Strathclyde, Glasgow, UK.

CHAPTER 11

THE SENSITIVITY OF SOLUTIONS TO TERMINAL CONDITIONS: SIMULATING PERMANENT SHOCKS WITH QUEST II[1]

Werner Roeger and Jan in't Veld

1. INTRODUCTION

In applied economic modelling work one is often interested in the long run effects of certain policy measures. An example of this is the evaluation of the potential benefits of certain structural economic reforms, such as changes in taxation or the removal of trade barriers, on output and employment. Another example is the long run impact of monetary shocks on the price level, which constitutes a simple test of money neutrality in a model.

From a purely technical point of view, simulating permanent shocks is a rather straightforward exercise in non-forward-looking models. In recent years though, the macroeconomic profession has moved away from such models and started to analyse policy issues by formulating models where economic agents solve intertemporal decision problems based on rational forward looking expectations. Analysing long run effects of policy changes with these types of models is more difficult. Typically an algorithm for solving a forward looking model requires it to be reformulated as a two-point boundary-value problem, with not only the initial conditions for the predetermined state variables, but also the terminal conditions for the jumping variables specified. Any solution is subject to these two sets of conditions. Determining the initial conditions is of course simple; they are known from history and moreover they are invariant to policy shocks. As regards the terminal conditions however, the situation is different as these depend on the nature and the size of the shock. In this paper we look at the nature of terminal conditions and their role in model solution. Terminal conditions are intimately linked to long run properties of the model and can most usefully be exploited if the model attains a steady state. We therefore will restrict our discussion to models with long run steady states.

Our discussion proceeds as follows. First, we present the steady state and solution of a simple linear model with forward looking expectations. This allows us to illustrate the problems in a more rigorous fashion and link it to the macroeconomic literature, which deals with the linear case nearly exclusively. We restrict our discussion to well-behaved models, i.e. models which are stable and which do not allow multiple solutions. This leaves us with two types of dynamic

[1] The views expressed in this paper are those of the authors and should not be attributed to the European Commission.

models, namely models with and without unit roots.[2] Since unit roots play a crucial role in macroeconomic time series and there exist various economic models generating unit root properties (e.g. models of endogenous growth, insider outsider models, some open economy models with infinitely lived consumers and interest parity etc.) we will briefly discuss methods of solving these models as well. This section is followed by a discussion of numerical methods in the non-linear case and the importance of terminal conditions is demonstrated in this context. We discuss three different strategies in which macromodellers often deal with terminal conditions in practice. We conduct a sensitivity analysis and compare the simulation results of these three strategies by applying them to a medium-sized macro model. We illustrate the differences by considering three different permanent shocks and show how the simulation results compare for each of these shocks.

2. LINEAR EXAMPLE: MODEL OF A SMALL OPEN ECONOMY

The early theoretical literature about forward looking expectations has evolved mainly within a framework of small linear models. In the linear case one can derive a closed-form solution of the model and analyse conditions of stability and uniqueness of the solutions. It is therefore most illustrative to start our discussion with a small linear model. Consider the following simple model of a small open economy. There is a representative agent who maximises the intertemporal utility function over consumption C_t

$$\sum_{t=0}^{\infty} \beta^t \log(C_t) \qquad \beta = \frac{1}{1+\theta} \tag{1}$$

where θ is the rate of time preference, subject to net foreign asset constraint

$$F_{t+1} = (1+r_t)F_t + Y_t - C_t \tag{2}$$

where F_t is the net foreign asset position of the economy, and Y_t is an exogenous income stream. The goods produced in the domestic economy are perfect substitutes for goods produced abroad, thus purchasing power parity holds and interest rates are equal to a constant world rate up to a risk premium which depends negatively on net foreign assets

$$r_t = r^* - aF_t \qquad a \geq 0. \tag{3}$$

The first order conditions of this maximisation problem yield the familiar Euler equation for consumption

$$E_t C_{t+1} = \beta(1+r_t)C_t \tag{4}$$

---

[2] Under unit roots we understand the presence of eigenvalues equal to one, i.e. a systems property and not a property of the system due to unit roots in exogenous variables.

In order to ensure that a steady state exists for all values of a, the rate of time preference is assumed to be equal to the world interest rate ($\theta = r^*$). In addition the transversality condition

$$\lim_{t \to \infty} (1+r)^{-t} F_t \tag{5}$$

holds, which rules out explosive paths.

The static steady state values of the endogenous variables (F^*, C^*) are given as a solution to the following system of equations

$$-(r^* - aF^*)F^* = Y - C^* \tag{6a}$$

$$\beta(1 + r^* - aF^*) = 1 \tag{6b}$$

If $a > 0$, net foreign assets are zero in the steady state and consumption equals current income. An indeterminacy arises if $a = 0$, because equation (6b) can no longer be used to solve for F^*. As will be shown below, this indeterminacy is more apparent than real, however, it complicates the solution.

The dynamic solution of this model can easily be analysed if we consider a linear approximation as follows

$$\begin{bmatrix} F_{t+1} \\ E_t C_{t+1} \end{bmatrix} = \begin{bmatrix} 1+r & -1 \\ -\beta a C^* & 1 \end{bmatrix} \begin{bmatrix} F_t \\ C_t \end{bmatrix} + \begin{bmatrix} Y_t \\ 0 \end{bmatrix} \tag{7}$$

with initial condition $F_{t=0} = F_0$.

In an influential paper, Blanchard and Kahn (1980) have stated the conditions under which a non-explosive and unique solution exists. There are two requirements, the predetermined variables must have a stable backward solution for given values of the jumping variables, while the jumping variables must have a stable forward solution, for given initial conditions. This is the case, since there exist eigenvalues with $\lambda_1 < 1$ and $\lambda_2 > 1$ if $a > 0$. In the absence of a risk premium effect (a=0), the system exhibits unit root behaviour ($\lambda_1 = 1$) for consumption. The consequences of this will become clear when we look at the solution of this system. As shown by Blanchard and Kahn, the solution can be represented as follows (Solution 1)

$$F_t = \lambda_1 F_{t-1} + Y_{t-1} + (1 + r^* - \lambda_1) \sum_{i=0}^{\infty} \lambda_2^{-i-1} E_{t-1} Y_{t+i-1} \tag{8a}$$

$$C_t = (1+r^* - \lambda_1)F_t + (1+r^* - \lambda_1)\sum_{i=0}^{\infty} \lambda_2^{-i-1} E_t Y_{t+i} \tag{8b}$$

for given value F_0. In our discussion we will assume that we are interested in a solution for t in the interval between 1 and T. Equation (8a) clearly shows that the unit root or the indeterminacy of the steady state solution only means that the steady state will depend on the initial condition, i.e. the system exhibits hysteresis.[3]

For the discussion of the non-linear case it is useful to write the solution in a slightly different way. Define the present value of discounted future income between period t and t' as

$$E_t H_{t,t'} = \sum_{i=0}^{t'} \lambda_2^{-i-1} E_{t-1} Y_{t+i-1} \tag{9}$$

Using this definition, the dynamics of the system between period 1 and T can be characterized as follows (Solution 2)

$$F_t = \lambda_1 F_{t-1} + Y_{t-1} + (1+r^* - \lambda_1)\left\{E_{t-1} H_{t-1,\Delta T} + \lambda_2^{-\Delta T} E_{t-1} H_{T+1,\infty}\right\} \tag{10a}$$

$$C_t = (1+r^* - \lambda_1)F_t + (1+r^* - \lambda_1)\left\{E_t H_{t,\Delta T} + \lambda_2^{-\Delta T} E_t H_{T+1,\infty}\right\} \tag{10b}$$

with $\Delta T = T - t$ and for a given value of the initial condition F_0 and the terminal condition $H_{T+1,\infty}$. The terminal condition summarises the present value of future expected income after period T. From the point of view of model solution, formulation (10a, 10b) has two interesting properties. First, conditional on the selection of the terminal condition, the model can be solved in a standard backward looking fashion. Second, the impact of the terminal condition on the solution is discounted by the term $\lambda_2^{-\Delta T}$. This implies that the impact of the terminal condition on the solution at date t can be arbitrarily small if the solution horizon (T) is chosen large enough.

3. SOLUTION IN THE NON-LINEAR CASE

From the last section it is clear that in the linear case, a solution of a forward looking model can easily be obtained for standard time series representations of exogenous variables. Unfortunately, in the non-linear case a closed form solution does generally not exist for forward looking models. However,

[3] It will generally be possible to obtain a solution in that case as well, by properly transforming the model such that the unit root is eliminated. This means one can use the fact that though there is a unit root in the system, endogenous variables will nevertheless be cointegrated. This means that it is possible to solve the system for ratios of endogenous variables and then transform this solution back to levels. In the example given above one can define $f_t = F_t / C_t$ and solve for the dynamic evolution of the net asset to consumption ratio. This ratio has a forward looking solution and no unit root.

a non-linear model can be brought into a form which resembles (10) and standard numerical solution techniques, developed for the solution of standard backward looking models, can be applied after choosing values for the terminal condition. Two broad classes of solution methods are used in macro modelling practice. The first stacks the system of equations and then solves the stacked model, while the second applies iterative methods.

The first method has been proposed by Hall (1995), Laffarque (1990), then developed by Boucekkine (1995) and Juillard (1996), and can be most easily explained in terms of solution 2 in the previous section. Let a non-linear dynamic model with forward looking expectations be given by

$$f_t\left(y_{t-1}, y_t, E_t y_{t+1}, x_t\right) = 0 \tag{11}$$

with initial condition y_0 and a transversality condition. Here, y_t (nx1) and x_t (kx1) are vectors of endogenous and exogenous variables respectively, f_t is a vector of n nonlinear dynamic equations. This model can be represented in a way similar to (10a,10b) by stacking this system for T+1 periods. Of course, the presence of predetermined state variables y_{t-1} and forward looking expectations (jumping variables) $E_t y_{t+1}$ introduces simultaneity across time periods, therefore we write the model as follows

$$F(z,x;t) = \begin{bmatrix} f_0(z_1, x_1) \\ \vdots \\ f_t(z_t, x_t) \\ \vdots \\ f_T(z_T, x_T) \end{bmatrix} = 0 \tag{12}$$

with initial condition y_0 and terminal condition y_{T+1} where $z_t=(y_{t-1}, y_t, E_t y_{t+1})$. This formulation resembles closely a standard non-linear system of difference equations, analogous to equations (10a) and (10b). Thus this stacked system of equations can be solved simultaneously for the vector $z=[z_1, \ldots, z_T]$ by Newton-Raphson subject to the predetermined variable y_0 and the terminal condition y_{T+1}.[4]

The basic Fair-Taylor (1983) algorithm deals with the simultaneity problem by breaking it into parts and then relies on an iterative scheme to achieve convergence. In the Type I iterations, values for the expectations variables are taken as given and the model is solved period by period by conventional solution methods conditional on these predetermined expectations. Fair and Taylor suggest a Gauss-Seidel algorithm but in principle other algorithms could be used. In the Type II iterations these expectations variables are then updated by the solution values derived in the first stage and the process is repeated until the expectational variables

---

[4] Since T must be chosen large enough such that the solution is close to a steady state in period T, F(.) becomes very large. Since most of the off diagonal elements in this system are zero, sparse matrix techniques can be applied in order to save computer memory.

are consistent with the model solution.[5] With unknown terminal conditions, Type III iterations are then needed to test whether extending the simulation horizon affects the solution (the "extended path" method). This involves extending the simulation horizon by one period at the time till no change occurs anymore and the solution has converged.

4. TERMINAL CONDITIONS

The discussion so far has shown that the additional complication for the solution of forward looking models can be reduced to selecting appropriate terminal conditions. They must be chosen for the expectational variables beyond the simulation horizon to tie down the solution path of the model to approximate the unique saddle path. Choosing the terminal condition analytically is generally impossible in the non-linear case. However, one can exploit the steady state properties of the stable solution. This property tells us that values of the forward looking variables must be close to their steady state solution if T is large enough. Thus, the terminal condition can simply be selected by calculating the steady state solution in a "static simulation".[6] The correct strategy is therefore to calculate first the steady state solution of a permanent shock and impose this as a terminal condition.

In practice, however, macromodelers have often resorted to other methods when simulating permanent shocks. It is most common among the profession to 'ignore' the issue in the sense that one assumes in a simulation of a permanent shock that there is no change in the terminal conditions. Others attempt to exploit certain properties of the steady state and impose these as terminal conditions. The example we will consider below is that of constant growth rates in the steady state. Our analysis will be conducted under the assumption that the model can be formulated in efficiency units and reaches a steady state growth path in the long run. Of course, the methods discussed can also be applied to the level of the variables, but it would slightly complicate the notation.

Method 1: Equilibrium solution of model *(Terminal Condition in Levels- TCL)*

The theoretically correct approach is to use the equilibrium values as terminal conditions. These can be derived from an equilibrium steady state counterpart of the dynamic model. Prior to simulating the dynamic model (11), the equilibrium counterpart to the dynamic model is calculated, *i.e.* a system is set up which gives the long run solution of y_t to any vector x^* of exogenous variables,

---

[5] There exist several variants of this algorithm which use incomplete inner iterations (so-called accelerated Fair-Taylor algorithms). Solutions of the inner loop are updated with every outer loop and therefore the convergence criteria for the inner loop are set looser relative to the outer rational expectations loop. This incomplete inner iterations methodology avoids unnecessary calculations but is basically a variant of the Fair-Taylor method (see Fisher (1992)).

[6] Note that this is only possible in the absence of unit roots. In the presence of a unit root there exist a multiplicity of solutions. As seen above a stable solution exists but it can no longer be expressed independently from the initial condition and therefore we cannot use the (static) equilibrium counterpart of the dynamic model to calculate values for the terminal condition. But note that a solution can be obtained by transforming the model into ratios (see footnote 2).

where x* denotes the long run level of the exogenous variables. Let this system be given by

$$f^{S}(y^{*},x^{*}) = 0 \tag{13}$$

and let y* be the long run solution for y_t. To give an example, suppose the vector y_t can be split into l predetermined state variables and m jumping variables contained in the vectors y^s_t and y^j_t and let the dynamic model be represented by

$$\left.\begin{aligned} y^s_t &= Ay^s_{t-1} + By^j_t + \gamma_1 x_t \\ E_t y^j_{t+1} &= Cy^s_{t-1} + Dy^j_t + \gamma_2 x_t \end{aligned}\right\} \tag{14}$$

Now define $\Pi = \begin{bmatrix} A & B \\ C & D \end{bmatrix}$. The steady state version of this model would be given by

$$\begin{bmatrix} y^{s}* \\ y^{j}* \end{bmatrix} = (I - \Pi)^{-1}\gamma X^{*} \tag{15}$$

Using this detour it is possible to calculate the long run solution implied by a given dynamic model by running a simple simulation of the model $f^{s}(..)$ in order to calculate y* for the long run values x* of the exogenous variables. The dynamic simulation can then be computed by imposing the solution values $y^{j}*$ from this static model on the terminal conditions y_{T+1}.

This method, which is used by e.g. Minford et al. (1979) and Masson et al. (1990), certainly has the advantage that the solution procedure is theoretically consistent. However, it has the disadvantage that the solution method becomes very cumbersome and requires the maintenance of two models which should be identical up to the dynamic specification. When such an equilibrium counterpart of a dynamic model is available, this is clearly the optimal strategy, but in practice it can be laborious to derive a steady state counterpart of the model.

Method 2: Initial Baseline Values ***(No Terminal Condition - NTC)***

This approach, supported by Fair and Taylor in their original 1983 paper but equally applicable to the stacked time method, suggests that any arbitrary condition can be used as long as it is far enough into the future not to affect the period of interest. For example, one could use the initial set of values for the expectations variables from the baseline and assume that imposing these as terminal conditions will not affect the solution. To verify stability of the model, this could then be tested in Type III iterations.

This is obviously a theoretically incorrect way of dealing with the problem. However, it could be justified in practice as it is unlikely that the terminal condition will have a big impact on the solution at the beginning of the simulation. We have seen in the previous section that the effect of the terminal condition on the solution at period t is discounted by $\lambda_2^{-\Delta T}$ (λ_2>1), therefore one would expect that choosing an incorrect value should not affect the solution very much, at least for dates far enough from the terminal date.[7] Therefore, if it is possible to run simulations over a long enough horizon, it is likely that the solution reaches a steady state at some point before it then departs from the steady state as the (incorrect) terminal condition exerts its influence on the solution. If one ignores the solution after the model has reached the steady state, then nothing would be lost by applying this method. In that regard a comparison of this solution method with theoretically more adequate methods is instructive since it will illustrate whether, and over which time horizon, this solution might be close to the correct solution. The big advantage of this method is of course its simplicity. However, the computational costs can be excessive, since applying this method may require very long simulation horizons in order to obtain reliable results over the adjustment period, as models often exhibit protracted adjustment lags towards a new steady state.

Method 3: Constant Growth Rates Condition ***(Terminal Condition in Differences - TCD)***

This third method consists of exploiting certain properties of the steady state solution for the definition of the jumping variables. Knowing that the model reaches a steady state implies a certain knowledge about the change of variables between two successive periods. If the system is formulated in efficiency units, for example, then we know that in the steady state, the percentage change of y_t^j is equal to zero for any shock and any steady state reached by the model solution.[8] If we define a new vector of jumping variables $\dot{y}_t^j = y_t^j - y_{t-1}^j$, then $\dot{y}_{T+1}^j = 0$ if we choose T large enough such that the model reaches a steady state in period T. In terms of the example given above, this amounts to the following specification.

$$\left.\begin{aligned} y_t^s &= Ay_{t-1}^s + By_t^j + \gamma_1 x_t \\ y_t^j &= Iy_{t-1}^j + I\dot{y}_t^j \\ E_t\dot{y}_{t+1}^j &= Cy_{t-1}^s + (D-I)y_t^j + \gamma_2 x_t \end{aligned}\right\} \tag{16}$$

Notice that in this system of equations, the variable $\dot{y}_{t+1}^j$ is the jumping variable, while y_t^j has now become a predetermined state variable. Thus the model can be reformulated such that the terminal conditions are invariant to the policy shock. This seems to be the most elegant solution. There is only a small cost associated with it, namely the model must be extended by adding m equations defining the vector $\dot{y}_t^j$.

---

[7] Conditions for this to happen in general were given in Fisher and Hughes Hallett (1998).

[8] This holds for QUEST II which is formulated in efficiency units. However, this method also works if all variables are specified in levels. In that case the vector $\dot{y}_{T+1}^j$ contains the values of the steady state growth rate of the jumping variables.

5. SENSITIVITY ANALYSIS

In order to illustrate the differences between these three alternative methods we compare their results when they are applied to a macro economic model. As shown above, the effect of the terminal condition depends crucially on the size of the eigenvalues. To add some realism to our analysis, we want to illustrate the three methods by applying them to a medium scale macroeconomic model, rather than a small theoretical model as often used in the literature. We use a smaller experimental version of the Commission's QUEST II model, which consists of two regions, namely the US and EU15. The behavioural equations in the model are based on microeconomic principles of intertemporal optimising behaviour of households and firms and the supply side of the economy is modelled explicitly via a neoclassical production function. This feature of the model assures that its long run behaviour resembles closely the standard neoclassical growth model. There are two major departures from the neo-classical model in the long run. Because firms are not perfectly competitive but can charge mark-ups over marginal costs, the long run level of economic activity will be lower than that predicted from a model with perfect competition. Also, the model economy will not reach a steady state equilibrium with full employment because of important frictions and imperfect competition in the labour market. To capture these labour market imperfections, a bargaining framework is used to characterise the interaction between firms and workers. The short run behaviour of the model economy will be influenced by standard Keynesian features since the model allows for imperfectly flexible wages and prices, as well as adjustment costs for labour and investment.[9]

The QUEST model contains several forward looking variables. The uncovered interest parity condition has a lead in the exchange rate, the Fisher equation contains a lead in prices, and the long term interest rate is determined by a term structure relationship to short term interest rates. Moreover, the model assumes overlapping wage contracts with a duration of 4 quarters which gives rise to three leads in wages. Human wealth, or life cycle income, appears with a lead in the model as it is represented by the current and expected future net income stream.[10] Finally, the shadow price of capital, or Tobin's Q, reflects the present discounted value of the marginal revenue from investment and forms the sixth forward looking variable in the model. Each of these variables require a terminal condition to be specified in simulations.

The qualitative nature of the solution is similar to what we would obtain by running the complete model. The simulation results therefore are representative in terms of the speed of adjustment as well as the impact on the endogenous variables in QUEST II under money supply targetting. The simulations were run with a horizon of more than 100 years. It should be stressed, as will be seen below, that it is

---

[9] The model is described in some detail in Roeger and in't Veld (1997). The full QUEST model contains almost 1000 equations and simulations are run on a RS/6000 workstation, with a simulation horizon of 70 years. The smaller version used here contains 101 equations and can be run over a longer horizon on a PC. It is therefore more suitable for illustrating the alternative methods of simulating permanent shocks. The simulations presented here were run on a Pentium with 32 megabytes of RAM.

[10] A life cycle hypothesis is adopted for consumption. As shown, for example, by Buiter (1988), consumption is not a random walk in that case. Thus the model does not contain a unit root.

generally not necessary to run simulations over that time horizon. It is done here to be on the safe side in ensuring that the model had reached a steady state solution.

The solution method used to simulate the model is the Laffarque-Boucekkine-Juillard (LBJ) algorithm, as implemented in the Portable TROLL software system by Hollinger (1996). All simulations were started in the year 2000 and run over 110 years. We consider three different permanent shocks and illustrate the effects of the terminal condition for each of these shocks. The types of policy shocks we are considering are a permanent increase in total factor productivity (TFP) of 1 per cent, a permanent increase in the money supply of 1 per cent and a permanent reduction in government purchases as a share of GDP of 1 per cent, combined with a reduction in the debt to GDP ratio by 10 percentage points. The focus here is not so much on the economic interpretation of these shocks but more on the technical aspects of the model solution and we have opted for this wide spectrum of shocks to show the robustness of the alternative strategies to a broad spectrum of policy interventions.

Technology-Shock:

Charts 1.a and 1.b give the results of a permanent shock to TFP of 1 per cent of GDP. In terms of model properties a technology shock has a multiplier of 1.67 per cent, i.e. the steady state solution of the equilibrium counterpart of the model gives a 1.67 per cent increase in GDP. It can be seen from Chart 1.a that the path of GDP when a constant growth rate assumption is imposed as terminal condition (TCD) is identical to that when the steady state level is substituted as terminal condition (TCL). Both reach the steady state value of 1.67. On the other hand, the solution under NTC (ignoring the terminal condition) reveals a severe endpoint problem. The good news, however, is that even under NTC the solution does not depart significantly from the correct solution for around one half of the simulation horizon and approaches the steady state. What is also clear from these charts is that it takes the economy about 3 years to complete 75 per cent of the adjustment (Chart 1.b). This is an interesting feature in the light of some recent discussion in the RBC literature on the typical adjustment of GDP (see e.g. Cogley and Nason (1995)).

Money-Shock:

A permanent increase in the money supply should lead to a proportional increase in the price level and have no real effects in the model in the long run. Charts 2.a to 2.d give the results for GDP and the price level of a permanent increase in the money supply of 1 per cent. It is clear that also in this case the solution does not differ significantly under TCL and TCD. Again, there is an endpoint problem with the baseline values are used as terminal conditions (NTC) which, however, does not have a severe influence on the first 50 years of the simulation. Again the steady state solution is reached like with TCL and TCD and the solution only departs after 50 years from the steady state.

With respect to model properties, this solution shows that money is neutral in the long run, with the increase in the money supply leading to a proportional increase in the price level. But monetary policy can have a strong short run impact with a short run multiplier of money on GDP of close to one (Chart 2.b). It takes about 2 years for 75 per cent of the price level adjustment to be completed (Chart 2.d).

Fiscal-Shock:

As shown in Chart 3, the three methods yield similar results for fiscal shocks compared to the two previous experiments. It is, however, visible that it takes the model longer to reach the long run solution (3.a) and there seems to be some small endpoint problems also associated with the solution methods TCL and TCD. It is interesting to notice that TCD does best in this case. We attribute this to the fact that the discrepancy between the steady state solution and the solution value from the dynamic simulation is larger if the terminal conditions are formulated in levels instead of first differences. It can also be seen that the solution under NTC deviates from TCL and TCD already after 10 years. Thus it is not generally true that NTC replicates the correct solution over one half of the simulation horizon.

This experiment also shows the typical adjustment of QUEST II in the case of a fiscal shock. Under monetary targeting, the short run fiscal multiplier is very small and the negative output effect of a fiscal contraction would disappear within the first five years. The negative short run effects could be reduced further by a slightly more expansionary monetary policy (*i.e.* inflation targetting) and/or a reduction in distortionary taxes.[11] It can also be seen that the long run GDP effects of a cut in government purchases and a reduction in the debt stock are rather modest. Notice, however, that this experiment consists of reducing lump sum taxes of households, thus the increase is mainly in private consumption. In other work on the long run effects of fiscal policy we found that a cut in government expenditure of the same order of magnitude would lead to an increase in GDP of 0.35 per cent (and of employment by 0.82 per cent) if it would be accompanied by a reduction in labour taxes and it would lead to a GDP-effect of 1.3 per cent (but no sizeable employment effect) if it would be accompanied by a reduction in corporate taxes (Roeger and In 't Veld (1997b)).

The last simulation shows the potential dangers associated with ignoring the terminal condition problem. The small model used here can be simulated over more than 100 years, but for larger models, like e.g. the full QUEST II model, one is constrained by the memory capacity of the computer. When simulations are run over shorter horizons the end-point problem associated with the NTC method becomes much more acute. To illustrate this we have repeated the above scenario of a fiscal consolidation but simulated it over a much shorter horizon of 50 years. For comparison the "correct" solution (TCD simulated over more than 100 years) is included in the charts, as is the NTC solution simulated over the long time horizon. The NTC50 method already deviates from the other solution paths in the first years of the simulation, while the end-point distortion renders the results over the last 25 years useless (chart 4.a). As can be seen from Chart 4.b, even the short run results are affected by the end-point problem. The TCD method gives much better results

---

[11] On the other hand, in the case of nominal interest rate targeting the fiscal multiplier could also be larger. See, for example W Roeger and J in't Veld (1997a).

over a 50 years simulation horizon, with the short run results close to the longer TCD solution. However, even now there is a small price to pay for imposing terminal conditions too early, as the TCD50 solution does not reach the correct steady state solution at the end of the simulation (0.075 as compared to 0.097). This clearly indicates that 50 years is not enough to achieve a new steady state equilibrium and a longer simulation horizon is required.

6. CONCLUSION

In this paper we have shown the importance of the terminal condition in simulating models with forward looking expectations and considered ways macromodelers deal with them in practice. It is clear that terminal conditions influence the solution of forward looking dynamic models. Despite the fact that it is theoretically incorrect, the often applied strategy of ignoring the problem and assuming it will not affect the solution too much, seems to work reasonably well over an extended simulation horizon and could be applied if there is enough computer memory available to allow for such long simulations. In practice though this is often not the case. Although the bias may not seem a serious problem in the case of the technology shock and the monetary shock, the fiscal shock, which involves a longer adjustment to a new steady state, clearly indicates that model simulations over shorter horizons can give misleading results if changes in the terminal conditions are not taken into account. Exploiting steady state properties like constant growth rates can approximate the correct solution method of imposing equilibrium values quite well. Our simulation results show that this method is both easy to impose on an existing model and seems to have the most reasonable properties.

REFERENCES

Blanchard, O J and C M Kahn (1980), "The Solution of Linear Difference Models under Rational Expectations", *Econometrica*, Vol. 48, pp.1305-1311.

Boucekkine, R (1995), "An alternative Methodology for Solving Nonlinear Forward-Looking Models", *Journal of Economic Dynamics and Control*, Vol. 19, pp. 711-34.

Cogley, T and J M Nason (1995), "Output dynamics in Real-Business-Cycle Models", *American Economic Review*, Vol. 85, pp. 492-511.

Fair, R C and J B Taylor (1983), "Solution and Maximum Likelihood Estimation of Dynamic Nonlinear Rational Expectations Models", *Econometrica*, Vol. 51, pp. 1169-85.

Fisher P (1992), "Rational Expectations in Macroeconomic Models", Kluwer Academic Publishers, Dordrecht.

Juillard, M (1996), "DYNARE: A Program for the Resolution and Simulation of Dynamic Models with Forward Variables Through the Use of a Relaxation Algorithm", *CEPREMAP Working paper no. 9602*, Paris.

Laffargue, J P (1990), "Résolution d'un Modèle Macroéconomique avec Anticipations Rationneles", *Annales d'Economie et Statistique*, Vol. 17, pp. 97-119.

Masson P, S Symansky and G Meredith (1990), "Multimod Mark II: A Revised and Extended Model", *Occasional Paper No. 71*, International Monetary Fund, Washington D.C.

Minford A P L, K G P Matthews and S Marwaha (1979), "Terminal Conditions as a Means of Ensuring Unique Solutions For Rational Expectations Models With Forward Expectations", *Economic Letters*, Vol. 4, pp. 117-20.

Roeger, W and J in't Veld (1997a), "Expansionary Fiscal Consolidations and Monetary Policy", mimeo.

Roeger, W and J in't Veld (1997b), "Effects of Taxation in QUEST II", in: Taxation and Economic Performance, OECD Report.

Roeger, W and J in't Veld (1997c), "QUEST II: A Multi Country Business and Growth Model", Economic Papers no 123, European Commission, Directorate–General for Economic and Financial Affairs.

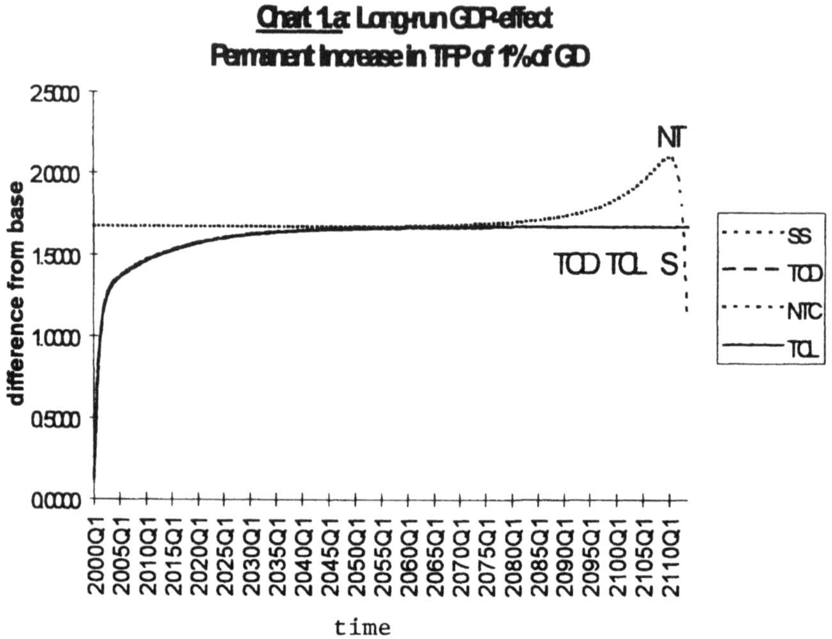
Chart 1.a: Long-run GDP-effect
Permanent Increase in TFP of 1% of GD
2.5000
2.0000
1.5000
1.0000
0.5000
0.0000
difference from base
NT
TCD TCL S
SS
TCD
NTC
TCL
2000Q1
2005Q1
2010Q1
2015Q1
2020Q1
2025Q1
2030Q1
2035Q1
2040Q1
2045Q1
2050Q1
2055Q1
2060Q1
2065Q1
2070Q1
2075Q1
2080Q1
2085Q1
2090Q1
2095Q1
2100Q1
2105Q1
2110Q1
time

Chart 1.b: Short-run GDP-effect
Permanent Increase in TFP of 1% of GD

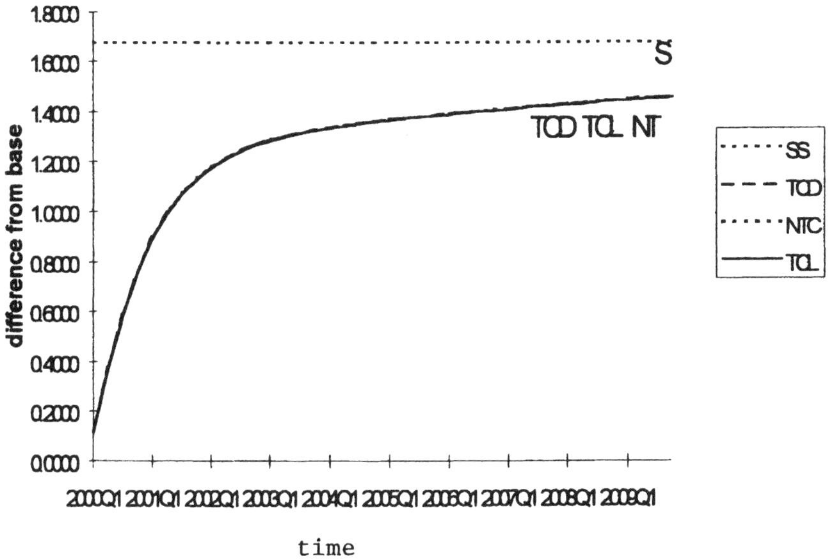

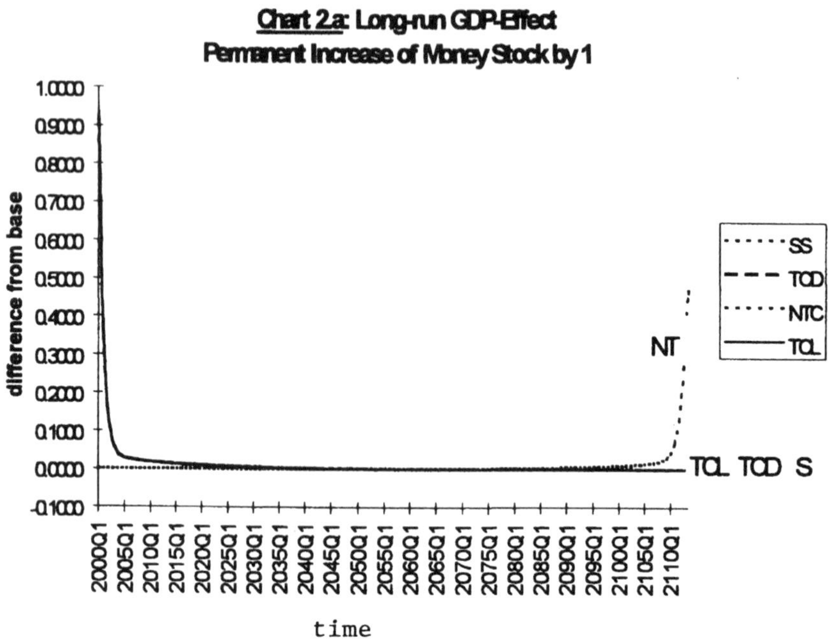
Chart 2.a: Long-run GDP-Effect
Permanent Increase of Money Stock by 1
difference from base
1.0000
0.9000
0.8000
0.7000
0.6000
0.5000
0.4000
0.3000
0.2000
0.1000
0.0000
-0.1000
SS
TCD
NTC
TCL
NT
TCL TCD S
2000Q1
2005Q1
2010Q1
2015Q1
2020Q1
2025Q1
2030Q1
2035Q1
2040Q1
2045Q1
2050Q1
2055Q1
2060Q1
2065Q1
2070Q1
2075Q1
2080Q1
2085Q1
2090Q1
2095Q1
2100Q1
2105Q1
2110Q1
time

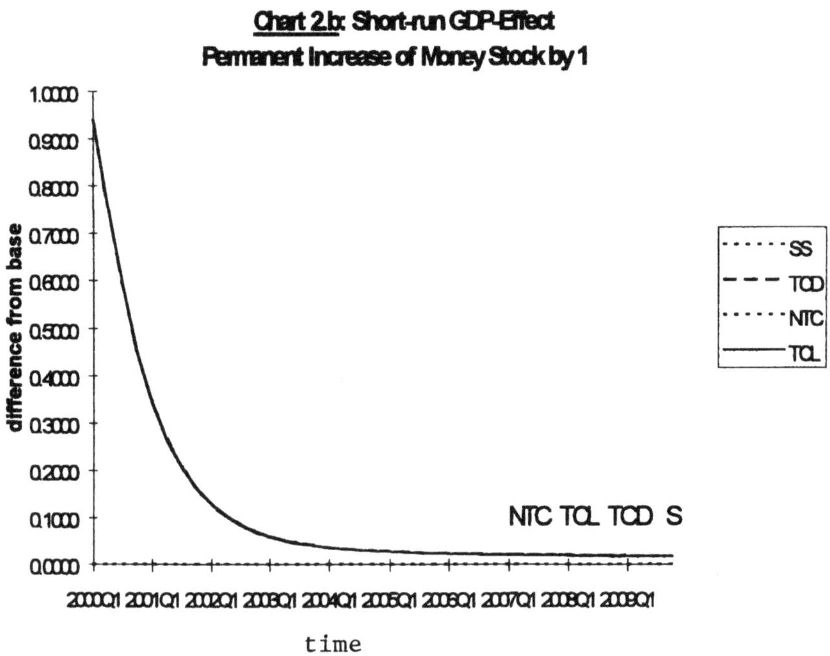
Chart 2.b: Short-run GDP-Effect
Permanent Increase of Money Stock by 1
difference from base
1.0000
0.9000
0.8000
0.7000
0.6000
0.5000
0.4000
0.3000
0.2000
0.1000
0.0000
SS
TCD
NTC
TCL
NTC TCL TCD S
2000Q1 2001Q1 2002Q1 2003Q1 2004Q1 2005Q1 2006Q1 2007Q1 2008Q1 2009Q1
time

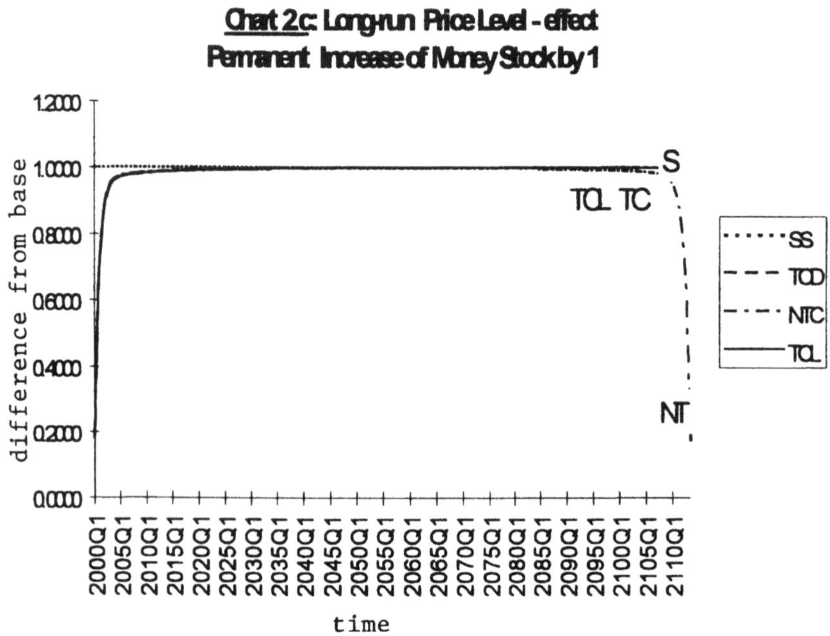
Chart 2c: Long-run Price Level - effect
Permanent Increase of Money Stock by 1
difference from base
time
SS
TCD
NTC
TCL

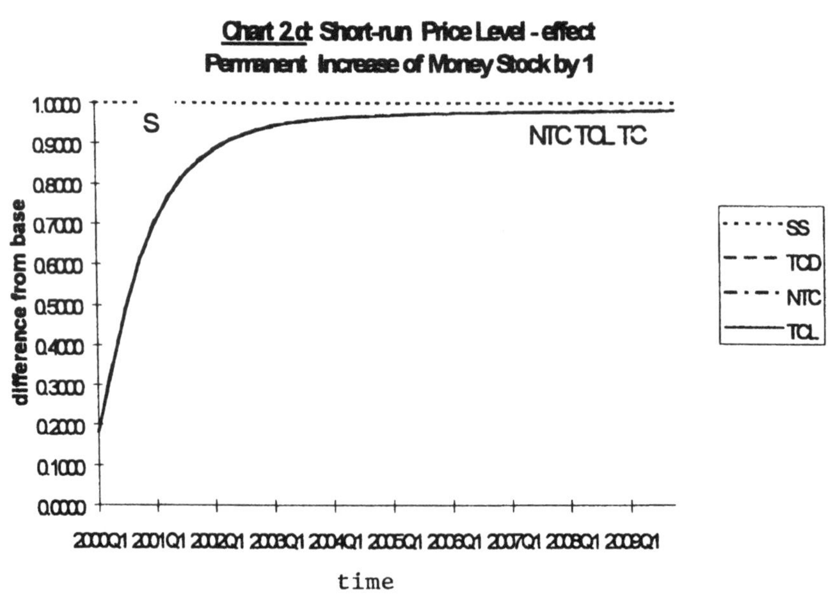
Chart 2d: Short-run Price Level - effect
Permanent Increase of Money Stock by 1
difference from base
time
SS
TCD
NTC
TCL

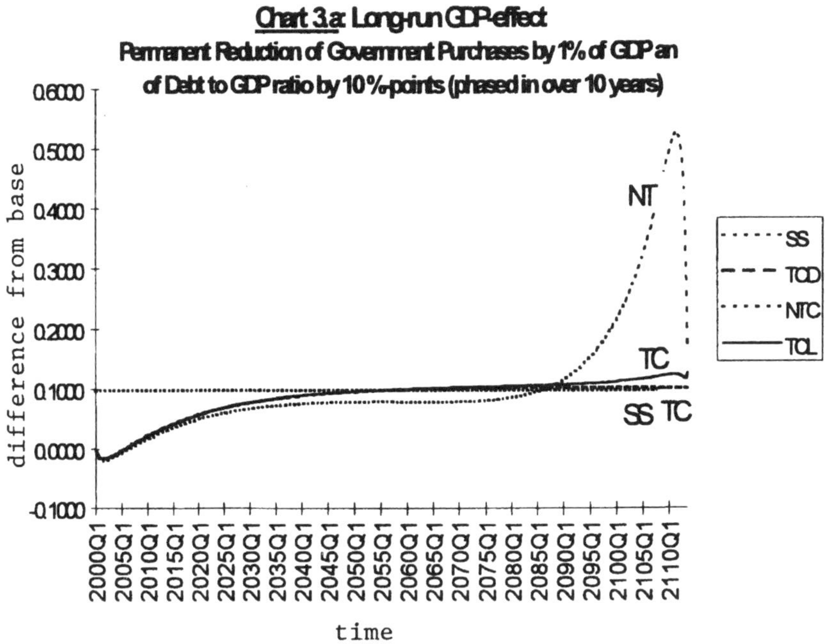
Chart 3.a: Long-run GDP-effect
Permanent Reduction of Government Purchases by 1% of GDP an
of Debt to GDP ratio by 10%-points (phased in over 10 years)
difference from base
0.6000
0.5000
0.4000
0.3000
0.2000
0.1000
0.0000
-0.1000
NT
TC
SS TC
SS
TCD
NTC
TCL
2000Q1
2005Q1
2010Q1
2015Q1
2020Q1
2025Q1
2030Q1
2035Q1
2040Q1
2045Q1
2050Q1
2055Q1
2060Q1
2065Q1
2070Q1
2075Q1
2080Q1
2085Q1
2090Q1
2095Q1
2100Q1
2105Q1
2110Q1
time

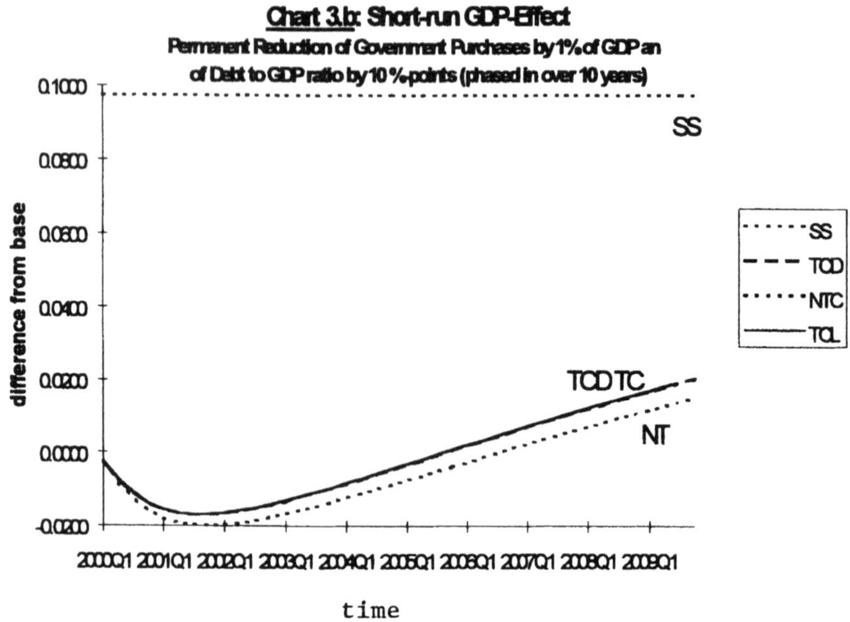
Chart 3.b: Short-run GDP-Effect
Permanent Reduction of Government Purchases by 1% of GDP an
of Debt to GDP ratio by 10 %-points (phased in over 10 years)
difference from base
0.1000
0.0800
0.0600
0.0400
0.0200
0.0000
-0.0200
2000Q1 2001Q1 2002Q1 2003Q1 2004Q1 2005Q1 2006Q1 2007Q1 2008Q1 2009Q1
time
SS
TCD TC
NT
SS
TCD
NTC
TCL

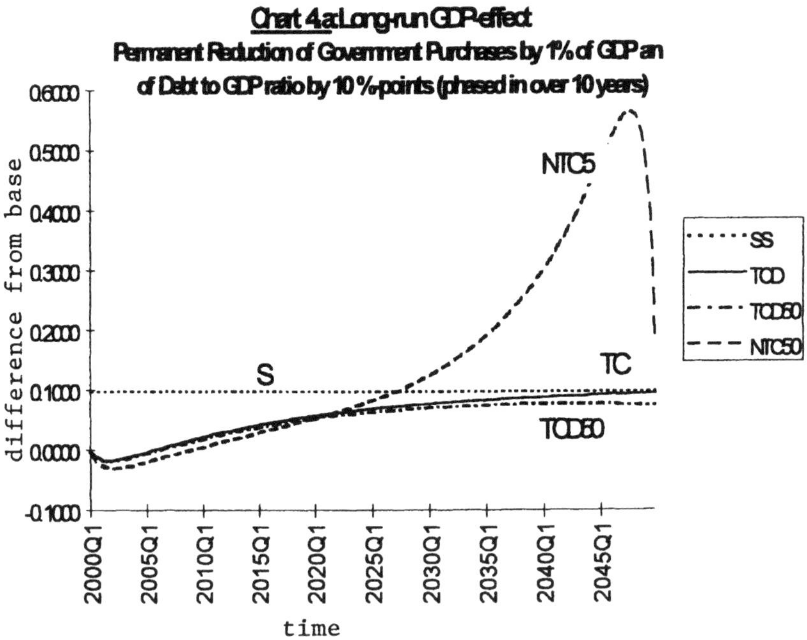
Chart 4a: Long-run GDP-effect
Permanent Reduction of Government Purchases by 1% of GDP an
of Debt to GDP ratio by 10 %-points (phased in over 10 years)
0.6000
0.5000
0.4000
0.3000
0.2000
0.1000
0.0000
-0.1000
difference from base
NTC5
S
TC
TCD60
SS
TCD
TCD60
NTC50
2000Q1
2005Q1
2010Q1
2015Q1
2020Q1
2025Q1
2030Q1
2035Q1
2040Q1
2045Q1
time

Chart 4b: Short-run GDP-effect Permanent Reduction in Government Purchases by 1% of GDP and of Debt to GDP ratio by 10% points (phased in over 10 years)

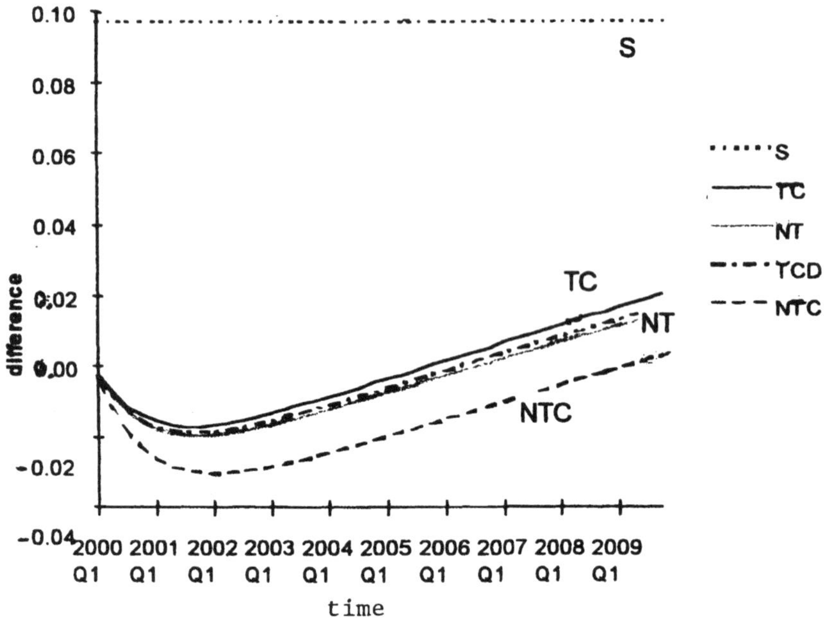

CHAPTER 12

SOLVING LARGE SCALE MODELS UNDER ALTERNATIVE POLICY CLOSURES: THE MSG2 MULTI-COUNTRY MODEL

Warwick J McKibbin[1]

1. INTRODUCTION

This paper explores a number of issues in the design and use of the MSG2 multi-country model for policy simulation analysis. A brief overview of the MSG2 model is presented in Section 2. The use of large scale models with rational expectations such as the MSG2 model has required the development of new numerical algorithms. The solution algorithm that is used to solve the MSG2 model, as well as several other multi-country models including the G-Cubed model (see McKibbin and Wilcoxen (1995)), is summarized in Section 3. In Sections 4 and 5 the impact of alternative assumptions about fiscal and monetary closure rules are explored in more detail. In particular the standard assumptions used in the MSG2 model of a incremental interest payments rule for fiscal are compared to other assumptions frequently used in other global models such as a debt targeting rule and a fiscal conservatism rule. In addition, rules for monetary policy such as a fixed stock of money rule, a nominal income rule and an inflation target are compared. Both sets of policy closure assumptions are compared focusing on Australia but the insights generalize across the other countries in the model. It is shown that these assumptions can have some important implications for both the long run and short run impacts of fiscal and monetary policy. A summary is presented in Section 6.

2. AN OVERVIEW OF THE MSG2 MULTI-COUNTRY MODEL

Full documentation of the MSG2 model and an analysis of its properties and tracking performance can be found in McKibbin and Sachs (1991). The model has undergone a number of changes since that earlier version and information on the latest model can be found on the world wide web at http://WWW.MSGPL.COM.AU A summary of the key features of the model are presented in table 1 and the coverage of the model is listed in table 2. The version used in this paper is the "Asia model" version 42I (see McKibbin (1996)).

The MSG2 multi-country model is a fully specified dynamic intertemporal general equilibrium model (DIGEM) with careful treatment of stock-flow relations such as the cumulation of investment into capital stocks and the cumulation of fiscal deficits into net asset stocks. Both the short run demand and supply sides of the

[1] The views expressed are those of the authors and should not be interpreted as reflecting the views of the trustees, officers or other staff of the Brookings Institution, or the Australian National University.

major economies are incorporated. In the long run, supply is determined by neoclassical growth theory. The model incorporates a number of financial markets such as share markets and markets for short and long bonds in each of the industrial regions where prices are determined by intertemporal arbitrage relations as well as long run sustainability conditions on fiscal deficits and current account positions. In addition, the assumption of rational expectations in these financial markets as well as some forward looking behavior in real spending decisions means the effects of anticipated policy changes are well handled by this model. The regimes that are included in the model are explicitly modeled and since we use a structural model with rational expectations, the model is essentially immune from the Lucas (1974) Critique. The model version in this paper has regional/country coverage for the United States, Japan, Germany, the United States, Japan, Germany, the United Kingdom, the rest of the EMS (denoted REMS),[2] Australia, the Rest of the OECD (denoted ROECD),[3] non-oil developing countries (denoted LDCs),[4] high income Asia,[5] other Asia,[6] oil exporting countries (denoted OPEC),[7] and eastern European economies including the former Soviet Union.[8]

It is important to note that investment and consumption behavior is modeled as a weighted average of intertemporal optimizing behavior (with rational expectations of the future path of the global economy), and backward looking behavior based on current income. Thus expected changes in policy and changes in future stocks of assets leads to an initial (although quite damped) response of households and firms. Investment is based on the cost of adjustment approach of Lucas (1967) and Treadway (1969) which yields a model with investment partially determined by Tobin's q, along the lines of the work of Hayashi (1982). A full derivation of the model can be found in McKibbin and Sachs (1991).

Apart from the shocks and underlying model structure, the results also depend on the assumptions about fiscal and monetary closure, or more specifically the fiscal and monetary regimes in place in each economy. In this paper, policy closure assumptions are changed in the Australian module with a given set of plausible fiscal and monetary closure assumptions in other countries. For example, in all other countries, fiscal policy is assumed to be implemented such that all governments maintain a fixed share of government spending to GDP and adjust taxes to service any changes in debt (the incremental interest payments rule discussed below). The fiscal deficit adjusts endogenously to any changes in real activity or interest rates. The details of the alternative policy closures in Australia as discussed in the next Section.

---

[2] This block consists of Belgium, Denmark, Ireland, Italy and Luxembourg.

[3] This group of countries consists of Austria, Canada, Finland, Iceland, New Zealand, Norway, Portugal, Spain, Sweden and Switzerland.

[4] Non-Oil Developing countries are based on the grouping in the IMF Direction of Trade Statistics less countries explicitly modelled as noted elsewhere.

[5] This group consists of Hong Kong, Korea, Singapore, Taiwan.

[6] This group consists of China, Indonesia, Malaysia, Philippines and Thailand,

[7] Oil exporting countries are based on the grouping in the IMF Direction of Trade Statistics.

[8] These countries are Bulgaria, Czechoslovakia, Eastern Germany, Hungary, Poland, Romania, Yugoslavia, and the former USSR.

Table 1.
Main Features of the MSG2 Model

- both the demand and supply side of the major economies are explicitly modelled;

- demand equations are based on a combination of intertemporal optimizing behavior and liquidity constrained behavior;

- the supply side takes explicit account of imported intermediate goods especially the role of imported capital goods in investment in economies;

- major flows such as physical investment, fiscal deficits and current account imbalances cumulate into stocks of capital, government debt and net external debt which in turn change the composition and level of national wealth over time.

- Wealth adjustment determines stock equilibrium in the long run but also feeds back into short-run economic conditions through forward-looking share markets, bond markets and foreign exchange markets.

- Asset markets are linked globally through the high international mobility of capital.

Table 2.
Regional Coverage of the MSG2 Model Used in this Paper
(version 42I)

Regions (preceded by country code)

Structural	
(U)	United States
(J)	Japan
(G)	Germany
(K)	United Kingdom
(E)	Rest of the EMS (denoted REMS)
(A)	Australia
(R)	Rest of thc OECD (denoted ROECD)
(H)	High Income Asia
(Z)	Other Asia
Non-Structural	
(O)	oil exporting countries (denoted OPEC)
(L)	non-oil developing countries (denoted LDCs)
(B)	eastern European economies and the former Soviet Union (denoted EFSU).

Sectors

one good in each country/region.

3. THE MSG2 SOLUTION ALGORITHM

The MSG2 model (as well as the G-Cubed Model) is solved using software developed by McKibbin (1987) for solving large models with rational expectations on a personal computer.[9] The model version in this paper has approximately 1300 equations in its current form with 26 costate variables. To describe the solution procedure we begin by observing that from a mathematical standpoint, the MSG2 model is a system of simultaneous equations which can be written in the form:

$$Z_t = F(Z_t, S_t, C_t, X_t) \tag{1}$$

$$S_{t+1} - S_t = G(Z_t, S_t, C_t, X_t) \tag{2}$$

$$C_{t+1} - C_t = H(Z_t, S_t, C_t, X_t) \tag{3}$$

where Z is a vector of endogenous variables, S is a vector of state variables, C is a vector of co-state variables, X is a vector of exogenous variables, and F, G and H are vector functions. The first step in constructing the baseline is to use numerical differentiation to linearize (1) though (3) around the model's database (which is for 1987). We then transform the model into its minimal state space representation by using (1) to find a set of equations f() that allow us to eliminate Z from (2) and (3):

$$S_{t+1} - S_t = G(f(S_t, C_t, X_t), S_t, C_t, X_t) \tag{4}$$

$$C_{t+1} - C_t = H(f(S_t, C_t, X_t), S_t, C_t, X_t) \tag{5}$$

The linearized model is then in the form:

$$dS_{t+1} = (I + G_Z f_S + G_S) dS_t + (G_Z f_C + G_C) dC_t + (G_Z f_X + G_X) dX_t \tag{6}$$

$$dC_{t+1} = (I + H_Z f_C + H_C) dC_t + (H_Z f_S + H_S) dS_t + (H_Z f_X + H_X) dX_t \tag{7}$$

The eigenvalues of this system of equations are then calculated to ensure that the condition for saddle-point stability is satisfied (that is, that the number of eigenvalues outside the unit circle are equal to the number of costate variables). Following that we compute the model's stable manifold as follows. For convenience, define Γ:

[9] For a more detailed description of the algorithm, see Appendix C of McKibbin and Sachs (1991). The software developed for solving this model has been written in the GAUSS programming language.

$$\Gamma = (I + H_Z f_C + H_C)^{-1} \tag{8}$$

Using Γ we can rewrite (7) to give dC_t in terms of the other variables:

$$dC_t = \Gamma dC_{t+1} - \Gamma(H_Z f_S + H_S) dS_t - \Gamma(H_Z f_X + H_X) dX_t \tag{9}$$

Substituting (9) into (6) gives:

$$\begin{aligned} dS_{t+1} = {} & (I + G_Z f_S + G_S - \Gamma(H_Z f_S + H_S)) dS_t + (G_Z f_C + G_C)\Gamma dC_{t+1} \\ & + (G_Z f_X + G_X - \Gamma(H_Z f_X + H_X)) dX_t \end{aligned} \tag{10}$$

Applying (9) recursively and using (10) allows us to find an expression for the stable manifold for the costate variables in terms of changes in current state variables and all current and future changes in the exogenous variables. The expression will have the following form:

$$dC_t = \Phi\, dS_t + \sum_{i=t}^{T} \Theta_i dX_i + \Omega\, dC_T \tag{11}$$

where Φ, Θ_i, and Ω are matrices of constants. We evaluate Φ, Θ_i, and Ω numerically; in general, their closed-form expressions will be quite complicated. Once this is found the model can be solved quickly and easily for different experiments because the new values of the costate variables can be calculated simply by evaluating (11). These values can then be inserted into (1) to calculate the other endogenous variables.

The algorithm also allows for calculation of time consistent close loop optimal policy rules although these are not discussed in this paper.[10]

4. ALTERNATIVE FISCAL AND MONETARY CLOSURE ASSUMPTIONS

In this Section, the role of the fiscal and monetary closure assumptions are explored in some detail. A number of alternative closures are possible including a full range of optimization assumptions for fiscal and monetary policy following the large literature on the design of optimal fiscal and monetary regimes.[11] Indeed the model used in this paper has contributed to that literature both from the point of view of a single country or region (Argy et al (1989)) as well as from a global perspective (Henderson and McKibbin (1993), McKibbin and Sachs (1988,1991). In this paper rather than focus on optimal rules as in the above studies, the focus is on the impact of simple rules for fiscal and monetary policy on the model properties. In particular three alternative fiscal regimes are considered and what these mean for the impact of changes in monetary policy in the model.

---

[10] See McKibbin (1987) for an overview of the optimization algorithm.

[11] See for example Bryant Hooper Mann (1993) and Brandsma and Hughes Hallett (1989) and Kydland and Prescott (1977).

i) Fiscal Regimes

Consider the budget constraint facing a government summarized in equation (12).

$$DEFN_t = G_t - T_t + i_t B_t \tag{12}$$

DEFN is the fiscal deficit ; G is total government spending on goods and services as well as infrastructure investment (which is included in the MSG2 model but unchanged for all simulations below); T is total tax revenue from income taxes, corporate taxes, import duties etc; i is the nominal interest rate and B is the stock of government debt. The last term (iB) is therefore the interest payment on outstanding government debt.

In the MSG2 model, variables are expressed in per efficiency units. In the above expression assuming lower case letters are upper case variables expressed in per efficiency labor units (i.e. g=G/Y) and adjusting the deficit for the inflation component of interest payments on the debt we get the following equation:

$$defi_t = g_t - t_t + r_t b_t \tag{13}$$

where r is the real interest rate defined as the nominal interest rate (i) less expected inflation ($r_t = i_t - {}_t\Pi_{t+1}$). Note that this expression has adjusted each variable in equation (1) by deflating by GDP plus it has subtracted the inflation component of interest payments on government debt .

The link between debt and the fiscal deficit is the familiar relationship

$$dB_t / dt = DEFI_t \tag{14}$$

To convert this to the same units as above it can be shown that given b=B/Y and assuming a population plus productivity growth rate equal to n, that:

$$db_t / dt = defi_t - nb_t \tag{15}$$

Thus debt (relative to GDP) in the MSG2 model evolves according to the budget constraint:

$$db_t / dt = g_t - t_t + (r_t - n)b_t \tag{16}$$

Imposing the condition that debt has finite value

$$\lim_{t\to\infty} b_t e^{-(r_t - n)t} = 0 \tag{17}$$

we can rewrite equation (16) as the intertemporal budget constraint of the government:

$$b_0 = \int_0^{\infty} (t_s - g_s)\, e^{-(r-n)s} ds \tag{18}$$

Equation (18) shows that the value of debt (relative to GDP) in period 0 is equal to the integral of the future stream of tax revenue less the future stream of government spending.

What is required to impose this intertemporal budget constraint in any model is a reaction function for either some component of spending or taxes such that (18) is satisfied.

The regimes considered in this paper are dealt with in greater detail in Bryant and Long(1996a,1996b) and the reader is referred to those papers for an analysis of the steady state and dynamic implications of each regime. In this Section I summarize the regimes.

The first regime considered is the regime used in the MSG2 model which is referred to in Bryant and Long (1996a) as the **incremental interest payments rule** (IIP). In the following notation a superscript b refers to the baseline value of a variable. Thus r_t^b is the baseline value if r in period t. This rule is shown in equation (19):

$$t_t = t_t^b + r_t b_t - r_t^b b_t^b \tag{19}$$

In this rule a lump sum tax (t) is adjusted to any changes in the interest servicing costs relative to baseline during simulation.

From the above summary of the government budget constraint it can be seen that assuming t=rb in equation (16) gives:

$$db_t / dt = g_t - nb_t \tag{20}$$

or in the steady state when db/dt=0, we have:

$$b_t = g_t \;/ n. \tag{21}$$

Thus in an economy in which taxes only cover interest costs of the debt, the steady state stock of debt to GDP in the case of the IIP rule is dependent on the steady state level of government spending adjusted by the underlying real growth rate. In terms of the simulations below any change in government spending will lead to a permanent change in the ration of debt to GDP. In the MSG2 model the long run growth rate of population plus labor augmenting technical change is 3% thus a 2 percent of GDP reduction in government spending will eventually reduce government debt by approximately 66% (=100*2/.03)

The second rule is the closure rule assumed in a number of models such as the IMF MULTIMOD model. This is referred to as the **debt targeting rule**.

$$\tau_t = \tau_{t-1} + \alpha_1 (b_{t+1} - b_{t+1}^T) + \alpha_2 ((b_{t+1} - b_{t+1}^T) - (b_t - b_t^T)) \tag{22}$$

The instrument in this rule is the income tax rate (t) rather than tax revenues relative to GDP (t). The current tax rate (t) is set equal to the previous period tax rate plus two terms. The first term in the gap between the actual debt at the end of period t less the desired debt at the end of period t. Targeted variables are indicated by a T superscript. Note that in this particular implementation we assume that the targeted debt is equal to the baseline debt. The second term is the derivative feedback term, that is the change in the gap between the actual and desired stocks of debt. This last term is also the fiscal deficit plus the term nb when there is underlying real growth in the economy. In the simulations below I assume the same values for a_1 (= 0.04) and a2 (=0.3) as Bryant and Long (1996a). In this rule any changes in the economy that change the fiscal deficit in the short run have not effect on the long run stock of government debt relative to GDP.

The third rule shown in equation (23) is **strict fiscal conservatism** in which the government is assumed to hit a desired debt stock exactly in every period. This is equivalent to equation (22) with very large feedback coefficients.

$$b_t = b_t^T \tag{23}$$

ii) Monetary Regimes

Monetary policy in this model is assumed to be implemented with a feedback rule for interest rates on some target variable (either the stock money relative to target, the level of nominal income relative to target, or the rate of inflation relative to target). In this paper we take an extreme value for each feedback coefficient such that the target variables are targeted exactly. An alternative approach is either to use an arbitrary coefficient to capture partial adjustment or one can calculate an "optimal" feedback coefficient such that some objective function written in terms of ultimate target variables is maximized (see McKibbin (1993)). In that earlier paper the "optimal" degree of adjustment for a monetary target rule, given the historically estimate variance covariance matrix of shocks, was found to be exact targeting on money.

The three monetary regimes use in this paper are summarized in equations (24) through (26). Take equation (24) for example. This has that the short term nominal interest rate (i) equal to the baseline nominal interest rate (i^b) plus a coefficient times the gap between the actual stock of money (M) and the target stock of money (M_t^T).

The money target is:

$$i_t = i_t^b + \beta_1(M_t - M_t^T) \tag{24}$$

The Nominal income (or nominal GDP) target is:

$$i_t = i_t^b + \beta_2(PY_t - PY_t^T) \tag{25}$$

Inflation target is:

$$i_t = i_t^b + \beta_3(\pi_t - \pi_t^T) \tag{26}$$

5. THE CONSEQUENCES OF FISCAL AND MONETARY CLOSURES

The results for each of the simulation are contained in Figures 1 through 10. For each policy change there are three sets of graphs (with an additional set of graphs for the fiscal shift, discussed below). All variables are expressed as deviations from what otherwise would have occurred along the baseline of the model. The deviation units differ across variables. GDP, employment, output price, nominal effective exchange rate and real effective exchange rate are expressed as percentage deviation from baseline. Inflation, short term nominal interest rates, short term real interest rate and (where they are presented) real and nominal rate of return on ten year bonds are all expressed as percentage point deviation from baseline. Thus a value of 1 is a 100 basis point rise in the variable. The fiscal deficit, government debt stock, current account balance and trade balance are all expressed as percent of baseline GDP deviation from base.

A. The Consequences of the Fiscal Regime for Changes in Monetary Policy

i) Reduction in the targeted price level by 2%

The first simulation is a reduction in the targeted level of prices by 2%. This is implemented by reducing the nominal anchor. In this simulation it is assumed that the money supply is the nominal anchor and it is reduced by 2% immediately in 1996. Over time the price level falls to the desired level 2 percent lower than that which would otherwise have been. Figures 1 through 3 contain the results for this scenario under the three assumptions for fiscal policy outlined above. In the Figures, the "rB rule" is the incremental interest payment rule (IIP rule); "B target" is the debt targeting rule and "B fixed" is the fiscal conservatism rule.

In understanding the results for monetary policy it is useful to first focus on the overall adjustment for all three regimes and then focus on the differences between regimes. In doing this it is helpful to first analyse the IIP regime ("rb rule" in the Figures) because this the standard fiscal regime in the MSG2 model and is most comparable to other studies with this model.

The outcome for prices can be seen in the bottom right hand panel of Figure 1. Prices fall (relative to baseline) by 0.8 percent during 1996 and gradually reach the new desired level by the year 2000. The policy is implemented by raising short term nominal interest rates (Figure 3) such that the new target path for money is achieved exactly. The result of the rise in interest rates with sticky wages is to sharply raise real interest rates (Figure 3). This appreciates the exchange rate in both real and nominal terms as foreign financial capital flows into the Australian economy attracted by higher real and nominal rates of return. Higher real interest rates dampen private investment directly through a higher cost of funds and also through a tightening of short run liquidity constraints on firms and households. In addition, the rise in the real exchange rate dampens foreign demand for Australian exports. Each factor acts to temporarily reduce GDP. The fall in aggregate demand reduces prices. In addition the appreciation of the exchange rate lowers the cost of imported consumption goods as well as the cost on imported intermediate goods which further reduces inflation (defined in terms of the consumer price index) temporarily. With sticky nominal wages the fall in aggregate demand and rise in the real wage reduces employment proportionately more than the fall in GDP.

The impact of the shock on the balance of payments can be considered in a number of ways. This is also where the fiscal policy assumptions are more important. One way to think through the adjustment process is through the expected theoretical effects on exports and imports which depend on their price and income elasticities. The fall in aggregate demand in Australia should reduce the demand for imports directly. On the other hand the stronger real exchange rate should raise the demand for imports since imported goods become relatively cheaper in Australian dollars. On the export side the effect is clearer. The stronger real exchange rate (i.e. the higher the relative price of Australian goods to foreign goods) tends to lower the demand for exports and there are no foreign income effects from the Australia policy change. Thus exports should fall. These factors taken together imply that the results for the trade balance are ambiguous in theory.

An alternative, equally valid but nonetheless useful, way of thinking through the adjustment process is to realize that the current account adjustment will be determined by the shifts in public and private saving and investment in Australia. On the investment side we have assumed that public infrastructure investment spending is constant. Private investment spending falls slightly because of the temporary rise in real interest rates (which raises the real interest rate on 10 year bonds) and the slowdown in economic activity which reduces expected future output in the near term as well as tightening cash flow of firms. Public saving tends to fall since government spending is fixed and the slowdown in economic activity tends to reduce tax revenue thus increasing the budget deficit all other things unchanged. Private saving tends to fall as well as some households attempt to smooth consumption as income falls temporarily. Therefore the effect on the current account is also ambiguous from this approach (as expected given they are two sides of the same story). The key insight is that it is clearer how the fiscal regime can be important when thinking through the saving/investment channel. This is through the effect of the fiscal regime on the response of public saving.

Indeed now consider the differences in results across the fiscal regimes. The results for real GDP do not differ much across these versions of the fiscal regimes. The key point from examining the differences in GDP are that the fiscal conservatism rule leads to a larger output loss in the short run since the tendency to run a budget deficit as revenues fall leads to a rise in tax rates so as to keep government debt unchanged. Thus the monetary contraction is accompanied by an endogenous fiscal contraction, relative to the other fiscal regimes. In the other regimes, in the short run, fiscal policy is allowed to be counter cyclical.

Greater differences can be found in the adjustment of fiscal and trade deficits. From Figure 2 it is clear that the incremental interest payments rule (IIP) allows a larger fiscal deficit to emerge than the other rules in the short run. The debt target rule allows a short run increase in the fiscal deficit however this rule returns the debt to the baseline level whereas the government debt is permanently higher under the IIP rule. The implication of this is that the fiscal deficit that emerges under the debt target rule must be reversed by running a fiscal surplus during the period shown which dampens economic activity during that phase of adjustment. The fiscal conservatism rule shows the assumption that the fiscal deficit and the stock of government debt remain unchanged at baseline.

The impacts on the trade balance are quite different under the different fiscal regimes. Under the IIP rule the trade balance deteriorates because public saving falls relative to the regime of fiscal conservatism. Indeed the trade balance improves under the fiscal conservatism rule because public saving is unchanged and the fall in private investment is larger than the fall in private saving. These results are interesting although the magnitudes of the differences are relatively small.

The effect on financial prices are more different than the real effects of the alternative regimes. In particular we find an interesting result in the case of the strict fiscal conservative rule. In this case note that the nominal interest rate does not change. This is because we have held the supply of bonds fixed as well as assuming that domestic and foreign bonds a perfect substitutes (i.e. uncovered interest rate parity holds). Thus with a fixed supply of bonds and an infinitely elastic demand for bonds, the domestic price of bonds (i.e. the inverse of the nominal interest rate) cannot change. This implies through the interest parity condition that the nominal exchange rate jumps to its long run value of a 2% nominal appreciation instantly. The implication from the money demand function is that the nominal transaction variable (in this case nominal GDP) must fall by exactly the fall in the money supply. The other implication of this rapid adjustment of nominal asset prices is that with sticky wages, the fluctuations in prices are manifested in changes in real interest rates and real exchange rates rather than in nominal interest rates and nominal exchange rates.

A final point to note is that there is a small long run depreciation of the real exchange rate in the case of the IIP rule because the earlier build of domestic government debt translates into a small build up of foreign debt which need to be serviced in the long run. This is achieved by having slightly higher exports relative to imports as compared to the baseline. Thus the in the long run there is a real depreciation relative to baseline. This effect is absent from the other two regimes that target debt stocks because the long run stock of government and foreign debt returns to baseline.

ii) Reduction in the Targeted Inflation rate of 1%

The results for a change in policy that is a permanent reduction in the targeted rate of inflation of 1% are shown next in Figures 4 though 6. The adjustment process is similar to that for the change in the price level target however several points stand out. Firstly, the real GDP and employment reductions are larger (when re-scaled to the initial period change in inflation) and remain below baseline for longer in the case of the inflation target. As expected, prices continue to fall by 1% per year which differs from the first simulation in which prices converged to a new lower level. In addition the changes in fiscal deficits, government debt and current account adjustment is more spread out for the inflation shock.

The other major differences can be seen in the financial prices in Figure 6. The permanent fall in the targeted rate of inflation and therefore a fall in the expected rate of inflation, has the effect of reducing the nominal interest rate in 1996 compared to the rise in nominal interest rates under the price level target. Indeed as we found above, the rule of strict fiscal conservatism causes nominal interest rates to adjust immediately to there new long run value which in this case is a fall of 1% immediately rather than returning exactly to baseline as for the price level shock.

b) The Consequences for Fiscal policy of the Monetary and Fiscal Regimes

This Section explores the impact of a fiscal contraction of 2 percent of baseline GDP that is unanticipated and permanent under a range of assumptions about fiscal and monetary regimes. In Figures 7 through 10 results for four regimes are presented. The IIP regime (labeled "rB rule" in the Figures) is assumed for fiscal policy under the monetary target, nominal income target and inflation target regimes. In addition these Figures contain the money target regime under both the IIP fiscal regime as well as the government debt targeting regime. In the case where the fiscal regime is the debt stock target, it is also assumed that the targeted stock of debt to GDP falls by 20% of GDP when the contraction in fiscal spending is announced.

The difference between results in Figures 7 through 10 stand out more than in the earlier Figures. That is the monetary and fiscal regimes appear to be important for the impact of fiscal policy. The fiscal contraction is implemented when announced rather than phased in over time. A phasing in would be preferable in this model in order to smooth the adjustment costs in the process of resource reallocation.. A sharp fiscal shock is chosen to make the adjustment clear.

Consider the standard MSG2 closure in which the IIP fiscal regime and money target rule operates. The cut in government spending reduces aggregate demand in the Australian economy. The expected increase in public saving (Figure 8) reduces real interest rates and depreciates the real and nominal exchange rates. The movement in financial prices acts to stimulate private investment and net exports but this is insufficient in the short run to offset the direct negative effects of the spending cuts on GDP. The reduction in 10 year bond rates are smaller than the reduction for a comparable (defined in terms of GDP) cut in US fiscal deficits (see McKibbin and Bagnoli (1993)) because Australia is small in global capital markets and the rise in government saving has negligible effects on world interest rates and therefore only temporary effects on Australian real interest rates. Given the assumption of an open capital market, the real interest rate in Australia eventually returns to the world real interest rate. This also happens for a U.S. fiscal consolidation except that the world interest rate does not remain unchanged in the U.S. case.

The fall in aggregate demand in Australia tends to reduce prices but the exchange rate appreciation tends to raise the price of imported intermediate inputs as well as imported final goods so that prices actually rise.

Now consider the role of the monetary regimes in changing this basic adjustment story. As inflation rises through the exchange rate depreciation, the inflation target regime implies a monetary contraction. This worsens the loss in real GDP and employment because the fiscal contraction is accompanied by a monetary contraction. The movement in nominal interest rates in Figure 9 show that a policy of unchanged nominal interest rates is consistent with an inflation target. However in the other regimes which have less GDP loss and less loss in employment the nominal interest rate is allowed to fall by up to 120 basis point in the case of a nominal income target. Thus if the goal of the policy regime is in smoothing output as well as inflation fluctuations an appropriate policy response to the fiscal adjustment would be to lower nominal interest rates by between 70 and 120 basis points in 1996 and then gradually reverse this through 1997 onwards. This type of response is induced by a nominal income targeting regime but not by a pure inflation targeting regime.

Figures 7 through 9 also give an indication of the role of the fiscal regimes. The money target can be compared under both the IIP rule and the bond target rule in these Figures. The initial output effects under both fiscal rules are similar although by 1998 the debt target rule becomes more expansionary. This is because the contraction in government spending begins to be offset by a tax cut as the ratio of debt to GDP levels out at the new desired level of 20% below baseline. Under the IIP rule the level of debt to GDP continues to fall until it reaches approximately 40% of GDP below what otherwise would have been. This can be seen clearly in Figure 8.

5. CONCLUSION

This paper has presented the model solution technique and considered the interdependence of monetary and fiscal closure rules using a global simulation model although focussing in particular on the Australian economy. It is found that for a policy shift in either fiscal or monetary policy, the fiscal and monetary closure rule in place can have important implications for the outcomes of the policy shift. In the case of monetary policy, the real consequences of the monetary shock appear to be less sensitive than the financial market reactions. Indeed it is shown that with perfect international capital mobility and extreme fiscal conservatism, the short term nominal interest rate is determined independently of the price level target of the monetary authority but is dependent on the inflation target.

The nature of the monetary closure rule in place during a substantial fiscal consolidation is shown to be important. Indeed the results suggest that a strict inflation target is likely to lead to excessive output losses relative to a rule that targets nominal income when there is a significant fiscal consolidation in the Australian economy.

REFERENCES

Argy, V, McKibbin W J and E Siegloff (1989), "Exchange Rate Regimes for a Small Economy in a Multi-Country World". *Princeton Studies in International Finance*, no 67, December.

Brandsma, Andries and Andrew Hughes Hallett (1989), "Macroeconomic policy design with incomplete information", *Economic Modelling*, Vol. 6, pp. 432-446.

Bryant, R, Hooper, P, and C Mann (eds) (1993), *Evaluating Policy Regimes: New Research in Empirical Macroeconomics*, Brookings Institution, Washington DC.

Bryant, R and L Zhang (1996), Intertemporal Fiscal Policy in Macroeconomic Model: Introduction and Major Alternatives. Brookings Discussion Paper in International Economics #123, Washington DC.

Bryant, R and L Zhang (1996), Alternative Specifications of Intertemporal Fiscal Policy in a Small Theoretical Model. Brookings Discussion Paper in International Economics #124, Washington DC.

Currie, David and Simon Wren-Lewis (1990), "Evaluating the extended target zone proposal for G3", *Economic Journal*, Vol. 100, pp. 105-23.

Hayashi, F (1982), "Tobins Marginal q and Average q: A Neoclassical Interpretation", *Econometrica*, Vol. 50, pp. 213-224.

D W Henderson and W McKibbin (1993), "An Assessment of Some Basic Monetary Policy Regime Pairs: Analytical and Simulation Results from Simple Multi-Region Macroeconomic Models", in Bryant R, Hooper, P, and C Mann (1993) *Evaluating Policy Regimes: New Research in Empirical Macroeconomics*, Brookings Institution, Washington DC.

Kydland, Finn and Edward Prescott (1977), "Rules Rather than Discretion: The Inconsistency of Optimal Plans", *Journal of Political Economy*, Vol. 85, pp. 473-491.

Lucas, R E (1967), "Adjustment Costs and the Theory of Supply", *Journal of Political Economy* Vol. 75, pp. 321-334.

Lucas, Robert (1976), "Econometric Policy Evaluation: A Critique", in Brunner Karl and Alan Meltzer (eds.) *The Phillips Curve and Labour Markets*, Amsterdam: North-Holland.

McKibbin, W (1993), "Stochastic Simulations of Alternative Monetary Regimes in the MSG2 Model", in Bryant R, Hooper P, and C Mann (1993) *Evaluating Policy Regimes: New Research in Empirical Macroeconomics*, Brookings Institution.

McKibbin, W J (1996), *The MSG Multi-country Model version 41I: User Manual*, McKibbin Software Group Inc, Arlington VA, USA

McKibbin, W J (1987), "Solving Rational Expectations Models With and Without Strategic Behavior", Reserve Bank of Australia Research Discussion Paper 8706, Canberra.

McKibbin, W and P Bagnoli (1993), "Fiscal Deficit Reduction: An Evaluation of Alternatives", Brookings Discussion Paper in International Economics #101, Washington DC.

McKibbin, W J and J Sachs (1988), "Comparing the Global Performance of Alternative Exchange Arrangements", *Journal of International Money and Finance*, Vol. 7, pp. 387-410.

McKibbin, W J and J Sachs (1991), *Global Linkages: Macroeconomic Interdependence and Cooperation in the World Economy*, Brookings Institution, Washington DC.

McKibbin, W and P Wilcoxen (1995), "The Theoretical and Empirical Structure of the G-Cubed Model", Brookings Discussion Paper in International Economics #118, The Brookings Institution, Washington DC.

Mitchell, P Sault, S, Smith P and K Wallis (1995), "Comparing Global Economic Models", Global Economic Institutions Working Paper #7, London: CEPR.

Smith, P and K Wallis (1994), "Policy Simulations and Long Run Sustainability in Forward Looking Macroeconometric Model", ESRC Macroeconomic Modelling Bureau Discussion Paper #34, University of Warwick, UK.

Taylor, J (1993), *Macroeconomic Policy in a World Economy: From Econometric Design to Practical Operation*. New York: WW Norton & Company.

Treadway, A (1969), "On Rational Entrepreneurial Behavior and the Demand for Investment", *Review of Economic Studies*, Vol. 36, pp. 227-239.

Figure 1: Consequences of a 1 percent Reduction in the Target Rate of Inflation

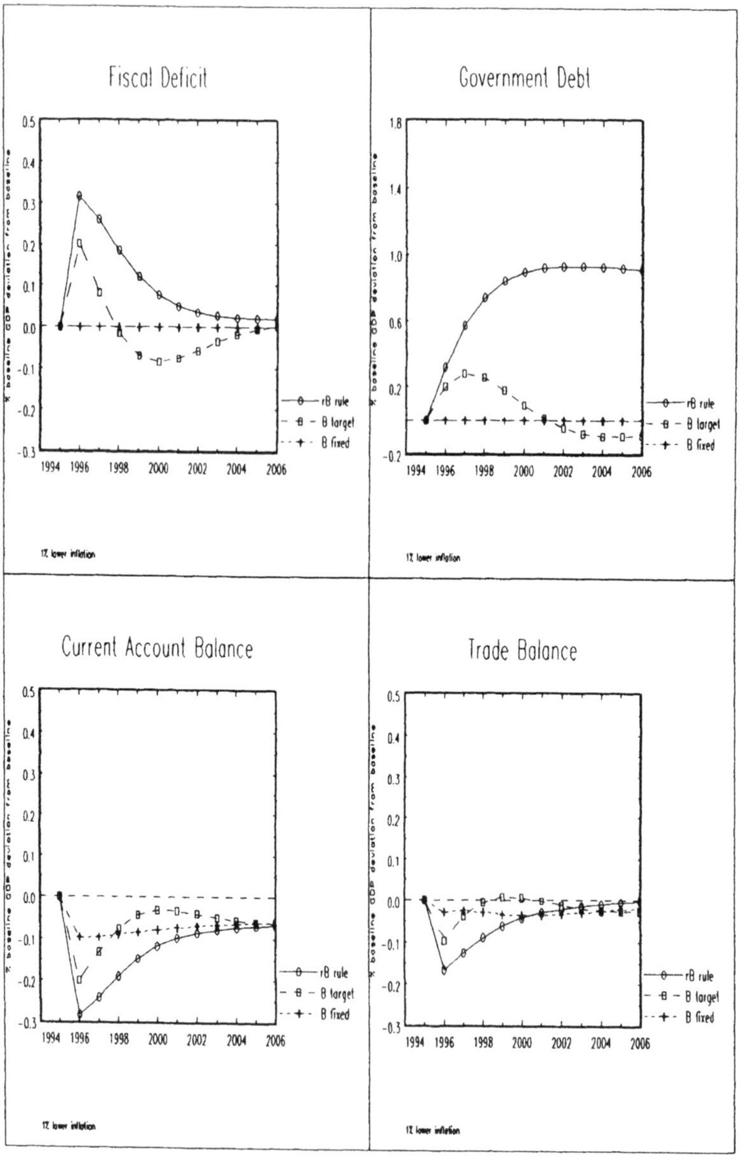

Figure 2: Consequences of a 1 percent Reduction in the Target Rate of Inflation

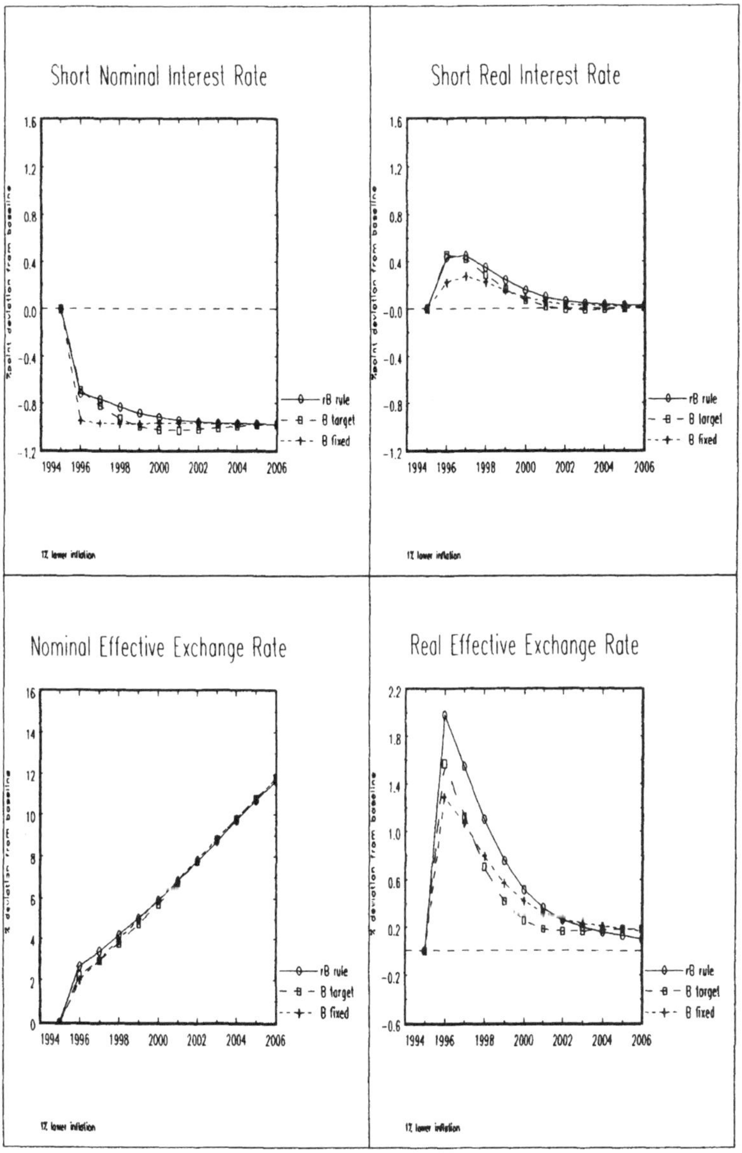

Figure 3: Consequences of a Permanent 2% of GDP Reduction in Government Spending on Goods and Services

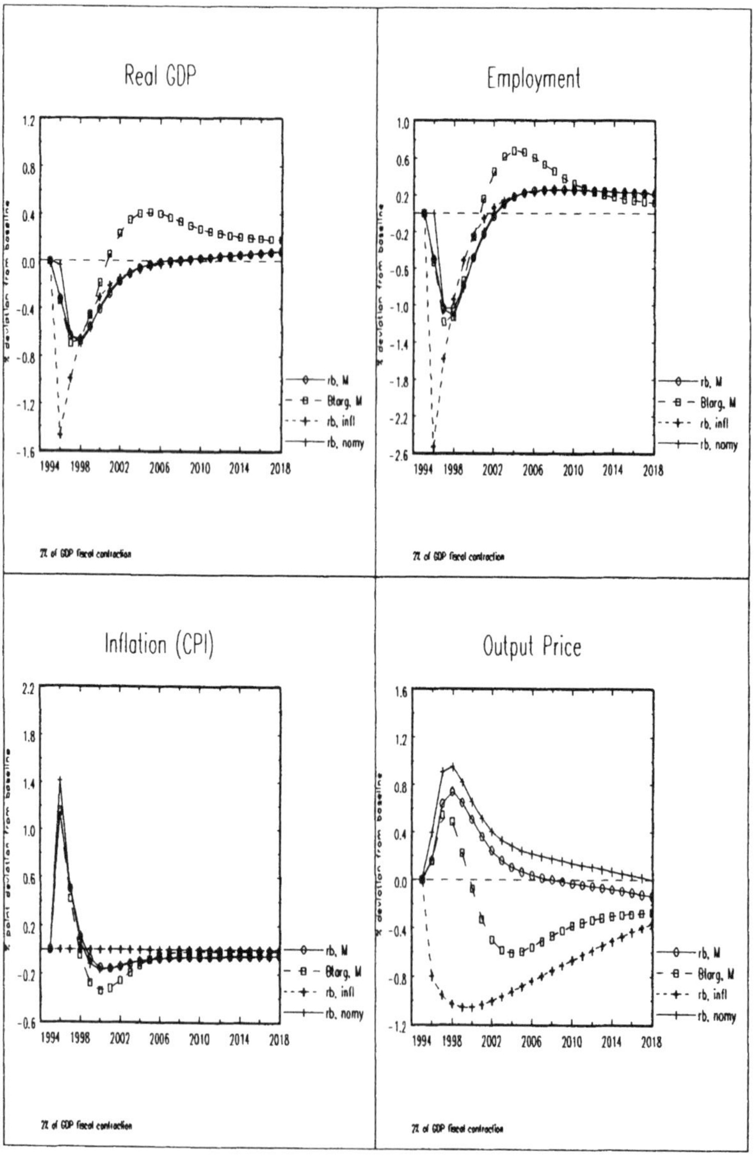

Figure 4: Consequences of a Permanent 2% of GDP Reduction in Government Spending on Goods and Services

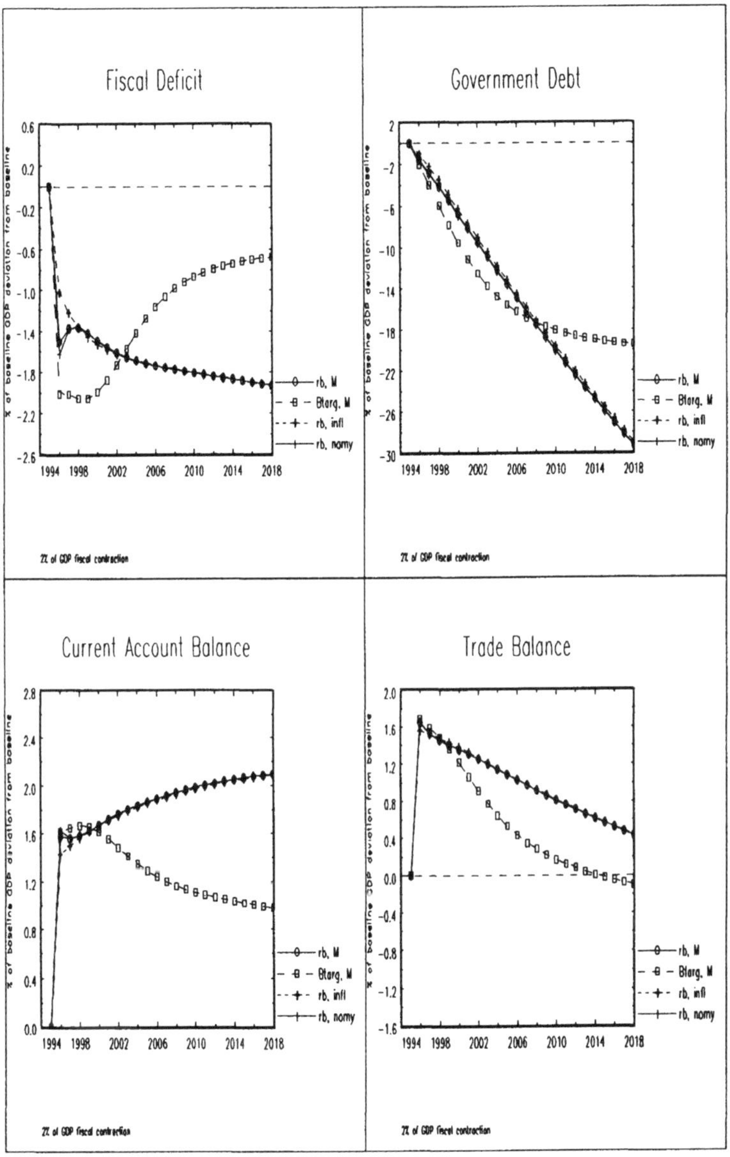

SUBJECT INDEX

AUTHORS' INDEX

Advances in Computational Economics

1. A. Nagurney: *Network Economics.* A Variational Inequality Approach. 1993 ISBN 0-7923-9293-0
2. A.K. Duraiappah: *Global Warming and Economic Development.* A Holistic Approach to International Policy Co-operation and Co-ordination. 1993 ISBN 0-7923-2149-9
3. D.A. Belsley (ed.): *Computational Techniques for Econometrics and Economic Analysis.* 1993 ISBN 0-7923-2356-4
4. W.W. Cooper and A.B. Whinston (eds.): *New Directions in Computational Economics.* 1994 ISBN 0-7923-2539-7
5. M. Gilli (ed.): *Computational Economic Systems.* Models, Methods & Econometrics. 1996 ISBN 0-7923-3869-3
6. H. Amman, B. Rustem, A. Whinston (eds.): *Computational Approaches to Economic Problems.* 1997 ISBN 0-7923-4397-2
7. G. Pauletto: *Computational Solutions of Large-Scale Macroeconometric Models.* 1997 ISBN 0-7923-4656-4
8. R.D. Herbert: *Observers and Macroeconomic Systems.* Computation of Policy Trajectories with Separate Model Based Control. 1998 ISBN 0-7923-8239-0
9. D. Ho and T. Schneeweis (eds.): *Applications in Finance, Investments, and Banking.* 1999 ISBN 0-7923-8294-3
10. A. Nagurney: *Network Economics: A Variational Inequality Approach.* Revised second edition. 1999 ISBN 0-7923-8350-8
11. T. Brenner: *Computational Techniques for Modelling Learning in Economics.* 1999 ISBN 0-7923-8503-9
12. A. Hughes Hallett and P. McAdam (eds.): *Analysis in Macroeconomic Modelling.* 1999 ISBN 0-7923-8598-5

KLUWER ACADEMIC PUBLISHERS – DORDRECHT / BOSTON / LONDON